THE LIBERATION MOVEMENT
IN RUSSIA
1900–1905

Soviet and East European Studies

Editorial Board

Soviet and East European Studies

Rudolf Bićanić, *Economic Policy in Socialist Yugoslavia*

A. Boltho, *Foreign Trade Criteria in Socialist Economies*

Asha L. Datar, *India's Economic Relations with the USSR and Eastern Europe, 1953–1969*

Sheila Fitzpatrick, *The Commissariat of Enlightenment*

Galia Golan, *The Czechoslovak Reform Movement*

Naum Jasny, *Soviet Economists of the Twenties*

Vladimir V. Kusin, *The Intellectual Origins of the Prague Spring*

Donald Male, *Russian Peasant Organisation before Collectivisation*

T. M. Podolski, *Socialist Banking & Monetary Control: The Experience of Poland*

P. Wiles (ed.), *The Prediction of Communist Economic Performance*

THE LIBERATION MOVEMENT
IN RUSSIA
1900-1905

SHMUEL GALAI

Lecturer in Russian History
Tel-Aviv University

CAMBRIDGE

AT THE UNIVERSITY PRESS

1973

Published by the Syndics of the Cambridge University Press
Bentley House, 200 Euston Road, London NW1 2DB
American Branch: 32 East 57th Street, New York, N.Y.10022

© Cambridge University Press 1973

Library of Congress Catalogue Card Number: 73–186252

ISBN: 0 521 08499 7

Printed in Great Britain by
Alden & Mowbray Ltd
at the Alden Press, Oxford

Contents

This book is dedicated to the memory of a brilliant young scholar and very dear friend, Robert Szereszewski (30 December 1936 – 5 June 1967). He possessed the rare quality of rejoicing in the achievements of his friends more than his in own, and the appearance of this work in print would have given him much pleasure.

Acknowledgments

This book is based in part on a PhD thesis I completed for London University in December 1967. Neither this study nor the dissertation could have been written without the generous assistance of several institutions, and the help and encouragement of individuals. It is, therefore, a pleasure for me to have the opportunity of acknowledging my immense debt to them.

I am especially indebted to the London School of Economics and Political Science for enabling me to work on my thesis under the supervision of Professor Leonard Schapiro, the best intellectual mentor one could hope for, and for providing me with a two-year Leverhulme Graduate Entrance Studentship for Overseas Students. I am also most grateful to the Friends of the Hebrew University of Jerusalem and the Humanitarian Trust for their generous financial aid during my stay in London and my travels. I owe a particular debt to the former secretary of the London office of the Friends, Dr W. Zander, who showed great interest in my work and provided constant encouragement. I also wish to thank Mrs A. Glaser and Miss G. Stein of that institution for their kindness in moments of despair.

I am very grateful to the staff of the British Museum Reading Room and Newspaper Library (Colindale); the library of the London School of Economics and Political Science (the British Library of Political and Economic Science); the library of the School of Slavonic and East European Studies (University of London); the Helsinki University Library; the Bibliothèque de Documentation Internationale Contemporaine (University of Paris), and to the Houghton, Widener, Law School and Russian Research Center, libraries of Harvard University. I also owe thanks to Professor S. Perlman, former Dean of the Faculty of Humanities, Tel-Aviv University, for providing me with a research grant, which facilitated preparation of the final script for publication, and to Professor Z. Yavetz, Chairman of the Department of History (now also Head of the School of History, Tel-Aviv University) for

Acknowledgments

considerately lightening my teaching load while I was engaged in this same activity. My thanks to Mrs Sarah Horowitz for typing and re-typing the manuscript with great patience and care.

I owe a debt of gratitude to all the people who read and commented on my script, and in particular to Professor Schapiro, who, although he did not always agree with my conclusions, constantly encouraged me to write this book, and followed its evolution with great critical skill and considerable patience. I am also grateful to Mr Harry Willets, Fellow of St Antony's College, Oxford, and to Professor John Keep, of the Department of History, Toronto University, who were my examiners at London University; their constructive criticism of my PhD thesis was invaluable to me in preparing this book. My thanks are also due to my colleagues and friends, Professor Israel Getzler of La Trobe University, Australia and Dr Jonathan Frankel of the Hebrew University, Jerusalem, for their critical appreciation of my script. I am also most grateful to Professor Richard Pipes, Director of the Harvard University Russian Research Center, who gave generously of his time to read and comment on the manuscript. Also deserving of thanks is Mrs Christine Linehan of the Cambridge University Press for her helpfulness throughout the writing of this book. If, despite all this invaluable help, the book still suffers from factual mistakes and errors of judgment, my own shortcomings are to be blamed.

Finally, I would like to express my gratitude to my family. To my mother, who encouraged me to pursue my studies, despite the fact that, as a consequence, she spent several lonely years. To my two children, who saw little of me for extended periods of time, and, above all, to my wife, without whose encouragement, forbearance and assistance this study could never even have been begun.

SHMUEL GALAI

Cambridge, Massachusetts
February 1972

Unless otherwise indicated, all dates throughout this book are given
in the Old Style (thirteen days behind the western calendar in the
twentieth century and twelve in the nineteenth). For transliteration, the
author has used the 'British system',* and departed from it only with
regard to the accepted or traditional spelling of the names of famous
people.

As far as references to works appearing in the bibliography are
concerned, the following system has been employed. In cases where
there is no author, the reference usually contains the first word of the
title in italics. In all other cases the author's surname in italics is used
as a reference. Where more than one work by the same author is
mentioned in the bibliography, Roman and Arabic figures or letters of
the alphabet are employed to indicate which particular work is being
quoted. For example: *Kuskova* VI*a* stands for Kuskova, E. D., 'Davno
Minuvsheye', *Novyy Zhurnal*, XLV (1956), pp. 129–80; *Milyukov* V₆
stands for Milyukov, P. N., 'Rokovyye Gody', *Russkiye Zapiski*
(September 1938), pp. 108–24.

* For the 'British system' of transliteration of the cyrillic alphabet see: W. K. Matthews,
'The Latinisation of Cyrillic Characters', *The Slavonic and East European Review*, XXX (1952),
pp. 531–48.

Abbreviations

A.R.R.	*Arkhiv Russkoy Revolyutsii*
Brokgaus	*Entsiklopedicheskiy Slovar*
Brokgaus supp.	*Entsiklopedicheskiy Slovar: Supplementary vols* I–II
B.S.E. I	*Bolshaya Sovetskaya Entsiklopediya* (Moscow 1926–47)
B.S.E. II	*Bolshaya Sovetskaya Entsiklopediya*, 2-ye izd. (Moscow 1949–57)
D.i.M.	*Revolyutsiya 1905–1907gg v Rossii. Dokumenty i Materialy*
G.D.	*Gosudarstvennaya Duma. Sistematicheskiy Svod Uzakoneniy i Rasporazheniy Pravitelstva*
Granat	*Entsiklopedicheskiy Slovar*
K.A.	*Krasnyy Arkhiv*
K.i.S.	*Katorga i Ssylka*
K.L.	*Krasnaya Letopis*
M.S.E.	*Malaya Sovetskaya Entsiklopediya*
O.D.	*Obshchestvennoye Dvizheniye v Rossii v Nachale XX-go Veka*
P.R.	*Proletarskaya Revolyutsiya*
P.S.Z. II	*Polnoye Sobraniye Zakonov. Sobraniye 2-e*
P.S.Z. III	*Polnoye Sobraniye Zakonov. Sobraniye 3-e*
S.A.	*S.A. Muromtsev. Sbornik Statey* (Moscow 1911)
S.O.	*Gosudarstvennaya Duma. Stenograficheskiye Otchety*
Spb	St Petersburg
Yubileynyy Sbornik	Veselovskiy, B.B. and Frenkel, Z.G. (eds), *1864–1914, Yubileynyy Zemskiy Sbornik*
Za Sto Let	Burtsev V. L. (comp.), *Za Sto Let (1800–1896)*

Introduction

It is now generally accepted that the Liberation Movement (referred to from the beginning as the 'Liberal Movement'[1]), which emerged in Russia at the turn of the twentieth century, played a very important role in the political events which culminated in the First Russian Revolution (of 1905). But little has been known until now about the origins, composition, organizational framework and significance of the 'liberalism' of this movement.

The emergence of the Liberation Movement coincided with the establishment of the other two main oppositional forces in tsarist Russia – the Russian Social-Democratic Workers Party, or RSDRP (*Rossiyskaya Sotsial-Demokraticheskaya Rabochaya Partiya*), and the party of Socialist Revolutionaries, or SR. All three were, to a large extent, a by-product of the dichotomy which characterized the policies of the autocratic regime during the last two decades of the nineteenth century and the first few years of the twentieth century. On the one hand it conducted a dynamic economic policy, the aim of which was the rapid industrialization of Russia, and, on the other, it displayed an ultra-conservative attitude towards social and political questions.

Russian autocracy was a more arbitrary and oppressive regime than any of the absolutist states of the West had ever been.[2] It became even more despotic in the period 1881–1904. All sections of the population, except to some extent the nobility, were denied personal freedom and political rights. Freedom of speech, of the press and of conscience were non-existent. Discrimination against minorities was intensified and transformed into the official policy known as 'russification'. The urban working class created in the wake of industrialization, was denied the right to form trade unions and/or to strike The legal status of the peasants, who still constituted the bulk of the population, was inferior

---

[1] See, for example, *Osvobozhdeniye* (1902), no. 1, pp. 5, 7, 10.
[2] For a very brief illuminating description of the peculiar features of autocracy see *Schapiro*, pp. 7–9.

I

even to that of the town dwellers with their meagre rights, and furthermore the peasants were forced to shoulder the main burden of the
industrialization drive. But it was the intelligentsia[1] which more than
any other section of the population resented and rebelled against the
tsarist despotism. The dynamic economic policy of the government
provided this class, for the first time in Russian history, with potential
mass support for its struggle against autocracy.

It was the prospect of at long last gaining the support of the peasantry
which encouraged those intellectuals who belonged to the Populist*
camp to establish the SR Party. At the same time, the inability of the
workers to redress their legitimate grievances within the legal framework of autocracy provided the Marxists with a powerful incentive for
the establishment of the RSDRP. Though the two parties differed
profoundly on questions of ideology and tactics, they had two things
in common: first, they both believed that ultimately autocracy could
only be destroyed through the use of violence; secondly, that at least
in theory, political freedom was, for both, only a means of achieving
social equality.

During the formative period of these two parties a sizeable group of
radical intellectuals began for the first time since the Decembrists,[2] to
regard political freedom not only as a means but also as an end in itself.
The members of this group came from both the Populist and Marxist
camps. The former rallied round the editorial board of *Russkoye
Bogatstvo* (Russian Wealth) and were known as 'Legal Populists'. The
latter became known, at the turn of the century, as 'Economists' and
'Legal Marxists'.† In addition to their belief in political freedom as an
aim in its own right, these people shared two other assumptions. They
believed that the use of violence was not the sole means by which
autocracy could be overthrown. (Hence the nickname 'legal', employed
by their revolutionary critics, the word standing not for legal oppositional activity, which was then an impossibility, but for their readiness
to rely mainly on non-violent means.) Secondly, they were temporarily
disillusioned with the masses, i.e. the peasants and the industrial
workers, and were seeking allies in other strata of the population. These

[1] For the origins of this term see *Seton-Watson*, p. 225.
* The term 'populism' is employed by the author in the traditional sense. For a re-
appraisal of this term see *Pipes* IIa, pp. 29–30, 84–6, and below.
[2] The most detailed account in English of the Decembrists is found in *Mazour*. See also
Raeff IV and *Schapiro*, pp. 23–38.
† The term 'Legal Marxism' was apparently coined, by Lenin, immediately after his
break with Struve, i.e. not before the end of 1900. It was used by him and by his Marxist-
orthodox allies in a derogatory sense. (See Pipes II, pp. 74n.–75n. and Pipes IIa, p. 124.)

allies were discovered not in the ranks of the rising bourgeoisie, as might have been expected on the basis of developments in Western and Central Europe, but among those nobles who were active in the elective local government institutions (zemstvos). And it was with the aid of these nobles (hereafter referred to as zemstvo radicals) that the Liberation Movement was launched.

This partnership constituted one of the distinguishing features of the Russian 'Liberal Movement'. The other was the political and social programme of its leaders which, by the beginning of 1905, had also become that of the majority of its rank-and-file members and supporters. It was not 'liberal' in the sense that the programmes of liberal parties and groups in nineteenth-century Western and Central Europe were. The co-ordinating centre of the Liberation Movement (the Union of Liberation) was not interested in partial reforms (such as individual freedoms, the rule of law and the establishment of a representative legislative assembly, elected by a restricted franchise) guaranteed by a constitution granted from above. What it aimed at was the destruction of autocracy by pressure exerted from below and its replacement by a fully democratic regime and what is now known as a 'welfare state'. The Liberation Movement was, therefore, radical–democratic in character, and on practical questions (as distinct from final objectives) it differed from its revolutionary contemporaries mainly as regards means. Even this difference was almost totally eradicated at the beginning of 1905.

The first two chapters of this book describe in detail the beginnings of zemstvo radicalism, the economic and political reasons for the emergence of an oppositional movement among the zemstvo nobility at large, and the growing influence of the former in this movement at the beginning of the twentieth century. Chapters 3 and 4 trace the origins of the democratically inclined intelligentsia. Part One of the book should, therefore, be regarded as a lengthy introduction, placing the Liberation Movement in historical perspective. Part Two describes the actual process by which the Liberation Movement came into being, the organizational framework which enabled the radicals to dominate it and its offensive against the autocratic government. Part Three brings the story to its unhappy conclusion. It starts by describing the stages by which the Liberation Movement achieved supremacy among the forces struggling against autocracy, and ends with the Movement's disintegration without having achieved its main aim – the replacement of autocracy by a constitutional–democratic regime.

3

PART ONE: ORIGINS

I

The origins of zemstvo radicalism*

Zemstvo radicalism was the offspring of what was referred to in Liberation Movement circles as the 'Constitutionalist Movement of 1878–81' or the 'First Zemstvo Movement'. The development of this group was therefore inextricably connected with the establishment and evolution of the institutions of elective local government.

The Law of 1 January 1864,[1] which provided for the establishment of the zemstvos, was born of both administrative necessity and political considerations. The old local government machinery, established by Catherine II's 1775 Edict on the Provinces, had started to disintegrate at the beginning of the nineteenth century,[2] but reform was not regarded as urgent as long as half Russia's population was composed of serfs[3] who were under the absolute jurisdiction of the nobility. Realizing that once these serfs were emancipated further delay would become impossible, Alexander II appointed a special committee in 1859 to make plans for the reform of local government.[4] This committee was faced with the task of organizing the local government machinery so as to enable it to administer a peasant population which would be doubled after emancipation. It also had to find ways and means of reflecting the new legal status of the liberated serfs in the composition and activities of the reformed local government institutions. And lastly, it was necessary to find ways of compensating the nobility for its loss of

* As used in Russia, the term *zemstvo* stood not only for the institution, but also for its elected councillors. Hence the widespread use of such terms as zemstvo movement, zemstvo liberalism etc. The present writer has chosen to coin the term zemstvo radicalism.

[1] *P.S.Z.* II, vol. 39, part I, no. 40457.

[2] See, for example, Speranskiy's proposals for reforms: *Speranskiy*, pp. 192–3, *Raeff* I, pp. 146–7.

[3] For the relevant figures see *Blum*, p. 420.

[4] Information on the deliberations of this committee, at first under the chairmanship of N. A. Milyutin and from 1861 under the chairmanship of P. A. Valuyev, can be found, *inter alia*, in *Avinov*, pp. 1–16, *Brokgaus*, vol. XII, pp. 533–4, *Samoderzhaviye i Zemstvo* I, pp. 63–76. See also *Fischer*, pp. 10–11, *Seton-Watson*, pp. 34–51. The first three sources somewhat exaggerate the importance of the differences of opinion between the liberal and conservative members of the committee.

political and legal rights over the peasantry, without, at the same time, endangering the foundations of autocracy.*

The outcome of the committee's deliberations was embodied in the 1864 Zemstvo Law, which provided for the establishment of zemstvo institutions at two levels: provincial (*guberniya*), and district (*uyezd*). Each institution consisted of an assembly of elected councillors and an executive board, chosen by the assembly. The decree (*ukaz*) to the Ruling Senate which accompanied the Law, defined the task of the zemstvos as participation in the management of public affairs, related to the economic needs and well-being of the local population of *every* province and *every* district.[1] Zemstvo institutions were, however, only established in less than two-thirds of the provinces of European Russia. In those thirty-four provinces where they were set up, the government and its local agents gave a very narrow interpretation to the right of participation in the management of local public affairs. But despite all the restrictions, the zemstvos proved an administrative success. During the fifty-three years of their existence, they raised the standard of education and public health, improved the road network and extended statistical and agronomical aid to the peasants in their provinces on a scale that the notoriously inefficient tsarist bureaucracy could not and would not match.[2]

As for the committee's second task, to give legal expression to the new status of the peasantry, it was fulfilled in the electoral provisions of the law. Elections to the zemstvo assemblies were held once every three years (usually in the autumn). The district zemstvo assemblies were elected first and their members subsequently elected representatives to the provincial zemstvo assemblies. The electorate was divided into three curiae for the district elections, and, for the first time in the annals of modern Russia, the division into curiae did not correspond to the classification of Russian society into three estates. It was based (para. 23 of the Law) on differences of interest (town and country) and ownership of land (privately owned and allotment land). To make this point of departure from previous practice absolutely clear the legislators added an appendix to the above paragraph. In this they stated that 'peasants who privately own non-allotment land amounting to... have the right to vote in the (first) curia'. As long as this stipulation

---

* Alexander II's close advisers entertained no illusions about his political intentions. They knew all along that he was as dedicated to the principle of autocracy as his predecessors.

[1] *P.S.Z.* II, vol. 39, part I, no. 40457 (italics added).

[2] For a detailed account of the activities of the zemstvos during the first forty years of their existence, see: *Veselovskiy* V *a–b*, VI, VII.

existed in the statute book (it was abolished in 1890), the zemstvos had the reputation of being 'non-class institutions',[1] but the satisfaction it afforded the liberated serfs was mainly theoretical. In practice the nobility dominated the zemstvos from the very beginning.

For a start, the number of councillors of noble origin was more than twenty times greater than was warranted by the percentage of nobles in the rural population.[2] Secondly, and more significantly, the nobles completely dominated the zemstvo provincial executive boards.[3] In contrast to the assemblies, which usually met once a year for a period not exceeding two weeks, the executive boards were in permanent session and conducted all the business of the zemstvos. The provincial boards were the most important, since they co-ordinated and, to some extent, supervised the activities of the district boards in their respective

[1] See, for example, *Avinov*, p. 5.

[2] The classification of the zemstvo councillors of district assemblies by class origin during the first and second three-year periods ('first' and 'second' after the establishment of the zemstvos), as well as on the eve of the 1890 zemstvo reform, was as follows:

	First period	Second period	1883–6
Nobles	42.5%	44.9%	42.4%
Peasants	38.5	37.4	37.4
Clergy	1.0	0.5	2.3
Others	18.0	17.2	16.9
	100.0	100.0	100.0

(Source: *Brokgaus*, vol. XII, p. 536)

As one moves up from the district to the provincial level, the percentage of nobles among the councillors rises sharply. According to one modern historian, it was as high as 76% in the late 1880s. (See *Fischer*, p. 9.)

For the relevant figures on the class-division of the rural population of European Russia on the eve of the emancipation of the serfs, see *Rashin* II, pp. 258–9.

[3] The predominance of nobles in the provincial boards is reflected in the following data:

The composition of zemstvo boards, 1883–6 according to the class origin of their members

	District boards		Provincial boards		Total	
	No.	%	No.	%	No.	%
Nobles	553	44.0	98	73.6	651	47.0
Peasants	389	31.0	2	1.5	391	28.0
Others	321	25.0	33	24.9	354	25.0
Total	1,263	100.0	133	100.0	1,396	100.0

(Source: *Brokgaus*, vol. XII, p. 538)

7

provinces. This predominance of the nobility was both natural and to a certain extent encouraged by the central authorities, since Alexander II and his advisers hoped thereby to compensate the nobles for their loss of rights over the peasantry. At the same time they wanted to prevent them from exploiting the zemstvos in order to undermine autocracy, and therefore included in the Law various restrictions in order to forestall this danger.

The Law restricted the activity of the zemstvos to a narrow field of local needs, and also vested the governors with what in reality amounted to veto powers over this activity. Para. 48 of the Law gave the governors of zemstvo provinces the right to veto the election of chairmen of zemstvo boards,[1] while para. 9 granted them the 'right to suspend the implementation of any decision of a zemstvo instititution which stands contrary to the law or to the *general needs of the state*'.[2] It is true that the zemstvos were entitled to appeal to the Senate against such a decision (para. 11), but this right was almost entirely theoretical. Most of the appeals were rejected, and even in those cases where the Senate ruled against the governors, the time-lag between the appeal and the Senate decision was so great that the victory was more moral than practical.[3] The Law also prohibited any co-ordination of activity between zemstvos from different provinces, explicitly stating that 'the sphere of activity of every zemstvo institution is limited by the boundaries of its respective province' (para. 3).

The government, however, was not satisfied with the restrictions imposed in the original Zemstvo Law and soon supplemented them. In 1866 it limited the powers of the zemstvo to impose taxation, and on 13 June 1867, it imposed censorship on zemstvo publications, once again emphasizing that all inter-provincial contacts were prohibited.[4]

It was later claimed, particularly by Witte, that, short of outright abolition, no amount of government restrictions could prevent the zemstvos from endangering the existing regime. This argument was

---

[1] *P.S.Z.* II, vol. 39, Part I, no. 40457.

[2] Ibid. (italics added).

[3] D. N. Shipov, the chairman of the Moscow zemstvo provincial board, related an instance of a successful appeal by the Moscow zemstvo assembly against an unlawful decision of D. N. Sipyagin, then Governor of Moscow. Sipyagin announced his decision on 23 August 1893, the zemstvo decided to appeal to the Senate at the first session following the decision – December 1893/January 1894, and the Senate gave its ruling on 8 February 1897. See *Shipov* II, pp. 107–8.

[4] A summary of governmental legislation on zemstvo matters during the period 1864–89 can be found in *Samoderzhaviye i Zemstvo* I, pp. 79–81, 85–7 and *Yubileynyy Sbornik*, pp. 31–3, among other sources. Cf. *Fischer*, pp. 12–13.

based on the assumption that, as elected institutions, the zemstvos were incompatible with the autocratic principle of government.[1]

The zemstvos were indeed at loggerheads with the government when Witte advanced this theory at the end of the nineteenth century, but not for the reasons he gave. Elective institutions had existed in Russia since the days of Catherine II, without having the slightest effect on autocracy. It was only after Witte's industrialization drive had considerably impoverished the nobility, and the general policy of repression, combined with bureaucratic incompetence, had made a violent revolutionary upheaval a dangerous possibility, that a rapidly growing number of zemstvo activists* took the path of active opposition to the government. Clear support for this theory is evident in the almost complete isolation of the zemstvo radicals up to the mid-1890s, their rapidly expanding influence from then till autumn 1905 and their abrupt loss of all support in the zemstvos immediately afterwards through the nobility's growing fear of a *Pugachovshchina*.[2]

The constitutionalist movement† of 1878–81, which fathered zemstvo radicalism, was initiated by Ivan Ilyich Petrunkevich. He was born in 1843 in the Borzdna district of the 'Little Russian' (Ukrainian) province of Chernigov to a family of the old nobility which owned a substantial estate there.[3] His interest in social and political questions was inherited from his father, who was active in public affairs and became the first president of the reformed Poltava circuit court. In his memoirs Petrunkevich noted that as a very young man, in the early 1860s, he became convinced of the need to establish a constitutional regime in Russia. Clearly aware of his country's backward state he realized[4] that this ultimate goal could only be achieved after arduous and protracted effort. As the first step towards the goal he envisaged the abolition of all legal estate distinctions and privileges, the equalization of all citizens before the law and the assimilation by the masses of the new political principles through their participation in elected local government.[5] He

---

[1] *Samoderzhaviye i Zemstvo* I, pp. 25–6, 96, 198 ff.

* The term 'zemstvo activists' is used in this book as an equivalent to the Russian term *zemskiye deyateli*. As in the case of 'intelligentsia', this term implied more than an occupational description. Only those councillors and zemstvo executive board members who regarded their position not only as an occupation but also as a mission were called *zemskiye deyateli*.

[2] For the extent of the reactionary backlash in the zemstvo milieu, see below.

† The term 'constitutionalist' is used by the author to describe individuals or groups who believed in the need to replace autocracy by a constitutional regime.

[3] See *Brokgaus supp.* vol. II, p. 404 and *Rodichev* IV, p. 317.

[4] *Petrunkevich* II, pp. 41–2.   [5] Ibid.

was therefore eager to become a member of the Chernigov zemstvo immediately after its establishment.[1]

In 1868 he was elected (by the third, i.e. peasant curia) councillor of the Borzdna district zemstvo assembly and was subsequently elected to the Chernigov provincial zemstvo assembly.[2] A year later he became a JP when this post was established in Chernigov, and before the year was out he had become chairman of the provincial panel of JPs, an office he occupied for ten years until his career was cut short by his arrest on 27 April 1879[3] for organizing illegal political activity. He was drawn to engage in this activity through his growing conviction that the approaching political crisis would endanger the whole fabric of Russian society and that only the abolition of autocracy could solve the crisis.[4]

The assassination of the chief of the gendarmerie, N. V. Mezentsev, on 4 August 1878,[5] convinced Petrunkevich that a wave of terror was imminent and that something must be done without delay. The panic-stricken reaction of the government, which on the 20th of the same month published an appeal to the population for help in its fight against 'a band of evilly disposed elements',[6] provided him with an opportunity for action. As he put it in his memoirs:

It became apparent to me that the struggle between the government and the revolutionary movement had entered a new phase...which might endanger not only the old regime which had outlived its usefulness...but also the steadily growing rapprochement with the culture and civilization of Western Europe... Was the government, while appealing to the population for help in its struggle against the revolution, contemplating the accomplishment of the second and final liberation? Obviously not! Hence the choice which faced us was between enrolment in the police force and the defence of liberty.[7]

Petrunkevich naturally chose the latter course, since, for all his aversion to terror, he regarded it as a lesser evil than the government policy. He believed that the government, because of its reactionary and repressive policies, was both responsible for the appearance of terror on the Russian scene, and had the means to put an end to it. As long as the government was not willing to use these means, namely to change its policy, he was prepared to provide shelter for individual terrorists, as well as to establish contacts with their organization.[8]

---

[1] The zemstvo institutions were introduced into Chernigov in 1865. See ibid. p. 13.
[2] Ibid. p. 45.   [3] Ibid. pp. 60–2, 114 and *Rodichev* IV, pp. 317–18.
[4] *Petrunkevich* II, pp. 90–1.   [5] Ibid. p. 96.
[6] Ibid. pp. 94–5 and *Venturi*, pp. 616–17, 839. The full text of this appeal is found, among other places, in *Bogucharskiy* I, pp. 19–21.
[7] *Petrunkevich* ibid. pp. 96–7.   [8] Ibid. pp. 98–100.

In a series of conversations with his friend Lindfors, Petrunkevich elaborated a three-stage plan of action; the first stage involved discovering the extent to which 'society'* shared his political views. If the response proved positive, he would proceed to the second stage: the use of the 'government appeal' as a starting point for the organization of public opinion and the voicing of demands for reforms through the medium of zemstvo assemblies, the press and the clandestine publication of political literature. Stage three would consist of establishing contacts with the revolutionaries with the aim of trying to persuade them to stop their campaign of terror for a limited period so as to enable the public-opinion campaign to gather momentum.[1]

It is not known whether at this stage Petrunkevich was already contemplating a more ambitious plan, namely the foundation of a liberal–constitutionalist party and the establishment of a united front with the revolutionaries, in case the Tsar refused to yield to public opinion. He met with very little success even in the execution of this limited plan.

Shortly after talking over their programme, Petrunkevich and Lindfors left for Kiyev to assess the political mood of society. There they met leaders of the Ukrainophile movement as well as representatives of other national movements,[2] who apparently approved of Petrunkevich's plan of action and offered help. They provided him with an occasion – the centenary of the birth of the Ukrainian poet Kvitko-Osnovyanenko – for the public airing of his political views and undertook to arrange a meeting between him and the terrorists.[3]

The 'Kvitko Anniversary' was celebrated with great pomp in Kharkov, and a commemorative banquet was held on the night of 18 November 1878[4] at the mansion of a local citizen, B. G. Filonov. About fifty people were present – the cream of Kiyev and Kharkov society – and Petrunkevich delivered his first political speech, which transformed him overnight from a local zemstvo activist into a well-known figure. The exact contents of his speech have not survived, but although sources differ with regard to details, they all seem to agree that it included a condemnation of both government and revolutionary terror,

---

* The term 'society' is employed by the author as an equivalent to the Russian *obshchestvo*. It refers to all educated people in Russia, except for those belonging to the higher echelons of the bureaucracy on the one hand and the working classes (including servants) and the revolutionary intelligentsia on the other.

[1] *Bogucharskiy* I, p. 401 (Petrunkevich's letter to the author).

[2] *Bogucharskiy* ibid. pp. 406–7, *Shakhovskoy* II, p. 453.

[3] *Petrunkevich* II, p. 98.

[4] In an autobiographical article Petrunkevich erroneously wrote that the Kvitko celebrations were held in October. See *Kizevetter: Pamyati Goltseva*, p. 104.

as well as an appeal to the government to put an end to the political crisis by initiating radical reforms.[1] Such political demands, however vaguely worded, had not been voiced publicly in Russia since the early 1860s. This aspect of the speech, more than its content, caught the imagination of the audience. According to Petrunkevich, only one participant expressed disapproval of what he had said, while all the others gave him a prolonged standing ovation accompanied by the cry: 'Such a speech is long overdue.'[2]

After obtaining assurances that the Kharkov provincial zemstvo assembly would include political demands among the final resolutions at its next session,[3] Petrunkevich and Lindfors returned to Kiyev, where the Ukrainophiles arranged a meeting between them and a group of southern terrorists. The meeting took place on 3 December 1878 at the home of V. L. Bernshtam, a well-known Ukrainophile.[4] Petrunkevich's remarks on this occasion have not been preserved, but it is known that he tried to persuade the revolutionaries to halt the terror campaign. He himself claimed (in a letter to Bogucharskiy and in his memoirs)[5], that he thought this would enable the public opinion campaign to gather momentum. Another possibility is that he was already thinking in terms of a united front of all oppositional and revolutionary groups on the basis of a minimum constitutional programme, and thought that temporary cessation of terrorist activity would facilitate the organization of his own supporters.[6] It is clear, however, that the negotiations failed because the revolutionaries stipulated unrealistic conditions for suspension of the terror campaign.[7]

---

[1] The main source for the banquet is Petrunkevich himself, but while he stated in a letter to Bogucharskiy that the main purpose of the Chernigov people at the banquet was to raise publicly the 'question of the struggle for political freedom and for a constitution' (*Bogucharskiy* I, p. 398), he mentions in his memoirs only two political demands voiced in his speech: condemnation of terror on both sides and the demand for political reforms from above (*Petrunkevich* II, p. 99). Cf. *Belokonskiy* II, pp. 11–12 and *Fischer*, p. 33.

[2] *Petrunkevich* II, pp. 99–100.   [3] *Shakhovskoy* II, p. 453.

[4] See *Petrunkevich* II, p. 101, *Bogucharskiy* I, p. 402. For the source of the legend about the existence of a 'liberal organization' at the time of the negotiations see *Kennan*, pp. 25–6. Kennan's version of the meeting between the two sides (but not of the 'liberal organization') is based on information he received from Petrunkevich in summer 1884 (*Bogucharskiy* II, pp. 255–6) and on a letter Petrunkevich sent him on 20 December 1886 (see G. Kennan's archive, Library of Congress). This letter was brought to the author's attention by R. Pipes.

[5] *Bogucharskiy* I, p. 402, *Petrunkevich* ibid. p. 101.

[6] *Debogoriy-Mokriyevich*, pp. 300–1.

[7] For a summary of the above negotiations, see *Venturi*, pp. 617–18, 818. This description suffers, however, from two faults. First, it is based solely on Petrunkevich's version of the meeting. Secondly, throughout the English version, as well as the original (*Il Populismo Russo*, p. 1001 and index), his name is misspelled as Petrushevsky.

Undeterred by this failure, Petrunkevich returned to the implementation of the second stage of his plan, namely the organization of
a public-opinion campaign. First he tried to secure the support of a
section of the press for this campaign. He contacted the editors of two
'thick journals'*, *Otechestvennyye Zapiski* and *Vestnik Yevropy*, and
one daily, *Molva*. The editors of the latter two were too timid to agree
to such a dangerous proposition,[1] while N. K. Mikhaylovsky, who met
Petrunkevich on behalf of *Otechestvennyye Zapiski*, refused to co-
operate with him because of ideological differences. According to
Petrunkevich: 'Nikolay Konstantinovich asked me a direct question:
Could I assure him that all the land would be given away to the
peasants?' To this Petrunkevich replied that although he personally
favoured such a solution of the land question and was prepared to do
everything in his power to bring it about, only the constituent assembly
would have the right to give a final answer to the land problem. '"In
that case", objected N.K., "the people will not give a damn for your
landowners' constitution. When the people take state power into their
own hands, they will produce their own brand of constitution which
you will never be able to grant them."'[2]

Having failed to secure the support of even a single newspaper,
Petrunkevich turned to the organization of a zemstvo campaign.
Although he was somewhat more successful in this endeavour than in
his encounters with the press and the revolutionaries, his achievements
were nevertheless very limited. All in all, five[3] out of a total of thirty-
four zemstvo provincial assemblies adopted resolutions containing
demands for reforms, while the majority of the remaining twenty-nine
pledged their full support for the government and called for the adoption of draconian measures against the terrorists.[4] Moreover, Petrunkevich was unsuccessful in his efforts to persuade the all-important
Moscow zemstvo to adopt a progressive resolution,[5] and of the five

---

* The term 'thick journals' (*tolstyye zhurnaly*) was applied at the time to those periodicals
in which social and political questions could be raised legally, the latter by oblique reference.
Since the daily and weekly press was rigorously censored, the intellectuals who were inclined
towards opposition wrote mainly for the monthlies and bi-monthlies. Hence their 'thick-
ness'.

[1] *Petrunkevich* II, pp. 103–4, *Bogucharskiy* I, pp. 398–9

[2] *Petrunkevich* II, p. 105, *Kizevetter: Pamyati Goltseva*, pp. 107–8. Cf. *Bogucharskiy* I,
pp. 399n.–400n. *Billington*, pp. 113–14.

[3] Kennan exaggerated when he wrote that the number of zemstvo 'constitutional'
addresses was eight to ten (*Kennan*, pp. 27–9). To be exact, four zemstvo assemblies
followed Petrunkevich's lead, while one – Poltava – adopted its resolution before he started
his campaign.

[4] See *Petrunkevich* II, p. 453.   [5] Ibid. p. 103.

addresses which did call for reforms (Poltava, Kharkov, Chernigov, Tver and Samara) only that of Tver included radical demands.[1]

The first to raise political questions was the zemstvo provincial assembly of Poltava.[2] In an oblique reference to the government appeal of 20 August 1878, it stated that

only by combining the efforts of the government and society will it be possible to destroy the root of all evil and to overcome the propaganda launched by the enemies of the government and society...But at present Russia lacks a legal basis for the achievement of such an amalgamation of forces, an amalgamation which should combine the efforts of the government and of all the zemstvos of the Empire.[3]

The address of the Kharkov zemstvo, which followed chronologically, stressed the same point:

The Zemstvo would like to unite its forces, not only for the sake of its own economic needs, but also for the sake of the country as a whole, so that its support will be of real value to the government.[4]

This vague and oblique language succeeded to such an extent in obscuring what was in reality a demand for the convocation of a *zemskiy sobor* that, Kennan's later evidence notwithstanding,[5] the Poltava and Kharkov addresses went unnoticed except by the Ministry of the Interior.[6] The latter immediately instructed all the governors of zemstvo provinces to prevent the recurrence of such acts of insubordination.[7] The order as such, more than its actual content, was responsible for the different fate of the Chernigov zemstvo address. This document[8] was written by Petrunkevich and approved almost unanimously by a 'private' meeting of all the zemstvo councillors.[9] It

[1] See *Kennan*, pp. 11, 27–9, *Petrunkevich* II, pp. 453–5, *Samoderzhaviye i Zemstvo* I, pp. 102–4, *Za Sto Let*, pp. 143–6, *Belokonskiy* II, pp. 11–15.

[2] Rodichev incorrectly states that the first address was submitted by the Kharkov zemstvo. See *Rodichev* III, pp. 6–7.

[3] *Petrunkevich* ibid. p. 454.

[4] *Belokonskiy* II, p. 13. Witte's assertion that the Kharkov address ended with the words: 'Grant your own faithful people what you granted the Bulgars' (*Samoderzhaviye i Zemstvo* I, p. 102) and Svatikov's statement (in his preface to Kennan's book) that the Poltava and Kharkov addresses included clear-cut constitutional demands (*Kennan*, p. 11), are not borne out by the other sources, including Kennan himself (ibid. p. 27) or by the later evidence of Petrunkevich himself. But the history of the zemstvo movement of this period was so intermingled with myth that even D. I. Shakhovskoy accepted the above assertions without reservations (*Shakhovskoy* II, p. 453).

[5] *Kennan*, p. 27.

[6] See *Petrunkevich* II, p. 100.

[7] *Kennan* ibid. *Samoderzhaviya i Zemstvo* I, p. 104.

[8] The fullest summary of the Chernigov address is found in *Za Sto Let*, pp. 143–6.

[9] *Petrunkevich* ibid. p. 108.

contained three main demands: the liberation of secondary and higher education from government interference, the granting of freedom of speech and of the press, and the establishment of a public order based on law.

Until these demands were fulfilled, the address continued, the answer to the appeal of government and Tsar[1] for help must be negative:

Therefore the Zemstvo of the Chernigov Province notes with inexpressible regret its complete inability to take any measures whatsoever in the struggle against evil, and considers it its civic duty to inform the government accordingly.[2]

Strongly worded as this address was, compared with the previous ones, it would not have achieved fame had it not been for the intervention of the authorities. When Petrunkevich tried to read the address at the plenary session of the zemstvo assembly, the chairman, acting in accordance with the governor's instructions, closed the meeting and dispersed the councillors and the public with the help of gendarmes.[3]

Immediately after this incident, Petrunkevich left for Tver, a town which was renowned for the radicalism of its nobility.[4] There Petrunkevich was met by, among others, his brother Michael, the Bakunin brothers, the youthful F. I. Rodichev (who became one of his earliest followers). Together with Rodichev (who then occupied the dual positions of Vesyegonsk district zemstvo board chairman and district marshal of the nobility, province of Tver*), he drafted the

[1] On 20 November 1878 Alexander II appeared before a meeting of representatives of all estates in Moscow and appealed to them 'to help in his efforts to prevent the young generation from following the lead of unreliable persons' (*Samoderzhaviye i Zemstvo* I, p. 101).

[2] Cited in *Fischer*, p. 35.

[3] *Kennan*, p. 27, *Petrunkevich* II, pp. 108–9. However, in his letter to Bogucharskiy (already quoted), Petrunkevich denied that the gendarmes actually entered the hall itself: 'They were waiting in the dining room and in the chairman's room' (*Bogucharskiy* I, p. 401). But even so, their presence could be interpreted in only one way, namely that the authorities were ready to use force if necessary.

[4] The radical tradition of the Tver nobility went back to the 1840s and had already reached full expression at the time of the great reforms. On 2 February 1862, the Tver assembly had adopted, by an overwhelming majority, a resolution calling for the convocation of an 'assembly of elected representatives of the whole people without distinguishing between estates'. See *Fischer*, p. 30, *Samoderzhaviye i Zemstvo* I, p. 64, *Rodichev* III, pp. 2–4. A brief summary of the history of this radical tradition is found in *Seton-Watson*, pp. 47–8 and *Fischer*, pp. 28–31. For a more detailed treatment of the subject see *Petrunkevich* II, pp. 166–78, 197–200, 289–90.

* Rodichev, who was to play a leading role in the Liberation Movement, was born in 1856. At the age of twenty he volunteered for the Serbian army and participated for a short period in the war against Turkey. On his return to Tver in 1877 he was elected marshal of the nobility of the Vesyegonsk district as well as chairman of the district zemstvo board. His association with Petrunkevich did not at first affect his public career. He held this dual

address of the Tver provincial zemstvo assembly.[1] This address contained the only almost direct demand for a constitution voiced at the time. Although it refrained from the explicit use of the word 'constitution',* it nevertheless made its demands perfectly clear as may be seen from the following passage:

His Majesty the Emperor, in his concern for the welfare of the Bulgarian people after their liberation from the Turkish yoke, found it necessary to grant them real self-government, personal immunity, independence of the courts and freedom of the press. The Zemstvo of Tver province dares to hope that the Russian people, who carried all the burdens of the war with such readiness and with such utterly devoted love of their own Tsar-Liberator, will be permitted to enjoy the same blessings since, according to the words of His Majesty himself, only they can give the people the opportunity to progress along the path of gradual and lawful development.[2]

After the approval of the address by the Tver zemstvo assembly, Petrunkevich left for Moscow, where, with the help of the 'Tver people', he succeeded in organizing a 'congress of zemstvo activists and well-known public figures'.[3] The congress opened on the last day of

post until 1890, when he resigned in protest against the introduction of the office of land captain. After his resignation, the government changed its attitude toward him and when in the following year he was elected chairman of the Tver provincial zemstvo board, his election was nullified by I. N. Durnovo. (See *Brokgaus supp.* II, p. 542. For his later activity see below.)

[1] *Petrunkevich* II, p. 112, *Rodichev* III, p. 7: IV, p. 319.

* As far as the tsars were concerned, the word 'constitution' remained taboo till the bitter end of the monarchy. This taboo was one of the factors (though a minor one) preventing an understanding between the government and the Cadets in autumn and winter 1905/6.

[2] *Samoderzhaviye i Zemstvo* I, p. 104, *Belokonskiy* II, p. 15. The Bulgarian constitution was destined to play some considerable part in the constitutional movement of 1904–5, mainly through the not always successful usage which P. N. Milyukov made of it. See below.

[3] Information on the theme of this congress is incomplete. In contrast to the Kvitko banquet and the zemstvo addresses, which were reported at the time, and the meeting with the terrorists which soon became common knowledge, although the identity of the participants did not, no reliable information on the Moscow congress reached the public or the authorities before 1910. Although rumours circulated at the time in Moscow, they were either not persistent enough to spark off a police enquiry or, if such an enquiry was held, it produced no results. This can be deduced from the fact that no accusations regarding participation in the congress were included in the indictment against Petrunkevich when he was arrested shortly afterwards, nor were they raised against any other participant. It is true that a police document of the period – 'The Memorandum on Anti-governmental Associations Which Are Not Too Harmful' (*sic*!) – mentions congresses held in Moscow. But it contains such a conglomeration of truths, half-truths and inventions that not even the police, its compilers, dared act upon it. (For the story behind this memo see *Galai* [unpub.] p. 584n.) The first reliable printed evidence on the conference is found in Petrunkevich's autobiographical article in *Kizevetter: Pamyati Goltseva*, pp. 108–10, published in 1910. [That it was still unknown in 1909 can be deduced from the fact that it was not mentioned in *Kornilov* II (see esp. pp. 241–6).]

The main source of information on the congress remains Petrunkevich. Apart from his

March or the first day of April 1879 in the apartment of a Moscow JP, Prince S. M. Kropotkin. It lasted two or three days and was attended by some thirty to forty people. Although the zemstvo delegates present represented only three provinces[1] – Tver, Chernigov and Moscow – they were in the majority, mainly because the Tver zemstvo alone sent ten delegates (among whom were the brothers A. A. and P. A. Bakunin, M. I. Petrunkevich and F. I. Rodichev); I. I. Petrunkevich and A. F. Lindfors represented Chernigov. Among the other delegates were the Ukrainophile V. L. Bernshtam, Professor M. M. Kovalevsky and V. A. Goltsev. The main topics discussed were tactics and organization. Ideological questions were settled beforehand and apparently only confirmed constitutionalists were invited.[2] As regards tactics, it was decided, apparently unanimously, to follow the path of the zemstvo addresses, but the organizational question almost split the congress.

Some of the delegates wanted to establish a conspiratorial society aimed at setting up a constitutional regime, while others opposed this vehemently as too dangerous. They suggested instead holding an annual conference of a similar type at which political questions would be discussed as they arose. Although this point of view prevailed,[3] the constitutionalists were nevertheless unable to implement even so mild a programme at this time. On the day the congress ended, a new attempt on the Tsar's life was made* to which the security authorities reacted for once with unusual vigour.[4] All those suspected of 'political unreliability', regardless of their class or occupation, were rounded up and Petrunkevich, the father of zemstvo radicalism, found himself under arrest on 27 April 1879.[5] Before his arrest, however, he succeeded in smuggling his pamphlet, *Blizhayshiye Zadachi Zemstva* ('The Immediate Tasks of the Zemstvo'),[6] out of the country.

contribution to *Kizevetter : Pamyati Goltseva* (ibid.), he deals with it in a letter to Boguchar-skiy (*Bogucharskiy* I, p. 398) and in his memoirs (*Petrunkevich* II, pp. 102–3, 112). Boguchar-skiy later succeeded in obtaining evidence from other participants and the story of the congress as outlined above is based mainly on his article (*Bogucharskiy* II, pp. 250–1). Rodichev's later reminiscences, on the other hand, are most unreliable on its proceedings. (See *Rodichev* III, p. 8, *Rodichev* IV, pp. 319–20.)

[1] Belokonskiy was letting his imagination run riot when he wrote that sixteen zemstvos were represented at the congress. (See *Belokonskiy* II, p. 16.)   [2] *Fischer*, p. 37.

[3] *Bogucharskiy* II, p. 251, *Fischer*, p. 37. Shakhovskoy's assertion to the contrary (*Shakhovskoy* II, p. 453) is erroneous.   * Soloviev's attempt of 2 April 1879.

[4] *Shakhovskoy* II, p. 454, *Fischer*, p. 38.   [5] *Petrunkevich* II, p. 114.

[6] A complete reprint of the pamphlet is found in *Petrunkevich* II, pp. 453–6. In the reprint in *Yubileynyy Sbornik*, pp. 429–35, the words 'constituent assembly' are missing for obvious reasons. For a brief but incomplete summary in English of this pamphlet see *Fischer*, pp. 35–7.

This pamphlet, which according to Petrunkevich's original plan was intended to be the first of a series of clandestine constitutional publications (which never materialized), had no practical impact at the time. (It was apparently written in the first half of March 1879[1] and first published only in 1883.[2]) Nevertheless it is of vital importance for understanding the subsequent development of the Liberation Movement. It contains in a nutshell the political ideals which guided the activists of the radical wing of zemstvo constitutionalism a generation later, the author himself serving as a living link between the two periods. Written on the eve of the Moscow congress, the pamphlet reflected both Petrunkevich's disillusionment with the zemstvos and his fast-growing radicalism.

After attacking the zemstvos for their cowardly replies to the government's appeal[3] Petrunkevich put forward two principles which were to become the tenets of faith of the radical wing of the Liberation Movement a generation later: the rejection of the idea of a constitution from above, and belief in the need for support from below. In his own words:

Although we choose the zemstvo as the basis of the (constitutional) movement, nevertheless we do believe that the efforts of the whole Russian people will be combined harmoniously for the achievement of its freedom... We reject any constitution granted from above and insist, instead, on the convening of a constituent assembly.[4]

The arrest of Petrunkevich terminated that stage of the 'First Zemstvo Movement' in which a conscious effort was made to organize a constitutional force in the country. It did not, however, end the political crisis, which became more and more acute. The Tsar, in his frantic efforts to put an end to the rising tide of terror (of which he was now the chief target) called on Count M. I. Loris-Melikov to save the situation. First he appointed him head of the specially created 'Supreme Administrative Committee' (12 February 1880) and then, six months later, made him Minister of the Interior. On assuming office, Loris-Melikov announced his intention of opening a new era in the relations

---

[1] The date is indicated by the following sentence: 'At this moment we hear of the murder of Prince Kropotkin' (*Petrunkevich* II, p. 453). Prince D. N. Kropotkin was Governor of Kharkov and was assassinated on 9 March 1879. (See *Za Sto Let*, part II, p. 98. Venturi mistakenly gives the date as 9 February 1879.)

[2] In *Volnoye Slovo* no. 56. For the adventurous history of this pamphlet before and after publication (Petrunkevich rediscovered it only in 1911), see *Petrunkevich* II, pp. 111–12, *Bogucharskiy* I, pp. 413–14; II, p. 252, *Yubileynyy Sbornik*, pp. 435–6 (Dragomanov's preface to the pamphlet).

[3] *Petrunkevich* II, pp. 453–5.

[4] Ibid. p. 456.

between government and society (which became known as the era of the 'dictatorship of the heart') and he specifically stated that the zemst- vos would enjoy greater freedom of action.[1] This declaration provided a new lease of life for the 'First Zemstvo Movement', although no new attempt was made to organize a constitutional force in the country. It enabled liberals and constitutionalists of varying shades of opinion, as well as certain zemstvo assemblies, to voice some of their demands.

The first to exploit Loris-Melikov's statements were a group of Moscow constitutionalists, consisting of university lecturers and mem- bers of the staff of *Russkiya Vedomosti*. S. A. Muromtsev, the future president of the first Duma, V. Ya. Skalon and A. I. Chuprov prepared on behalf of this group, a memorandum on the causes of the current political crisis, which they handed to Loris-Melikov on 25 March 1880.[2] They listed the main grievances of 'society', some of which were already familiar, i.e. lack of personal freedom and immunity,[3] lack of respect on the part of the government for the law and its officers,[4] and imposition of ever-increasing restrictions on the zemstvos.[5] New plaints against 'the recently opened crusade against the educated classes (the best elements of our society)'[6] and the 'unequal distribution of the taxation burden among the various classes of Russian society'[7] were added. The authors of the memorandum then went on to state:

The only solution to the current political crisis lies in the establishment of an inde- pendent assembly of representatives of the zemstvos, which will participate in the governing of the nation and in the drafting of the indispensable guarantees of personal immunity and of freedom of thought and expression.[8]

The zemstvo addresses which followed were less outspoken than that of the Moscow constitutionalists. Even the Tver zemstvo refrained from 'constitutional' hints in its congratulatory cable to Loris-Melikov on 19 December 1880.[9]

The assassination of Alexander II introduced an element of urgency into the deliberations of the extraordinary sessions of the zemstvos. But even then none of the assemblies went beyond the demand for the convocation of a *zemskiy sobor*, while at the same time emphasizing their aversion to terror and their support for the government and for

---

[1] *Samoderzhaviye i Zemstvo* I, pp. 107–8, *Rodichev* III, p. 9.
[2] 'Statement of 25 Prominent Moscow Citizens'. Full text found in *Kennan*, pp. 30–48. For Muramtsev's role in its composition see *Milyukov* IV, pp. 30–1. See also *Rodichev* III, p. 10 and *Fischer*, pp. 65–7.
[3] *Kennan*, pp. 30, 36–41.   [4] Ibid. p. 35.   [5] Ibid. pp. 37–9.   [6] Ibid. p. 35.
[7] Ibid. p. 45.   [8] Ibid. p. 47.   [9] *Samoderzhaviye i Zemstvo* I, p. 110.

the course of 'law and order'. Thus, for example, the appeal of the Novgorod zemstvo assembly to the new monarch included the following sentence:

We beg you to give society the opportunity to participate in the struggle against the enemies of the Russian people and humbly ask Your Imperial Highness to sound out the free voice of Russia.[1]

The Tver zemstvo reminded Alexander that

the invincible and mighty strength that the Russian Tsar and the Russian people always found in times of trouble was derived from a union between the representatives of the land and the Supreme Power.[2]

Other zemstvos adopted similar resolutions but they were not allowed a free rein for long. The new Tsar very soon succeeded, with the aid of Pobedonostsev and Count D. A. Tolstoy, in imposing his notorious reign of reaction.[3] From now on all government measures, except in the field of industrialization, were aimed at undoing as many as possible of the political and social achievements of the 'era of the great reforms'. The main target of the government's wrath were those measures aimed at bringing about greater equality between the estates, the idea of equality being regarded by Alexander III and Tolstoy, as by their spiritual mentor K. P. Pobedonostsev, as one of the 'greatest evils of our time'. They hoped to reverse the trend towards equality by intensifying the grip of bureaucracy (and particularly of the Ministry of Interior) on society, and by restoring to the nobility many of its pre-emancipation privileges.

The first to suffer from these policies were the institutions of higher and secondary education. Tolstoy and his henchman, Delyanov, the new Minister of Education, replaced the 1863 university statute with the draconian 1884 Law of Higher Education. The new law greatly increased the powers of government inspectors over both students and faculty bodies, and transferred the authority to nominate professors, deans and rectors from the universities to the Ministry of Education.[4]

---

[1] *Samoderzhaviye i Zemstvo* I, p.118. [2] Ibid. Cf. *Rodichev* III, p.12, *Zayonchkovskiy*, p.317.

[3] As mentioned above, the 'First Zemstvo Movement' was also known in Liberation Movement circles, and is still referred to by some modern historians as the 'Constitutionalist Movement of 1878–83'. The latter description, however, is quite erroneous since it implies that the Movement existed until 1883, while in fact it was dissolved in 1881. The 'constitutionalist activity' of 1881–3, such as the publication of *Volnoye Slovo* and the 'establishment' of the 'Zemstvo Union' did not, in fact, represent a genuine movement, but was a product of the not-always successful machinations of the 'Holy Brotherhood'. For the story behind these activities see *Galai* (unpub.), Appendix A, pp. 550, 573–88.

[4] *Seton-Watson*, p. 475.

Three years later, Delyanov raised the entrance fees to universities, *gimnazii* and incomplete *gimnazii*, so as to make them less accessible to children from the lower orders. Not content with these measures, he sent his notorious 'cooks' circular' in the same year to all officials of the Ministry of Education in the provinces. In it he urged them to prevent 'children of coachmen, servants, cooks, washerwomen, small shop-keepers and persons of a similar type' from obtaining secondary or higher education.[1] According to the calculations of a well-known modern historian of Russia, Delyanov's efforts bore fruit. From 1882 to 1895 the number of pupils in *gimnazii* and incomplete *gimnazii* dropped from 65,751 to 63,863, while the percentage of children of nobles and officials in these schools increased from 47 per cent to 56 per cent.[2] After completing his 'reform' of the educational system, Tolstoy turned his attention to the peasantry and the zemstvos. In 1889 the office of JP was abolished in the zemstvo provinces, and in the rural areas its functions were transferred to the newly created offices of 'land captain' (*zemskiy nachalnik*). The land captains were officials of the Ministry of the Interior and were drawn from the hereditary nobility of the districts in which they served.[3] A year later, after Tolstoy's death,[4] a new zemstvo law was published.

The Zemstvo Law of 12 June 1890[5] differed from the original law on three important points: it severely curtailed the independence of these institutions, it abolished their 'non-class' character, and it almost abolished the elective principle as far as the peasants were concerned. The chief provisions for curtailing the independence of the zemstvos were: the granting of an 'absolute veto' over a large range of zemstvo activities to the Minister of the Interior and the governors;[6] a substantial expansion of the 'suspensive veto' powers of the governors by way of curtailing the rights of the zemstvos to appeal to the Senate against their decisions;[7] the appointment of the governors as 'guardians' of the zemstvos,[3] and the establishment of special committees under their chairmanship, with a majority of government officials on their boards, to enable them to supervise day-to-day activities.[9] The district marshals

[1] Ibid. p. 476.   [2] Ibid.   [3] Ibid. p. 467.
[4] Before his death, Tolstoy prepared a draft for a new zemstvo law which, if accepted, would have abolished the zemstvos in all but name. See: *Alvincv*, pp. 2c–1, *Samoderzhaviye i Zemstvo* I, pp. 136–41 and *Zayonchkovskiy* I, pp. 40?–11.
[5] *P.S.Z.* III, vol. X, part I, no. 6927.   [6] Ibid. para. 12, 81–4, 94.
[7] Ibid. para. 87, 89.   [8] Ibid. para. 5.
[9] Ibid. para. 8–12, 36, 47–9. The committees were called *Gubernskoye Po Zemskim Delam Prisutstviye* (Provincial Office on Zemstvo Affairs).

of the nobility and some categories of local officials were declared *ex officio* chairmen and members respectively of the 'zemstvo assemblies'.[1] The chairmen and members of the zemstvo boards were made equal in status to government officials,[2] and were subjected to all the limitations of governmental service.[3]

The non-class character of the zemstvos was abolished through the classification of the three electoral curiae according to the estate division of Russian society:[4] the barring of members of the lower classes from the top position in the zemstvos – namely chairmanship of the provincial boards;[5] the expansion of noble representation and a drastic reduction in the representation of non-gentry landowners and peasants.[6] The elective principle in the peasant curia was severely curtailed by para. 51, which stated that governors were to appoint peasant councillors from lists of candidates submitted by peasant electors.

But despite their great theoretical significance, these elaborate provisions had almost no practical consequences. The electoral clauses of the Law fixed the total number of district councillors at 10,229.[7] Their distribution by class was as follows:[8] Curia A (1st electoral assembly – nobles)[9] 57.1 per cent; Curia B (2nd assembly – 'poor' nobles and others, excluding peasants)[10] 13.3 per cent; Curia C (rural assemblies – peasants)[11] 29.6 per cent. If one adds to the representatives chosen by the first curia those nobles chosen by the second, one may assume that at least 60 per cent of zemstvo district councillors were of noble origin, and that the percentage was even higher in the provincial assemblies. But striking as they are, these figures do not in fact represent a significant change. The percentage of nobles among the total number of district councillors may have been lower before the promulgation of the 1890 law,[12] but they constituted a much higher percentage – 76 per cent – among the provincial councillors, and what was most important, they then completely dominated the zemstvo provincial executive boards.

---

[1] *P.S.Z.* III, vol. X, part I, no. 6927, para 56–7.   [2] Ibid. para. 124.   [3] Ibid. para. 132, 134.
[4] Ibid. para. 14–16, 24, 28, 31.   [5] Ibid. para. 117.
[6] For a statistical summary see *Lazarevskiy* III, pp. 65–6.
[7] *Brokgaus*, vol. XII, p. 537.
[8] Ibid. The percentage applies to 9,523 councillors, or the total number of district councillors in thirty provinces. Because the statistical significance of the remaining councillors is small, one can assume that these figures apply to the total number of district councillors.
[9] *P.S.Z.* III, vol. X, part I, no. 6927, para. 24.
[10] Ibid. para, 31.   [11] Ibid. para. 15, 51.   [12] See above.

Moreover, the new law was designed to ensure the nobility's preponderance in the zemstvos, only because Alexander III and his close advisers believed the nobility to be 'the most reliable class in Russia', i.e. the social bulwark of autocracy.[1] When this assumption proved false, all the restrictions imposed by the new law were powerless to prevent the zemstvos from becoming centres of oppositional activity.

The first cracks in the monolithic and reactionary facade of Alexander III's reign appeared only a year after the publication of the new Zemstvo Law, mainly as a consequence of the traumatic effect of the 1891–2 famine on the Russian educated classes.[2] The famine suddenly exposed both the stagnation of Russian agriculture which, on the threshold of the twentieth century, was still completely dependent on the vagaries of nature, and the cruelty and incompetence of the tsarist government. I.A. Vyshnegradskiy, Witte's predecessor in the Ministry of Finance (1887–92), who initiated the industrialization drive, also introduced an ingenious method of indirect taxation as a means of increasing exports. This increase was necessary for the attainment of a favourable balance of payments, a prerequisite for putting the rouble on the gold standard. Since grain was the main Russian export commodity, Vyshnegradskiy's officials collected the taxes in the autumn, when grain prices were low, thus forcing the peasants to sell a larger proportion of their crop in order to raise the money.[3] This meant that a larger amount of grain was available for export, but at the same time it left the peasants with insufficient grain reserves to see them through the lean years. Hence, a particularly bad harvest in 1891 resulted in a national calamity of unprecedented magnitude. At first the government tried to conceal the gravity of the situation from the public. It was only when their inability to cope with the emergency became apparent to all that they agreed to accept help from individuals and non-governmental institutions.

Educated society reacted to the famine in two ways. A small minority, composed mainly of students, tried to exploit it for the propagation of revolutionary ideas and the fostering of peasant disturbances in the famine-stricken provinces.[4] The response of the majority was much more conventional. Relief committees sprang up in many parts of Russia (one of these was headed by L. Tolstoy), money was raised and

---

[1] See *Avinov*, p. 20, *Robinson*, pp. 131–2 and *Seton-Watson*, pp. 466–8.

[2] See, for example, *Korolenko* v, *Petrunkevich* II, pp. 275–7, *Struve* VII, p. 353. Cf. *Fischer*, p. 72 and below.

[3] See *Seton-Watson*, p. 518, *Von Laue* III, pp. 26–7.

[4] See *V. Obolonskiy*, pp. 196–209 and below.

volunteers distributed food and clothes and supplied medical help to the affected areas. It was mainly through their work on the relief committees and in the famine areas that many members of the upper classes first discovered the wretched conditions under which the peasants lived (and died) in Russia. Some of them were so appalled by the realities of peasant life that they turned to anti-government activity in order to change them. Among the latter[1] were Prince Peter D. Dolgorukov, who immediately joined the tiny radical group formed by Petrunkevich, and who was later to become one of the most important leaders of the radical wing of the Liberation Movement, his brother Pavel D. Dolgorukov, who held somewhat less radical views at the time, and Count P. A. Geyden, the chairman of the Imperial Free Economic Society, who later became one of the leaders of the moderate constitutionalists.

The new mood generated by the famine brought the zemstvo radicals out of their shell, but they were able to return to full activity only after the death of Alexander III. The change of rulers which occurred on 20 October 1894 gave Petrunkevich and his followers the first opportunity since the late 1870s of exploiting the zemstvo institutions as sounding boards for the propagation of their ideas.

The zemstvo assemblies usually held their regular sessions in the autumn, and were thus the first public institutions able to comment on Nicholas II's accession to the throne. The great majority of the assemblies sent conventional messages of goodwill to the new monarch. Nine of them – Tver, Tula, Ufa, Poltava, Saratov, Tambov, Orel, Kursk and Chernigov[2] – added to their messages various hints about the need for reforms, but only the Tver assembly included demands which could be and were immediately interpreted as constitutional. The other eight assemblies (except, to some extent, for Chernigov) mainly requested the removal of various obstacles to zemstvo activity imposed by the 1890 law. They also asked for the right to appeal directly to the monarch, a right enjoyed by the provincial assemblies of the nobility.

The Tver zemstvo address was drafted by Petrunkevich and his followers: his brother Michael, A. A. Bakunin, A. A. Golovachev, F. I. Rodichev and several others.[3] Petrunkevich, who had lived alternately in Moscow and Tver since his release from prison and exile in 1886,

---

[1] See *Peter Dolgorukov*. pp. 300–1.

[2] The list of zemstvo assemblies as well as a summary of their decisions and the reaction of Nicholas II can be found in *Mirnyy*, pp. 3–15. It was then reprinted in *Samoderzhaviye i Zemstvo* I, pp. 164–6, *Belokonskiy* II, pp. 50–2, etc.

[3] *Petrunkevich* II, p. 289.

had been a member of the Tver provincial assembly since 1890.[1] It was therefore in his capacity as a zemstvo councillor that he seized the opportunity to make some of his ideas public, a thing he had been unable to do for more than sixteen years. Since he and his followers were well aware that the majority of the Tver zemstvo provincial councillors were not yet ready to adopt a clear-cut constitutional resolution, they deliberately watered down their demands. But even the final draft, which was presented to the Assembly by Rodichev, was approved only by a narrow majority.[2] This draft read in part as follows:

Your Imperial Majesty, in these momentous days when you begin your *service* to the Russian people, the Zemstvo of the Tver Province greet you as your loyal subjects ...At one with all the Russian people, we are filled with gratitude and hope for the success of your labours towards the accomplishment of the great aim which you have set yourself – to build up the happiness of your loyal subjects...

We trust that our happiness will increase and grow firmer under an *unflinching adherence to the laws* on the part both of the people and *of the authorities*. For the laws, which in Russia embody the expression of the sovereign will, must be placed above the accidental intentions of individual representatives of the government. We ardently believe that the rights of individuals and of public institutions will be steadfastly safeguarded.

We look forward, Sire, to its being possible and right for public institutions to express their views on matters concerning them, so that an expression of the requirements and thoughts of *representatives of the Russian people*, and not only of the administration, may reach the heights of the throne... We believe that in intercourse with representatives of all classes of the Russian people... the power of Your Majesty will find a new source of strength.[3]

In theory this address did not go beyond the demand for the establishment of a *Rechtsstaat* and the convocation of a consultative assembly and hence, technically speaking, there was nothing in it which could be interpreted as a demand for the limitation of the autocratic powers of the Tsar. In reality the borderline between a consultative and a legislative assembly was less well-defined. Since the convening of the Estates-General by Louis XVI, the supporters of absolutism had been aware of the ease with which one could be transformed into the other. Hence they were as vehemently opposed to the introduction of a consultative representative institution as to the convening of a legis-

---

[1] Ibid. pp. 248–67. After his release Petrunkevich was barred from entering St Petersburg and five South Russian provinces, including his native Chernigov. The ban was lifted only at the end of 1904. (Ibid. p. 244.)

[2] *Petrunkevich*, ibid. pp. 289–90.

[3] English translation in *Struve* VII, pp. 349–50 (italics added).

lative assembly. It was therefore only natural that the young Tsar's advisers interpreted the Tver address as a demand for the replacement of autocracy by a constitutional regime. This interpretation, as well as the fact that such demands had not been publicly voiced for more than a decade, was undoubtedly responsible for the exaggerated reaction of the government to this message of goodwill.[1]

F. I. Rodichev was the first to suffer the consequences. He was deprived of all his civil rights, i.e. the right to participate in estate or public assemblies or in the election of representatives to such assemblies.[2] Nicholas then exploited the occasion of his marriage reception, held on 17 January 1895*, in order to deliver a public rebuke to all those members of society, and especially to 'certain zemstvo activists', who expected him to transform autocracy into a less absolutist and arbitrary regime. Addressing the assembled representatives of the nobility, zemstvos, town dumas and the Cossack army, he uttered two sentences which transformed the Tver Address episode into a landmark in the annals of the Liberation Movement:

I am aware that of late, in some zemstvo assemblies, the voices of persons who have been carried away by *senseless dreams* of the participation of zemstvo representatives in the affairs of internal administration, have been heard. Let it be known to all that, while devoting all my energies to the good of the people, I shall maintain the principle of autocracy just as firmly and unflinchingly as did my unforgettable father.[3]

This speech (Petrunkevich's later evidence notwithstanding[4]) went down very badly with the audience, annoyed the liberally minded bureaucrats, and infuriated public opinion (i.e. society).[5] It also brought about a resounding reply two days later in the form of 'An Open Letter to Nicholas II' from zemstvo constitutionalist circles.

You have uttered your word and it will now resound all over Russia, all over the civilised world. Till now you have been unknown to anybody. Since yesterday you have become a known quantity about whom there is no longer any room for 'sense-

---

[1] That the government over-reacted to the Tver Address because it interpreted it as a demand for a constitution is confirmed by the following entry in Lamsdorf's diary (19 January 1895): 'A certain zemstvo assembly (Tver) hinted about its constitutional longings and because of this all the deputations at the reception were scolded.' (*Lamsdorf*, p. 26.)

[2] *Brokgaus supp.* II, p. 542, *Petrunkevich* ibid. p. 290.

* The wedding ceremony itself took place on 14 November 1894.

[3] *Struve*, p. 350. (Italics added.) The Russian text is found, among other sources, in *Polnoye Sobraniye Rechey Nikolaya II, 1894–1906*, p. 7, *Za Sto Let*, p. 264, *Petrunkevich* II, p. 290.

[4] *Petrunkevich* II, p. 290.

[5] See *Lamsdorf* ibid. and *Struve* ibid.

less dreams'...At none of the zemstvo meetings has there been a single voice raised against the autocratic government...It was only a question of removing that wall of bureaucracy and court that separates the Tsar from Russia.* Such are the aspirations of the zemstvo members which you, who have just mounted the throne, inexperienced and ignorant as you are, have dared to brand as 'senseless dreams'... If the autocracy identifies itself, both in words and deeds, with the omnipotence of officialdom, if it depends on completely silencing the public and on a permanent enforcement of the supposedly temporary Emergency Defence Act, *then its game is lost, it is digging its own grave*...You have begun the struggle, and the struggle will not be long in coming.[1]

With the exception of the very small band of Petrunkevich's followers, no one was aware at that time of the identity of the very unusual group of people[2] hidden behind the name 'zemstvo constitutionalist circles'. The main author of the open letter was the twenty-five-year-old Peter Berngardovich Struve, already a well-known Marxist.[3] He had become famous four months earlier on the publication, in St Petersburg, of his *Critical Notes on Russia's Economic Development*,[4] the first major Marxist contribution to the Marxist–populist controversy of the mid-1890s.[5] Struve was assisted in the composition, hectographing and distribution of the 'Letter' by a small circle of personal friends. This group consisted of: A. N. Potresov, one of the founding-fathers of Russian social-democracy;[6] A. M. Kalmykova, in whose house Struve lived at the time, and who became a devoted Marxist under his influence,[7] and four constitutionally inclined zemstvo activists – Prince D. I. Shakhovskoy, a future leader of the radical wing of the Liberation Movement,[8] K. K. Bauer, Alexandra A. Steven and F. I. Rodichev, who was kept informed of events by Shakhovskoy.

The role played by Struve, and to a much lesser extent by Potresov, in the publication of the 'Open Letter' throws important light on the still fluid state of radical politics in Russia at that time. It also substanti-

* The phrase 'wall of bureaucracy' (*sredosteniye*) became very popular with the leaders of the Liberation Movement on the eve of the 1904–5 Revolution and during its first phase. Some of them, like Shipov, used it because they believed in its existence, while others did so because it provided a good disguise for attacks on autocracy itself.

[1] *Struve* VII, pp. 352–4, Russian text found in *Struve* I. Italics added.
[2] For the list of people and their contribution to this enterprise, see *Struve* VII, pp. 351–2, 354–8.
[3] A comprehensive biography of Struve has recently appeared in print. See *Pipes* IIa.
[4] See *Struve* IV and *Struve* V, p. 581.   [5] See *Keep*, p. 30, and below.
[6] See below, and also *Getzler*, pp. 45 ff., *Keep*, pp 34, 67 ff., *Nikolayevskiy* II, *Schapiro* I, pp. 35 ff.
[7] For Kalmykova's intimate relations with Struve and her role in Russian Marxism, see *Lenin* II, vol. 46, pp. 598–9, *Pipes* IIa, pp. 24n. 25–7, 72–3, 76–9, 170–5.
[8] See below.

ates some of Struve's later claims about his motives for embracing Marxism,[1] as well as revealing basic traits in his character which were to characterize his political behaviour through most of his life.

Struve's motives for embracing Marxism were quite different from those of his much more famous contemporary, Lenin, or even of Potresov. For the latter two, one of the main attractions of Marxism lay in its social content. Hence their gravitation towards orthodoxy in the second half of the 1890s.[2] Struve, on the other hand, had already made it clear in the preface to *Critical Notes* that he 'does not see himself as bound by the letter and code of any doctrine. He is not infected by orthodoxy.'[3] He subscribed to Marxism at that time mainly because it offered a 'scientific solution' to the twin problems of liberating Russia from the yoke of autocracy and from the misery of its backward state.[4] Beside historical determinism, the most attractive feature of the 'Marxist solution' for Struve and like-minded Russian radicals lay in the role it assigned to the industrial workers. The theory which regarded the proletariat as the most revolutionary class in Russia seemed to promise them the support of a section of the 'people' in their struggle with tsarism at a time when disillusionment with the 'revolutionary potential' of the peasantry was at its height. But the banner of opposition to the existing regime was raised in the winter of 1894–5 not by the industrial workers but by some of the zemstvo assemblies. Struve immediately took note of this development and shifted his attention for a while to these institutions.[5] He was to repeat this performance, but with more lasting effect, when similar circumstances arose at the turn of the century.[6]

His role in the publication of the 'Letter' clearly demonstrated Struve's ability to work simultaneously with people from different social backgrounds and of varying political creeds. It also revealed his capacity to adapt his arguments and style to the political levels of various strata of Russian society. These traits were to prove important assets at the time of the formation of the Liberation Movement, but prior to this development and particularly after it they served as liabilities, since they were to a great extent responsible for Struve's inability to become a 'straight' party man. This in part accounted for the distrust which the founding-fathers of Russian Marxism displayed

---

[1] See *Struve* V, pp. 576–8 and below.   [2] See below.
[3] *Struve* IV, pp. viii–ix. This statement was one of the reasons for Lenin's savage criticism of Struve's book at the time. See below.
[4] See *Struve* V, pp. 577–8.   [5] See *Struve* VII, pp. 350–1.   [6] See below.

towards him in the second half of the 1890s.[1] his progressive loss of influence in the Liberation Movement from about 1903 onwards, and his isolation in the Cadet Party.

These events however still lay in the future. In the meantime, the Tver Address, Nicholas's speech and the 'Open Letter' aroused great hopes among Russian émigrés abroad from both the Marxist and populist camps. Plekhanov and Akselrod, who together with Vera Zasulich formed the Liberation of Labour Group, had by then already developed their theory of the 'two-stage revolution'. According to this theory, the proletariat was due to play a leading, but not exclusive, role in the 'first', i.e. 'bourgeois' stage.[2] They were therefore eagerly awaiting the appearance of a bourgeois–liberal movement as the prerequisite for the success of the revolution. Although the *zemtsy*, whom they believed to have written the 'Open Letter', were only progressive landowners and not captains of industry, banking and commerce, they chose to regard this event as only the beginning of a process. Hence Plekhanov's jubilation (premature, as he was soon to discover) on receiving the news about the developments in the zemstvo milieu. One can sense this excitement in his correspondence with Engels. In a letter dated 20 February 1895 he wrote *inter alia*:

Our zemstvo has become enlivened. You have undoubtedly heard about the Tver zemstvo petition. That of the Chernigov zemstvo is even more emphatic. The young idiot at the Winter Palace has rendered a great service to the revolutionary party by his speech.[3]

A fortnight later (3 March 1895 N. S.) Plekhanov returned to the same theme:

At the present moment, so-called 'society' is being aroused against Nicholas II...I enclose herewith the reply of the Russian liberals to Nicholas's famous speech. The letter was reprinted in London, but it is authentic; it was circulated all over Russia before it came to London. You will see from the letter that we can hope for better times.[4]

A little later, after receiving news about the outbreak of strikes in Russia, Plekhanov wrote again:

You know already that Mr Nicholas the younger has proved himself to be an ultra-

---

[1] Even Vera Zasulich, Struve's greatest admirer in the Liberation of Labour Group, admitted privately in late 1897 that although he was abler than Lenin, the *'praktiki'* and the 'Samarans', Struve lacked the ability to conform to a party line and hence his unreliability. See *Gruppa* VI, pp. 188–9, 197, and below.

[2] See below.   *Gruppa* II, p. 333.

[4] Ibid. pp. 336–7. Apart from the first sentence, the English translation is taken from *Struve* VII, p. 359.

reactionary... The revolutionary movement is now stronger than it has been in the past decade. It is becoming hot in Russia.[1]

The news of developments in the zemstvos was welcomed no less enthusiastically by the populist, S. M. Kravchinskiy-Stepnyak.* On receiving a copy of the 'Open Letter', he wrote in one of the 'Express Leaflets' (*Letuchiye Listki*) of the 'Fund of the Russian Free Press' that although the 'zemstvo people' were not yet demanding a democratic constitution, their actions proved that they had already entered upon the 'right' path of opposition to the autocratic regime. Moreover, he continued, the promptness of their reply to Nicholas's speech demonstrated that they already represented a substantial force in the country: 'They are organized: the speech was delivered on 17 January 1895, and by the 19th the reply had already been prepared, hectographed and despatched.'[2]

Plekhanov and Kravchinskiy were, of course, entirely wrong about the authorship of the 'Open Letter', the number of the 'liberals' and the strength of their organization. None of the zemstvo assemblies, except to some extent Chernigov,[3] followed Tver's example, nor did Petrunkevich's radical circle succeed in utilizing their initial triumph for the launching of a zemstvo–constitutional newspaper.[4] As a consequence, the exaggerated hopes aroused among the exiled revolutionaries soon gave way to deep disappointment with zemstvo liberalism. This disillusionment was particularly acute in Marxist circles, since the political apathy displayed by the overwhelming majority of zemstvo activists after Nicholas's speech stood in glaring contrast to the growing unrest among the workers of St Petersburg. The industrial unrest in that city, which began in mid-1895, culminated in the famous textile strike of 24 June–17 July 1896.[5] This resulted, on the one hand, in the enactment of the $11\frac{1}{2}$-hour working–day law (2 June 1897) and, on the other, in the establishment of the St Petersburg Union of Struggle for the Emancipation of the Working Class, which laid the foundation for the Russian Social-Democratic Movement.[6]

These developments more than overshadowed the Tver Address and the Tsar's reaction to it. This explains why Struve did not follow up his

---

[1] *Gruppa* ibid. pp. 337–8.

* S. M. Kravchinskiy (1852 – December 1895), a leader of the 'southern terrorists', assassin of Mezentsev and one of the founders of the 'Fund of the Free Russian Press' in London. He was run over by a train.

[2] Quoted in *Struve* VII, p. 359.   [3] *Mirnyy*, pp. 14–15.

[4] *Petrunkevich* II, pp. 294–7, *Shakhovskoy* I, p. 200.   [5] *Russkiy Kalendar* 1897, p. 323.

[6] *Keep*, pp. 39–49. *Schapiro* I, pp. 24–9. For a different point of view see *Pipes* II, pp. 76–125.

'Open Letter' for the time being with new ventures into the field of 'liberal politics' but plunged himself wholeheartedly into the more promising field of social-democratic activity.[1] Many like-minded radicals, who later broke with orthodox Marxism, followed his example.

But although the stature of the zemstvo radicals diminished in the eyes of the revolutionaries between 1895 and 1898, they became increasingly important in their own milieu through two developments. The white-collar employees of the zemstvos (the 'Third Element'[2]) were becoming increasingly active and influential, and were proving helpful to the zemstvo radicals in their efforts to capture the hearts and minds of their fellow councillors. At the same time, the nobility was becoming more susceptible to oppositional ideas because of the worsening agricultural crisis and the first signs of unrest in the cities.

Despite the various governmental restrictions, the 1890s witnessed a sharp rise in the economic and welfare activity of the zemstvos. This was most evident in the fields of primary education, public health and veterinary services, where expenditure more than doubled during the decade. Nor did activity in other fields lag far behind.[3] This created an

[1] See *Kindersley*, pp. 51–2, 180–7, 192–7.

[2] The other two elements being the government officials ('First') and the elected councillors ('Second'). The phrase 'Third Element' was coined by Konoidi. Vice-Governor of Samara, at the opening of the regular meeting of the Samara provincial zemstvo assembly in December 1899. See *Yordanskiy*, pp. 44–6, *Kaufman*, p. 267, *Belonkonskiy* II, pp. 71–2, *Bryukhatov*, pp. 191–2. See also *Fischer*, p. 61, who mistakenly gives Konoidi's seat of office as Saratov.

[3] The following table shows the increase in zemstvo expenditure in the last two decades of the nineteenth century:

Zemstvo expenditure and its allocation in the years 1880–1900

	1880		1890			1900		
	Thousand roubles	%	*Thousand roubles*	%	*Increase over 1880* %	*Thousand roubles*	%	*Increase over 1890* %
Total	35,074	100	47,047	100.0	33.0	88,294	100.0	88.0
Support of govt institutions (including maintenance of prisons)			12,679	26.8	—	7,751	8.7	40.0
Maintenance of zemstvo admin.			3,982	8.4	—	8,677	9.8	118.0
Public health			10,505	22.5	—	24,322	27.6	131.0
Primary education			7,226	15.3	—	15,557	17.6	115.0
Veterinary services			711	1.6	—	1,734	2.0	143.0
Other expenditure			11,944	25.4	—	30,253	34.3	160.0

(Source: *Karavayev*, pp. 166–7, 170)

unprecedented influx of statisticians, physicians, veterinary surgeons, teachers, agricultural experts and other professional employees into the zemstvo provinces. At the end of the decade their numbers had reached the 70,000 mark, which meant that there were roughly fifty hired employees to every elected member of a zemstvo executive board.[1] Even if these white-collar workers had held no political beliefs, their sheer numbers, their superior education and expertise would have enabled them to exert great influence on the conduct of zemstvo affairs.[2] Their vested interest in the enlargement of the scope of their work made them natural allies of the more progressive zemstvo councillors. Since the vast majority of these professional *intelligenty* were extremely politically minded, they became a very powerful factor.

The most influential and radical of these white-collar workers were the statisticians, who by the nature of their work came into close contact with the peasants (this for many of them being the main reason they had become statisticians in the first place).[3] They were followed closely by the teachers, agriculturalists and physicians. Their political creed, which was a mixture of economic populism and political democratism,[4] was sometimes too radical even for Petrunkevich,[5] not to mention less radical zemstvo constitutionalists. But this did not, on the whole, prevent close co-operation between these two groups.

The 'Third Element' influenced the day-to-day work of the zemstvos through the various bureaux and councils – statistical, economic, health, education etc. – established by the different provincial and district boards.[6] The contacts between these bureaux and the boards were usually handled by the more progressive members of the latter. Some of the bureau heads were themselves nobles who, after receiving formal education, had chosen to become hired employees of the zemstvos, sometimes serving simultaneously as councillors. In these cases the ties between the elected progressive councillors and the professional employees were naturally closer.[7] The case of Prince D. I. Shakhovskoy serves as an example of such collaboration and its consequences.

Shakhovskoy, who was to play an important role in the establishment of the Union of Liberation, the Union of Unions and the Cadet Party,

---

[1] *Bryukhatov*, p. 190.

[2] See *Samoderzhaviye i Zemstvo* I, pp. 162–3 for an appreciation of this fact by a hostile source.

[3] *Kaufman*, p. 261, *Belokonskiy* II, p. 36, *Peshekhonov* IV, pp. 308, 315–16, 320, 324–5.

[4] *Peshekhonov* ibid. pp. 320–1.   [5] See *Petrunkevich* II, pp. 311, 314.

[6] *Cherevanin* I, p. 270.   [7] See *Fischer*, p. 62, *Veselovskiy* VI, p. 476.

started his public career as the head of the Education Department of the Vesyegonsk district zemstvo board (Tver province). He was offered this post by F. I. Rodichev (who was chairman of the board in the years 1877 to 1890).[1] During his term of service (1886–90), there was close co-operation between the education bureau and the zemstvo board, which helped intensify educational activity in the Vesyegonsk district, and the education bureau was also utilized by its head as a sounding board for the expression of general political demands. Shakhovskoy, however, was not content with this and also participated in the economic and statistical activities of the Vesyegonsk zemstvo. A clash between the zemstvo and the administration was inevitable, and in 1890 Shakhovskoy was forced to resign his post.[2] He then returned to his native province of Yaroslavl, where for a time he served as an elected zemstvo councillor.[3] Nor was he the only person for whom the borderline between the position of hired employee and elected councillor was almost non-existent.

In addition to exerting indirect influence on the political behaviour of the zemstvo activists through its growing domination of the day-to-day activity of the zemstvos, the 'Third Element' also wielded direct influence on their minds. Till the mid-1890s there were few opportunities for the very small group of zemstvo radicals to exert influence over the vast majority of the non-committed councillors, in the absence of a free press etc. The situation changed quite drastically with the influx of large numbers of radically minded *intelligenty* into the provinces. In almost every zemstvo province house-circles sprang up in which constitutionalist and socialist ideas (the latter mainly of the populist trend) were discussed freely. They were also discussed in oblique terms, well understood by the educated classes, at professional conferences and meetings.[4] All this political activity could not but make the 'Second Element' (the elected councillors) more perceptive to constitutional ideas, and that at a time when the economic policy of the government was arousing growing opposition in this sphere.

[1] See above.
[2] *Shakhovskoy* I, pp. 198–9, *Brokgaus*, vol. 39, p. 226. Although the available sources do not imply any connection between the resignations of Shakhovskoy and Rodichev, which took place in the same year, it is possible that such a connection existed.
[3] *Shakhovskoy* I, pp. 199–200.
[4] See *Belokonskiy* II, pp. 36–9, 48; *Veselovskiy* III, p. 305.

2

The beginnings of the zemstvo oppositional movement

The last decade of the nineteenth century was characterized by the unprecedentedly high rate of industrial expansion in Russia (8 per cent per annum)[1] encouraged by S. Yu. Witte, and by the stabilization of the monetary system on the gold standard.[2] But it also witnessed the severe aggravation of the endemic agricultural crisis,[3] and these developments were not unconnected.

As in other backward countries, the agricultural crisis in Russia manifested itself in a very low output growth rate which barely kept pace with the increase in population, and in its complete subjection to the vagaries of nature. According to the calculations of a modern economic historian, the average annual rate of growth of agricultural output in the Russian Empire was less than two per cent during the period 1861–1913.[4] In years in which natural disasters occurred, and these were particularly frequent towards the end of the century, output either stood still or declined. In the same period the total population of the Empire more than doubled (from 74 million in 1858 to 129 million in 1897 and 175 million in 1913), and the rural population increased proportionately, continuing to constitute almost 90 per cent of the total.[5] At the end of the nineteenth century there were some 97 million peasants in the rural population as against less than one and a half million nobles (according to the 1897 census)[6], and even in the best of years they could barely maintain their standard of living at the very low pre-emancipation level. They were in dire straits in those

---

[1] See *Gerschenkron* III, p. 156.

[2] For a detailed study of Witte's economic policy and its impact on Russia see *Von Laue* III.

[3] There exists an extensive historical literature on the agricultural crisis in nineteenth- and early twentieth-century Russia. See, *inter alia, Gerschenkron* I, *Goldsmith, Lyashchenko,* pp. 57–89, *Robinson.* See also *Seton-Watson,* pp. 393–404, 506–17.

[4] See *Goldsmith,* pp. 441–3.

[5] For the relevant figures see ibid. p. 444, *Lyashchenko,* p. 115 and *Seton-Watson,* pp. 534–5, 662.

[6] See *Seton-Watson,* pp. 534–5.

years when harvests were bad or crops failed, ever before they were forced to pay the price of industrialization.

The nobles too paid a heavy price for the stagnation of Russian agriculture, though in different fashion. According to the calculations of a well-known historian of Russian agriculture, the nobility lost about one-third of their privately owned land during the period of 1877–1905 (for which records are available).[1] Since most of their income was derived from agriculture, the loss of land inevitably led to impoverishment.

The backwardness of Russian agriculture was caused mainly by two factors. The first and foremost was the fact that serfdom survived in Russia till 1861. This institution maintained the peasant masses in a state of enslavement, and for centuries they lived a life of abject ignorance and profound apathy. But this situation apparently played havoc with their masters as well. There are strong grounds for belief that the habits acquired by the Russian nobility during the very long period of serfdom were among the main factors responsible for their lack of business initiative. They failed to introduce new methods of cultivation and to adapt themselves to the economic requirements of the post-emancipation era.[2]

The second factor was the nature of the 1861 emancipation settlement,[3] which liberated the peasants from the personal rule of the nobles and bestowed legal identity upon them. Instead of ameliorating their situation, it perpetuated the problem until well into the twentieth century. The settlement adversely affected the peasants in three ways. To begin with, it failed to abolish the peasant estate or to equate its legal status to that of urban sections of the population. Almost all legal disputes between peasants were dealt with in special rural district (*volost*) courts,[4] and they were obliged to continue paying poll tax (one of the stigmas of servitude) till it was abolished in the mid-1880s.[5] Together with Asiatic natives, soldiers and sailors, they remained liable to corporal punishment. (This was legally abolished, under growing revolutionary pressure, in August 1904[6] but was in fact widely applied as a suppressive measure during the 1905 upheaval and its aftermath.) Such measures as the replacement of JPs by land captains in 1889 and

[1] See *Robinson*, pp. 130–1.   [2] Ibid. pp. 129–37.
[3] On the emancipation settlement see *Gerschenkron* I, pp. 706–63, *Robinson*, pp. 64–95 and *Seton-Watson*, pp. 334–48, 393–404.
[4] See *Seton-Watson*, p. 356.
[5] See *Lyashchenko*, p. 179 and *Gerschenkron* I, p. 769.
[6] See *Galai*, p. 95 and below.

the enactment of the 1890 Zemstvo Law only worsened the legal status of the peasants.

Secondly, the land received by the peasants at the time of their emancipation was not regarded as private property nor was it granted to individual peasant households. Instead, it was allotted (hence the term 'allotment land' or *nadelnaya zemlya*) to the peasant communes[1] for perpetual use.[2] This arrangement created a powerful stumbling block to the introduction of modern methods of cultivation. The commune assemblies were authorized to determine the rotation of crops[3] and, as might have been expected of illiterate peasants, they preferred the obsolete three-field system to more modern methods of cultivation. Moreover, at the turn of the century about eighty per cent of all the communes still held their land in repartitional tenure (*obshchinnoye vladeniye*).[4] In these communes the situation was even worse, for the arable land was periodically redistributed among the peasant households as the number of households and of persons per household changed. At the time of redistribution not only quantity but also quality was taken into account. Thus the traditional three fields were subdivided into innumerable strips (*cherespolositsa*), increasing the wastefulness of the system, and the improvement of the soil was openly discouraged. Hence, despite the fact that the average peasant plot in Russia was, even at the beginning of the twentieth century, much larger than its western European counterpart,[5] it was too small to supply even the most basic needs of those who lived on it.

Thirdly, the communes were also made responsible for delivering redemption payments to the government for the land allotted to the peasants at the time of emancipation, as well as for all other direct taxes. For this purpose they were invested with collective responsibility (*krugovaya poruka*) over their individual members. This arrangement resulted in the severe restriction of the freedom of movement of the peasants since the departure of a peasant from the commune meant that the remaining members had to shoulder an additional tax burden. Thus it was very difficult for the individual peasant to improve his economic lot through migration to cities or to less-populated regions.

Hemmed in by these restrictions, the only way in which the peasants

[1] For the origins and development of the peasant commune in Russia before 1861 see *Blum*, pp. 24–6, 94–7, 234–5, 328–9, 504–35.
[2] See *Gerschenkron* I, pp. 722–56, *Robinson*, pp. 66–93, *Seton-Watson*, pp. 346–8, 393–404.
[3] See *Seton-Watson*, p. 399.
[4] See *Gerschenkron* I, p. 745, *Robinson*, p. 215, *Seton-Watson*, p. 513.
[5] See *Robinson*, pp. 97–8, *Seton-Watson*, pp. 507–8.

could raise their standard of living was by acquiring additional land, which was a difficult, costly and slow process. Since the rural population was expanding much more rapidly than the areas of land available, the average peasant plot had shrunk.[1] This led to hidden unemployment, which began to manifest itself at the end of the nineteenth century in the form of 'peasant land hunger'.

The situation of the agricultural sector of the economy was further exacerbated by two external developments: the world price of grain began to fall in the 1870s and reached rock bottom in the mid-1890s,[2] while natural disasters caused very poor harvests in Russia in 1891, 1897, 1898 and 1901.[3]

This was the state of affairs when Witte began to force Russian agriculture to pay the price of industrialization. The main burden was naturally borne by the peasants, who paid the lion's share of both direct and indirect taxes.[4] Although Vyshnegradskiy's 'ingenious' system of collecting taxes in the autumn was discontinued after the 1891-2 famine, the combination of high taxes and poor harvests proved calamitous for the peasants. The following passage in the report of the State Comptroller, Lobko, for 1902 illustrates how heavy was the burden of industrialization for the peasantry:

At present there is no more doubt that the crisis is caused by the artificial and excessive growth of industry in recent years. Industry, based on a *protective tariff*, extensive government orders and the speculative increase in cheap foreign capital, has grown out of proportion to the development of the consumers' market, which consists chiefly of the mass of agricultural population to which 80% of our people belong...In view of the inadequacy of the government measures, the negative sides of the protective system show up all the more strongly in the agricultural population. The chief burden of that system rests undoubtedly upon the agricultural masses...They have to bear almost the whole burden of direct and indirect taxes.[5]

Nor did the nobles escape unscathed. The combination of low grain prices, dear money and high tariffs on important goods[6] accelerated the pace of their economic decline. Moreover, this decline was that much

---

[1] See *Gerschenkron* I, p. 768-76.

[2] See *Gurko*, pp. 57-8, *Veselovskiy* III, p. 232 and *Von Laue* III, p. 115.

[3] See *Von Laue* III, p. 211 and above.

[4] For the relevant figures on direct and indirect taxes and on the regressive character of the Russian ordinary state budget see *Seton-Watson*, pp. 529n., 530n.

[5] Cited in *Von Laue* III, p. 220. (Italics added.)

[6] Vyshnegradskiy's tariff of 1891 turned Russia into the most protectionist country in the world at the time. See *Seton-Watson*, p. 518.

more painful because it stood in flagrant contrast to the social ascendancy of the nobility during Alexander III's reign.

The peasants reacted to their rapidly worsening plight mainly in two ways. They failed to meet their tax obligations in full and as a consequence went into heavier and heavier arrears. Secondly, their desire to get hold of the estates of the nobles was intensified. Since they did not hold most of their land as private property, they had no respect for the private property of others, and especially of their former oppressors. This attitude to the 'land of the nobles' found its first open expression in the peasant disturbances of spring 1902.[1]

The initial reaction of the nobles to their predicament was more or less traditional. Fortified by their estate privileges and assisted by a powerful party inside the government led by I. N. Durnovo,[*] they tried to defend their economic position against the onslaughts of Witte's policies by exercising pressure behind the scenes, but to no avail. The Ministry of Agriculture and State Domains, under the well-meaning but weak A. S. Yermolov,[2] which was established in March 1894 for the specific purpose of defending their interests against the encroachments of the Ministry of Finance,[3] proved a failure. Their opposition to the introduction of the gold standard was crushed[4] and the conference of the marshals of the nobility, which met in St Petersburg in November 1896, produced no practical consequences. Its participants were even prevented from distributing among their local followers the final memorandum of the conference, which contained a sharp attack on Witte's policies, though they were able to convey their feelings to the Tsar by securing an audience for M. A. Stakhovich, marshal of the nobility of Orel province.[5] The Special Conference on the Needs of the Landed Nobility – the only tangible achievement of the nobles' campaign, which was established under the chairmanship of I. N. Durnovo on 13 June 1897 – fared no better. Many of its participants submitted requests for subsidies and this enabled Witte to dismiss the whole venture as another example of the parasitical tendencies of the noble estate, living off all other classes.[6] Although the Conference continued to meet for more than four years, it never

---

[1] See below.
[*] Minister of the Interior 1889–95, Chairman of the Council of Ministers 1895–1903.
[2] See *Gurko*, pp. 69–73, *Polovtsev* I, pp. 123–4.
[3] *Brokgaus*, vol. 19, pp. 358–9, *Veselovskiy* III, p. 300; VI, p. 377.
[4] See *Von Laue* III, pp. 139–44, *Suvorin*, p. 129.
[5] *Von Laue* ibid. p. 172, *Suvorin* ibid. p. 136.
[6] See *Witte* VIII, pp. 422–3.

recovered from Witte's initial blow, and was quietly dissolved on 1 January 1902.[1]

The failure of the nobles to redress the balance between industry and agriculture through their traditional forms of representation had far-reaching political consequences. Some of them lost hope in the possibility of protecting their own estate interests in isolation from other classes. They joined the ranks of the zemstvo activists,[2] who were prepared to use the zemstvo institutions for the protection of the interests of all farmers, the mass of peasantry included.[3] The others, who constituted the vast majority, who were unable or unwilling to abandon the path of narrow class interest, withdrew from politics altogether. They thus cleared the way for the transformation of the zemstvos into centres of that oppositional activity which became known as the 'zemstvo movement'. This began as a semi-official affair, initiated by a most loyal believer in autocracy, D. N. Shipov.

Dmitriy Shipov was born in 1851 into a well-to-do noble family. At the age of twenty-one he received from his father a substantial estate in the Volokolamsk district of Moscow province, where he established his home. Shipov became involved in zemstvo affairs in 1877, when he was elected to the Volokolamsk district zemstvo assembly and then to the Moscow provincial zemstvo assembly. In 1891 he was elected chairman of the Volokolamsk district zemstvo board and two years later he was elected to the most important zemstvo job in the country, chairman of the Moscow provincial zemstvo board. He remained in this post till April 1904, when his re-election was vetoed by Plehve because of his 'oppositional' activity.[4]

By the time the nobility were beginning to despair of the government, Shipov had arrived at what may best be described as a liberal-Slavophile *weltanschauung*.[5] Despite his own claim to the contrary,[6] he shared many Slavophile beliefs. He approached politics from a religious point of view and believed that pre-Petrine autocracy was far superior to the western regimes which were based on rationalistic and positivistic principles. At the same time he did not maintain, as did the

---

[1] *Von Laue* III, pp. 172–3, *Gurko*, pp. 60–2.

[2] See for example M. A. Stakhovich's transformation from spokesman of the noble *fronde* to one of the founders of *Beseda* and one of the leaders of the zemstvo movement at the turn of the century (*Shipov* II, p. 135, *Mikheyeva*, p. 241).

[3] *Veselovskiy* III, p. 304; VI, pp. 368–72. See also below.

[4] See *Shipov* II, pp. 3–7, 12–24, 233–5 and below.

[5] For a very valuable but slightly different interpretation of Shipov's views see *Schapiro*, pp. 143, 147–51.

[6] See *Shipov* II, pp. 269–70.

Slavophiles, that this resulted from the intrinsic superiority of the Russian people and the Orthodox Church to their western counterparts, but rather regarded it as an accident of history. As a consequence he was prepared to see Russia adopting some of the better features of western societies, while at the same time rejecting the principles on which they were based. Hence he was not only a Slavophile but also a liberal.

Shipov's beliefs are clearly outlined in his extremely valuable memoirs.[1] He tells the reader that he approached politics from the viewpoint of evangelical Christianity, believing in the equality of men and in human progress. He measured progress not by material achievements but by the extent of advancement towards the achievement of the ultimate goal of Christianity, the establishment of a world kingdom based on love. This goal could be achieved only by each individual recognizing his moral obligation to his fellow-men and not insisting on his own rights as opposed to the rights of others.

Shipov's main criticism of the liberal–constitutional doctrine was directed, therefore, not against its emphasis on the importance of the individual, his freedom and happiness, which he fully accepted, but against its assumption that this, as well as the happiness of mankind as a whole, could be achieved through the fulfilment of the individual's self-interest. It was this assumption, he wrote, which had led the constitutionalists to adopt the doctrine of the rights of the citizen and man and the sovereignty of the people. And, human nature being imperfect, this had led to endless social strife and political struggle. The holding of continual elections to the highest offices in the constitutional state exacerbated this strife – both because any election campaign inevitably leads to a rise in the political temperature and because the winners were bound to use their newly acquired power for the benefit of their own faction, thus inevitably increasing the resentment of the losers. Furthermore, power corrupts its holders, and power achieved for a limited period after a struggle could corrupt even more.

Hence Shipov's preference for hereditary autocracy. His ideal autocrat had nothing in common with the autocracy of his time. He was envisaged as standing above the political turmoil and social strife of the state, looking upon his unlimited supreme power as an obligation entrusted to him by the entire people, and using his power in consultation with his subjects and for their benefit. This he could achieve only

---

[1] The following summary of Shipov's views is based on *Shipov* II, preface and pp. 136–50 267–73. See also *Vinogradov*.

by being constantly informed of the needs of the people and by constant encouragement of individual involvement in public life.

Shipov was convinced that a state ruled by such an autocrat would fulfil the basic requirements of Christianity: moral solidarity would flourish between ruler and ruled and peace and harmony, based on mutual love, common good and truth would reign. The old Russian state had fulfilled the first part of the above requirements, but the reforms introduced by Peter the Great had put an end to the solidarity between Tsar and people and thus prepared the ground for the current political crisis. But fortunately for Russia, wrote Shipov, those reforms and the subsequent unhealthy development of the Russian state (excluding the reign of Alexander II)[1] had not destroyed the Christian outlook of the Russian people, nor had it imbued them with a consciousness of 'human rights'. Hence, he concluded, it was still possible to reform the Russian regime and base it on healthier principles than those upon which its western counterparts rested.

Had Shipov's opposition to the introduction of a constitutional regime into Russia been based only on the above theoretical assumptions, it would not be difficult to dismiss him as a Slavophile obscurantist whose religious–political views bore no relation to the realities of Russian life. (This, indeed, was the line adopted by many of his constitutionalist opponents in the Liberation Movement, especially Milyukov.[2]) But Shipov was too much of a pragmatist to oppose the introduction of a constitutional regime into Russia only for theoretical reasons. He appears to have been more influenced by practical considerations.

Shipov the political pragmatist was a great admirer of England. Although his memoirs display a lack of understanding of English society and English political structure, he was nevertheless correct in his observation that because England had not experienced a revolution for many a year, the changes which her regime had undergone had proved more lasting than the political changes on the Continent. His ideal was to see Russia developing on the same lines as England,[3] and he insisted that this could only be achieved through co-operation between the Tsar and society. To insist on constitutional limitations to autocracy would prevent such co-operation from the very beginning. The Tsar would never agree to such proposals of his own free will, while any attempt to try to force his hand would aggravate the political crisis instead of solving it.[4] In order to achieve reforms from above

---

[1] *Shipov* II, pp. 81–3. [2] See below. [3] *Shipov* II, p. 271. [4] Ibid. p. 149.

through co-operation between the Tsar and society, Shipov reasoned, society would have to put forward only such demands as would not imply limitations on his autocratic powers. At the same time the reforms requested would have to be far-reaching enough to satisfy the most urgent needs of society and thus restore the moral solidarity between Tsar and people. Such reforms would have to include: the replacement of the unrestricted and arbitrary rule of the bureaucracy by the rule of law;[1] the abolition of all legal estate distinctions and the equalization of all citizens before the law:[2] a guarantee of individual freedom of conscience, thought, speech and the right to participate in local government through elected representatives:[3] the release of the elected local government institutions from bureaucratic tutelage and the restoration to the zemstvo of its original non-class character, abolished by the law of 1890;[4] the gradual introduction of small zemstvo units for the benefit of the peasantry[5] and the admission of elected representatives of the people into the central governing bodies of the state. This, he thought, could be achieved either through the restoration of the institution of *zemskiye sobory* (implying, under the given conditions, the establishment of a separate institution of elected representatives) or through the admission of elected representatives into the State Council.[6] But in either case the elected representatives would serve the state only in a consultative capacity and in accordance with the Slavophile axiom 'Supreme power belongs to the Tsar; opinion – to the people.'

Shipov did not maintain that all these reforms should be implemented at once, nor did he hold that the first step in this direction should consist of government legislation. He believed that, as a start, the best method of action would be to widen the scope of the zemstvos within the existing legal framework. This would have the added advantage of corresponding to the wishes of the zemstvo activists and to the needs of the agricultural population, especially the nobles, in their hour of distress. His work as chairman of a zemstvo executive board, however, brought him face to face with the basic distrust of the bureaucracy for this institution, and he concluded that it was necessary to establish an all-zemstvo organization in order to overcome this opposition to the expansion of zemstvo activity. Such an organization would co-ordinate the activities of the various zemstvo boards, thus creating a united front against the bureaucracy.[7] As a beginning he proposed arranging

---

[1] *Shipov* II pp. 134, 151.   [2] Ibid. pp. 142, 167.   [3] Ibid. pp. 81–3, 151.   [4] Ibid.
[5] Ibid. pp. 167–8, *Melkaya Zemskaya Yedinitsa*, pp. 332–3 and below.
[6] *Shipov* II, pp. 147–9, 151–2.   [7] Ibid. pp. 57–60, 62, 67.

frequent meetings of the chairmen of zemstvo provincial executive boards. This plan met with the unanimous approval of the chairmen at their meeting in Moscow in May 1896[1] at the time of the coronation of the Tsar.[2]

The government was anxious, almost from the outset, to prevent the emergence of such a union[3] but, to its own misfortune, was not known for the co-ordination or consistency of its policies. To take one example, the newly appointed (15 October 1895) Minister of the Interior, I. L. Goremykin, vetoed such an inoffensive proposal as presenting the royal couple with a coronation present from all the zemstvo assemblies because of the danger that it might become a precedent for joint zemstvo actions in the future.[4] Shortly afterwards the same man agreed to Shipov's suggestion regarding the convening of zemstvo provincial board chairmen.[5]

The first of these meetings, widely referred to in the zemstvo movement as the First Zemstvo Congress,[6] was held in Nizhniy Novgorod on 8–11 August 1896[7] while the All-Russian Exhibition was taking place there.[8] The gathering was attended by more than half the zemstvo provincial board chairmen (nineteen out of a total of thirty-four) as well as some invited participants (Prince Peter D. Dolgorukov, chairman of a district zemstvo board; Count P. A. Geyden, President of the Free Economic Society and some others) and its main topics of discussion were the worsening of the agricultural crisis and the day-to-day activity of the zemstvos.[9] But it first discussed the question of the co-ordination of zemstvo activity. Encouraged by Goremykin's consent to the meeting, the assembled chairmen arrived at a far-reaching organizational plan. They decided to hold annual meetings of chairmen (the next one to be held in March 1897 in St Petersburg) and to estab-

---

[1] Ibid. pp. 67–8.
[2] The coronation took place on 14 May 1896 but the festivities, culminating in the notorious Khodinka Catastrophe of 18 May 1896, went on for a fortnight. (See *Russkiy Kalendar* 1897, pp. 322–3 and below.)
[3] See above.
[4] *Belokonskiy* II, pp. 56–7, *Shipov* II, pp. 63–7.
[5] *Shipov* ibid. pp. 68–9.
[6] Ibid. p. 70, *Peter Dolgorukov*, p. 303. Belokonskiy, on the other hand, claims the title of 'First Zemstvo Congress' for the Congress of Activists in the Field of Agronomic Aid to the Local Economy which opened in Moscow on 10 February 1901 (*Belokonskiy* II, p. 84, *Russkiy Kalendar* 1902, p. 263). But this congress was not a pure zemstvo affair. On the contrary, it was dominated by the 'Third Element'. (See below.)
[7] *Shipov* ibid.
[8] Opened on 28 May 1896. (*Russkiy Kalendar* 1897, p. 323.)
[9] *Shipov* ibid. pp. 70–2, *Belokonskiy* ibid. pp. 58–9, *Dolgorukov* ibid.

lish a permanent bureau affiliated to the zemstvo board of Moscow province, under the chairmanship of D. N. Shipov[1], to prepare the agenda for forthcoming meetings. Should a meeting of chairmen decide to petition the government, they promised to ensure that all zemstvo provincial assemblies would send identical petitions.[2]

The fact that an official of the Ministry of Finance addressed the meeting on economic matters of mutual interest led the participants to believe that Goremykin's attitude was an indication of a change of policy on the part of the government rather than an isolated gesture by a 'liberally inclined' minister.[*] They left Nizhniy Novgorod with the feeling that at long last the government had become aware of the need to remove artificial obstacles from the path of the zemstvos.[3] Their feeling of satisfaction soon evaporated when they learned, several months later, of the Minister of the Interior's *volte face*.

The Nizhniy Novgorod congress and its decisions greatly alarmed government circles in St Petersburg, and Goremykin realized that he had blundered in agreeing to Shipov's proposal to hold annual conferences of provincial zemstvo board chairmen. He therefore immediately ordered the dissolution of the newly elected bureau and prohibited the holding of any zemstvo conferences in the future, including that already scheduled to be held in St Petersburg.[4]

This abrupt change of policy came as a grave shock to Shipov. First, being himself a sincere man, he expected his fellow-men to adhere to his own high moral code of behaviour. Hence he regarded Goremykin's decision as an act of personal betrayal and decided to sever all connection with him. In his own words: 'After losing all confidence in the words and intentions of I. L. Goremykin I never again approached or met him during his tenure of office as Minister of the Interior.'[5] Secondly, and more significantly, Goremykin's change of policy came at a time when Shipov had despaired of co-operation with the bureaucracy in another field. Besides being chairman of the Moscow provincial

---

[1] The bureau elected by the conference consisted of five chairmen of provincial zemstvo boards: (1) D. N. Shipov (Moscow), Chairman (and secretary of meeting); (2) V. V. Khvoshchinskiy (N. Novgorod), (as host acted as chairman of the meeting); (3) V. P. Markov (St Petersburg); (4) N. A. Rachinskiy (Smolensk); (5) S. A. Khvostov (Orel). (*Shipov* II, p. 70.)

[2] *Shipov* ibid. and *Belokonskiy* II, pp. 58–9.

[*] Strange as it may seem, Goremykin, the arch-reactionary premier of 1906 and 1914–16, was thought at the time to be a liberal Minister of the Interior. See *Gurko*, pp. 77–8, *Shipov* II, p. 80, *Von Laue* III, p. 157. This opinion was not shared by his government colleagues. See *Polovtsev* III, p. 121.

[3] *Shipov* ibid. p. 73.   [4] Ibid. pp. 76–80.   [5] Ibid p. 80.

zemstvo board, he was also a member of the Agricultural Council of the Ministry of Agriculture and State Domains, where his performance was so impressive that, in February 1896, Yermolov offered him the directorship of the Ministry; Shipov declined because of his preference for zemstvo activity.[1] But by autumn of the same year he had become utterly disappointed in the Council. He and other zemstvo activists had joined it in order to fight Witte's economic policies with maximum effectiveness, but the task now appeared futile to him and he resigned. As he himself explained:

After becoming convinced during the 1896 regular session of the Agricultural Council that the participation of public representatives in its meetings was of merely decorative value and that they...were in the minority compared to the representatives of the Ministry and other bureaucratic departments, I announced my resignation from the Council in the following year.[2]

Shipov's break with Goremykin and his resignation from the Agricultural Council proved to be a turning point in the development of the zemstvo movement. His despair of the possibility of reforming the government's economic policy from within gave the task of extending the scope of zemstvo activity special urgency in his eyes. He had previously regarded it mainly as the first step on the road towards bridging the gap between Tsar and Society. Now he began to believe that it was also the only means of defending the civil and economic interests of the agricultural population from the consequences of Witte's policies. But, as was shown above, he advocated the establishment of an all-zemstvo organization as the prerequisite for expansion of zemstvo activity and as long as he believed that the government might consent to this, he refused to indulge in 'illegal 'activity. This was why he successfully opposed the proposal raised at Nizhniy Novgorod that the future zemstvo congresses be opened to rank-and-file councillors. Such a move, he argued, would transform the meetings into large gatherings and might be interpreted by the government as 'unlawful' activity.[3]

Goremykin's change of policy, however, made it abundantly clear that the government would never consent to the establishment of an all-zemstvo organization. So Shipov abandoned his adherence to the very narrow field of legal and semi-legal activity and became willing to co-operate with the more radical zemstvo elements in order to help extricate these institutions and Russian society as a whole from their

---

[1] Ibid. pp. 60–1.   [2] Ibid. p. 62.   [3] Ibid. pp. 70–1.

plight. His change of mind was instrumental in opening before Petrunkevich and his followers the door to all-zemstvo activity which Nicholas II had tried to close for ever in his notorious speech of 17 January 1895.

Before finally embarking on this new path, Shipov felt it necessary to warn the government against the consequences of its policy. The opportunity arose when, despite Goremykin's prohibition, another meeting of chairmen of zemstvo provincial boards was held on the occasion of the unveiling of the monument to Alexander II in Moscow on 16 August 1898.[1] The mood of the meeting, which lasted three days, was much more belligerent than in 1896. It reflected the growing deterioration in relations between the government and the zemstvo milieu, as well as the fact that many of the participants had been exposed a few months earlier to an intensive dose of radical influence, administered by representatives of the St Petersburg intelligentsia and the 'Third Element' during the public debates on the agricultural crisis, held by the Free Economic Society in March 1898.[2] Shipov, who had exercised a restraining influence during the Nizhniy Novgorod meeting, now delivered what amounted to an oppositional speech, in spirit if not in form. After praising Alexander II for his courage in carrying out far-reaching reforms despite strong opposition from the influential 'reactionary party',[3] he attacked the Zemstvo Law of 1890 and formulated the credo of the zemstvo liberal Slavophiles at the time: 'We, the zemstvo people, strongly believe that local needs can be satisfied only by extensive individual participation in public life within the framework of the historically formed Russian regime.'[4]

His speech was a warning as well as an assurance directed at the Tsar above the heads of his bureaucracy. It warned him against the bureaucracy's reactionary tendencies as well as against any procrastination in the introduction of the much-needed reforms, lest even the most moderate elements of society be alienated from the government. At the same time it assured him that the demands of the moderates could be met within the framework of autocracy. But the warning as well as the assurance went unheeded. The government rejected the only practical demand put forward by that meeting and supported by the great majority of all zemstvo assemblies – namely for the publication of a zemstvo newspaper.[5] It also attacked the very premise of Shipov's

[1] *Shipov* ibid. p. 80, *Russkiy Kalendar* 1898, p. 273.
[2] *Veselovskiy* VI, pp. 507–8 and *Osvobozhdeniye* I, pp. 63–5.
[3] *Shipov* II, pp. 81–3.   [4] Ibid. p. 83.   [5] Ibid. pp, 86–90.

speech: the belief that free development of elected local government was compatible with autocracy. The exponent of this view was none other than the then powerful Minister of Finance, S. Yu. Witte.

In a secret memorandum[1] to the Tsar, written in reply to I. L. Goremykin's proposal to extend the zemstvo system to the western provinces of the Empire,[2] Witte stated that elective local government was incompatible with autocracy[3] and submitted an impressive amount of theoretical and historical material in support of this view.[*] Although his argument was neither new nor theoretically provable,[4] it achieved its immediate aim: Goremykin's proposals were rejected and he lost his post.[5]

Because of the important role this memorandum played in the development of the Liberation Movement, and because of its repercussions on Witte's political future, it is worth pausing a while to examine Witte's motives for writing it. He himself implied at the time that Goremykin's proposals were only the pretext and not the reason for the writing of the memorandum. The main reason, according to him, was his desire to force the government to clarify its position. He insisted on this explanation not only in public but also in private. In public, i.e. in his memorandum, he could only hint at what he had in mind. He urged the government in general terms to be sincere and to state precisely what its plans for the future were: did it want to introduce a constitutional regime into Russia, or did it intend to preserve autocracy? If the former were true, then and only then should it encour-

---

[1] Despite its classification, the memo was anything but secret. Many duplicated copies were distributed by Witte among the higher echelons of the bureaucracy and to various public figures (*Shipov* II, p. 128, *Witte* VII, p. 369). Some copies found their way to the press, which during 1898/9 hotly debated the central issue: was elective local government incompatible with autocracy? (*Veselovskiy* VI, pp. 512–14). Hence, in describing Struve's publication of the memo under the title *Samoderzhaviye i Zemstvo* as 'sensational' (*Fischer*, pp. 106, 230), Fischer is somewhat exaggerating. A better adjective would be 'timely'. Struve published and prefaced the first two editions of *Samoderzhaviye i Zemstvo*. (See *Bibliography*.) A third edition was published by Cherevanin in St Petersburg in 1908. The whole work, plus a preface and an appendix, was published in 1914 by Witte himself under the title *Po Povodu Neprelozhnosti Zakonov Gosudarstvennoy Zhizni*. (See *Bibliography*.)

[2] Goremykin did not propose to introduce the full zemstvo system into the western provinces, but only provincial zemstvos. (See *Veselovskiy* V, p. 511.) That Witte's memo was written in reply to Goremykin's proposals is underlined several times in this work. See *Samoderzhaviye i Zemstvo* I, pp. 168–9, 177–85, 210–12

[3] Ibid. pp. 25–6, 96, 198 ff.

[*] This, incidentally, had an important side-effect. It made his memorandum an important source on the history of the zemstvos in the nineteenth century.

[4] See above.

[5] *Shipov* II, p. 130. Goremykin was replaced by D. S. Sipyagin on 20 October 1899. (*Witte* VII, p. 135.)

age the development of the zemstvo system. If not, then it should not encourage false hopes among the zemstvo people by extending the zemstvo system to the western provinces.[1]

In private Witte could be more specific. In two letters to Pobedonostsev he explained what he had had in mind when he called on the government to clarify its position. First, he explained, 'our position is based on insincerity and on the desire to reconcile the irreconcilable, to achieve popularity without losing virginity'.[2] Then he pointed out what seemed to him the source of this insincerity. Many members of the bureaucracy, he wrote to Pobedonostsev, believed that 'by travelling along the road of zemstvo self-government, it will be possible to induce the Tsar to cross, unconsciously, the borderline between autocracy and self-government'.[3] Such an attitude, he explained (and was later echoed by V. A. Maklakov[4]), was alien to his nature and damaging to the state, and hence his desire to clarify the issue by writing his memorandum.

Although it is true that there was a streak in Witte's character which drove him to try and clarify political issues when it was not only undesirable but even disastrous to do so,[5] nevertheless it is hardly conceivable that, at the height of his power, Witte would have found the time or the inclination to write a political tract on the desirability of being honest!

Plehve, the notorious Minister of the Interior (1902–4),* for one, did not believe in such a possibility and said as much to Shipov. According to him, Witte's main motive in writing the memorandum was his desire to bring about the downfall of Goremykin and he was and remained a great believer in the principle of elective government[6] (i.e. in constitutionalism). Plehve, however, overstated the case against Witte. It is true that in mid-1902, when Plehve made this statement,[7] Witte had become disillusioned with autocracy and as a consequence had changed his mind about constitutionalists in general and in particular about the advocates of strong and independent zemstvo institutions as a prelude to constitutional changes.[8] But this was not the case in 1898

---

[1] *Samoderzhaviye i Zemstvo* I, pp. 210–12.
[2] *Witte* III, p. 102 (letter of 28 August 1898).
[3] Ibid. pp. 104–5 (letter of October 1898), 'self-government' being a synonym for a constitutional regime.
[4] *Maklakov*, vol. II, pp. 252–9.
[5] Such as his intervention in the drafting of the decree of 12 December 1904. See below.
* For Plehve's role and policy see below.
[6] *Shipov* II, p. 178.
[7] Ibid. p. 170.
[8] Ibid. pp. 186–8, *Chermenskiy* II, pp. 47–9.

when he composed his notorious memorandum; he then still believed in the progressive role of autocracy, since he relied on support from the autocratic rulers of Russia to crush the opposition of the nobility to his policy of industrialization.[1] Hence his attack on Goremykin and on the zemstvos (which he regarded as a mere extension of the assemblies of the nobility[2]) was much more sincere than was thought at the time.[3]

It was an open secret that relations between Witte and Goremykin were very strained,[4] but it was also well-known that while in power, Witte's relations with people were influenced more by political than by personal considerations. Gurko, a high-ranking bureaucrat at the time, who was far from being an admirer of Witte, admitted that 'to Witte, power was not an end in itself or even a means of satisfying his personal ambition and of assuring his material well-being. He sought power so that he might use his great constructive ability...[5] He hated his enemies with a bitter hatred and he cherished no illusions about his friends.'[6] Nevertheless, Gurko continued, Witte was prepared to co-operate with them as long as they supported his policies.[7] Unfortunately for Goremykin, Witte and Russia, Goremykin did not support his policies. The main bone of contention between them was the peasant question.

Witte, who by that time had realized that his plans for the further industrialization of Russia would be increasingly hampered by the backwardness of Russia's agriculture, began, at first unnoticed by the wider public, to devote more and more attention to this problem. But while Goremykin, Durnovo and other representatives of 'rural interests' in the government spoke only on behalf of the landed nobility, Witte, who regarded the nobility with contempt, applied himself from the first to the solution of the much more urgent and infinitely more important question of the plight of the peasantry. Anticipating Stolypin by eight years, Witte urged the Emperor, in a personal letter written in October 1898, to abolish the communes and to grant the peasants full legal rights, including full property rights on the allotment land they cultivated.[8] Six months later, in the teeth of Goremykin's opposition, he forced through the Committee of Ministers a decision urging the Tsar to appoint a special conference on the peasant question.[9]

Goremykin's opposition was in no small way responsible for the fact

---

[1] See *Samoderzhaviye i Zemstvo* I, pp. 205–6, *Von Laue* III, pp. 158–9.
[2] *Gurko*, p. 63. [3] See, for example, *Maklakov*, vol. II, p. 255.
[4] See for example *Polovtsev* III, p. 121. [5] *Gurko*, p. 76. [6] Ibid p. 66. [7] Ibid.
[8] See *Witte* VIII, pp. 429–34, *Von Laue* III, pp. 174–5, *Polovtsev* III, p. 123, *Shebunin*, p. 186.
[9] *Witte* VIII, pp. 427–8, *Polovtsev* III, p. 126, *Von Laue* III, pp. 173–4.

that both Witte's ventures were unsuccessful. The former's opinion on the peasant question carried special weight with Nicholas, because the Ministry of the Interior was responsible for peasant affairs.[1] Witte realized that as long as Goremykin remained at his post, his plans for the solution of the peasant question would not be implemented. Hence his supposed hatred of Goremykin[2] and his desire to replace him by someone more congenial to himself and to his policies.

Goremykin's project to extend the zemstvo system to the western provinces of the Empire came as a gift from heaven to Witte. By providing him with the pretext for writing his lengthy memorandum on the incompatability of the zemstvo and autocracy, it enabled him to kill two birds with one stone. It gave him the opportunity of accusing Goremykin by implication of liberal and constitutional tendencies and thus undermining his position in the eyes of the Tsar.[3] At the same time it made it possible for him to deliver a blow against the nobility, hiding behind a facade of 'gentry liberalism', which he regarded as the real source of opposition to his peasant policy.

If Witte had been more perceptive of developments in Russian society, he would have known by then (as he discovered a few years later[4]) that far from reflecting the narrow class interests of the nobles, the zemstvo activists shared his own basic belief in the urgency of the peasant problem as well as many of his conceptions about its remedy. But as it happened, Witte's revelation came too late and his memorandum achieved the opposite of what he had intended: in the long run it undermined his own position more than Goremykin's and was a blow against autocracy and not against 'gentry liberalism'.

As far as Witte himself was concerned, he alienated the progressive public forever by attacking the zemstvos[5], while at the same time failing to satisfy the reactionaries. The latter were disappointed because he had not urged the abolition of the existing zemstvo institutions, merely opposing the extension of their scope of activity and the introduction of similar institutions into other provinces.[6] The general mistrust of Witte thus generated played into the hands of his personal enemies who, like Plehve, accused him of playing a double game and of being prepared to sacrifice everything for the sake of power.

[1] See *Gurko*, pp. 79–80, *Von Laue* III, p. 223.
[2] *Polovtsev* ibid.
[3] See *Gurko*, p. 81, *Von Laue* III, p. 162.
[4] See below and *Shipov* II, pp. 186–8.
[5] See *Maklakov*, vol. II, p. 254, *Petrunkevich* II, pp. 327–9.
[6] *Witte* III, p. 103.

In addition, Witte's memorandum proved to be the direct cause of the establishment of *Beseda* (Symposium),[1] the first organized group of what soon became known as the Liberation Movement, and which was to help to prepare the ground for autocracy's ultimate destruction.

Shipov and his liberal Slavophile supporters were flabbergasted when they learned about Witte's memorandum. At first they regarded it as a manifestation of the utmost folly on Witte's part.[2] It was bound, or so they thought, to put an end to any possibility of reforming autocracy from within and thus prepare the way for its total destruction from below. On second thoughts, Shipov came to the conclusion that the memorandum constituted not folly but high treason. He reasoned that Witte was too clever a man not to understand the consequences of his deeds. Hence he became convinced that Witte's main motive for writing the memorandum was his secret desire to bring about the downfall of autocracy, preferably by an 'explosion from below'.[3]

No wonder, therefore, that Shipov, the faithful supporter of autocracy, was aroused by his interpretation of Witte's motives to immediate action. It became clear to him that autocracy needed to be preserved from its official supporters as well as from the follies of the incumbent autocrat.[4] The question was – how? To find an answer to this, he approached various prominent public figures. Although not all those who agreed to discuss the matter shared his political views, all shared

---

[1] Despite the important, if not crucial role it played during the formative stage of the Liberation Movement, *Beseda* has been almost entirely neglected by the historians and writers of memoirs of the period. Until very recently the main sources on *Beseda* were: (1) Shipov's memoirs (*Shipov* II, pp. 128–36, 150–5), where he described in great detail the establishment of that circle without actually naming it; (2) Maklakov's highly controversial memoirs (*Maklakov*, vol. II, pp. 291–7). Although Maklakov sheds interesting light on this circle, his preoccupation with proving his case against the Liberation Movement deprives his memoirs of much of their importance as a historical source.

Brief references to *Beseda* are also found in the following books and memoirs, among others: *Belokonskiy* II, p. 80; *Peter Dolgorukov*, p. 304; *Fischer*, pp. 124–5; *Gessen* I, pp. 161–5; *Shakhovskoy* IV, pp. 103–5; *Smith* (unpub.), pp. 34–5, 159–61.

Two articles recently published in the Soviet Union – *Chermenskiy* II and *Mikheyeva* – throw new light on *Beseda* and add much to our knowledge of the origins of the Liberation Movement. Both articles are based on the *Beseda* archives (Chermenskiy also quotes other archives) which are located, according to the authors, in *Gosudarstvennyy Istoricheskiy Muzey v Moskve, Otdel Rukopisey* F. 31 op. 1 d. 142. The present author did not succeed in gaining access to the quoted archives, hence the picture of *Beseda* as drawn here is far from complete. Professor Pipes, who has seen the archives, did not, however, find them very revealing.

[2] See for example A. S. Suvorin's letter to Witte (*Witte* VII, pp. 369–76).

[3] *Shipov* II, pp. 128–30.

[4] Ibid. pp. 132–4.

his growing fear that

unless, in the shortest possible time, the necessary reforms are accomplished from above...the sovereign will be forced by the course of events and under the impact of the rapidly growing oppositional mood in the country, to agree in the very near future to a much more radical change in our regime.[1]

The discussions which began immediately after the contents of Witte's memorandum became known to Shipov, fathered the semiconspiratorial circle, *Beseda*.[2] At first its membership was restricted to a very small group of 'public men', the majority of whom were active in zemstvo affairs and/or marshals of nobility:[3] N. V. Davydov, Prince Pavel D. Dolgorukov,* N. A. Khomyakov,† V. O. Kluchevskiy, R. A. Pisarev,‡ F. D. Samarin,§ D. N. Shipov, M. A. Stakhovich,¶ Prince P. N. Trubetskoy, ‖ and Prince S. N. Trubetskoy. Between them, these ten men played a leading role in three out of the four ideological groups which existed by then among the zemstvo activists.

Davydov, Khomyakov, the famous historian Kluchevskiy, Stakhovich and Prince P. N. Trubetskoy shared Shipov's political views which, as described earlier, amounted to liberal Slavophilism. These people believed that since the assassination of Alexander II, the rulers of Russia had done everything in their power to discredit the autocratic regime. They blamed these rulers and not society for the growing lack of mutual confidence.[4] Moreover, Goremykin's *volte face* and Witte's assault on the zemstvos proved to them the impossibility of reforming autocracy within the existing legal framework. Hence, unlike the more conservative Slavophiles, they did not believe that a mere change of heart and policy on the part of the government would suffice to forestall the approaching political crisis. Instead, they emphasized the urgent need for institutional reforms from above as the only means which might prevent the destruction of autocracy from below.[5]

At first the conservative Slavophiles were represented in *Beseda* by F. D. Samarin. They, like the liberal Slavophiles, came to the conclusion at the turn of the century that Russia was approaching a political

---

[1] *Shipov* ibid. p. 134.   [2] For a note on the origins of *Beseda* see below *Appendix A*.
[3] The list of names is found in *Shipov* II, p. 135.
* Marshal of the nobility of the Russkiy district (Mos. province), 1893–1906, *B.S.E.* I, vol. 23, p. 50.
† Marshal of the nobility of the Smolensk province, 1887–97, *Veselovskiy* VII, p. 518.
‡ Member of the Tula provincial zemstvo board.
§ Councillor of the Moscow provincial zemstvo assembly, *Veselovksiy* VII, pp. 525–6.
¶ Marshal of the nobility of Orel province.
‖ Marshal of the nobility of Moscow province. Half-brother of S. N. Trubetskoy.
[4] *Shipov* II, pp. 81–4, 131–5.   [5] Ibid. p. 135 and above.

crisis and that only reforms introduced from above could save the existing regime from destruction.[1] But they differed from the latter in their diagnosis of the causes of the crisis and consequently of the reforms needed for its solution. What the conservatives wanted were reforms which would bring about a change in policy while leaving intact the institutional framework of state and society. Hence, while demanding the restoration to autocracy of its original *zemskiy* character[2] (*zemskiy* being a synonym for the unity between tsar and people) they were opposed at this time to the convocation of a *zemskiy sobor*. While emphasising the urgent need for the extensive development of local government, they avoided any reference to the principle of elected representation and were actively opposed to the abolition of the class character of the zemstvo or to a change in the legal rights of the various estates.[3]

Samarin expounded the conservative Slavophile position to Shipov at one of the first meetings of *Beseda*. The approaching political crisis, he said, was not so much a consequence of the policy of the government as of the predominance of negative ideological currents in society. Hence the distrust which the government showed towards society, and which was without doubt one of the causes of the crisis, was justified to a large degree by the negative attitude which the leaders of public opinion were displaying towards the religion of their fathers, the history, beliefs and mode of life of their people and above all towards the autocratic regime itself. The solution to the crisis lay not in institutional reforms but in a change of heart on the part of society and a change of heart and policy on the part of the government. The government needed to recover belief in itself and in its own importance and the Tsar had to use his power and authority for the restoration of the original *zemskiy* character of autocracy. The first step in this direction, Samarin explained to Shipov,

has to be the strengthening and enlargement of all those local organs of the government in which the chief role belongs to people who are *drawn from the population* and not to bureaucrats. Only by the most extensive development of local self-government will it be possible in the given conditions to preserve autocracy.[4]

At the same time he believed that the introduction of the principle of representation into the central organs of government, even in its mildest, consultative form, might lead to the eventual establishment of a con-

[1] Ibid. p. 134.   [2] Ibid. p. 152.
[3] See below and *Veselovskiy* VII, p. 256.
[4] *Shipov* II, p. 152 (italics added).

stitutional regime which would constitute a great evil, and that such measures must be avoided.[1]

The remaining three founding-fathers of *Beseda* – Prince Pavel D. Dolgorukov, Prince S. N. Trubetskoy and R. A. Pisarev – belonged to the moderate constitutionalists. (The radicals remained the only group of politically minded zemstvo activists who were not represented in the 'Symposium' at this stage.)

The moderate constitutionalists, like the liberal Slavophiles, wanted to achieve reforms from above in order to prevent a revolution from below. However, in contrast to the latter, they believed that only the granting of a constitution would be able to satisfy society and thus prevent a revolutionary upheaval. Their position was explained to Shipov by Prince S. N. Trubetskoy, the professor of philosophy and future first elected rector of Moscow University. According to Shipov,

he found the idea of the restoration of the ideal autocracy to be utopian. He did not think it possible to put an end to the arbitrariness of the government without limiting it by a well-defined legal order and regarded the replacement of autocracy (*prikaznyy stroy*) by a constitutional regime as the only solution to the existing political crisis.[2]

At the foundation stage of *Beseda*, the main preoccupation of its members was the search for ways and means of undoing some of the damage done by Witte's memorandum. In July 1900, Shipov and Khomyakov suggested the following plan of action: to compose a petition to the Tsar proving the falsehood of Witte's conclusion that the zemstvo was incompatible with autocracy; to submit the petition for signature to all the marshals of the nobility, chairmen of zemstvo provincial boards, mayors of the greater cities and distinguished 'public men'; to present the petition to the Tsar through an elected delegation or one of his close associates.[3] The circle approved the plan and asked Shipov to compose the petition.[4] In doing so he formulated, in a nutshell, the political programme of what became known at the end of 1904 as the zemstvo minority. He started out by postulating that the combination of 'a locally self-governing land with an autocratic Tsar at its head is the only historically true course of our political life and the strongest bulwark of genuine autocratic power'.[5] Then he explained that the precondition for such a state of affairs was the existence of mutual confidence between the governor and the governed.

---

[1] *Shipov* ibid. pp. 153–4.   [2] Ibid. p. 154.   [3] Ibid. p. 135 and *Chermenskiy* II, p. 44.
[4] *Shipov* ibid. pp. 135–6, 149–50.   [5] *Chermenskiy* II, p. 44.

Such confidence could be derived only from close communion between the autocratic Tsar and the people. This communion was broken when genuine autocracy was replaced by the autocracy of the bureaucracy. In order to restore the ideal state of affairs the Tsar would have to guarantee to the people freedom of conscience, thought and speech, and to allow elected representatives of public institutions to participate in the legislative work of the State Council and its committees.[1]

Although the petition was never sent to the Tsar, because its demands appeared too radical to Samarin and not radical enough to S. N. Trubetskoy,[2] the debate which it aroused transformed *Beseda* into the semi-conspiratorial circle which played so important a role in the development of the Liberation Movement.

The debate, which continued for the better part of winter 1900–1,[3] aroused great interest and membership of the circle rose from ten to between forty and fifty.[4] By force of circumstances the majority of the new members were either moderate or radical constitutionalists and Shipov and his supporters were reduced to a small minority. The following, admittedly incomplete, list of *Beseda* members[5] shows the extent of the constitutionalist domination of the circle from 1901 onwards:

Constitutionalists:* M. V. Chelnokov, Prince Pavel D. Dolgorukov, Prince Peter D. Dolgorukov, Count P. A. Geyden, F. A. Golovin, F. F. Kokoshkin, N. N. Kovalevskiy, Prince G. E. Lvov (the future chairman of the provisional government), N. N. Lvov, V. A. Maklakov, Yu. A. Novosiltsev, V. M. Petrovo-Solovovo, I. I. Petrunkevich, R. A. Pisarev, Prince D. I. Shakhovskoy, A. A. Stakhovich, A. A. Svechin, G. S. Tolstoy, Prince E. N. Trubetskoy, Prince S. N. Trubetskoy, V. I. Vernadskiy, and Yershov.

Liberal Slavophiles: N. V. Davydov, N. A. Khomyakov, V. O. Kluchevskiy (who was, apparently, not a member for long), D. N. Shipov, M. A. Stakhovich and Prince P. N. Trubetskoy.

Conservative Slavophiles: Count V. A. Bobrinskiy, F. D. Samarin, and Count P. S. Shermetyev. (Samarin apparently left the circle soon afterwards.)

---

[1] *Shipov* II, pp. 150–2.   [2] Ibid. pp. 152–5.   [3] Ibid. p. 135.
[4] *Chermenskiy* II, p. 44, *Mikheyeva*, p. 241.
[5] The list was composed on the basis of information found in *Chermenskiy* II, pp. 44, 46, 50, *Peter Dolgorukov*, p. 304, *Shipov* II, p. 135 and *Mikheyeva*, pp. 241, 243. Professor Pipes, who has studied the *Beseda* archives, has corroborated this list with the following exceptions: N. N. Kovalevskiy, I. I. Petrunkevich, V. I. Vernadskiy, V. O. Kluchevskiy, P. N. Trubetskoy and F. D. Samarin.   * Zemstvo radicals and moderate constitutionalists.

55

Although constitutionalists dominated *Beseda*, they never transformed it into a purely constitutional organization[1] but kept it uncommitted. The reason for this was very simple and practical. They
were thus able to exercise some influence over the government through
the contacts which the liberal Slavophiles, D. N. Shipov and M. A.
Stakhovich, or the moderate constitutionalists such as Count P. A.
Geyden and Prince S. N. Trubetskoy, had with various ministers and
high-ranking officials. Secondly, they could steadily increase their
influence over the non-*Beseda* zemstvo activists, among whom the
liberal Slavophiles, and not the constitutionalists, constituted the
majority until the end of 1904.

Prince Peter D. Dolgorukov put the case for the continuation of
Beseda as an uncommitted political group succinctly when replying in
1902 to a suggestion that *Osvobozhdeniye*, the illegal organ of the
Liberation Movement, be made the circle's official mouthpiece. He
declared that 'the way has to remain open for us to influence by word
those who do not agree with us, constitutionalists, those who still
believe in autocracy (Shipov, M. Stakhovich and others)'.[2] Shipov and
his supporters were still indispensable to the zemstvo radicals and they
remained so till the Zemstvo Congress of November 1904.[3] For that
reason *Beseda* continued to meet two to four times a year at least until
February 1905 if not until the establishment of the Cadet Party in
October of that year.[4] It is true that its importance declined rapidly
after the establishment in November 1903 of a 'front organization' of
the Union of Liberation inside the zemstvo, the 'Union of Zemstvo
Constitutionalists'.[5] Till then, however, it had enabled the constitutionalist minority to exercise for the first time considerable influence
on the political attitude of the non-constitutionalist majority of the
zemstvo activists as well as on some members of the government, and
had also been instrumental in consolidating the ranks of the zemstvo
constitutionalists themselves.[6]

This aspect of *Beseda* activity, despite being emphasised by the
various authors of memoirs, was overshadowed by its publication

[1] See *Shakhovskoy* IV, pp. 103–4 and below.
[2] *Chermenskiy* II, p. 46. See also *Mikheyeva*, pp. 241–2.
[3] See *Petrunkevich* II, pp. 356–7 and below.
[4] Although Mikheyeva (ibid. p. 241) maintains that *Beseda* continued to meet till the
establishment of the Cadet Party, as does Maklakov (*Maklakov* II, p. 296), the last reported
meeting of this circle was held on 20 February 1905 (*Chermenskiy*, p. 19).
[5] See below.
[6] *Shakhovskoy* IV, p. 104.

activity[1] because of the dearth of factual material, and some contemporary writers have even claimed that publication was its main business. But now it is known that not only did *Beseda* play an important role in the launching of *Osvobozhdeniye*[2] by providing a meeting place for zemstvo constitutionalists and sympathizers, but also organized the zemstvo campaign of 1902.[3] With the intensification of the political crisis in 1902–3, it even ventured into the field of oral and written propaganda, especially among the peasants.[4]

On the basis of these facts it is understandable why *Beseda* was so important to the constitutionalists and why, for the sake of preserving its unity, they were prepared to compromise with Shipov's group of liberal Slavophiles. But why were the latter prepared to remain in the circle while realizing that it mainly served the ends of the constitutionalists? The answer to this lies in the government's policy. The government, especially after Plehve became Minister of the Interior in April 1902,[5] seemed to be more afraid of true supporters of autocracy, like Shipov and his friends, than of the revolutionaries. (Plehve thought he could keep the latter in hand by perfecting the police apparatus.) As a consequence, Shipov's group had no choice but to co-operate with the constitutionalists, especially as they were prepared for the time being not to force *Beseda* to adopt their political programme and to work for the achievement of the common goal: widening the scope of zemstvo activity and defending the civic and economic interests of the agricultural population.[6]

---

[1] For *Beseda*'s publication activity, conducted mainly in co-operation with *Pravo*, see below and *Gessen* I, pp. 161–4; *Fischer*, p. 230.
[2] *Chermenskiy* II, p. 50, *Mikheyeva*, p. 243.   [3] *Chermenskiy* ibid. pp. 46–7.
[4] *Mikheyeva* ibid.   [5] See below.   [6] *Chermenskiy* II, p. 47, *Mikheyeva*, p. 243.

3

The birth of the democratic intelligentsia

It is necessary to realize clearly that the course of Russian historical development brought about a most peculiar relationship between socialism and liberalism. In all other countries socialism grew up on the soil already prepared by evolution of the regime of legality based on the principles of liberalism and democracy. It was not so in Russia where, after the Decembrists, who were as yet quite unaffected by the ideas and yearnings of socialism, all the ensuing struggle for political reforms became closely intertwined with socialist tendencies and ideas. (*Struve* v, p. 573)

Russia's intelligentsia, for all its love of freedom and hatred of the tsarist regime, was not known for its admiration of the 'bourgeois' freedom of the West. The populists, whose indeterminate ideology dominated the thought of the radical intelligentsia until the mid-1890s if not later, cared very little at the height of their power for such things as constitutions, civil liberties or parliamentary rule.[1]

It was only on the eve of the political débâcle of populism, and as a direct consequence of the peasants' lack of response to the appeals and exhortations of the movement 'to go to the people' that the founders of the ill-fated People's Will Party (*Narodnaya Volya*) and their supporters among the 'Legal Populists' discovered the importance of civil liberties and democratic institutions.[2] But even then they looked upon them as means, albeit indispensable ones, for the achievement of their old goals: the establishment of a just society in which the land, the factories and the workshops would belong to the people.[3] As one of the founders of the People's Will explained at the time:

The function of the social-revolutionary party does not include political reforms.

[1] For a classical analysis of the reasons behind the antagonism which the Russian intelligentsia felt toward Western-type liberalism, see Sir Isaiah Berlin's introduction to *Venturi*, esp. pp. viii–x.
[2] *Venturi*, pp. 649–65, *Schapiro* 1, pp. 6–7. As far as N. K. Mikhaylovskiy, the central figure of 'Legal Populism' was concerned, his attitude towards liberalism and constitutionalism at that time was ambivalent, to say the least. See above and *Billington*, pp. 104–19, *Mendel*, pp. 83–8.
[3] *Schapiro* ibid., *Venturi*, pp. 677–8.

Such reforms ought to be exclusively the task of those who call themselves liberals. But here in Russia these people are utterly impotent. Whatever the reasons, they are quite incapable of giving Russia free institutions and guarantees for rights of the individual. Yet such institutions are so indispensable that all activity becomes impossible without them. And so the social-revolutionary party must take upon itself the function of destroying despotism and giving Russia the political forms within which a 'struggle of principles' will become possible [1]

But even this conditional recognition of the importance of political freedom was soon forgotten in the wake of the reckless terror campaign launched by the new party. 'What had proclaimed itself as a political movement', writes a well-known authority on Russian revolutionary movements, 'in the end proved to be a conspiracy and nothing more.'[2]

It took the crushing defeat of *Narodnaya Volya*, the decade of reaction which followed and a new disillusionment with the masses during the 1891–2 famine year to bring about an attempt by the veterans of the populist movement of the 1870s and their young supporters to launch a party for which political freedom was to be not only a means but also an end in itself. In order to emphasise their break with terror as a political weapon and their preoccupation with personal and political liberty, they decided to call their organization The People's Rights Party (*Partiya Narodnogo Prava*).[3]

The significance of the party launched by these people in summer 1893[4] lay not in its immediate achievements, which were nil, but in the important role it played in the emergence of the Liberation Movement. This party did for the intelligentsia section of the Liberation Movement what the 'First Zemstvo Movement' of 1878–81 had done for the zemstvo–constitutionalist wing – it provided it with the majority of its leaders and with the basis for its radical programme. During its short lifetime contacts were established between the future leaders of these two wings and the foundation for their future collaboration was laid.

---

[1] *Venturi*, pp. 654–5. This reasoning was later echoed by the Marxists, who, at least in theory, substituted the working class for the socialist-revolutionary party. See below.

[2] *Schapiro* I, p. 7.

[3] Despite its importance for understanding the Liberation Movement, the People's Rights Party has not yet been extensively studied. The main available sources on this organization are *Aptekman* and *Iz Obzora*. References to the party are found, among other places, in *Brokgaus supp.* vol. II, p. 241, *Billington*, pp. 158–c. *Chernov* III, pp. 75–80; IV, pp. 41–3, 63–8, 94–6, 182, 187–90, 195–7, *Fischer*, pp. 93–4, *Kuskova* VIa, p. 179; *d*, pp. 161–3; *e*, pp. 178, 184–6, *M.S.E.* vol. V, col. 575, *Mendel*, pp. 94–6, 287, *Mitskevich* III, pp. 179–81, *Spiridovich*, pp. 43, 219, *Stepnyak*, pp. 118–22, *Yarmolinski*, p. 339 *Yegorov*, p. 374, *Za Sto Let*, pp. 260–2.

[4] *Aptekman*, pp. 196–7.

The People's Rights Party, like the Union of Liberation a decade later, was composed of a small core of members and a much larger periphery of active supporters and sympathisers. The practical leadership of the party was in the hands of Mark Natanson[1] and two of his political friends; N. S. Tyutchev and V. O. Aptekman. All three were veteran populists who had not belonged to *Narodnaya Volya* (Natanson and Tyutchev were arrested before it was established while Aptekman, at the time of the split of *Zemlya i Volya*, joined *Chernyy Peredel*).[2]

The theoretical leadership was provided by N. K. Mikhaylovskiy, the leading figure in 'Legal Populism', and his followers on the editorial board of *Russkoye Bogatstvo*: N. F. Annenskiy, the well-known writer V. G. Korolenko and A. V. Peshekhonov.[3] Mikhaylovskiy supported Natanson almost from the beginning in his efforts to launch the People's Rights Party. Although he never joined it officially, he helped to draft its programme and became editor-in-chief of its publications.[4] Peshekhonov became a member of its council,[5] while Vladimir Korolenko and Annenskiy, although not officially members of the party, were exponents of its ideology in Nizhniy Novgorod where they lived at the time.[6] Annenskiy, who was head of the Statistical Bureau of the Nizhniy Novgorod provincial zemstvo board in the period 1887–95,[7] also extended material support to many party members and active supporters.

Another group which played an important role in the People's Rights Party came from the Ryazanov circle. This group, named after its

---

[1] All the available sources except one attribute to Natanson the leading role in this party. See *Aptekman*, pp. 187–9, 196 *Brokgaus supp.* vol. II, p. 241, *Chernov* III, pp. 75–7; IV, pp. 41–3, 187–91, *Kuskova* VIa, p. 179; *d*, pp. 158–9; *e*, pp. 184–6. Only the police claimed that Tyutchev was the initiator and main leader of the party. See *Iz Obzora*, p. 229. It appears, on the basis of the available evidence, that the police were mistaken in this instance.

[2] See *B.S.E.* I, vols 3, cols 187–8; 41, col. 302, *B.S.E.* II, vol. 43, p. 550. See also *M.S.E.* vol. 5, col, 575.

[3] Mikhaylovskiy became co-editor of *Russkoye Bogatstvo* in 1892, and together with Annenskiy, Korolenko, Peshekhonov and V. A. Myakotin, who joined them later, he dominated this newspaper from then until his death in 1904. See *Billington*, p. 195, *Fischer*, pp. 91–3.

[4] See *Aptekman*, pp. 189–90, 194–6, 200, 202, *Aleksandrov*, pp. 15–17, *B.S.E.* I, vol. 39, cols 521–3, *Mendel*, p. 95, 287, *Billington*, pp. 157–9. Billington however, mistakenly implies that Mikhaylovskiy participated in the party's foundation conference. This mistake arose from the confusion of this conference (held in summer 1893 in Saratov) with a student meeting in St Petersburg in spring 1893 at which Mikhaylovskiy was the chief speaker. (See *Aptekman*, pp. 195–6.)

[5] *Iz Obzora*, pp. 321–2.

[6] *Aptekman*, pp. 191–3, *Kuskova* VId, p. 197, *Mitskevich* III, pp. 66–9.

[7] *Brokgaus supp.* vol I, pp. 122–3.

recognized leader and principal host, A. I. Ryazanov,[1] was formed after the collapse of another clandestine student group, the Astyrev circle in Moscow. N. M. Astyrev (1857–94) achieved great fame at the time by writing the 'First Letter to Hungry Peasants' in which he incited them to a jacquerie. He and almost all the members of his circle were arrested on 30 March 1892 shortly after the clandestine publication of the 'Letter'.[2]

The Ryazanov circle rapidly became the central student circle in Moscow,[3] the students being attracted to it mainly by its openness. Ryazanov, who by then was already a convinced Marxist, did not try to impose his newly adopted political creed on his followers. Thus the group encompassed Marxists, such as Ryazanov, M. Lyadov (N. N. Mandelshtam) and S. I. Mitskevich, and people like S. N. Prokopovich and his common-law wife, E. D. Kuskova, who were in the process of becoming Marxists after losing their faith in populism. It attracted young *Narodovoltsy* like Victor Chernov, and (apparently for the first time in the annals of Russian student movements) convinced constitutionalists like P. I. Kuskov (then still husband of E. D Kuskova) and A. N. Maksimov (close friend and room-mate of S. N. Prokopovich). Through Kuskov and Maksimov (who married into the Bakunin family), Prokopovich, Kuskova, Chernov and other members of the Circle came into contact with I. I. Petrunkevich's zemstvo radical circle in Tver and the liberal circle in Moscow (S. A. Muromtsev and others). The establishment of the People's Rights Party in summer 1893 put an end to the existence of the Ryazanov circle. Apart from the convinced Marxists (Mitskevich, Lyadov, Ryazanov, Vinokurov etc), who concentrated on organizing workers' circles, all its members joined or became active supporters of the new party.[4]

The People's Rights Party also acquired a following among radical *intelligenty* who at the time of its formation did not belong to any particular circle. A. I. Bogdanovich, the author of *Nasushchnyy Vopros* (The Current Question), the Party's only surviving printed work[5] with the exception of its programme, belonged to this group. So did

---

[1] *Kuskova* VIe, p. 178, *Lyadov*, p. 42.

[2] See *Aleksandrov*, p. 20, *B.S.E.* I, vol. 3, cols 710–11, *Chernov* IV, pp. 148–9, *Lyadov*, pp. 52–3, *Kuskova* VIf, pp. 176–7.

[3] *Chernov*, ibid. p. 123.

[4] *Chernov* IV, pp. 123, 142–4, 156–75, 182–97, Iz *Obzora*, pp. 230, 232–5, *Kuskova* VIe, pp. 178–82, 184–6, 196–7, *Lyadov*, pp. 42, 53–4, 63–5, *A.I.Ryazanov*, pp. 132–6, *Vademecum*, p. 28, *Vinokurov*, pp. 32, 38.

[5] *Aptekman*, pp. 199–201.

V. Ya. (Yakovlev) Bogucharskiy, the famous historian of the populist era,[1] and V. V. Khizhnyakov, future Permanent Secretary of the St Petersburg Free Economic Society (1903–10),[2] a life-long friend and political ally of Kuskova and Prokopovich. All four were to become leaders of the Union of Liberation.

These groups and individuals were brought and kept together as a result of their disillusionment with the 'people' after their encounter with unadorned reality in the famine year 1891–2. This led to scepticism as regards the populist tendency to idealize and idolize the masses and to their subsequent realization that what Russia needed first of all was political freedom.

The shock of the encounter with the people and the disillusionment it created was particularly great among those who were followers of P. F. Nikolayev, like Kuskova. Nikolayev, who was the sole survivor of the Astyrev circle, addressed to the young radicals a 'Letter from an Old Friend' (*Pismo Starogo Druga*). He advised them to utilize the déclassé urban elements (*bosyaki*) in famine- and epidemic-ravaged provinces as a spearhead in the attack on the existing political and social order. (Because of this advice, he and his followers were known at the time as the *Bosyatskiy* movement.[3])

Kuskova almost paid with her life for heeding this foolhardy advice. During the cholera epidemic which followed the 1891–2 famine in Saratov, she and a friend, who were working as nurses, tried to transform the pogrom staged against medical personnel into a riot against the authorities. They were soon recognized and were on the point of being lynched when the police saved them from the hands of a savage mob. Although the mob eventually attacked the police and sacked the governor's house, they did so for the wrong motives, namely because of the authorities' defence of the *intelligenty*.[4] For her role in this riot and especially for her part in the distribution of Nikolayev's 'Letter from an Old Friend', Kuskova was sentenced in 1893 to one month's imprisonment and three years' police supervision.[5] The punishment

---

[1] *B.S.E.* I, vol. 6, col. 623. [2] *Iz Obzora*, p. 242.

[3] On the *Bosyatskiy* movement and Kuskova's participation in it see *Chernov* IV, pp. 148–57, *Granat*, vol. 26, col. 258 and *Mitskevich* III, pp. 113–14. Mitskevich, however, does not mention Kuskova but only her future husband, P. I. Kuskov. This movement was completely discredited after the cholera riots in Saratov and many of its participants, including P. F. Nikolayev, joined the People's Rights Party (*Chernov* ibid. pp. 156–7, 192–3, *Mitskevich* ibid. p. 67).

[4] Kuskova's role in the cholera riot in Saratov is described vividly in *Chernov* III, pp. 53–5; IV, pp. 94–6, *Kuskova* VI*d*, pp. 161–8. The riots in general are described in *Aptekman*, pp. 193–4 and *V. Obolenskiy*, pp. 223–7. [5] *Kuskova* VI*e*, pp. 177, 181; *f*, pp. 167–8.

inflicted on her by the hated government was nothing compared to the emotional crisis she must have undergone as a consequence of the treatment she received from her beloved people.

Although Kuskova's experience was not typical, even those radicals who did not follow Nikolayev's advice to exploit the famine *à la* Bakunin, were appalled by the ignorance, superstition, hatred of educated people and blind devotion to the Tsar displayed by the peasants.[1] At a time when Mikhaylovskiy was writing that 'governors-general, ministers and governors have led Russia to the brink of an abyss',[2] the peasants not only continued to believe in the goodwill of the Father-Tsar (*Batyushka-Tsar*) but were also convinced that the people who came to their rescue did so on his personal orders.[3]

Vladimir Korolenko remarked at the time that before these 'ignorant and barbaric masses' could be of any use to the revolution, it would be necessary to educate them and 'to awaken in them the self-awareness of citizens'.[4] But how could one arouse this self-awareness in a country where the vast majority of the population had no rights whatsoever, and where even those rights existing were not guaranteed by law?

And so the question of achieving political rights was raised again, as in 1879, but this time with an important difference. The founders of the People's Will still believed in the spontaneous socialism of the Russian peasants, and the achievement of political freedom meant to them the establishment of the best conditions for the realization of this socialism. The founders of the People's Rights, on the other hand, had lost for a time all hope in peasant socialism and as a consequence began to regard political freedom not only as a means but as an end in itself. At the same time, they did not lose their belief in the virtues of socialism and this led them to define political freedom as equal to socialism. As a consequence, their ideological break with populism was less drastic than it may have appeared from their own statement. The break found full expression in the following passage from the ideological declaration of the new party, *Nasushchnyy Vopros.*[5]

It is time for us to wake up. It is time to shake off the yoke of the decayed ideas of populism, culture-bearing (*Kulturnichestvo*) and the propagation of small deeds. It

---

[1] *Aptekman*, pp. 188–9.   [2] *Billington*, p. 158.

[3] *Aptekman* ibid. p. 189, *Obolenskiy* ibid. pp. 211–2.

[4] *Mitskevich* III, p. 68, *Kuskova* VIf, p. 154.

[5] Although this declaration was written by Bogdanovich, it was debated, amended and finally approved by the Council of the People's Rights Party and by Mikhaylovskiy. Hence the views expressed in it represented the official view of the party and not the private views of Bogdanovich. (See *Aptekman*, pp. 199–200.)

is time also to get rid of the condescending worship of the mythical 'people' (*narod*)
...Life itself calls us... to the struggle for political liberty, which was never hostile
to anything but absolutism. For absolutism it spells death, for the people – *conditio
sine qua non* for public life. And as far as socialism is concerned, political freedom
and socialism are not only not incompatible but are, on the contrary, complementary
and mutually dependent...*Political freedom is not only the first step towards the
achievement of socialism, but also the conditio sine qua non for its existence.*[1]

The programme of the People's Rights Party, which was adopted at
its foundation congress at Saratov in summer 1893,[2] anticipated, almost
point for point, the programme of the Liberation Movement which its
leaders helped to organize a decade later. Its main novelty lay not only
in the fact that it proclaimed the achievement of political liberty to be
the main aim of the new party, but also in the description of the means
by which this goal was to be attained. For the first time in the annals of
Russian parties, it declared organized public opinion to be the main
weapon in the struggle against autocracy. The authors of the programme
were aware that its novelty might not be to the liking of the populist
intelligentsia, their main source of potential support. They therefore
opened the programme[3] by explaining the reasons why the achievement
of political freedom was the main goal of the new party:

There are moments in the life of states when one question occupies the foremost
place, thrusting into the background all other interests, however essential they
might be in themselves...Such a moment Russia is now living through and the
question, determining her future destiny, is the question of political freedom.

The programme then proclaimed the aim of the newly founded party
to be the 'replacement of autocracy by free representative institutions'.
But, it continued,

since there is not and cannot be a hope that the government will willingly enter upon
the path indicated, there is one course remaining for the people: to oppose the force
of *organized public opinion* to the inertia of the government and the narrow dynastic
interests of autocracy...The party has set itself the task of uniting all oppositional
elements in the country and of organizing an active force which should...attain the
overthrow of autocracy and secure for everyone the rights of citizen and man. These
rights include:

[1] *Aptekman*, p. 201. Italics in text.   [2] Ibid. pp. 196–7.
[3] *Iz Obzora*, pp. 235–6. The full text of the programme is found in *Za Sto Let*, pp. 260–2
and an English translation is given in *Stepnyak*, pp. 118–21. (Italics added.) This translation,
however, is not only very poor but is in some instances misleading. The author of this book,
while using the English translation for reasons of convenience, has checked its meaning by
constant comparison with the original text.

representative government on the basis of universal suffrage;
freedom of religious belief;
independence of the courts of justice;
freedom of meeting and association;
inviolability of the individual and of his rights as a man;
the right of self-determination for all the nationalities entering into (the) composition (of Russia).

The publication of the programme, in the form of a manifesto, on 19 February 1894[1] proved to be the swan-song of the newly formed party. The secret police were aware of the activities of its organizers almost from the very beginning, and allowed them to continue uninterrupted in order to obtain maximum information on their contacts.[2] The publication of the manifesto now made the continued existence of the party too dangerous a proposition in the eyes of the authorities. But the police waited another two months, collecting sufficient additional information to enable them to destroy the newly born party at one stroke. On the morning of 21 April 1894 they struck simultaneously in five towns where members and supporters of the party lived: Orel (the headquarters of the party), Kharkov, Moscow, Smolensk (where its printing press was located) and St Petersburg. The majority of the party members – fifty-two in all – were arrested and the printing press was seized. Among those arrested were M. Natanson, N. S. Tyutchev, Victor Chernov, V. V. Khizhnyakov, and A. V. Peshekhonov.[3] Those who escaped arrest either suspended all illegal activity for the time being (the *Russkoye Bogatstvo* group) or left the country (Kuskova and Prokopovich).

The blow inflicted by the police proved irrevocable as far as the party as an organization was concerned. But for many of the members the bonds of personal friendship and common political heritage forged during the short period of its existence proved stronger than the new political alliances they entered into as a consequence of the advance of Marxism. It is no accident that Kuskova and Prokopovich were the first to raise the banner of revolt against Russian orthodox Marxism[4] or that, among the five representatives of the radical intelligentsia on the board of the first elected Council of the Union of Liberation, four (Annenskiy, Bogucharskiy, Peshekhonov and Prokopovich)[5] were former members or supporters of the People's Rights Party.

[1] *Iz obzora*, p. 236.　　　　　　　　　　　　　　[2] Ibid. pp. 228–34.
[3] Ibid. pp. 235–8, *Chernov* III, pp. 77–80, B.S.E. I, vol. 50, col. 537.
[4] See below.　　　　[5] M.S.E. vol. 8, cols. 257–8, *Shakhovskoy* IV, p. 117 and below.

Origins

The party's liquidation coincided with the triumph of Marxism in its struggle with populism* for the hearts and minds of the Russian radical intelligentsia. The magnetic appeal of Marxism for young radicals derived mainly from two factors: it provided a more plausible explanation than populism for the realities of Russian life, and it appeared to promise success in the struggle against autocracy where populism had so patently failed.

The Marxist–populist controversy in the mid-1890s[1] was focused at first on the question of the economic development of Russia. The populists claimed that capitalism, synonymous at the time with industrialism, was an alien element on Russian soil. Like Lobko some years later they quite rightly maintained that the rapid process of industrialization which Russia was undergoing had been produced by artificial means: the high protective tariff, numerous government orders (and subsidies) and the influx of foreign capital. Their conclusions, however, appeared wrong even at that time.

The populists claimed that neither high tariffs nor government orders nor foreign capital could protect industry in the long run from the consequences of the lack of domestic and foreign markets. They were apparently unaware of the teachings of Marx and F. List on these questions, nor did they take into account developments in Germany and Japan at the time, and they therefore identified the home market with private consumption. Their claim was that the home market was shrinking since the standard of living of the peasants, who constituted the overwhelming majority of private consumers in Russia, was on the decline. This they regarded as a direct consequence of the economic policy of the government, which was forcing the peasants to pay the price of the artificial growth of industry. A decreasing home market, they reasoned, was bound to bring about the closing of foreign markets to Russian industry, since the advanced countries of the West, based as they were on extensive domestic markets, would always produce

* The term 'populism' is employed here in the traditional sense. As Professor Pipes has noted, this traditional meaning was formulated mainly by Struve, during his controversy with the ideological opponents of social-democracy. (See Pipes IIa, pp. 28–30, 84–6.)

[1] There is an extensive literature on the Marxist–populist controversy as well as on the role played by the leading protagonists – the Marxists G. V. Plekhanov, P. B. Struve, V. I. Lenin, N. A. Berdyayev, S. N. Bulgakov and M. I. Tugan-Baranovskiy and the Populists N. F. Danielson, V. P. Vorontsov and S. N. Yuzhakov. (N. K. Mikhaylovskiy, who was himself critical of many populist ideas, held an intermediary position.) Accounts in English of this controversy are found, inter alia, in Baron I, pp. 141–7, Billington, pp. 161–72, Keep, pp. 27–36, Kindersley, pp. 5–28, 146–79, Mendel, pp. 37–76, 123–64, Schapiro I, pp. 13–15 and Von Laue II. See also Pipes IIa, pp. 79–100.

industrial goods at a cheaper price and of higher quality. Hence the populists regarded the government's economic policy as self-defeating, and Russian capitalism as doomed to failure.

The Marxists were quick to point out the main flaw in this economic analysis, namely the identification of the domestic market with private consumption. They claimed, with ample justification, that private consumption accounted for only a small part of the domestic market.[1] Government expenditure and investment in the expansion of industry ('heavy industry') were much more important for the development of the home market than was private consumption. Since both were expanding on an unprecedented scale during the 1890s, economic facts bore out the Marxist claim that capitalism had come to stay or, to use a modern term, reached the point of no return.

The excitement which this controversy generated in intellectual circles was aroused not so much by these somewhat academic arguments as by their political implications. In claiming that capitalism was doomed in Russia, the populists were in fact restating in economic terms their old belief in the uniqueness of its development. What set Russia apart from the West, in their view, were the peasant commune and the *artel* (cottage industry). The predominance of these two institutions in rural Russia made it possible for her to become a socialist state or society without going through a bourgeois state of development. They stressed possibility rather than certainty, one of the main common denominators of populism being its rejection of historical determinism and its emphasis on the importance of individual free will.

According to the materialist conception of history as expounded by Marx in his *Preface to a Contribution to the Critique of Political Economy*, written in 1859, it was ostensibly impossible to skip a stage in history. Marx stated that there were four consecutive stages discernible in the history of mankind in the pre-socialist era: 'In broad outlines, Asiatic, ancient, feudal and modern bourgeois modes of production can be designated as progressive epochs in the economic formation of society.'[2] Engels later reiterated this statement, applying it to Russia. In a famous reply[3] to the well-known Russian Jacobin, Peter M. Tkachev,[4] he wrote that not even Russia could achieve socialism without first going through a capitalist stage of development.[5]

---

[1] See especially *Kindersley*, pp. 146–54. [2] See *Marx* I, p. 329.
[3] See *Marx* II, pp. 46–56 and *Blackstock*, pp. 203–15, 273–4.
[4] For a recent biography of Tkachev in English see *Weeks*.
[5] See *Marx* II, pp. 46–7, *Blackstock*, p. 205.

Marx himself, however, in contrast to Engels, was extremely cautious in his pronouncements on this question. In two letters, one to Mikhaylovskiy (1877) and the other to Vera Zasulich (1881), as well as in the preface to the second Russian edition of the *Communist Manifesto* (published in 1882) to which Engels added his signature, Marx made it clear that he did not regard his materialist conception of history as a universal law binding all countries and societies.[1] In fact he explicitly stated that it was applicable to Western Europe alone, and at least partially recognized the uniqueness of Russia's development.[2] Because of the existence of the peasant commune, he wrote, Russia could be transformed into a socialist society without passing through the bourgeois stage of development — on certain conditions. It could only happen if the government policy of forced industrialization (which, according to Marx, commenced in 1861) did not succeed in making capitalistic relations an important element in the economy by the time the revolution occurred. Otherwise, Marx wrote, 'once Russia has crossed the threshold of the capitalist system, it will have to submit to the implacable laws of such a system, like the other Western nations'.[3] The second condition was that the Russian revolution 'sound the signal for a proletarian revolution in the West, so that each (revolution) complement the other'.[4]

The question of the proper relation between the Russian and European revolutions was to play an important role in the subsequent development of Marxist theory and practice in Russia. At the time of the Marxist–populist controversy, however, the first condition was the more important. Had the populists been able to prove their claim that capitalism was doomed in Russia, they could have exploited the authority of Marx in order to overwhelm his Russian disciples, whom they generally described as 'apologists of capitalism'.[5] But, as has been shown, the populists failed to convince their audience of the correctness of their economic analysis and, as a consequence, they lost the battle for the hearts and minds of the Russian radical intelligentsia.

By proving that Russia had crossed the threshold of the capitalist system, the Marxists were able to argue that from then on the country would develop according to the rules of historical materialism. This prognosis was tremendously appealing to the majority of the Russian radical intelligentsia at the time.

---

[1] The texts of the letters, their unpublished drafts as well as the story behind their writing and comments on the history of the preface, are found in *Blackstock*, pp. 216–28, 274–83.
[2] See *Blackstock*, pp. 217, 275, 278–9.　　　　　　　　　　　　　　[3] Ibid. p. 217.
[4] Ibid. p. 228, *Marx* I, p. 24.　　　　　　　　　　　　　[5] See *Struve* V, p. 581.

For a start the determinist features of historical materialism assured the young radicals of the support of the forces of history in their struggle against autocracy. Such an assurance was for them preferable to the populist voluntarism which had failed so disastrously in 1881 and again in 1891–2.

Secondly, contrary to populist expectations at the time,[1] the determinist elements did not turn Marxism into an ideological cloak for political passivity. Instead of encouraging its Russian adherents to rely on the forces of capitalism to destroy autocracy and prepare the ground for the socialist revolution in the distant future, Marxism provided them with a very strong stimulus for immediate action. This was achieved mainly through the efforts of George Plekhanov and, to a lesser extent, Pavel Akselrod, who had been preoccupied since the early 1880s with applying Marxist theory to Russian conditions.[2] The outcome of their efforts became known at the turn of the century as the theory of the 'hegemony of the proletariat' in the bourgeois revolution.[3] By then it had become the official doctrine of Russian orthodox Marxism and it remained such till the emergence of Leninism and Trotskyism some years later.

The 'hegemony' theory attempted to apply to Russian conditions two postulates which formed part of classical Marxism as developed in Western Europe. First, it took the dictum of historical materialism – 'No social order ever perishes before all the productive forces for which there is room in it have developed and new, higher relations of production never appear before the material conditions of their existence have matured in the womb of old society itself'[4] – and interpreted it in accordance with Russian needs as the authors understood them. Accordingly, the hegemony theory maintained that Russia would have to undergo a thorough capitalist transformation before it would be ripe for a socialist revolution. Such a transformation could be achieved only if Russia's feudal superstructure, which corresponded to its pre-capitalist phase of development, were superseded by a bourgeois one. Because of the nature of the tsarist regime, it claimed, such a development could be brought about only through revolution. From this there followed the dictum that Russia was faced with a 'two-stage revolution', a 'bourgeois–democratic' stage to be followed after a more or less lengthy interval, by a socialist one.[5] The authors of the 'hegemony'

---

[1] See, for example, *Keep*, p. 18.

[2] For the crucial role played by Plekhanov and to a lesser extent by Akselrod, in the development of Russian Marxism, see *inter alia*, *Baron* I, II, *Keep*, pp. 15–26, *Schapiro* I, pp. 8–13.   [3] See *Schapiro* ibid. and *Akselrod* I, III.

[4] *Marx* I, p. 329.   [5] See *Keep*, pp. 21–5 and *Schapiro* I, p. 9.

theory, however, like the founders of the People's Will, believed that the Russian bourgeoisie was too weak for the task of accomplishing its own revolution.[1] This belief led them to their own interpretation of the second postulate of classical Marxism, namely the theory of the proletariat.

The founding-fathers of Russian Marxism adhered whole-heartedly to the dictum that the proletariat was the most revolutionary class in modern, i.e. bourgeois, society. They believed, however, that it was also the most revolutionary class in Russian society, which on the whole was still far from modern, arriving at this conclusion on the basis of an analysis of the autocratic regime. Under tsarism, they thought, there were no prospects for either progressive labour legislation or legalization of trade unions and strikes. Since these were indispensible to the day-to-day economic needs of the working class, their absence must transform the Russian industrial workers into implacable enemies of autocracy. They admitted that, numerically, the Russian proletariat was still very small, but argued that this weakness was more than compensated for by the political awareness of the class and its readiness to respond to revolutionary propaganda. As a result, according to Plekhanov and Akselrod, the industrial workers formed the most revolutionary class in tsarist Russia.[2] Hence the proletariat was bound to play a leading role in the 'bourgeois–democratic' revolution. They therefore regarded it as obligatory for the Russian revolutionary intelligentsia to help to organize and join the Social-Democratic Workers Party, the only party able, in existing conditions, to lead the fight against autocracy;[3] it also followed that it was in the interests of the other two oppositional strata in Russia – the professional intelligentsia and the liberal landowners – even if they developed political parties of their own, to concede the leading role in the forthcoming 'bourgeois–democratic' revolution to the SD Workers Party. In other words, Plekhanov and Akselrod claimed for the SD Party the right and duty to exercise 'hegemony' in the first, i.e. anti-tsarist stage of the revolution.[4]

It is not difficult to understand why this theory proved so attractive to many Russian radicals in the mid-1890s. The assumption that the proletariat was the most revolutionary class in Russia promised them the support of a section of the 'people' in their struggle with autocracy

[1] See *Akselrod* I, pp. 15–16; III, pp. 10–11, 15.

[2] See, *inter alia, Keep*, pp. 19–21, *Kuskova* II, pp. 26–7, *Prokopovich*, pp. 55–6.

[3] See *Plekhanov: Sochineniya*, vol. II, pp. 359–60, *Akselrod* I, p. 19.

[4] See *Akselrod* I, pp. 3–20, 24–6, 29–34; III, pp. 15–18, 22–3. For a somewhat later definition of 'hegemony' see *Lenin* II, vol. IV, p. 332 and *Perepiska* vol. II, pp. 141–2.

at a time when disillusionment with the populist worship of the peasants was at its height. At the same time, the theory of the two-stage revolution seemed to hold out the prospect that, after the overthrow of tsarism, Russia would enjoy a political regime on the lines of Western Europe for many years to come. Such a prospect greatly appealed to people like Kuskova, Prokopovich and Struve, who at that time were beginning to value the 'bourgeois' freedom of the West more and more.

Besides its ideological appeal, Marxism also enjoyed a psychological advantage over populism. All the leading exponents of Marxism inside Russia, except for Tugan-Baranovskiy (1865–1919), were in their early twenties at the time of the controversy, while their three chief protagonists, Danielson, Vorontsov and Yuzhakov were in their forties.[1] Since debates in the universities played an important role in the controversy, youth was a great asset. This initial advantage of the Marxists over their opponents was augmented by the fact that their analysis of the current situation corresponded more to the realities of Russian life than that of the populists.

The following episode may illustrate this point: Victor Chernov, the future leader of the SRs, who was a *Narodovolets* as well as a supporter of the People's Rights Party at the time of the Marxist–populist controversy, described in his memoirs a crowded student meeting he attended in Moscow in 1893. At this meeting the twenty-three-year-old Ulyanov (Lenin) defended the Marxist case against the onslaughts of V. P. Vorontsov. According to Chernov, Lenin's arguments were based on a rational analysis of the realities of Russian life and were delivered in a matter-of-fact tone of voice while Vorontsov behaved arrogantly. He poured scorn on his young adversary, refused to cite any facts in support of his position and instead referred Lenin (and the audience) to his own book and that of Danielson. Chernov, who could not be accused of a pro-Lenin bias, wrote later that 'this kind of argument could not impress us'.[2] Not surprisingly it was Lenin, and not Vorontsov, who won the day.[3]

The victory of Marxism seemed complete and irrevocable at the time. In reality, however, events took a different course. Five years after the publication of Struve's *Critical Notes on Russia's Economic Development*,[4] which signalled the triumph of Marxism, Populism

---

[1] N. F. Danielson (Nikolay-on) was born in 1844, V. P. Vorontsov (V.V.) was born in 1847 and the youngest of the three – Yuzhakov – was born in 1849.

[2] *Chernov* III, p. 74.   [3] Ibid.

[4] P. B. Struve, *Kriticheskiye Zametki k Voprosu ob Ekonomicheskom Razvitii Rosii*, St Petersburg 1894 (September: see *Keep*, p. 30).

began to enjoy a new renaissance[1] while the Marxist camp found itself in total disarray. This was caused, to a large degree, by the disillusionment of many of the founders and early adherents of Marxism with its orthodox dogma as a result of their contacts with the labour movement in Western Europe and of developments inside Russia.

In Western Europe, in contrast to Russia, economic and social developments did not bear out the Marxist analysis of contemporary society. Nowhere was the gap between Marxist theory and reality more apparent than in the case of the Marxist concept of the 'proletariat'. According to this theory, the proletariat was bound to bring about the socialist revolution because of its progressive impoverishment under capitalism and because it was becoming a numerical majority in society.[2] The process of impoverishment was bound to cause the proletariat to rise up against its oppressors, while its numerical superiority assured it of final victory as well as providing the revolution with its moral justification.[3]

Advanced capitalism, however, neither reduced the standard of living of the workers nor polarized society into two numerically unequal classes: a small class of capitalists (owners of the means of production) and an overwhelmingly large class of proletarians. If, rather than becoming impoverished, the workers improved their standard of living through trade union action and state legislation, did this not imply that they might have developed a stake in capitalism and in the nation-states? And if this was so, what remained of Marx's assertion in the *Communist Manifesto* that the proletariat was the most revolutionary class in modern society since 'the proletariat is without property. . . The proletarians have nothing of their own to secure and fortify[4]. . . The working men have no country.'[5] What of the claim that in a communist revolution 'the proletarians have nothing to lose but their chains. They have a world to win.'[6] If the proletariat was not going to become a majority in society, what remained of Marx's moral justification of the socialist revolution, derived from the assumption that while 'all previous historical movements were movements of minorities or in the interest of minorities, the proletarian movement is the self-conscious, independent movement of the immense majority in the interest of the immense majority?'[7]

---

[1] *Keep*, p. 33.   [2] *Marx* I, pp. 38–43.
[3] Hence the Marxist standard equation of the 'dictatorship of the proletariat' with the dictatorship of the vast majority over the small minority. See, for example, *Lenin* I, vol. 25, pp. 419–20.
[4] *Marx* I, p. 42.   [5] Ibid. p. 49.   [6] Ibid. p. 62.   [7] Ibid. p. 42.

At the beginning of 1898 Edward Bernstein's criticism[1] of Marx's main assumptions made a theoretical discussion of these questions unavoidable. Although Plekhanov claimed otherwise, the weakness of the orthodox position[2] then became apparent to all. The orthodox Marxists were unable to deny the fact that the polarization of modern society did not go as far as Marx had predicted or that the workers' standard of living had improved under capitalism. They tried to minimize the importance of Bernstein's criticism by 'biting away at figures'[3] as regards the lack of polarization and by trying to explain away the rising standards of living of the working class by inventing the theory of the 'relative impoverishment of the proletariat'. In the words of Plekhanov, 'the position of the worker worsens relatively even though his material position improves in the absolute sense'.[4] This was a very poor substitute for the theory of the absolute impoverishment of the proletariat which had such a revolutionary appeal to the young radicals, especially in Russia. It also failed to explain the growing 'opportunism' of the labour movement.[5]

The failure of orthodox Marxism to bridge the gap between Marxist theory and the realities of life resulted in the victory of 'revisionism' in Western Europe, in practice if not in theory.[6] In Russia, which was still in the initial stages of industrialization, it brought about the emergence of two diametrically opposed movements. On the one hand it gave birth to Leninism, which restored the revolutionary appeal of Marxism by substituting the party for the proletariat (in practice, if not in theory) and thus emptying it of its humanistic content.[7] On the other hand it contributed directly to the emergence of a democratically

---

[1] See *Bernstein*, esp. pp. x–xii, 101–8, 169–70, 205–13, 218–19, *Perepiska*, vol. I, pp. 189–96.

[2] For a brief and good summary of the orthodox–revisionist controversy and the role played by Plekhanov in it see *Baron* I, pp. 167–85.

[3] Cited in *Baron* I, p. 180.

[4] Cited in ibid. p. 181.

[5] *Bernstein*, pp. 196–7.

[6] See for example: *Perepiska*, vol. II, p. 58n.

[7] A more theoretical answer to the problem facing orthodox Marxism was given by Trotsky. On the basis of his experience in 1905, Trotsky came to the conclusion that contrary to Marxist thinking at the time, the revolutionary potential of the proletariat was neither a function of its impoverishment nor of its numerical strength, but rather of its ability to paralyze the capitalist economy. Hence, according to him, 'in an economically backward state the proletariat, although a small minority, might seize power much earlier than in an advanced capitalist country' (*Trotsky* II, p. 34). For all its outspoken 'daring', Trotsky's theory was still based on the assumption that the proletariat was destined by history to bring about the socialist revolution. Hence it was more conventional than Lenin's 'un-theoretical' organizational innovation.

orientated group among the social-democratic intelligentsia. The first among the Russian Marxists to give theoretical expression to their disillusionment with orthodox Marxism were E. D. Kuskova and S. N. Prokopovich.[1]

Kuskova and Prokopovich, whose life-long partnership has been compared by modern historians to that of Beatrice and Sidney Webb,[2] became attracted to Marxism while members of the Ryazanov circle.[3] Prokopovich, the less imaginative of the two, was drawn to Marxism as a result of statistical enquiries he conducted on behalf of the government among peasant-emigrants to Siberia from the famine-stricken provinces. According to Kuskova, these enquiries brought about his complete loss of faith in the revolutionary potential of the peasantry.[4] (As shown earlier, Kuskova's disillusionment with the 'people' occurred in more dramatic circumstances.) As a consequence Prokopovich became favourably predisposed to Marxism because of its emphasis on the revolutionary role of the proletariat.[5] Under his influence Kuskova too began to display interest in the new creed.

The establishment of the People's Rights Party, however, provided them with a timely and better alternative to populism than Marxism and they promptly joined it. Prokopovich nevertheless continued to develop his contacts with the Marxists. In the winter of 1893–4 he even undertook a trip to Switzerland where he apparently met Plekhanov and Akselrod. They supplied him with letters of recommendation and literature for the Marxist groups in Russia.[6] Hence, when the People's Rights Party was liquidated, he and Kuskova quite naturally turned to Marxism.

Prokopovich, who was pedantic by nature,[7] decided that before finally joining the Marxist movement, he and Kuskova should enlarge their knowledge of Marxism in general and of the labour movement in

---

[1] Although Struve already displayed revisionist tendencies in his book *Critical Notes on Russia's Economic Development* nevertheless it was Kuskova and Prokopovich who were the first to proclaim themselves adherents of Bernstein. Moreover, at the time they did so, Struve was writing the Manifesto of RSDRP, his most orthodox 'Marxist' composition (see *Kindersley*, pp. 197–202, *Mendel*, pp. 175–8). Thus, technically and historically speaking, Kuskova and Prokopovich were the first Russian revisionists.

[2] See *Fischer*, p. 109, *Keep*, p. 56.

[3] See above.

[4] *Kuskova* vie, pp. 180–1.

[5] *Kuskova* ibid.

[6] *Perepiska*, vol. I, pp. 92–4.

[7] *Kuskova* vif, p. 153.

particular.[1] On escaping from Russia, they made their way to Belgium[2] which was known at the time for its militant socialist and trade union movement and for the 'socialist university' (Université Nouvelle) which was formally opened in Brussels in spring 1894.[3] But if they expected their studies to strengthen their belief in their newly acquired creed, they were soon disappointed.

Being a statistician by profession as well as by inclination, Prokopovich began his study of the labour movement in the West by collecting data on the working class. Not surprisingly, a close examination of the real working class in Western Europe affected him in a similar way to his study of the real peasants in Russia. In both cases reality superseded myth. Just as his disillusionment with the mythical populist concept of the peasantry had predisposed him favourably towards Marxism, so his disillusionment with the Marxist myth of the proletariat resulted in the couple's loss of faith in Marxism and their eventual return to the democratic ideology of the People's Rights Party. As Prokopovich himself pointed out in the preface to his book *The Labour Movement in the West*[4] (which incorporated the results of his research): 'The author must confess that in the course of his research, he lost the better half of the theoretical preconceptions with which he started his investigations. The facts irrefutably demonstrated to him the incompatibility of many of the ideas with which he began his research with the real course of events.'[5]

Their growing doubts about the validity of Marxism were not yet strong enough to cause them to change their original plans. Hence, after what seems to have appeared to them a sufficient period of apprenticeship, they left Belgium for Switzerland. On their arrival there, they were first met by P. Akselrod and V. Zasulich who were then living in Zurich. Rumours about the 'heretical tendencies' of the couple must by then have reached the Russian émigrés and as a consequence,

---

1 *Kuskova* ixb.
2 Information on the whereabouts of Kuskova and Prokopovich during the period 1894–8 is found mainly in *Granat*, vol. 26, col. 258, *Kuskova* vif, p. 171; vig. pp. 131, 133–9; IX a & b, and *Perepiska*, vol. I, pp. 101, 174–5. Although the sources differ on many details, it is nevertheless possible to state on the basis of the information they reveal that Kuskova and Prokopovich left Russia in 1894, stayed for a brief period in Switzerland and from there moved to Belgium, where they lived until 1897. For an evaluation of the various sources as well as for a discussion of the fate of their private archives, see *Galai* (unpub.), pp. 129–30.
3 *Institut des Sciences Sociales* 1894–1900(?). See *Annales de l'Institut des Sciences Sociales* (Bruxelles), no. 1 (15 Juin 1894), pp. 1–3. *Balabanova*, pp. 23–24, *Kuskova* ixa, *Wolf* I, p. 65.
4 *Rabocheye Dvizheniye na Zapade*, St Petersburg 1899 (*Prokopovich* XI: see *Bibliography*).
5 Ibid. p. 1.

75

Akselrod and Zasulich were probably on their guard. But at his first meeting (since spring 1894) with the veterans of Russian Marxism, Prokopovich apparently tactfully avoided any criticism of their faith. This enabled Akselrod to write to Plekhanov on the same day that 'S. N. Prokopovich is entirely reliable from the political point of view'.[1]

As a consequence, the Liberation of Labour Group invited the pair to join the Union of Russian Social-Democrats Abroad, which had been established in 1895.[2] Kuskova and Prokopovich accepted the invitation,[3] and at first relations between the newly arrived couple and the Liberation of Labour Group which dominated the Union of Russian SD until November 1898[4] were very cordial. This in itself was no small achievement if one takes into account the nature and intensity of the émigré politics in which the Liberation of Labour Group was involved for so long.[5] But by the autumn their personal relations had begun to deteriorate, both sides contributing to the tension.[6] The fact that Prokopovich was unable to keep his political convictions to himself[7] for long, that his literary style was not to the liking of Akselrod and that his pedantry and 'gentlemanly' manners irritated the bohemian Zasulich,[8] all contributed to the growing personal friction.

The political co-operation between the two sides was not affected[9] by the situation for varied and numerous reasons. For once the question of ideological purity was not all-important. Prokopovich was no Bernstein but merely the 'philosopher from Brussels' as Vera Zasulich mockingly called him in a letter to Plekhanov.[10] Hence his criticism of various aspects of Marxism could be light-heartedly brushed aside. At the same time the veterans became aware of the intellectual superiority of Prokopovich (and Kuskova) over the other 'young' members of the

---

[1] *Perepiska*, vol. 1, p. 174. The editors' explanation that Akselrod used the phrase 'politically reliable' in connection with Prokopovich's attitude to the inter-group fighting in the Union of Russian SD (ibid. p. 175) is implausible. How could Prokopovich, newly arrived in Switzerland, have immediately found his way in the labyrinth of émigré politics?

[2] See *Otvet Redaktsii R.D.*, p. 73, *Frankel*, p. 273.

[3] See *Otvet* ibid. p. 75, *Kuskova* VIg, p. 143.

[4] *Frankel*, p. 266n.

[5] For accounts in English of the disputes between the Liberation of Labour Group and other Marxist émigré groups until 1897 see *Baron* I, p. 153, *Frankel*, pp. 270–3, *Keep*, pp. 42–3. For the Liberation of Labour Group version of these disputes see *Perepiska*, vol. I, pp. 72–91. For a hostile version see *Otvet Redaktsii R.D.*, pp. 70–5.

[6] A detailed account in English of the growing personal friction between the two sides is found in *Frankel*, pp. 273–6.

[7] *Gruppa* VI, p. 179.　　　　　　　　　　[8] Ibid. pp. 185–8, *Perepiska*, vol. I, pp. 179–81.

[9] See *Otvet Redaktsii R.D.*, pp. 62–3.　　　　　　　　[10] *Gruppa* ibid. p. 179.

Union of Russian SD. Inside the Union, the couple could perform important tasks while outside it they could become dangerous. Plekhanov admitted as much himself when he wrote: 'We have to do everything in our power so as not to alienate S. N. (Prokopovich). He might be useful, while in opposition he will harm us terribly.'[1] As far as Plekhanov was concerned, there may have been an additional reason for his unusual leniency towards Kuskova and Prokopovich – the fact that, unlike most of the other young members of the Union of Russian SD, they were genuine Russians.[2]

Be that as it may, from spring 1897 to summer 1898 Prokopovich and Kuskova played an important role in the Russian SD movement in exile. As it turned out, this was a very fruitful, if not always pleasant, period in their long lives of political activity. It was during this time that they finally broke with Marxism, made useful contacts and acquired conspiratory techniques which were of great help when they participated in the launching of the Liberation Movement shortly afterwards.

The couple met Struve, apparently for the first time,[3] during the International Congress on Questions of Legislation for the Protection of Labour which was held in Zurich on 23–30 August 1897(NS). Prokopovich and Struve were attached to the Russian delegation to this Congress, which was composed of P. B. Akselrod, A. Kremer and B. A. Ginsburg-Koltsov.[4] The published material does not reveal what kind of impression Prokopovich and Struve made on one another. But it is known that on the basis of the factual data presented both came to similar conclusions, namely that Marx's theory of the progressive impoverishment of the proletariat under capitalism, and hence the theory of the *Zusammenbruch*, no longer corresponded to reality.[5]

[1] *Perepiska*, vol. i, p. 182.

[2] For a short discussion of the background to Plekhanov's hostile attitude to the non-Russian i.e. Jewish members of the Russian Social-Democratic movement (except for the Jewish members of the Liberation of Labour Group) see *Franzel*, pp. 270–1. For a particularly virulent anti-Jewish outburst by Plekhanov see *Lenin* ii, vol. iv, pp. 338–9.

[3] This author has not found any reference to an earlier meeting between Struve and Prokopovich. It is, however, possible that such a reference is to be found in Struve's private archives, located in Russia, which cover the years 1897–1916 (*Lichnyye Arkhivnyye Fondy v SSSR*, vol. ii, p. 199). The author has not succeeded in gaining access to these archives. [4] *Perepiska*, vol. i, p. 177.

[5] Struve's 'heretical' conclusions are found in a lengthy report on the congress which he published on his return to Russia. For the relevant passages see *Struve* viii, pp. 414–16, *Kindersley*, pp. 130–1. Prokopovich, however, was not so fortunate with his report on the congress. The Liberation of Labour Group vetoed its publication (*Gruppa* vi, pp. 186–8, *Perepiska*, vol. i, pp. 179–82) because, as Zasulich put it, 'he intended to turn Marxism upside-down' (*Gruppa* ibid. p. 187). From this argument, as well as from the views expressed by Prokopovich a few months later (see below and *Prokopovich*, p. 55 *Perepiska*, vol. ii, pp.

77

The similarity of their theoretical conclusions did not result immediately in similarity of action. At that time Struve seems to have distinguished between developments in Western Europe and in Russia. He apparently believed that the theory developed by Marx in the *Communist Manifesto*, on the basis of his analysis of the socio-economic situation in Western Europe in the 1840s, was also applicable to the Russia of the 1890s. This enabled him to compose the Manifesto of RSDRP with inner conviction in the following year, and to remain a member of the Russian SD Movement until mid-1900.[1] Prokopovich, on the other hand, did not make such a distinction between East and West, and hence he and Kuskova found themselves in head-on collision with Plekhanov and Akselrod by the beginning of 1898. But despite the different political courses they pursued during the period immediately following the Congress, the acquaintance of Prokopovich and Kuskova with Struve did not prove useless. It was to be of great political value to both sides three years later.

In the meantime, despite their growing annoyance with the Liberation of Labour Group because of the latter's refusal to publish Prokopovich's lengthy report on the congress, he and Kuskova continued to play an active role in the affairs of the Union of Russian SD Abroad. They spent the winter of 1897–8 in Berlin, where, together with Ts. Kopelson, V. A. Bukholts and other members of the Union, they were responsible for all contacts with Russia.[2] The experience they thus acquired was later utilized by Kuskova in organizing a network for smuggling *Osvobozhdeniye* into Russia.[3]

The co-operation between the 'Belgian couple' and the Liberation of Labour Group came to an abrupt end in spring 1898. Encouraged by the appearance of Bernstein's 'revisionist' articles in January and beginning of February 1898[4] Prokopovich decided to bring his own theoretical objections to Marxism into the open.[5] By so doing he precipitated a major crisis in Russian Marxism which became known as the 'Economist controversy'.[6]

9–10) it is possible to deduce that his theoretical conclusions were at least as 'heretical' as Struve's.   [1] See below.

[2] See *Perepiska*, vol. I, pp. 207–8, *Gruppa* VI, p. 214, *Frankel*, p. 275.   [3] See below.

[4] Bernstein's famous articles in the series 'Problems of Socialism' which opened his revisionist campaign, were published on the following dates (NS): *Die Neue Zeit*, no. 16, 5 January 1898 and no. 18, 19 January 1898; *Vorvärts*, no. 23, 28 January 1898 and no. 32, 8 February 1898 (*Perepiska*, vol. I, p. 191).   [5] See *Perepiska*, vol. I, p. 204.

[6] The main accounts in English of the 'Economist controversy' are found in *Baron* I, pp. 186–207, *Frankel*, *Keep*, pp. 54–66 and *Schapiro* I, pp. 30–41. For a list of Russian-language publications on this controversy, see *Frankel*, p. 264n.

In a series of letters to Akselrod, apparently written in the second half of February 1898, Prokopovich invoked Bernstein's name in support of his own 'heretical' views.[1] About a month later, Kuskova also joined the fray.[2] With Bernstein's example before their eyes, Kuskova and Prokopovich opened their criticism of orthodox Marxism[3] by asserting their right to criticize it. 'Marxism is not a dead doctrine but a guiding theory which is developing and expanding. Criticism of Marxism and the working-out of several undeveloped questions is quite important at the present moment', wrote Kuskova to Akselrod.[4] She continued: 'Only... if the *Communist Manifesto* is to be treated like the Gospel can this appear to be heresy.'[5] Then, like Bernstein two months earlier,[6] she pointed out that the real working class differed considerably from the ideal picture of the proletariat as painted by Marx.[7] Like Lenin four years later in *What is to be Done?*[8] Kuskova denied that the workers were imbued with socialist consciousness: 'The workers know only two things!', she wrote, 'their clearly understandable concrete self-interest and their relative position vis-a-vis other classes in society.'[9] Unlike Lenin, she and Prokopovich did not regard this as a disadvantage. On the contrary, they were greatly impressed by the achievements of what Bernstein called 'democratic' and Prokopovich 'peaceful' working-class organizations – the trade unions, co-operatives, mutual-aid societies etc. – in the West and began to regard them as of more permanent value than the political fighting organizations so dear to the hearts of orthodox Marxists.[10] After criticizing the orthodox Marxist concept of the working class in general, they proceeded to challenge its validity as regards Russia in particular. By so doing they touched on Plekhanov and Akselrod's most sensitive spot, namely their theory of the 'hegemony' of the proletariat in the forthcoming 'bourgeois' revolution.

Kuskova and Prokopovich opened their attack on the 'hegemony'

---

[1] *Perepiska*, vol. I, p. 204 (letter from Akselrod to Plekhanov, 28 February 1898). The exact contents of these letters are not known to this day. The editors of *Perepiska* promised to publish the correspondence between Akselrod and Prokopovich in 1897–8 in a special appendix (*Perepiska*, vol. I, p. 205n.) However, in a postscript to the second volume they wrote that they had not done so because of 'technical difficulties' (*Perepiska*, vol. II, p. 289).

[2] See *Kuskova* II.

[3] See *Appendix B* below for a bibliographical note on Kuskova and Prokopovich's writings at the time.

[4] *Kuskova* II, p. 25. English translation based on *Fischer*, p. 111.

[5] *Kuskova* ibid. p. 26.   [5] See *Bernstein*, pp. 102–18, 218–19.

[7] See *Kuskova* ibid. pp. 17–18.   [8] See *Lenin* I, vol. 5, p. 375, *Schapiro* I, p. 38.

[9] *Kuskova* II, p. 21.

[10] See *Bernstein*, pp. xi–xvi, 104, 109–34, 139 ff., *Prokopovich*, pp. 45–7.

79

theory by rejecting the assumption that it was impossible to improve the conditions of the workers under autocracy. They claimed that the history of the latest economic strikes and the government labour legislation which followed showed that the workers could extract concessions from autocracy.[1] But if this was so, they asked, why then should the workers be more interested in the abolition of autocracy than the other classes? The answer was that they were not. They claimed, with justification, that the workers were primarily interested in improving their economic conditions[2] and not in the concept of political freedom, which was too abstract for the intellectual capacities of the majority of the Russian proletariat.[3] Even if a workers party were established in the near future in Russia, they argued, it would have to deal mainly with economic questions. (Hence the 'economist' label which was attached by the orthodox Marxists to this branch of 'heresy'.) Such a party, therefore, could not exercise 'hegemony' in the forthcoming 'bourgeois–democratic' revolution. Hence, according to them, the radical intelligentsia should look elsewhere for allies in its struggle against autocracy.

Their position on these questions was summed up by Kuskova in a letter to Kopelson:

As long as an intellectual identifies himself with the workers he has no right to impose upon them ideas which do not invoke a practical response from their side. But if he considers himself a democrat he has to identify himself with all the democratic circles, including the bourgeoisie...I have nothing against the political aspirations of such an intellectual. On the contrary. It would, however, be much better if he would actively try to fulfil his aspirations and if, without duplicity, without trying to identify his own aims with the aims of the working class, he would work in the circles of the liberal and especially radical bourgeoisie for the achievement of political freedom.[4]

As might have been expected Plekhanov could not let such a 'heretical' view remain unchallenged. But the violence of his reaction surprised not only his life-long collaborators, Akselrod and Vera Zasulich, but also Lenin.

When, in the second half of March 1898, Plekhanov discovered the connection between the heretical views of the 'Belgian couple' and Bernstein's 'revisionism', he demanded immediate action against

[1] See *Kuskova* II, pp. 26–7, *Prokopovich*, pp. 55–6.
[2] *Prokopovich*, pp. 41–5.
[3] *Kuskova* II, p. 20.
[4] *Kuskova* I, p. 151.

them.[1] In a series of letters to Akselrod, written in April 1898,[2] he insisted on the prompt expulsion of Kuskova and Prokopovich from the Union of Russian Social-Democrats Abroad. When Akselrod informed him that they intended to leave the Union before there was time to expel them,[3] Plekhanov demanded that they be declared non-members retrospectively. And he added: 'Prokopovich must be squashed.'[4] Moreover, against the better judgment of Akselrod and Zasulich, Plekhanov decided to widen the scope of his offensive by attacking the other members of the 'Berlin Group', though he was well aware that they did not share the couple's 'heretical' views. Their main sin, in Plekhanov's eyes, seemed to lie in their opposition to his high-handed manner of dealing with the 'Belgian couple'.[5] His personal vendetta against these people, which culminated in the publication of private correspondence in *Vademecum*,[6] brought about a split between the Liberation of Labour Group and the Union of Russian Social-Democrats Abroad, which led to the temporary but almost total isolation of the former.[7]

At first even Lenin was shocked by this vendetta. After his first encounter with Plekhanov in 1900 he wrote, *inter alia*:

Plekhanov displayed a hatred towards the Union Abroad people that bordered on the indecent (suspecting them of espionage, accusing them of being swindlers and rogues, and asserting that he would not hesitate to 'shoot' such 'traitors' etc.). The remotest suggestion that he went to extremes (for example my allusion to the publication of private letters – *Vademecum* – and to the imprudence of such a procedure) roused him to a high pitch of excitement and manifest irritability.[8]

But Lenin soon realized the political advantage which a witch-hunt

---

[1] On the basis of the published correspondence between Akselrod and Plekhanov it is possible to state that the latter did not become aware of the extent of the threat the 'Belgian couple's' views posed to Russian orthodox Marxism in general and to the 'hegemony' theory in particular, before mid-March 1898. Akselrod informed Plekhanov of Prokopovich's reliance on Bernstein in a letter of 28 February 1898, where he wrote *inter alia*: 'Our evolutionists *à la* S. N. Prokopovich and his entourage seek support in Bernstein. . .I am, therefore, of the opinion that you should read those letters in which Prokopovich's views are, so to speak, expressed popularly. If you agree, I will send them to you. . .(*Perepiska*, vol. I, p. 204).

In his reply to Akselrod's letters of 28 February and 15 March 1898, Plekhanov neither mentioned Prokopovich nor asked for his letters to be sent to him (ibid. pp. 208–9). He was, apparently, too preoccupied at the time with Bernstein to notice the importance of Akselrod's warning against revisionism from within. It was only a week or two later that he realized the seriousness of Prokopovich's 'revisionism' and then he immediately counterattacked (see ibid. vol. II, 5–6).

[2] See *Perepiska*, vol. II, pp. 8–10, 13–15, 18, 28.   [3] Ibid. p. 11.   [4] Ibid. p. 14.

[5] See *Frankel*, pp. 278–9.   [6] See *Bibliography* and *Appendix E*.

[7] See *Frankel*, pp. 280–2.   [8] *Lenin* I, vol. IV, p. 33. See also *Potresov* III, pp. 356–7.

against heretics might give the *Iskra* faction in its drive for supreme leadership of the Russian SD movement. As a consequence, he not only joined the campaign against 'Economism', but also carried it to such extremes that in the end it proved too much even for Plekhanov.[1] By then, however, Kuskova and Prokopovich were no longer concerned with these developments.

Realizing their inability to bring over the majority of the Union of Russian SD Abroad to their ideological point of view, and disgusted by the campaign of personal slander which Plekhanov and his henchman, Koltsov, had opened against them, they announced their withdrawal from the Union at the end of April 1898.[2] About two months later Kuskova left for Russia[3] and Prokopovich followed suit at the beginning of 1899. He was arrested at the border,[4] and the whole burden of explaining their views to the radical intelligentsia of St Petersburg fell upon Kuskova.[5] She took part in many heated debates there during the spring of 1899, the majority of which were held in A. M. Kalmykova's home.[6] During one of these discussions Kuskova put her main arguments down in writing, and thus unknowingly created the famous *Credo*.[7] In it she developed the ideas she had expressed in private in the letter to Kopelson:

What is there for the Russian Marxist to do?! The talk about an independent workers' political party merely results from the transplantation of alien aims and alien achievements to our soil. The Russian Marxist, so far, is a sad spectacle. His practical tasks at the present time are paltry, his theoretical knowledge, insofar as he utilizes it not as an instrument for research but as a scheme for activity, is worthless for the purpose of fulfilling even these paltry practical tasks. Moreover, these borrowed patterns are harmful from the practical point of view. Our Marxists, forgetting that the working class in the West entered political activity after that field had already been cleared, are much too contemptuous of the radical or liberal opposition activity of all other non-worker strata of society. The slightest attempt to concentrate attention on public manifestations of a liberal political character rouses the protest of the orthodox Marxists, who forget that a number of historical conditions prevent us from being Western Marxists and demand of us a different Marxism,

[1] See *Schapiro* I, pp. 33–40, *Frankel*, pp. 263–4, 284.
[2] See *Kuskova* I, p. 159. *Prokopovich* Ia, pp. 163–4, *Perepiska*, vol. II, pp. 11–43, *Gruppa* VI, pp. 204–15.
[3] See *Appendix B*.
[4] See *Prokopovich* ibid., *Kuskova* V, pp. 324–6; Ixc, *Gruppa* ibid. p. 242.
[5] *Potresov* III, pp. 38–9.
[6] *Lenin* III, vol. I, pp. 664–5.
[7] For the story behind *Credo* see: *Kuskova* V ibid., *Lenin* ibid., see also *Schapiro* I, pp. 34–5.

suited to, and necessary in, Russian conditions. Obviously, the lack in every Russian citizen of political feeling and sense cannot be compensated for by talk about politics or by appeals to a non-existent force. This political sense can only be acquired through education, i.e. through participation in that life (however un-Marxian it may be) which is offered by Russian conditions. . . For the Russian Marxist there is only one course open: participation in, i.e. assistance to, the economic struggle of the proletariat, and participation in liberal opposition activity.[1]

At first Kuskova's views made little impression.[2] However, she very soon won the support of a group of social-democrats headed by Struve, who became known as the 'Legal Marxists'.

[1] *Lenin* I, vol. 4, p. 174.   [2] See *Lenin* III, vol. I, p. 665.

4

The parting of the ways

If Struve 'ceases entirely to be a *Genosse*' – so much the worse for him. It will, of course, be an enormous loss to all the *Genosse* for he is a very talented and well-informed person, but of course friendship is one thing and duty is another, and this does not get rid of the need for war.   (*Lenin* II, vol. 46, p. 32)

Struve was never an orthodox Marxist in the sense that Plekhanov was. As long, however, as the behaviour of the Russian proletariat seemed to confirm the predictions of Plekhanov, he continued to belong to the mainstream of Russian Marxism. Till the beginning of 1899 Struve's position in the Marxist camp was similar to that of Lenin, Potresov and other leading Marxists inside Russia, except for the fact that he was mainly engaged in theoretical activity while they, from the very beginning, combined theoretical with practical illegal work in workers' circles. But even this difference was, according to Struve himself, due more to chance than to conscious design. While describing the activities of the first Marxist circles in Russia, he wrote in his memoirs *inter alia*:

That I did not then take a more active part in that propaganda and was not arrested as early as 1891 and have thus, as it were, remained outside 'practical' social democratic work, was due to chance, namely to the discovery and arrest of Golubev... Then towards the end of 1891, I fell seriously ill...and after a time in hospital went abroad.[1]

His theoretical work was not confined to legal activity (the Manifesto of RSDRP[2] and the 'Open Letter to Nicholas II' are his best-known illegal compositions of the 1890s); he also engaged in practical illegal work such as participation in the Russian SD delegation to the London Congress of the Socialist International, 27 July – 2 August 1896 (NS).[3]

This does not mean that there were no differences of opinion between Struve and the other leading Russian Marxists during the 1890s. The

---

[1] *Struve* v, p. 583. See also *Pipes* IIa, pp. 76, 121–5.   [2] See below.
[3] *Perepiska*, vol. I, p. 141.

reverse was true. His first major Marxist work – *Critical Notes on Russia's Economic Development* – had already brought Struve into conflict with some other leading Marxists at the time and especially with his contemporary, Vladimir Ilyich Ulyanov (Lenin). As was already mentioned, Struve stated in the preface to that book that he was not 'infected by orthodoxy'. And, indeed, the book was anything but 'orthodox'.

To begin with, Struve confessed in it that the philosophical basis of dialectical materialism was rather thin. Although he was not as yet questioning the validity of this theory, but only wrote of the need to 'improve it',[1] such a confession could hardly endear him to Plekhanov or to orthodox Marxists in general.

Secondly, he rejected Marx and Engels' definition of the state as 'an organization of economic class domination'. According to him, 'the state is first of all an organization of order' and as such could never 'wither away'.[2]

Thirdly (in the opinion of his later orthodox Marxist critics), he 'overemphasized' the positive role of capitalism. What offended them was not his description of the 'progressive' role of capitalism (the introduction of 'technical rationalization'[3]) in industry and agriculture (where he emphasised the progressive role of the big latifundia),[4] but the way he formulated his thoughts. This suggested that he regarded capitalism as a positive phenomenon.[5] Especially offensive to his critics was the concluding sentence of his book: 'Let us confess our cultural backwardness and let us go and learn from capitalism.'[6]

The most vehement and detailed criticism of Struve's book in the Marxist camp came from Lenin. He began his critical review – 'The Economic Content of Populism and its Critique in Mr. Struve's Book'[7] – by declaring himself, in contrast to Struve, an 'orthodox'

[1] *Struve* IV, pp. 43–6.   [2] Ibid. pp. 52–3. See also *Pipes* IIa, pp. 107–10.
[3] Ibid. pp. 224–5.   [4] Ibid. pp. 238–45.
[5] And, indeed, this was how Struve himself later interpreted his book. (See *Struve* V, pp. 582–3.)
[6] *Struve* IV, p. 288.
[7] This essay has an interesting history of its own. It was first delivered as a paper by Lenin – 'The Reflection of Marxism in Bourgeois Literature' – to a small circle of Marxists in the presence of P. B. Struve, against whom it was written. Among the other members of this circle was A. M. Potresov (for both Potresov and Struve it was their first meeting with Lenin). This paper became the basis for Lenin's much longer but less violently critical essay against Struve – 'The Economic Content of Populism and its Critique in Mr. Struve's Book' – which was published in spring 1895 in the Marxist miscellany, *Materials for the Outline of Our Economic Development*. This miscellany was held up by the censor and only about one hundred copies (from a total of 2,000) were saved by the compilers from the hands of the police and reached the public clandestinely. When Lenin reprinted his essay in 1907

Marxist.[1] Then he pointed out Struve's statements about the 'slenderness' of the philosophical basis of dialectical materialism[2] and his rejection of the Marxist theory of the state.[3] Yet his main criticism was directed, not against these 'heretical' statements but against Struve's description of the development of capitalism in Russia.[4] (Here he mainly objected to Struve's belief that the process of differentiation was only at the initial stage in the village.[5]) And he ended his criticism of Struve's book by taking him to task for his exaggeration of the progressive role of capitalism[6] and for failing to recognise the positive side of Populism (the Populists' care for the people, their theories about cooperation, etc.).[7]

Lenin's sharp formulation of the difference between his attitude to Marxism and Struve's view enabled both men to claim many years later that they were never close politically or personally. Thus in his memoirs, written forty years after the events, Struve described his relations with Lenin and Lenin's attitude to Marxism at the time in the following way:

This man (i.e. Lenin) was absolutely alien to me by his mentality...because of this I never was and never could be on terms of personal intimacy with him...[8] The impression which Lenin at once made upon me...and which remained with me all my life – was an unpleasant one...[9] In his attitude to his fellow-men Lenin breathed coldness, contempt and cruelty...Lenin's brusqueness and cruelty – this became clear to me almost from the outset, from our first meeting – was psychologically indissolubly bound up, both instinctively and deliberately, with his indomitable love of power...[10] his principal *Einstellung*...was hatred...The doctrine of the class war...proved congenial to Lenin's emotional attitude to surrounding reality. He hated not only the existing autocracy (the Tsar) and the bureaucracy, not only the lawlessness and arbitrary rule of police, but also their antipodes – the 'liberals' and the 'bourgeoisie'.[11]

On his part, Lenin was no less emphatic in his denials of the existence of any close ties between him and Struve in the 1890s.[12]

In reality, relations between Lenin and Struve at the time were quite

he added the title of his paper as a subtitle to the essay and it has been subsequently known as *The Economic Content of Populism and its Critique in Mr. Struve's Book: A Reflection of Marxism in Bourgeois Literature*. (See *Lenin* II, vol. 1, pp. 347, 592–3; vol. 16, pp. 97–8, *Nikolayevskiy* II, pp. 22–3, *Struve* V, pp. 590–1.) The full text of the article is reprinted in *Lenin* II, vol. 1, pp. 351–534.

[1] *Lenin* II, vol. 1, p. 352.   [2] Ibid. pp. 437–8.   [3] Ibid. pp. 438–40.
[4] Ibid. pp. 444–53.   [5] See esp. *Struve* IV, pp. 224–5.   [6] *Lenin* ibid. pp. 527–9.
[7] Ibid. p. 530.   [8] *Struve* V, p. 582.   [9] Ibid. p. 591.
[10] Ibid. p. 592. For a diametrically opposed description of the young Lenin see *Martov* III, pp. 268–9.
[11] *Struve* ibid. p. 593.   [12] See below.

different from their subsequent portrayal. In his memoirs, Struve confused Lenin's attitude to liberalism in the mid-1890s with his subsequent views at the turn of the century. And as far as Marxist philosophy was concerned, Struve refrained during the next couple of years from voicing his doubts too strongly. Thus he only returned to the question of the validity of dialectical materialism in 1897 (and finally rejected it only in 1899) and he restated his positive attitude towards the state only after his final break with Marxism. At the same time Lenin did not attach great importance to questions of philosophy until at least 1899, if not later.[1] Moreover, their differences on the question of the economic development of Russia were not as great as might appear from Lenin's attack. Both believed at the time in 'capitalism as a supposedly inevitable phase in Russia's economic development'.[2] And Struve's 'exaggeration' of the positive role of capitalism, especially as expressed in the concluding sentence of his book was, as he confessed later, written deliberately to provoke the Populists.[3] At any rate, by the beginning of 1896, if not before, Lenin and Struve had become close political comrades and apparently personal friends.[4]

Struve was Lenin's chief supplier of literature while the latter was in prison and in exile in Siberia (1896–1900).[5] And when Struve and M. I. Tugan-Baranovskiy[6] came under heavy fire from a group of

[1] In a letter to Potresov dated 2 November 1898, Lenin stated that he felt himself incompetent in the field of philosophy. See *Lenin* II, vol. 46, p. 15. See also *Pipes* IIa, p. 240.
[2] *Keep*. p. 39.   [3] *Struve* V, p. 582. See also *Pipes* ibid. p. 114.
[4] See *Lenin* II, vol. 46, p. 32 and below. For a different interpretation of their personal, though not political, relations see *Pipes* ibid. pp. 135–6. 237–40.
[5] See *Struve* VI, p. 72 and *Lenin* II, vol. 55, p. 32ff. Struve's activity in supplying Lenin with literature entailed some amount of direct correspondence between the two to the existence of which Lenin testified at the time. (See *Lenin* ibid. pp. 51, 156. See also *Pisatel* (writer) and *Ecrivain*, which were then two of Struve's pseudonyms.) However, not even one letter from Lenin to Struve is found in *Lenin* II, vol. 46 which covers Lenin's letters in the period 1893–1904. Moreover, when the editors of Lenin's Collected Works (*Polnoye Sobraniye Sochineniy*) were confronted with Lenin's own reference to a certain letter he sent to Struve at the time (*Lenin* II, vol. 55, p. 51) they laconically commented that 'the letter has not been preserved'. (Ibid. p. 477, n. 52.) It is, of course, possible that this particular letter was lost. However, the absence of any other letters to Struve in Lenin's Collected Works seems very curious, especially as Struve's private archives covering the above period are to be found in the Soviet Union. (See *Pipes* IIa, p. 140n.) And even if there are no letters from Lenin in these archives, it is still likely that Lenin kept copies of at least part of the correspondence. One cannot, therefore, escape the conclusion that this absence was deliberate on the part of party historians in the USSR. They, like Lenin himself, were very embarrassed by his friendship with Struve in the 1890s. Hence, apparently, their decision not to publish Lenin's letters to Struve.
[6] For the role played by Tugan-Baranovskiy in Russian Marxism in the 1890s see *Kindersley*, pp. 52–9.

Samara Marxists in spring 1897 for advocating high prices for grain (which according to both sides would be advantageous to the landowners of the larger estates being run on a capitalistic basis, and disadvantageous to the bulk of the peasantry), it was Lenin who came to their rescue.[1] According to Martov,

there was nothing left of [Lenin's] former mistrust of Struve's apologetics for capitalism...On the contrary, he became very mistrustful of the Samarans, suspecting them of a tendency to slur sentimentally over the question of the process of de-peasantizing the countryside...In this spirit he wrote and asked us...to restrain the Samarans from open attacks on Struve.[2]

Struve's closeness to Lenin did not prevent him from publicly revealing his 'unorthodox' attitude to Marxism. At the beginning of 1897, Struve adopted a critical approach to the philosophical foundations of Marxism[3] in his polemics with S. N. Bulgakov[4] over the question of free will and necessity (which arose in connection with the growing influence of neo-Kantianism). Towards the end of that year, anticipating Bernstein, Struve criticized Marx's theory of the progressive impoverishment of the proletariat and the theory of the *Zusammenbruch* and attacked Engels for his contribution to this theory.[5]

Both critical utterances were noted by the Russian orthodox Marxists at the time.[6] As a consequence even Vera Zasulich, his greatest admirer in the Liberation of Labour Group,[7] was forced to admit that although Struve was abler than Lenin, the *praktiki* and the Samarans, he lacked the ability to conform to a party line.[8] But generally, thanks to the fact that philosophy was not yet all-important to orthodox Marxist dogma, and that Struve confined himself to criticism of Marxist revolutionary theory in Western Europe alone, no great importance was attached to his utterances at the time.[9]

At first, this view of Struve's critical attitude to Marxism seemed to be justified. In contrast with 1897, 1898 was an 'orthodox' year as far as Struve's writings were concerned. He refrained from repeating any

---

[1] See *Martov* III, pp. 327–32, *Angarskiy*, pp. 100–5, *Kindersley*, p. 196.
[2] *Martov* ibid. English translation in *Kindersley*, p. 197.
[3] See *Struve* VIII, pp. 487–507, *Mendel*, pp. 167–71, *Kindersley*, pp. 112–18 and *Pipes* IIa, pp. 184–9.
[4] For Bulgakov's role in Russian Marxism see *Kindersley*, pp. 59–63.
[5] See *Struve* ibid. pp. 415–18, *Kindersley*, pp. 90, 130–1, and above.
[6] *Lenin* II, vol. 46, p. 15 and *Potresov* III, p. 34 (letter from Lenin to Potresov, 2 September 1898), *Gruppa* VI, pp. 188–9, 197 (letters from Zasulich to Plekhanov, 18 December 1897 and 10 March 1898 NS).　　　　[7] See *Gruppa* V, p. 199; VI, pp. 183–6, 189, 197 ff.
[8] *Gruppa* VI, pp. 189, 197.　　　　[9] *Gruppa* ibid. pp. 188–9, 197.

of his earlier 'heretical' views throughout the year,[1] and that at a time when Bernstein in the West and Kuskova and Prokopovich among the Russian SD abroad were opening their 'revisionistic' campaign. Moreover, in spring of that year Struve wrote his most orthodox-Marxist composition, the Manifesto of RSDRP. In this document, which he composed on behalf of the Foundation Congress of the Russian Social-Democratic Workers Party (RSDRP), held in Minsk on 1–3 March 1898,[2] Struve restated clearly and concisely the basic tenets of the 'hegemony' theory:

The further eastward one goes in Europe, the weaker, more cowardly and more abject the bourgeoisie becomes politically, and the more to its cultural and political tasks fall to the proletariat...Only the Russian proletariat can win itself the political freedom that it needs...The Russian proletariat will cast off the yoke of autocracy, thereby with greater energy to continue the struggle with capitalism and the bourgeoisie to the full victory of socialism.[3]

Despite Struve's later contrary assertions,[4] there seems no indication that he did not believe at the time in what he was writing in the Manifesto.[5] However, his belief in the 'hegemony' theory and hence his 'orthodoxy' were dependent to a very large extent on the political performance of the Russian proletariat and were consequently not destined to last long.

The year 1898 was a poor one from the point of view of the performance of the proletariat. It witnessed the first signs of recession after the unprecedented economic boom of the mid-1890s[6] and this was immediately reflected in the reduced militancy of the workers. The total number of strikers fell sharply[7] and although it rose again in 1899, the

---

[1] *Mendel*, pp. 175–8. Kindersley's assertion that the ideological differences between Struve and the orthodox Marxists came to light in autumn 1898 is somewhat inaccurate. Lenin's letter to Potresov (2 September 1898) on which it is based (*Kindersley*, p. 203) does not substantiate his assertion. In this letter Lenin was referring to Struve's philosophical writings in 1897. (See *Kindersley*, pp. 88–90, *Lenin* II, vol. 46, pp. 15, 474 (n. 17).)

[2] See *Keep*, pp. 52–3, *Kindersley*, pp. 197–8, *Struve* VI, p. 75.

[3] See *Struve*, English translation in *Kindersley*, p. 200.

[4] See *Struve* VI, p. 75 and *Davats*, p. 7.

[5] For a detailed analysis of the contradiction between Struve's political position at the time and his later evidence see *Kindersley*, pp. 197–201. See also *Keep*, p. 53n. and *Schapiro* I, p. 30. The latter two support Kindersley's conclusion that Struve expressed his political beliefs in the Manifesto and that in his memoirs, in Keep's words, he tried 'to disavow his revolutionary past'. In his recent biography of Struve, Professor Pipes also holds that as far as the question of the role of the proletariat in the 'bourgeois' revolution was concerned, Struve believed at the time in what he wrote in the Manifesto. (See *Pipes* IIa, p. 192.)

[6] See *Von Laue* III, pp. 216–17, *Keep*, p. 41.

[7] From 60,000 in 1897 to 43,000 in 1898 (see *Keep*, ibid.). This number represents only strikers in factories which were under the jurisdiction of government inspectors. These

new strike wave was defensive in character and took place not in Russia proper but in Poland.[1] In addition, the rise in the number of strikers in 1899 gave way to a very sharp decline in 1900, which was the calmest year in the decade 1893–1903 as far as industrial disturbances were concerned.[2]

The rapid decline in the militancy of the workers was that much more noticeable because of the growing spirit of opposition in society in 1898. The same year witnessed not only a growing militancy in the zemstvo milieu but also the intensification of unrest among the students, always an important barometer for measuring the mood of society in Russia.[3]

Smarting under the restrictions imposed upon them by the draconian 1884 Law of Higher Education, the students became restive towards the end of Alexander III's reign. As with the zemstvo radicals, this unrest achieved significance only after the Tsar's death. The shattering of hope for 'reforms from above' by the new ruler, the Marxist–populist controversy and the growing militancy of the industrial workers in 1895–6 were among the main factors contributing to this development. Then an incident occurred towards the end of 1896 which considerably increased the discontent among the students.

The festivities following Nicholas II's coronation on 14 May 1896 in Moscow culminated in a disaster of catastrophic proportions. A huge crowd, estimated at half a million people, gathered on the Khodynka field near the old capital awaiting the customary distribution of small gifts. Through the incompetence of the authorities, the crowd stampeded and as a result 1,389 people were killed and 1,301 injured.[4]

On 18 November 1896, the six-month anniversary of the Khodynka disaster, the students of Moscow University organized a procession to the cemetery where many of the victims were buried. Besides eulogizing the dead, the demonstrators demanded a public enquiry into the

factories, however, employed 70 per cent of all Russian factory-workers. Hence it is possible to assume that a relatively similar decrease in the number of strikes occurred in the remaining factories. For full statistical data on the strike movement in the 1890s see *Koltsov*, pp. 224–8. For a short and good summary see *Brokgaus supp.* vol. II, p. 704.

[1] The industrial unrest in Poland was caused, paradoxically, by the insistence of employers on the implementation of the law of 2 June 1897 for a 11½-hour-maximum working day. This law, which represented a positive gain for the industrial workers in Russia proper, was detrimental to the interests of Polish workers, who enjoyed a shorter working day (see *Kolstov*, p. 199).

[2] *Keep*, p. 41.   [3] See *Charques*, p. 66.

[4] For the casualty figures see *Von Stein* I, p. 484. See also *Russkiy Kalendar* 1897, pp. 322–3 and *Charques*, pp. 54–5.

tragic event and punishment of those found responsible for the catastrophe. As is generally the case, the forces of law and order over-reacted to this manifestation of discontent. The police blocked the way to the cemetery, dispersed the demonstrators by force and made more than 700 arrests.[1] The great majority of those arrested were expelled from the University.[2] The mass arrests and expulsions added fuel to the general feeling of discontent among the students. This unrest was to erupt into a full-scale confrontation between almost the entire student body of the Empire and the government at the beginning of 1899.

The students returned to their studies in autumn 1898 in a very defiant mood. The tension was particularly great at St Petersburg University. There, acts of insubordination on the part of the students towards the university authorities became an almost daily occurrence. By the end of January 1899 the atmosphere on the campus had become so tense that only a spark was needed to cause an explosion.[3] This was provided by the celebration held on 8 February, the eightieth anniversary of the founding of St Petersburg University. The behaviour of the students during the festivities greatly incensed the rector and, on the following day, he published a proclamation condemning the mis-behaviour on the campus. The student leaders retaliated by organizing a mass meeting (*skhodka*) at the university. The rector called in the police who, as usual, used too much force to disperse the assembled students. As a consequence the students went on strike and in a matter of days were joined by students in thirty universities and institutions of higher education all over Russia. By mid-February 1899 the number of strikers had reached the 25,000 mark.[4] The government reacted by demanding that the university authorities expel students who partici-pated in meetings or strikes, and by threatening to conscript all those expelled. To this effect it published 'temporary regulations on the conscription of students expelled from institutions of higher education for participation in mass disturbances' which were approved by Nicholas on 29 July 1899.[5]

The government decision to solve the student problem by suppres-sion alone achieved the opposite effect. It increased tension in the

---

[1] See *Dan*, p. 458.   [2] See *Charques*, p. 67.   [3] See *Cherevanin* I, pp. 268–72.
[4] Ibid. p. 273. For a detailed account of the student disturbances in 1899 see *Vanovskiy* I, *Libanov*, pp. 1–79, 95–103 and *Mogilyanskiy* III, pp. 217–39.
[5] See *Russkiy Kalendar* 1900, p. 286. The full text of these regulations is found in *Libanov*, pp. 84–6. It should be noted that Witte was one of the architects of these regulations. How-ever, in a letter to Pobedonostsev he put it on record that he did it only for the sake of pre-venting the use of more draconian measures. See *Witte* III, pp. 101–2 and *Suvorin*, p. 230.

universities and when, a year later, the Ministry of the Interior implemented the 'temporary regulations' a fresh outburst of student disturbances followed which had far-reaching repercussions on the political situation in Russia. These events, however, still lay in the future. Meanwhile, the unrest in the universities mainly affected developments in the revolutionary movement as a whole and in social-democratic circles in particular.

The political events of the second half of 1898 and the beginning of 1899 reversed the 1895 situation. Then, as has been shown earlier, the nascent oppositional movement in society (mainly in the zemstvo milieu) was soon overshadowed by developments among the industrial workers. In 1898 the opposite took place. These developments could not but have a profound effect on Struve, who had not followed up his first venture into liberal politics because the oppositional movement in society was overshadowed by the industrial strikes. His sudden change of attitude towards Russian orthodox Marxism apparently resulted from this reversal of roles as well as from the intensification of the 'revisionist' controversy in the West and the conspicuous role played by Plekhanov in the campaign against Kuskova and Prokopovich. (He must have received a first-hand account of this when Kuskova arrived in St Petersburg at the beginning of 1899.)[1]

This indeed was the way things looked at the time to Struve's personal friend and political ally, M. I. Tugan-Baranovskiy. In a letter he wrote to Potresov in March 1899,[2] Tugan-Baranovskiy described the Marxist camp in St Petersburg as being split into three factions. The first was composed of orthodox Marxists, the second of Kuskova and her followers, who advocated the abandonment of Marxism and 'the return to the former universal progressive programme'. A third faction was headed by Struve 'who occupies an intermediary position'. In Tugan-Baranovskiy's opinion, the main reason for this state of affairs lay in 'the lack of practical achievements' on the part of the Social-Democrats. And he continued, 'to this one has to add the reaction against Marxism outside Russia, which has found expression in Bernstein's articles and his book...(and the) upsurge in the spirit of "society" which was so characteristically expressed in the student disturbances.'[3]

Be that as it may, by the beginning of 1899 Struve had joined the

[1] See above. See also *Pipes* IIa, pp. 212–15.
[2] See *Potresov* III, pp. 38–9.
[3] Ibid. p. 38.

ranks of the revisionists. In a letter to Potresov dated 2 February 1899, he wrote:

The internal position of the monist (i.e. Plekhanov) is profoundly sorrowful and extremely tragic...It is tragic because he is defending hopeless positions: (1) the orthodox view of social evolution; (2) materialism, which is irrelevant to anyone and anything; (3) Hegelianism (dialectics etc.) which is also irrelevant to anyone and anything and completely bankrupt.[1]

Shortly after attacking Plekhanov and orthodox Marxism in private, Struve brought his revisionism into the open. Together with S. N. Bulgakov, N. A. Berdyayev (who abandoned Marxism in favour of neo-Kantian idealism[2]), S. L. Frank[3] and Tugan-Baranovskiy, Struve criticized every aspect of Marxism during the remaining months of 1899 and during 1900, beginning with economics and ending with philosophy.[4] However, despite the fast-growing criticism of Marxism by the 'Legal Marxists' (as the above group of writers soon became known), Struve and Tugan-Baranovskiy still believed that it was possible for them to remain members of the Russian SD movement. Their belief was based on the assumption that in the coming struggle with Plekhanov and his orthodox followers, not only Potresov but also Lenin would side with them.

Thus, in a letter to Potresov, dated 10 February 1899,[5] Struve wrote:

Tugan-Baranovskiy and Bulgakov...have essentially the same attitude towards orthodoxy as I have. They too, like myself, have now no sympathy for (Plekhanov's) literary activity...it is no mere chance that (Plekhanov) turns out to be spiritually isolated. I think that over the *Zusammenbruch* (Lenin) has not yet renounced orthodoxy, but I hope that this will come about sooner or later. Conservatism or half-heartedness in thinking is the only thing which can maintain a faith in *Zusammenbruch*, but (Lenin) has a lively mind which moves forward, and real intellectual conscientiousness.[6]

Tugan-Baranovskiy, writing later, was already less certain about such a possibility. In a letter to Potresov, written on 19 May 1899, in which he

[1] Ibid. p. 348.
[2] For the ideological development which brought about the abandonment of Marxism by Bulgakov and Berdyayev see *Mendel*, pp. 194–226. For their role in Russian Marxism see *Kindersley*, pp. 59–67 and above.
[3] For Frank's role in Russian Marxism see *Kindersley*, pp. 67–72.
[4] A summary in English of the criticism levelled against Marxism by this group is found in *Kindersley*, pp. 101, 105–6, 131–45, 156–75, 203–5, and *Pipes* IIa, pp 221–33, 292–307. For a good Russian résumé (although written from a Marxist point of view and hence hostile) see *Potresov* II, pp. 584–97.
[5] See *Nikolayevskiy* II, p. 33, *Pipes* IIa, p. 240n.
[6] *Nikolayevskiy*, ibid. English translation in *Kindersley*, p. 203.

informed him about his decision to join the ranks of the revisionists without reservation, he wrote *inter alia*: 'I write to you about all this because I now feel myself on political questions closer than ever before to those whom my critique of Marx might make angry. But try and convince people that you can criticize Marx and still remain a *Genosse*.'[1] But even then he still believed, as he explained in the same letter, that although the first reaction of the orthodox Marxists to his revisionism would be very hostile, nevertheless 'in less than two–three years they will agree with my point of view'.[2] In the beginning it seemed that Struve's assumptions about the attitude of the leading orthodox Marxists in Russia was right, at least as far as Lenin was concerned.

The first among the leading orthodox Marxists in Russia to sound the alarm about developments in St Petersburg was Potresov. This was mainly the result of a 'geographical accident'. Potresov's place of exile in the town of Orlov, province of Vyatka (now Kirov), was in European Russia, while his two partners in the future orthodox-Marxist triumvirate[3] – Lenin and Martov – were exiled to the remote Siberian province of Yenisey. Hence he was earlier – and better – informed than his two colleagues about the developments in the literary world of St Petersburg[4] and about the seriousness of the revisionist crisis in the West.

Potresov informed Lenin, apparently for the first time, about the revisionist crisis in St Petersburg and about Struve's attack on the *Zusammenbruch* theory in general and on Plekhanov in particular[5] in a letter dated 27 March 1897.[6] Lenin's reaction to this news, as can be deduced from his reply of 27 April,[7] was one of bewilderment rather than anger. Although he expressed opposition to Bernstein's 'revisionism', nevertheless, he attacked the critics of the *Zusammenbruch* theory mainly for the danger they posed to the Russian movement. As for Western Europe, Lenin only remarked that Bernstein's criticism of the *Zusammenbruch* theory was not well-founded.[8] But most revealing of all was his treatment of Struve. He expressed the opinion (was it wish-

---

[1] *Potresov* III, p. 44. [2] Ibid. [3] See below.

[4] See *Potresov* III, pp. 48–9, 346–7, 354 (n. 160), *Gruppa* VI, p. 242, *Nikolayevskiy* II, p. 33. See also *Pipes* IIa, pp. 240–1.

[5] The following description of the sequence of events is mainly based on four letters which Lenin sent to Potresov between 2 September 1898 and 27 June 1899. These were replies to Potresov's letters of 11 August and 24 December 1898 and of 27 March and 2 June 1899. Potresov's letters were not preserved but it is possible to get the gist of them from Lenin's replies. Lenin's letters are found, among other places, in *Lenin* II, vol. 46, pp. 14–33 and *Potresov* III, pp. 35–7, 39–43, 45–8. English translation in *Lenin* I, vol. 34, pp. 25–43.

[6] *Lenin* II, vol. 46, p. 22. [7] Ibid. pp. 22–8. [8] Ibid. p. 26.

ful thinking?) that his revisionist utterances were to a great extent a consequence of Bulgakov's growing influence over him.[1] Moreover, throughout the letter he referred to Struve as 'a *Genosse*'. Only after Lenin received, on 18 June, Potresov's next letter (dated 2 June)[2] did he change his tone as regards Struve. In this letter Potresov succeeded in impressing on him the 'seriousness' of the situation in St Petersburg and the inclination of Struve and the 'Legal Marxists' to return to a general-democratic platform as propagated by Kuskova.[3] Although Lenin still could not make himself believe that Struve had abandoned Marxism for good, he nevertheless declared that

If Struve 'ceases entirely to be a *Genosse*' – so much the worse for him. It will, of course, be an enormous loss to all the *Genosse* for he is a very talented and well-informed person, but of course friendship is one thing and duty is another, and this does not get rid of the need for war.[4]

Although Potresov sounded the alarm too early, as far as the 'Legal Marxists'' adoption of Kuskova's programme was concerned,[5] he nevertheless put his finger on the basic question over which Struve and his political friends eventually parted ways with the Social-Democrats, namely the question of the role of the proletariat in the forthcoming 'bourgeois' revolution. But, and here it differed from the case of Kuskova and Prokopovich, the final split between the two sides occurred not because of Plekhanov's insistence on the maintenance of the purity of the 'hegemony' theory, but because of Lenin's new interpretation of it. This however was discovered only in the coming year – as a consequence of the prolonged negotiations between the 'Legal Marxists' and their orthodox counterparts.

Potresov's warning brought about the conclusion of a political pact between him, Lenin and Yu. O. Martov, who were all due to end their terms of exile in the second half of January 1900.[5] The immediate aim of this triumvirate or, as they called themselves, the Literary Group (*Literaturnaya Gruppa*),[7] was the establishment of an illegal orthodox Marxist newspaper which would fight revisionism in all its various forms.[8] From the very beginning the triumvirate planned to co-operate closely with the Liberation of Labour Group[9] and Vera

[1] Ibid. p. 24. [2] Ibid. p. 28.
[3] Ibid. pp. 31-2. See also *Nikolayevskiy* II, pp. 34-5 and *Kindersley*, pp. 204-5.
[4] *Lenin* II, vol. 46, p. 32. English translation in *Lenin* I, vol. 34, pp. 41-2 and *Kindersley*, p. 205. [5] See *Nikolayevskiy* ibid.
[6] See *Potresov* III, p. 347 and *Getzler*, p. 44. [7] *Potresov* ibid. p. 355.
[8] See *Martov* III, p. 412, *Nikolayevskiy* II, pp. 35-6 [9] *Martov* ibid.

Zasulich even travelled illegally to St Petersburg to establish direct contact between the two groups.[1] But they nevertheless had not yet closed their minds to the possibility of simultaneous co-operation with other SD circles.[2] The most important among these were the 'Legal Marxists'. Their importance lay not only in the fact that they were headed by Struve, still highly esteemed by Lenin, but also in their contacts with 'society' whose oppositional spirit was on the rise. These contacts meant financial support for the new enterprise.[3] As long as the 'Legal Marxists' were prepared to accept the political programme of the Russian SD which Struve had composed only two years earlier in the form of the RSDRP Manifesto, Lenin and Potresov were prepared to regard them as a special group inside a future SD party.[4] Questions of philosophy and of Marxist theory were not as yet considered by them very important.

The 'Legal Marxists', on their part, were interested in such a bargain from the beginning. By now Struve must already have realized from his correspondence with Potresov that neither he nor Lenin was prepared to join the ranks of the revisionists.[5] But he apparently continued to believe that both sides still shared the immediate political aim of destroying autocracy and supplanting it by a 'bourgeois-democratic' regime, and that this common aim was more important than the disagreement on questions of Marxist theory.[6] This belief was shared by the other two 'Legal Marxist' ex-editors of *Nachalo*,*

[1] Vera Zasulich stayed illegally in St Petersburg for a few months at the beginning of 1900 and while there took part in many meetings which the newly arrived exiles held at the home of A. M. Kalmykova. (See *Potresov* III, p. 355, *Lenin* II, vol. 4, p. 479, *Gruppa* VI, pp. 245–8.)

[2] See *Martov* II, pp. 49–55.

[3] See ibid. pp. 55–8 and *Potresov* III, p. 64 (letter from Zasulich to Potresov, May 1900). See also *Pipes* IIa, pp. 248–50.

[4] Martov, the third member of the triumvirate, agreed very reluctantly to the policy of seeking an agreement with Struve and the 'Legal Marxists'. See *Getzler*, pp. 45–6.

[5] See *Nikolayevskiy* II, pp. 32–3 and *Pipes* IIa, pp. 212–15.

[6] See *Martov* II, pp. 55, 58–9.

* *Nachalo* was a Marxist monthly published legally in St Petersburg from January 1899. It was sponsored by the police but this fact was of course unknown to the editors. It existed for five months and only four issues (nos. 1–3, 5) reached the public, the April (no. 4) issue being suppressed by the censor. The editors of *Nachalo* were P. B. Struve, M. I. Tugan-Baranovskiy, V. Ya. Bogucharskiy, A. M. Kalmykova and V. G. Veresayev. (See *Potresov* III, pp. 349–50, *Nikolayevskiy* II, p. 30, *Perepiska*, vol. II, p. 75, *Kindersley*, pp. 92–104 and *Pipes* IIa, pp. 215–19.) The domination of *Nachalo*'s editorial board by the future leaders of 'Legal Marxism' was reflected in the monthly's policy. From the second issue onwards it adopted a growing revisionist tone, so much so that in a letter to Akselrod, dated 21 April 1899, Plekhanov wrote *inter alia*: 'The most urgent business of the moment is to fight Bernsteinism inside Russia. *Nachalo* is completely on his side.' (*Perepiska*, vol. II, p. 81.)

Tugan-Baranovskiy and V. Yakovlev (Bogucharskiy).[1] who had by now assumed the political leadership of that group together with Struve.[2]

As a consequence, when both sides met for a formal conference in Pskov at the end of March and the beginning of April 1900,[3] they arrived at the following agreement. The 'Legal Marxists' accepted[4] the SD programme as outlined in the 'Draft Declaration of the Editorial Board of *Iskra* and *Zarya*'[5] despite its savage denunciation of 'revisionism' and its strong emphasis on the theory of the hegemony of the proletariat in the 'bourgeois' revolution. They also undertook to keep the Literary Group supplied with literature, information and financial help, while the Group undertook to open the pages of its publications to articles expressing the 'Legal Marxist' point of view.[6]

This agreement was brought before the conference held between Lenin and Potresov and the Liberation of Labour Group in Switzerland in mid-August[7] to discuss co-operation in the publishing of *Iskra* and *Zarya*.[8] Its approval encountered the vehement opposition of Plekhanov,[9] who was not prepared to tolerate the creation of a situation in the Russian SD similar to that in its Western counterparts, where the 'orthodox' and 'revisionist' elements belonged to the same party.[10] Plekhanov retreated from his opposition under heavy pressure from Vera Zasulich[11] and only after the 'Legal Marxists' agreed to appear as a non-socialist Democratic–Oppositional 'Freedom' Group (*Gruppa*

---

[1] See *Martov* II and *Struve* VI, p. 77n.

[2] *Perepiska*, vol. II, p. 140.

[3] For the date of the meeting see *Lenin* II, vol. 4, p. 479, *Perepiska* II, p 140, *Struve* VI, p. 75. As to the participants, all sources agree that the orthodox side was represented by Lenin, Martov and Potresov (See *Martov* II. p. 58, *Lenin* ibid., *Perepiska* bid. and *Struve* ibid.). However, there is a slight contradiction in the sources regarding the composition of the Legal Marxist delegation. Some maintain that they were represented by all three political leaders – Struve, Tugan-Baranovskiy and Bogucharskiy (*Perepiska* ibid., *Struve* ibid.), while others claim that Bogucharskiy was not present (see *Lenin* ibid., *Martov* ibid.).

[4] For a vivid description of the negotiations which brought about the acceptance by the 'Legal Marxists' of the orthodox programme see *Martov* II, pp. 58–60.

[5] The text of the Draft Declaration is reprinted in *Lenin* II, vol. 4, pp. 322–33.

[6] See *Perepiska* ibid., *Struve* VI, pp. 75–6.

[7] The official conference was held on 24–28 August 1900 (NS). See *Potresov* III, p. 359 (n. 246).

[8] Lenin's most illuminating description of this conference – 'How the Spark was Nearly Extinguished' – is found, among other places, in *Lenin* II, vol. 4, pp. 334–52. English translation in *Lenin* I, vol. 4, pp. 333–49. See also *Potresov* II, pp. 356–7.

[9] See *Lenin* II, vol. 4, pp. 339–40, *Perepiska*, vol. II, p. 140.

[10] See *Lenin* ibid. p. 337, *Perepiska* ibid.

[11] *Potresov* III, pp. 73–4 (letter from Zasulich to Potresov from beginning of September 1900 (NS)).

Demokraticheskoy Oppositsii 'Svoboda').[1] Co-operation with such a group was, according to Plekhanov's concept of the 'hegemony' theory, not only permissible but also essential to the success of the bourgeois revolution.[2] As long as Lenin seemed to believe that the Freedom Group was merely an invention, intended to placate the imperious Plekhanov,[3] he continued to press for a quick agreement. However, when the negotiations between the 'legal' and the orthodox Marxists were resumed at the end of 1900, Lenin suddenly discovered that what was intended to be a face-saving formula, had become a reality. As a consequence, a complete change of roles took place between Lenin and Plekhanov. The former, who until then had been the chief advocate of co-operation with 'Struve and Co.' became their main opponent while Plekhanov, who till autumn 1900 had vehemently opposed such a policy, favoured an agreement between the orthodox Marxists and the Freedom Group.

The transformation of the Freedom Group from an artificial body into a real political organization took place some time in autumn 1900.[4] It seems that Struve resumed his contacts with the zemstvo radicals[5] during 1899. At any rate, by February 1900 these contacts had become strong enough for the latter to discuss with Struve the possibility of co-operation between the zemstvo radicals and the 'Legal Marxists' in the publication of an illegal liberal–constitutionalist newspaper.[6] But at this initial stage, neither side was prepared to commit itself fully. The 'Legal Marxists' were still hoping to arrive at a working agreement with the orthodox Marxist Literary Group, while the zemstvo radicals were apparently trying to persuade P. N. Milyukov, the future leader of the Cadets (who was never a Marxist and hence must have been more to their taste at the time),[7] to accept the editorship of such a newspaper.[8]

[1] See *Lenin* II, vol. 4, p. 480, *Perepiska* II, p. 140. See also *Pipes* IIa, pp. 258–9, *Struve* VI, pp. 76–7. [2] See *Perepiska* ibid. and above.
[3] For Lenin's (and Potresov's) revulsion from Plekhanov's dictatorial tendencies see *Lenin* II, vol. 4, pp. 334–52.
[4] The exact date, as well as all the various moves which brought about this transformation, cannot be established on the basis of the published material. It is, of course, possible that much valuable information on these developments is found in archives located in the Soviet Union. However, as indicated earlier the present author has been unable to verify this. Hence the picture of events as drawn here is far from complete.
[5] For Struve's earlier contacts with them see above. [6] See *Belokonskiy* II, p. 92.
[7] For Milyukov's beliefs and role in the Liberation Movement see below. See also *Pipes* IIa, pp. 310–11.
[8] See *Milyukov* v₃, pp. 116–17, *Petrunkevich* II, pp. 336–7 and *Shakhovskoy* IV, p. 85. Milyukov's assertion that D. Zhukovskiy approached him on behalf of the zemstvo radicals

By autumn 1900 the situation had changed considerably. The 'Legal Marxists' learned at the Pskov Conference that unless they had a firm organizational basis of their own, they would never be treated as equals by the Literary Group. Although, with the exception of Tugan-Baranovskiy,[1] the 'Legal Marxist' leaders continued their contacts with their orthodox counterparts and even bowed to Plekhanov's demand to declare themselves a non-socialist group, nevertheless they became determined never to conduct negotiations with them again from a position of weakness. As a consequence, the Freedom Group established political links with the 'ex-Economists', Kuskova and Prokopovich and the *Russkoye Bogatstvo* people.[2] The latter were of great importance at the time because of their domination of the Writers Union.

This body, officially designated The Russian Writers Union of Mutual Aid,[3] was established in 1897, and according to its statutes, its aim was to promote the professional interests of Russian writers (such as arbitration in disputes between writers and publishers), to preserve correct ethical relations between them, etc.[4] But from the very beginning, the professional aspect of the Writers Union was overshadowed by its political activity. This was bound to happen since, for one thing, the democratically orientated *Russkoye Bogatstvo* group occupied a dominant position in the Union from the very start. (Thus for example, Vladimir Korolenko, its leading figure at the time, was chairman of the Union's legal committee[5] and a member of its most important body, the Court of Honour.[6]) Secondly, many of the rank-and-file members of the Union were only marginally, if at all, connected with literature or journalism. Their chief qualification for membership, so it seems, was their radicalism, and this radicalism sometimes got the better of their judgment. For example, many of them opposed Chekhov's application for membership (which was supported by Korolenko) on the grounds that 'he described the peasants in *The Peasants* (*Muzhiki*) not according to radical principles'.[7] It was, however, a sign

and offered him the editorship in 1901 does not make sense in the light of Zhukovskiy's activity at the time (see below). Milyukov must have been approached before summer 1900.

1 After Pskov, Tugan-Baranovskiy reached the conclusion that it was impossible to come to an honourable agreement with the orthodox Marxists. As a consequence, he did not participate in the negotiations between the two sides which were resumed in Munich in winter 1900/1. See *Lenin* I, vol. 4, p. 381, *Lenin* II, vol. 4, p. 387n. and below.
2 For the *Russkoye Bogatstvo* group see above.
3 See *Russkiy Kalendar* 1902, p. 264. 4 *Korolenko* I, p. 81.
5 Ibid. p. 78. 6 Ibid. p. 81 and *Suvorin*, pp. 187–8, 204, 240.
7 *Suvorin*, p. 179.

of the times that despite such occasional lapses into bad taste, the influence of the Writers Union was constantly increasing, especially after the suspension of the activities of the Imperial Free Economic Society.

Founded in 1765 for the purpose of educating the landowning nobility in economic and technical matters, the Economic Society was transformed in the mid-1890s into a centre of oppositional activity.[1] Under the benevolent chairmanship of Count P. A. Geyden, it opened its doors to many prominent leaders of the socialist intelligentsia of both the populist and the Marxist camps. (Among the latter one finds Struve and Tugan-Baranovskiy who joined the Society in 1895.[2]) The leaders of the intelligentsia employed the open debates of the Society, in which many zemstvo activists participated, as a sounding-board for attacks on the economic policy of the government. Towards the end of the decade, the police began to consider these activities as very dangerous.[3] On the recommendation of Sipyagin, the Minister of the Interior, Nicholas signed an order on 8 April 1900, prohibiting the invitation of outsiders to the meetings of the Free Economic Society, pending the promulgation of new regulations. A general meeting of its members learnt of this order on 21 April and decided tacitly to suspend the main activities of the Society for the time being.[4]

As a result of this decision the Writers Union remained the only central institution where the radical intelligentsia of St Petersburg could discuss 'public' (i.e. political) questions almost openly. By establishing links with the *Russkoye Bogatstvo* people, the Freedom Group and the 'ex-Economists' appropriated the only political base available for their semi-legal activities. Together they were able to transform this base, the Writers Union, into the nucleus of what immediately became known as the Russian radical–democratic intelligentsia. Under the new leadership the influence of the Writers Union grew very rapidly. From mid-1900 the weekly dinners and occasional banquets organized by it became the central events in the political life of St Petersburg intelligentsia.[5] They also provided a convenient location

---

[1] See *Fischer*, pp. 57–8.   [2] See *Kindersley*, pp. 58–9.
[3] For a police indictment of the Free Economic Society see *Osvobozhdeniye* I, pp. 58–65 (*Doklad Dept. Politsii ob Imperatorskom Volnom Ekonomicheskom O-ve*).
[4] See *Brokgaus supp.* I, pp. 454–6, *Trudy Volnogo Ekonomicheskogo O-va* (1900), nos. 4–5, pp. 29–32.
[5] The activities of the Writers Union during the period from summer 1900 to spring 1901 are described in *Gessen* I, pp. 167–8, *Kaun* I, pp. 320–4, *Savelyev*, pp. 169–70, *Sverchkov* II, pp. 19–21 and *Tyrkova* II, pp. 59–64.

for meetings between its leaders and the zemstvo constitutionalists. The most notable of its banquets was that held on the night of 18–19 February 1901 to commemorate the fiftieth anniversary of the liberation of the peasants. It was attended not only by the cream of the radical literary world of St Petersburg but also by many radical intellectuals from the provinces, the most famous of whom was Maxim Gorky.[1]

After thus establishing a political base for the activities of the Freedom Group, Struve resumed his contacts with the zemstvo radicals. The idea of establishing political ties with them had become particularly attractive to him since the establishment of *Beseda*, and the zemstvo radicals were now more in favour of such connections than in February 1900. As their political importance increased they began to regard it as imperative to establish an illegal newspaper. Since, despite all their efforts to persuade him, Milyukov steadfastly refused to accept the editorship of such a paper,[2] Struve became almost indispensable to them. His stature must also have grown in their eyes because of the leading role the Freedom Group had assumed among the St Petersburg democratic intelligentsia. Thus the two groups grew closer together and by late autumn 1900 had apparently arrived at agreement. The zemstvo radicals undertook to finance an illegal newspaper abroad under Struve's editorship, which was planned to become, in due course, the mouthpiece of a 'liberal party'. They also provided him with a copy of Witte's secret memorandum against the zemstvos for immediate publication. On his part, Struve succeeded in obtaining the consent of the zemstvo radicals to an attempt to publish the newspaper in co-operation with the orthodox Marxists.[3]

The final negotiations between the Freedom Group and the orthodox Marxists opened in Munich on 28 December 1900 (NS) and they continued till the end of February or beginning of March 1901 (NS). The Democratic–Oppositional Freedom Group was represented at the negotiations by P. B. Struve, his wife A. N. Struve, and V. Ya. Bogucharskiy. The *Iskra* and *Zarya* editorial board was represented by Lenin, Potresov and Zasulich and, at the last stage, also by Akselrod and Plekhanov.[4]

As a consequence of the arrangements made by Struve on the eve of the negotiations, he arrived in Munich in a completely different mood

[1] See *Kaun*, p. 321 and *Savelyev*, pp. 170–1.
[2] See *Milyukov*, v̄3, pp. 116–17 and *Shakhovskoy* IV, p. 85.
[3] See *Lenin* II, vol. 4, pp. 386–8; vol. 46, pp. 90, 436 (n. 96), *Struve* VI, p. 79 and below.
[4] The fullest account of these negotiations is found in *Perepiska*, vol. II, pp. 140–4. See also *Lenin* II, vol. 4 pp. 386–8, 486–7 (n. 141), *Struve* ibid. p. 77 and below.

to that of Pskov. There he had been prepared to lean over backwards in order to achieve an agreement with the orthodox Marxists for the sake of the common struggle against autocracy. In Munich, however, he stood firmly by his principles and spoke from a position of strength. He made it clear from the very beginning that he would be satisfied by nothing less than virtual independence (political as well as financial) for his proposed newspaper, and that this newspaper was intended to become a focal point for the organization of a liberal party.[1]

Struve's new position came as a terrible shock to Lenin. As noted earlier, at that time Lenin did not yet attach much importance to questions of philosophy, especially if they were related to developments in Western Europe. Politics, particularly as far as Russia was concerned, were an entirely different matter. The relations between Social-Democrats and liberals, as defined in the 'hegemony' theory, undoubtedly belonged to the field of politics. Hence Lenin's sensitivity on these matters.

Lenin made his interpretation of the 'hegemony' theory perfectly clear in a letter to Potresov dated 26 January 1899. There he stated that liberals must be utilized, but never given equal rights.[2] However, as long as the prospect of the establishment of an independent liberal party in Russia remained a matter for theoretical speculation, Lenin was prepared to tolerate, albeit with great difficulty, Akselrod and Plekhanov's 'hegemony' theory.[3] But by the time of the opening of the Munich negotiations he had realized that what had seemed a theoretical possibility had suddenly become almost a reality. There he discovered for the first time that what Struve had in mind was no less than the establishment of an independent liberal party. This immediately brought his basic hostility towards the liberals to the surface and transformed him into a bitter, lifelong enemy of Struve. Both attitudes are clearly reflected in Lenin's own account of the first day of negotiations (written at 2 a.m., 29 December 1900, NS). This is a rare document of the greatest psychological significance.[4]

Lenin began his description of the opening of negotiations, with the participation of himself, Potresov, Vera Zasulich, Struve and his wife (Bogucharskiy joined them a few days later), by stating that 'it was historic as far as my life is concerned; it summed up, if not a whole

---

[1] See *Lenin* II, vol. 4, pp. 386–8; vol. 46, pp. 79–81 (Lenin's letter to Plekhanov, dated 30 January 1901, NS) and below.
[2] See *Lenin* II, vol. 46, pp. 20–1.   [3] Ibid.
[4] See ibid. vol. 4, pp. 386–8. English translation in *Lenin* I, vol. 4, pp. 380–2. See also *Struve* VI, pp. 78–9.

epoch, at least a page in a life history, and it determined my conduct and my life's path for a long time to come.'[1] Then Lenin revealed why he was using such an emphatic tone. He had been totally astounded by the fact that Struve was arguing from a position of strength. Struve opened the business part of the meeting by denouncing the Pskov agreement, stating that he and his friends were not prepared to write articles and give assistance to *Iskra* and *Zarya* for which the editorial boards could 'take them to task'. He and his friends, he declared, would co-operate with the orthodox Marxists 'only on terms of complete equality'. In order to achieve this, the Freedom Group insisted on the establishment of a 'third political periodical on an equal basis with the others'. He himself would be the editor of this periodical.[2]

Struve's demands, wrote Lenin, revealed 'the coarse haggling nature of the *common liberal* that lay hidden beneath the dapper, cultured exterior of this latest "critic"'.[3]

After coming to the conclusion that Struve had become a spokesman of 'Russian liberalism', Lenin decided to bring out into the open his position on co-operation with such a movement.

Everything became clear, and I said openly that the publication of a third periodical was out of the question, and that the whole matter reduced itself to the question of whether Social Democracy must carry on the political struggle or whether the liberals should carry it on as an independent and self-contained movement.[4]

After he had stated his case, Lenin wrote, the discussion turned to the question of the publication of Witte's secret memorandum. Struve and his wife refused to reveal the content of this document before the editorial board of *Iskra* and *Zarya* agreed to their terms of publication. They insisted that the connection of the board be merely technical, that it should not be granted editorial powers and that its name should not appear on the pamphlet. These demands appeared so 'insolent' to Lenin that he refused to participate in further discussions. Potresov and Zasulich continued to argue but 'I remained silent for the most part and laughed (so that the twin* could see it quite clearly) and the conversation soon came to an end'.[5]

From then on Lenin was an implacable opponent of any kind of agreement with the Freedom Group and a personal enemy of Struve. In his account of the first day of negotiations he had already called Struve a '"politician" of the purest water, a politician in the worst sense of the word, an old fox and a brazen huckster'.[6] Immediately afterwards

[1] *Lenin* I, ibid. p. 380. [2] Ibid. p. 381. [3] Ibid. italics added. [4] Ibid. pp. 381–2.
* Struve. [5] Ibid. p. 382. [6] Ibid. p. 380.

103

he began to refer to Struve in private correspondence as 'Judas'.[1] But since Akselrod, Plekhanov, Potresov and Vera Zasulich were in favour of an agreement,[2] Lenin had to bow to the will of the majority, though not before declaring that he 'washed his hands' of the whole business.[3]

The final agreement, signed after more than two months of bargaining, was never published. But the gist of it can be extracted from the available sources.[4] According to its terms, the Freedom Group was to publish a special supplement to *Zarya*, under Struve's editorship, to be called *Sovremennoye Obozreniye* (The Contemporary Review). It was to be devoted to attacks on the existing regime in Russia, and the editors of *Iskra* and *Zarya* were to be responsible for its printing, transportation and distribution. They also agreed to allow Struve and his friends to publish articles in their papers on condition that the latter refrained from dealing with social-democratic questions. In return, the Freedom Group undertook to cover the cost of publication and distribution of *Iskra*, *Zarya* and *Sovremennoye Obozreniye*. It also agreed to open the pages of the latter to the editors of *Iskra* and *Zarya* and, apparently very reluctantly, to permit the social-democratic papers to use material written for *Sovremennoye Obozreniye*.[5]

The agreement was to be accompanied by a declaration aimed at explaining to the supporters of each faction the need for the establishment of a 'united front' against autocracy. It was comprised of two documents, one composed by Plekhanov and the other written by Struve. The declaration as a whole was apparently approved by both sides.[6] Plekhanov explained that Russian social-democracy had always maintained that the oppressive tsarist regime could be destroyed only through the efforts of all the revolutionary and oppositional groups in Russia. Hence, he continued, social-democracy was always prepared to lend support to all groups fighting autocracy and striving for the establishment of political freedom in Russia. The Freedom Group, according to Plekhanov, deserved such support since its main aim consisted of trying 'to give political sense to the legal struggle against the...arbitrary power of the autocracy'.[7]

---

[1] *Lenin* I, vol. 34, pp. 55–7 and *Lenin* II, vol. 46, pp. 79–81 ff.

[2] *Lenin* II, vol. 4, pp. 486–7 (n. 141); vol. 46, p. 79, *Perepiska*, vol. II, pp. 139–44. Martov, who also opposed an agreement with Struve, was not present at the negotiations; he was still travelling in Russia. See *Getzler*, pp. 45–7.   [3] See *Lenin* II, vol. 46, p. 81.

[4] See *Pipes* IIa, 266–7.   [5] See ibid. and *Lenin* II, vol. 46, pp. 79–80.

[6] As in the case of the agreement, the full declaration was never published but, as is not the case with the agreement, an extensive summary of the declaration is found in *Potresov* II, pp. 615–16. See also *Pipes* IIa, pp. 267–9.

[7] *Potresov* ibid. p. 615. Ellipsis dots in original.

Plekhanov's explanation was quite consistent with the 'hegemony' theory as developed by him and Akselrod and as they had practised it in the past. Struve, in his section of the declaration, did not challenge this theory. He wrote:

Finally, we believe it necessary to stress that – like the Social Democratic group which joins us in the common task – we assign a prime political importance and mission to the Russian labour movement. In this movement, the political thought of the Russian intelligentsia has found a powerful ally, with whose growth henceforth the fate of political liberty will be indissolubly linked [1]

He also refrained from mentioning the fact that his main aim was to establish an independent liberal party. He must have known by then that such a development would be anathema to Lenin, and therefore apparently decided to refrain from mentioning it in order not to antagonize him too much.

Struve's tactics were quite successful as far as Plekhanov was concerned. By paying lip-service to the 'hegemony' theory, Struve enabled Plekhanov to sign the agreement and the joint declaration in good faith. But Lenin was not taken in. In a letter to Plekhanov, written on 30 January 1901 (NS), Lenin made a last-minute effort to prevent the signing of the agreement by stating that if it materialized, the 'hegemony' theory would become an empty phrase.[2] Since he failed to prevent the signing of the agreement, he waited for an opportunity to render it null and void. This opportunity was provided by one of Struve's financial backers, D. Zhukovskiy, who was later to play an important role in the launching of *Osvobozhdeniye*.[3]

Soon after the agreement was signed and the declaration regarding the establishment of the 'United Front' composed, Struve left for Russia. At the same time Zhukovskiy arrived in Western Europe with a certain amount of money which he intended to donate only to *Sovremonnoye Obozreniye*. The editors of *Iskra* and *Zarya* believed that their agreement with Struve entitled them to a share in this money. When Zhukovskiy refused point-blank to give them money, Lenin proclaimed it a breach of contract and succeeded in convincing the other editors to suspend the agreement and send Struve an ultimatum: money – or an end to the agreement.[4]

At the time this ultimatum was sent, Struve was in prison. He was arrested together with numerous other radical intellectuals while

[1] *Potresov* ibid. p. 616. English translation in *Pipes* IIa, pp. 268–9.
[2] See *Lenin* II, vol. 46, p. 78 and *Pipes* IIa, p. 267.   [3] See below.
[4] See *Lenin* II, vol. 46, p. 90 (Lenin's letter to Akselrod, dated 20 March 1901, NS).

participating in a street demonstration at Kazan Square, St Petersburg on 4 March 1901.[1] Thus the ultimatum did not reach him. At the same time, Dietz, the German publisher of *Zarya*, refused to publish the declaration because of his fear of legal complications.[2] These developments made it easy for Lenin to bury the whole matter.

In any case there are strong grounds for belief that the agreement between the orthodox Marxists and the Freedom Group would never have been implemented, even without Struve's arrest and Dietz's refusal. To begin with, there is no reason to believe that Struve would have yielded to the ultimatum. Secondly, judging by Struve's preface to Witte's memorandum (which Lenin was compelled to published in 1901 in pamphlet form, under the title *Samoderzhaviye i Zemstvo*[3]) and by Lenin's vicious attack on it,[4] there was no more room for co-operation between these two men and between their supporters.

In his preface to Witte's memorandum, Struve made it clear that the establishment of a liberal party was by then his main political aim.[5] The appearance in print of this preface can be seen therefore as signalling the final break between the Russian democratic intelligentsia and the SD movement. As has already been mentioned, the leaders of that intelligentsia regarded the radical elements in the zemstvo as their main partners in the struggle for political liberty.

Struve, who was closer to the zemstvo radicals than the other leaders of the democratic intelligentsia, hoped that the partnership between the two sides would very soon result in the establishment of a liberal party (on this particular point he was soon to be proved wrong).[6] He was well aware, however, of the fact that the zemstvo radicals represented only a very small minority of zemstvo activists.[7] Since Struve regarded the non-radical majority of zemstvo activists as potential rank-and-file members of the 'liberal party', he translated the general-democratic demands of the intelligentsia into a practical programme in his preface, adapted to their level of political consciousness.

Addressing himself to the task of politically educating the non-radical majority of zemstvo activists, Struve did not condemn their desire to achieve a compromise with the government without engaging in illegal activities. On the contrary, he explained to his readers that if the government would abolish the Emergency Laws, lift the ban on

---

[1] See below. [2] See *Lenin* II, vol. 46, pp. 88, 484 (n. 81), and *Struve* VI, p. 79.
[3] See *Lenin* ibid. pp. 90, 486 (n. 96) and *Bibliography*. [4] See below.
[5] *Samoderzhaviye i Zemstvo* II, pp. xli–xlii. [6] See below.
[7] For the definition of the term 'zemstvo activists' see above.

political activity, permit professional association of workers, give them the right to strike, and grant freedom of expression and religion, a compromise would be not only possible, but also desirable because the country was not yet ready for more radical reforms.[1] However, he continued, since the government, as everyone could see from Witte's memorandum, was bent on a different course, and was even contemplating the abolition of the zemstvo institutions, the chances for the establishment of an illegal liberal party were good. Although such a party would be composed of a very moderate rank-and-file membership, nevertheless, Struve explained, under the pressure of the SD or a labour party and because of its illegal status, it would soon adopt a radical programme and thus become an important political factor.[2] Then, turning the tables on his former political allies, and thus, as it were, turning the 'hegemony' theory on its head, Struve explained to his new audience that such a party might have a very good chance of becoming the political master of Russia. This might happen if the imminent struggle between the government and the SD Party ended in a deadlock.[3]

Struve ended his political discourse on a note less frightening and more acceptable to his audience. He explained that there was still time to avoid the final confrontation between the government and the revolutionaries. Everything depended on the government. If it changed its policy from an aggressively reactionary one to one of progressive reform, Russia would have a good chance of achieving freedom in an evolutionary and not revolutionary way.[4]

Struve's 'pedagogic' remarks and especially his attack on the 'hegemony' theory outraged Plekhanov. They must also have confirmed Lenin's innate distrust of the 'treacherous' liberals, since he accompanied Struve's pamphlet with a most vicious attack on the zemstvo constitutionalists in general and Struve in particular.[5] His conclusions had far-reaching repercussions. In the short run this attack rendered impossible any co-operation between the *Iskra* faction of RSDRP and

[1] *Samoderzhaviye i Zemstvo* II, pp. viii–xvi.
[2] Ibid. pp. xli–xlii.
[3] Ibid. p. xlii.
[4] Ibid. pp. xliv–xlv.
[5] See *Lenin* I, vol. 5, pp. 35–80 ('The Prosecutors of the Zemstvo and the Hannibals of Liberalism'). The final version of Lenin's lengthy article was somewhat toned down on the insistence of Plekhanov and Akselrod. (See *Lenin* II, vol. 46, pp. 127–35.) A most detailed and illuminating description of this final phase in the 'parting of the ways' between orthodox Marxists and the Freedom Group, and its subsequent historical importance, is found in *Pipes* IIa, pp. 271–9.

the emergent Liberation Movement. In the long run, Lenin's state of mind was, to a large extent, responsible for the fact that the Bolsheviks regarded the Russian liberals and democrats as more dangerous than autocracy.

5

The launching of the Liberation Movement

While Struve was negotiating with the orthodox Marxists in Munich, the oppositional mood of society in Russia was reaching boiling-point. D. S. Sipyagin, who replaced Goremykin as Minister of the Interior on 20 October 1899,[1] succeeded, during his relatively short term of office (he was assassinated on 2 April 1902),[2] in antagonizing almost every stratum of educated society. According to the well-informed Polovtsev,* Sipyagin was an 'idiot' whose chief qualification for his job was his belief in police rule and his submission to Witte.[3] His confidence in police rule was immediately reflected in the tightening of press censorship, which affected even such a loyal newspaper as *Novoye Vremya*.[4] At the same time, his belief in Witte led him to introduce a series of measures aimed at drastically curtailing the activities of the zemstvos.

The governmental measure which hit the zemstvo activists hardest was the 'Law Regarding the Fixation of Limits to Zemstvo Taxation' promulgated on 12 June 1900. Under this law, any increase of 3 per cent or more in zemstvo taxation of immovable property had to be approved in advance by the Ministers of Finance and the Interior.[5] Coming as it did shortly after the contents of Witte's secret memorandum had become known, the law could only be interpreted by the zemstvo activists as further proof of the intention of the government to abolish the zemstvo institutions altogether or to restrict their activity to such an extent that they would remain zemstvo institutions in name only. No amount of explanation by Witte that the reasons behind the

[1] *Witte* VIII p. 135.
[2] See *Russkiy Kalendar* 1903, pp. 313–14. *Polovtsev* I, pp. 130–3.
* A. A. Polovtsev, whose published diary (quoted frequently in this book) is an important source on behind-the-scenes activities in the tsarist government, was for nine years (1883–92) secretary and from 1892 member of the State Council. He was also an active member and later president of the Imperial Russian Historical Society.
[3] See *Polovtsev* I, p. 99, *Suvorin*, pp. 250, 266, 279. See also *Witte* IV, pp. 33–41.
[4] See *Suvorin*, pp. 223, 238, 259–63.
[5] *Veselovskiy* Va, p. 139; VI, pp. 533–4.

law were economic could make them alter their opinion that the main aim of the law was, in the words of Shipov, 'to impede the development of zemstvo activity'.[1]

The bitterness aroused by this measure increased the oppositional mood of the activists and made them more inclined to follow the lead of the zemstvo radicals and the 'Third Element'. This was reflected in the growing domination of *Beseda* by the constitutionalists and came to the notice of the public at the 'Congress of Activists in the Field of Agronomic Aid to the Local Economy'.[2] This Congress, which was held in Moscow on 10–19 February 1901,[3] was not a private affair, as were the zemstvo meetings of 1896 and 1898,[4] but a mass gathering of zemstvo activists and representatives of the 'Third Element'. The latter constituted the overwhelming majority of the 360 delegates who took part in the deliberations.[5] Among the former (of whom there were not more than thirty)[6] at least ten were members of *Beseda* and all of them played a leading role in the Congress. They were: N. A. Khomyakov (chairman of the Congress), D. N. Shipov (host of the Congress), M. V. Chelnokov, Prince Pavel D. Dolgorukov, Prince Peter D. Dolgorukov, F. A. Golovin, N. N. Lvov, R. A. Pisarev, Prince D. I. Shakhovskoy and A. A. Stakhovich.

The predominance of the 'Third Element' made it obvious to all the participants that the Congress would adopt radical resolutions. What was less obvious was the possibility that the majority of the zemstvo activists would side with the 'Third Element' in the plenum debates and would more or less follow the lead of the zemstvo radicals in private conclaves. This, however, was exactly what happened.

On the fourth day of the Congress (13 February) Shipov invited all the zemstvo activists present to an unofficial lunch, where they discussed the latest anti-zemstvo government measures. After explaining the gravity of the situation, Shipov tried to persuade the participants to adopt a plan of action which only a few months earlier had been rejected by *Beseda*, namely the sending of a petition to the Tsar. N. N. Lvov and other participants at the luncheon (there were no more than 25 people present) agreed to his suggestion, but only on condition that constitutional demands should be included in the petition. But because

---

[1] *Shipov* II, p. 122.
[2] The account of the composition, proceedings (official debates as well as private gatherings) and decisions of the Congress is based mainly on the following sources: *Melkaya* I, pp. 329–36, *Savelyev*, pp. 162–7, *Veselovskiy* Vb, pp. 145–6, 163–4; VI, pp. 553–4.
[3] *Russkiy Kalendar* 1902, p. 263.   [4] See above.   [5] See *Veselovskiy* VI, p. 553.
[6] For name-lists of delegates see ibid. pp. 553–4 and *Savelyev*, pp. 162–3.

Shipov neither would nor could incorporate such demands in his proposed petition, his suggestion was not accepted by the conclave.[1] The readiness of the zemstvo activist delegates to follow the lead of the radicals became even more apparent at the second meeting of the 'conclave' which was held on 15 February, the day after the assassination of the Minister of Education, N. P. Bogolepov.[2] This time, many speakers attacked Sipyagin and Witte personally – the former for his reactionary policies in general and for his mishandling of the student disturbances in particular, the latter for his economic policy and his anti-zemstvo campaign. All the speakers demanded the transformation of autocracy into a constitutional regime.[3]

At the same time as the zemstvo activists were holding their private luncheons, the representatives of the 'Third Element' were holding meetings, banquets etc. where demands of a much more radical nature were voiced.[4]

In contrast to the private gatherings of delegates to the Congress, its formal meetings dealt with what might appear a very prosaic matter, namely the question of the small zemstvo unit (*melkaya zemskaya yedinitsa*), that is, a separately elected lower-level zemstvo. In actual fact, this question, as debated at the Congress and later in the press, was anything but prosaic. The chief protagonists in the debate were Shakhovskoy, representing the point of view of the zemstvo radicals and the 'Third Element' on the one hand, and Shipov representing the views of the liberal Slavophiles on the other. The arguments they then voiced were employed by them and by their supporters time and time again during 1904–5 when they were openly debating the suitability of a constitutional system and a democratic franchise for Russia under the given conditions.[5]

Reduced to their bare essentials, the arguments put forward by both sides in defence of their respective proposals were as follows. Shipov was not opposed in principle to the establishment of small zemstvo units. On the contrary, as has been shown earlier, the restoration of the original non-class character of zemstvo institutions and the gradual introduction of small zemstvo units for the benefit of the peasants were corner-stones of the political programme of the liberal Slavophiles. He was opposed, however, to the suggestion, put forward by Shakhovskoy and his supporters, that these units should be introduced immediately, that they should be completely autonomous and that they should have

---

[1] See *Savelyev*, pp. 163–5.   [2] See below.   [3] See *Sevelyev*, pp. 166–7.
[4] See *Belokonskiy* II, p. 84.   [5] See for example *Shipov* I, pp. 16–29.

an entirely non-class character.[1] This, in the words of Shipov and his supporters, would mean letting the peasants run these units independently together with the 'Third Element'. The peasants, however, were still too ignorant and the 'Third Element' was still too radical in its outlook to undertake this without causing grave damage to the whole zemstvo system.[2] Hence, until the defects of the peasantry and of the 'Third Element' were eliminated, Shipov suggested the establishment of small economic units (*economicheskiya popechitelstva*) to be within reach of the peasants but directed and supervised by the district zemstvos.[3]

Shakhovskoy and his supporters did not deny that the peasants were ignorant nor that they might cause damage to the zemstvos if given complete independence. However, this seemed to them a price worth paying for the political education the peasants would obtain from running the small zemstvo units and for the transformation of the zemstvo into 'truly popular institutions' (*istinno-narodnyye uchrezhdeniya*).[4] They also vehemently defended the 'Third Element' from the implied attacks of the liberal Slavophiles and accused the latter of living in a world of make-believe.[5]

Eventually, the Congress approved Shakhovskoy's point of view by a huge majority[6] and adopted a resolution calling for the establishment of 'autonomous, non-class small zemstvo units'.[7] This resolution was of very great influence in the launching of the Liberation Movement.

By basing their legal political campaign in the next year on the demand for the establishment of small zemstvo units, the zemstvo radicals killed two birds with one stone. First, the campaign for the establishment of small zemstvo units proved a good substitute at a time when it was impossible to mention constitutional demands even indirectly in the legal press. One of its by-products was the beginning of co-operation between the zemstvo radicals and the editorial board of *Pravo*,* which laid the foundation for *Beseda*'s literary activity[8] as well as making *Pravo* the legal twin of *Osvobozhdeniye*.[9] Secondly, by

[1] See *Melkaya* I, p. 335. [2] Ibid. pp. 332–3. [3] Ibid. pp. 330–1. [4] Ibid. p. 333.
[5] Ibid. p. 334. [6] Ibid. p. 335. [7] *Veselovskiy* vb, pp. 163–4 (n. 1).
* *Pravo* (*Law*) was a juridical weekly which was published in St Petersburg during the period 1898–1917. Its official editors were V. M. Gessen and N. I. Lazarevich. Its editorial policy, however, was directed mainly by I. V. Gessen, V. D. Nabokov and other leading members of the Liberation Movement and future leaders of the Cadet Party.
[8] See *Gessen* I, pp. 161–5 and above. Appropriately enough, the first joint publication of *Beseda* and *Pravo* was the already quoted two-volume *Melkaya Zemskaya Yedinitsa* (see *Bibliography*).
[9] See *Gessen* I, pp. 166, 170–5.

demanding that the new zemstvo units be organized according to democratic principles, the radicals added to their existing bonds with the 'Third Element', an ideological dimension of great importance. For the great majority of the 'Third Element' constitutionalism without social content was not enough. But when the zemstvo radicals declared that the transformation of the zemstvos into 'truly popular institutions' (*istinno-narodnyye uchrezhdeniya*) was one of their political aims, they added social content to their political programme. This paved the way for their partnership with the 'Third Element' in one comprehensive political movement, the Liberation Movement, which was launched a few weeks after the Congress ended.

By the time the Congress dispersed, a crisis of the first magnitude was developing in the main cities of Russia. The tension in the universities, which had somewhat subsided after the initial flare-up at the beginning of 1899, rose again as a consequence of Sipyagin's rigid application of the regulations on conscripting recalcitrant students.[1] On the basis of these regulations more than two hundred students were forcibly drafted into the army in autumn 1900. This immediately caused the entire student community to rise up in arms, and the crisis reached boiling-point early in 1901.[2]

On 14 February 1901, Peter Karpovich, an expelled student, shot and mortally wounded the Minister of Education, N. P. Bogolepov.[3] The assassination of Bogolepov triggered off street demonstrations by students in Kharkov, Kiyev, Moscow (23–8 February 1901)[4] and other university towns. This wave of disturbances culminated in the notorious mass demonstrations in the Kazan Square in St Petersburg on 4 March 1901.[5] The cream of the St Petersburg radical intelligentsia participated in this demonstration side-by-side with the students. The former included almost all the leaders of the Writers Union, including Struve, who had just returned from Munich. The authorities, who had never before been faced with a demonstration of this size, decided to teach the participants a lesson and gave the Cossacks and the mounted police a free hand. As a consequence many of the demonstrators and by-standers, including the revered N. F. Annenskiy, were beaten, and about

---

[1] See above.
[2] See *Keep*, p. 70, *Cherevanin* I, pp. 275–80, *Savelyev*, pp. 172–80.
[3] See *Russkiy Kalendar* 1902, p. 264.
[4] For an account of the Moscow disturbances see *Materialy* VI₂, pp. 1–2, 9–17.
[5] *Russkiy Kalendar* 1902, p. 264. For eye- and ear-witness descriptions of this demonstration and its aftermath, see *Ivanov-Razumnik* IV, pp. 1–6, *Kaun* I, pp. 318–20, *Savelyev*, pp. 175–6, *Sverchkov* II, pp. 35–7, *Tyrkova* II, pp. 64–89.

1,500 of those present were arrested.[1] They included Annenskiy, Ivanov-Razumnik, Myakotin, Peshekhonov, Struve, Tugan-Baranov-skiy, Tyrkova-Williams[2] and scores of other radical intellectuals. For some of them it was not their first arrest but for others it was a baptism of fire which launched them on the road to active participation in the Liberation Movement.[3]

The maltreatment of the demonstrators by the Cossacks and the police shocked St Petersburg society to the core and produced a crisis of conscience in the highest echelons of the bureaucracy, which was becoming more and more exasperated by Nicholas II's conduct of affairs. The Vyazemskiy Scandal illustrates this point.

Prince Leonid Vyazemskiy was a scion of one of the oldest noble families in the land and a member of the State Council. There he passed his time in idleness and would certainly have failed to leave his mark on history were it not for the fact that he happened to be at Kazan Square on the fateful morning of 4 March 1901. There, according to his own account, he 'admonished the police agents and the Commandant of St Petersburg for their inhuman treatment of the students'.[4]

For his 'uncalled-for interference' he was sternly reprimanded and ordered to leave St Petersburg.[5] There can be little doubt that the sympathy displayed towards him by many of his fellow-councillors and by society more than compensated him for his punishment. At the general meeting of the State Council held on the day after the demonstration, he was hailed by many councillors as a hero,[6] while the following description of his deed, given in the *Refutation of the Official Account of the Kazan Demonstration*,[7] made him the darling of society for a while:

We assert that on 4 March, the police and Cossacks were given vodka in order to rouse them...the Cossacks appeared on the Square at the silent signal of Kleigels*
...and began to beat the crowd...having in no way warned them of their intentions...Thus Prince Vyazemskiy, member of the State Council, witnessed the beating of the writers Peshekhonov and Annenskiy, and his efforts to exhort the drunken mob were of no avail.[8]

[1] *Ivanov-Razumnik* ibid. p. 2, *Polovtsev* I, p. 82, *Tyrkova* II, pp. 64–89.
[2] See *Brokgaus supp.* I, p. 122; II, pp. 252, 496.
[3] See for example *Tyrkova* ibid. p. 90, *Osvobozhdeniye* (1902), no. 7, p. 106 and below.
[4] Cited in *Polovtsev* I, p. 82.   [5] Ibid. p. 84.   [6] Ibid. p. 82.
[7] The *Refutation* was apparently written by M. Gorky and it was distributed widely in St Petersburg. See *Kaun* I, pp. 322–3.
* N. V. Kleigels was the Commandant (*Gradonachalnik*) of St Petersburg. See *Gurko*, pp. 26, 605 (n. 8)
[8] Cited in *Kaun* I, p. 323.

The indignation of society and of many high-ranking bureaucrats and official supporters of the regime[1] created favourable conditions for the resurrection of personal terror as a revolutionary weapon. (Thus, on 8 March 1901, only four days after the Kazan Square demonstration, and less than a month after the assassination of Bogolepov, an attempt was made on Pobedonostsev's life.[2]) This, in its turn, helped to bring about the renaissance of political populism and contributed to the creation of the Socialist-Revolutionary Party (SR).[3] These events also set in motion a chain-reaction which brought the Liberation Movement into being.

The general excitement in St Petersburg society found clear expression at the extraordinary meeting of the Writers Union, convened several days later to discuss this event. The indignation of the participants knew no bounds when they learned of the manhandling of Annenskiy (who was allowed several days' liberty before his deportation from St Petersburg and was thus able to attend the meeting). According to an eye-witness, 'the enormous blue-black circle around his eye played a decisive role...at the evening meeting of the Union of Writers'.[4] As a consequence, the letter of protest which the meeting decided to send to the Minister of the Interior was couched in very strong terms.[5]

Sipyagin's reaction was immediate and predictable. On the orders of the Commandant of St Petersburg, the Writers Union was closed for good on 12 March 1901.[6] Thus Sipyagin left the capital's radical intelligentsia no alternative but to establish an illegal organization, and the inefficient police handling of the situation (they allowed the St Petersburg deportees to choose their place of exile) made the task very easy for them. Annenskiy and Myakotin, for example, chose Finland[7] and since their place of residence there was very close to the border, it immediately became a centre of activity for the St Petersburg intelligentsia.[8] Peshkhonov chose Pskov, which was not far from St Petersburg,[9] and Struve Tver,[10] Petrunkevich's home and the centre of zemstvo radicalism.

---

[1] See *Polovtsev* I, p. 82, *Suvorin*, pp. 224, 263, 278 f.
[2] *Russkiy Kalendar* 1902, p. 264.
[3] For the danger which these developments presented to the political influence of the SD movement see *Getzler*, pp. 53–4, *Keep*, pp. 74, 78–9.
[4] Cited in *Kaun* I, p. 324.   [5] Ibid. and *Shakhovskoy* IV, p. 84.
[6] *Russkiy Kalendar* 1902, p. 264.   [7] *Borkgaus supp.* I, p. 122; II p. 232.
[8] See *Gessen* I, pp. 198–9, *Milyukov* V₅, p. 110, *Belokonskiy* II, pp. 93–4.
[9] *Brokgaus supp.* II, p. 496.   [10] Ibid. p. 719.

Struve's arrival in Tver brought to its logical conclusion the agreement he had reached with the zemstvo radicals in autumn 1900 regarding the publication of an illegal constitutionalist newspaper (which was to have become, in due course, the mouthpiece of a liberal party). As a result of the events of February and March, both sides now regarded the establishment of such a newspaper and the launching of a liberal party as urgent and imperative. At the same time, Struve's experience in Munich must have finally convinced him of the impossibility of co-operating with the orthodox Marxists in such an endeavour. As a result, he and Petrunkevich decided to publish a completely independent newspaper. Struve put forward only one demand – complete independence in editing it – to which Petrunkevich quickly agreed. After agreeing on this point, and after apparently deciding on the name *Osvobozhdeniye* (Liberation) which resembled the Russian name of the Freedom Group,[1] both parties left Tver. Struve left illegally for Europe to organize the technical side of the publication, while Petrunkevich went to Moscow to obtain the approval of his friends to the agreement and to finalize the financial arrangements which enabled *Osvobozhenive* to appear in print a year later.[2]

On his arrival in Moscow, Petrunkevich submitted his agreement with Struve to a joint meeting of zemstvo radicals, the majority of whom were members of *Beseda* and Moscow liberals. The former included Prince D. I. Shakhovskoy and V. I. Vernadskiy, while the spokesmen of the latter were A. A. Kornilov* and P. I. Novgorodtsev.† The meeting gave its official approval to the agreement[3] and, as might have been expected, the financial side did not pose much of a problem for *Beseda*.[4] (When Shakhovskoy and N. N. Lvov left for Stuttgart in spring 1902 to visit Struve, they carried with them, besides the programmatic announcement of the newspaper,[5] 100,000 roubles.[6])

The approval of the agreement between Struve and Petrunkevich

---

[1] According to *Pipes* IIa, p. 314, Struve intended to call the paper *Liberty* (*Svoboda*), exactly the name of his group, but was unable to do so because the name had been appropriated by a splinter SR group. Hence his decision to call the paper *Osvobozhdeniye* which resembled the group's name.

[2] See *Shakhovskoy* IV, p. 85 and *Rodichev* IV, pp. 322–3. See also *Struve* VI, p. 81. For Struve's whereabout in Europe until *Osvobozhdeniye* began to appear see *Pipes* IIa, pp. 312–14.

* The well-known historian, who in 1904 became virtually co-editor of *Osvobozhdeniye*. (See *B.S.E.I.* vol. 34, cols 323–4.)

† Professor of Philosophy at Moscow University. See *Brokgaus supp.* II, pp. 294–5.

[3] See *Chermenskiy* II, p. 50, *Mikheyeva*, p. 243.   [4] See, for example, *Kuskova* XVIIIa.

[5] See below.   [6] See *Petrunkevich* II, p. 337.

paved the way for the next step towards the establishment of the Liberation Movement. This took the form of the establishment of 'Friends of Liberation' (*Druzya Osvobozhdeniya*) circles.[1] These circles became the nucleus of the illegal radical–constitutionalist movement, which derived its name from them (and from the newspaper) and hence became known as the Liberation Movement (*Osvoboditelnoye Dvizhen-iye*.)[2]

The establishment of the 'Friends of Liberation' circles was made possible by the fact that the zemstvo radicals and the leaders of the radical–democratic intelligentsia[3] shared a set of beliefs which enabled both sides to agree on a common programme of action.

To begin with, they believed in the need to establish in Russia a constitutional regime, i.e. a regime based on a written constitution which would provide for the existence of a representative assembly with full legislative powers. Secondly, apart from Milyukov[4] and several less important future leaders of the Union of Liberation, both sides subscribed to the democratic principle of universal suffrage, believing that the legislative assembly should be elected by all adult male Russian citizens. Thirdly, they believed that this regime could be established only by 'pressure from below', i.e. in revolutionary fashion through the convocation of a constituent assembly elected by universal suffrage, which would promulgate the constitution.

Fourthly, they thought that the constituent assembly should be convened, not through violence but by peaceful means, meaning that the existing autocratic government should and could be brought to its knees mainly by the organization of public opinion. They believed, however, that the difference between violent deeds and peaceful means was a tactical rather than a basic one. It is true that at the turn of the century all of them would have preferred a peaceful to a violent revolution.[5] However, as Petrunkevich pointed out as early as 1878[6] and Struve a generation later[7] the existing regime was based on violence and thus was also responsible for the violence of the revolutionaries. Hence they condoned the violence of the latter and as a consequence

---

[1] See *Belokonskiy* II, pp. 92–4. *Shakhovskoy* IV, p. 85.

[2] For a brief discussion of the sources on the history of the formation of the Liberation Movement see below, *Appendix C*.

[3] See above.

[4] For Milyukov's stand on the question of universal suffrage at that time, see *Milyukov* V₃, p. 118 and below.

[5] See *Kuskova* II, p. 20, *Prokopovich*, p. 56.

[6] *Petrunkevich* II, pp. 96–8.

[7] *Osvobozhdeniye* (1902), no. 7, p. 107.

(as they themselves pointed out at the time[1]) they stood for peaceful means mainly for very practical reasons, these means being dictated to them by the milieu in which they operated. Believing, however, that peaceful means would not suffice to bring about the convocation of a constituent assembly, they subscribed to what became known as the policy of 'no enemies on the left'. This policy aimed at co-ordinating the activities of the 'peaceful' opposition and the revolutionaries in order to bring the government to its knees, a prerequisite for the convocation of a constituent assembly.

Lastly, since the beginning of 1901 (since the Congress of Activists in the Field of Agronomic Aid to the Local Economy), the majority of the zemstvo radicals had added social content to their political programme.[2] Thus the only obstacle to co-operation between them and the radical intelligentsia of socialist inclinations was removed. Because of all these shared beliefs the establishment of the 'Friends of Liberation' circles went very smoothly and quickly. Shakhovskoy and Bogucharskiy were particularly active in the organization of these circles, the former among the zemstvo activists and the 'Third Element'[3] and the latter among the radical intelligentsia of the towns, and especially the capital.

Bogucharskiy came to this task by accident. Since he returned from abroad (where he participated in the negotiations with the orthodox Marxists) after 4 March 1901, he escaped being arrested with the majority of the other leaders of the Writers Union.[4] He utilized his freedom by travelling all over Russia, establishing contacts between the exiled leaders of the Union. His first stop was Tver where he learned about the agreement between Struve and Petrunkevich. From there he went to Finland where Annenskiy, Myakotin and Milyukov[5] were then living in exile, and it was there that the first circle of 'Friends of Liberation' was founded. This circle, which was later transformed into the St Petersburg branch of the Union of Liberation, included almost all the future leaders of its intelligentsia wing – Annenskiy, Bogucharskiy, Khizhnyakov, Kuskova, Myakotin, Peshekhonov (who must have joined it after his release from Pskov), Prokopovich and several others.[6] Besides providing the *Osvobozhdeniye* enterprise with solid literary backing, this circle contributed much in the field of

---

[1] Ibid., and *Kuskova* ibid., *Prokopovich* ibid. [2] See above.
[3] See *Tyrkova* II, pp. 113–14.
[4] *Belokonskiy* II, pp. 92–4.   [5] *Milyukov* v₃, pp. 115–16; v₅, pp. 109–110 and below.
[6] *Belokonskiy* ibid. The St Petersburg branch of the Union of Liberation was composed of the intelligentsia wing of the Union of Liberation Council and of its Technical Group.

conspiratorial contacts (especially in Finland)[1] and techniques, which later made it possible to deliver *Osvobozhdeniye* to all parts of Russia. (Kuskova and Prokopovich's earlier stay in Berlin was in no small way responsible for this). After the establishment of the 'Finnish' circle of 'Friends of Liberation', Bogucharskiy renewed his travels and visited Voronezh, Tula, Kursk, Kharkov and the Crimea, where similar groups were founded.[2]

While Bogucharskiy was travelling throughout Russia, Shakhovskoy and other zemstvo radicals, as well as members of the 'Finnish circle', were busy organizing groups of 'Friends of Liberation' among the 'Third Element' and the growing number of constitutionally inclined zemstvo activists. For this purpose they attended the Regional Congress on Domestic Crafts held in September 1901 in Poltava; the Tenth Congress of Natural Scientists and Doctors (one of its sections was composed of statisticians), held in St Petersburg at the end of 1901 and beginning of 1902, and the National Exhibition of Domestic Craft held there in March 1902.[3] As in the case of the Congress of Activists in the Field of Agronomic Aid to the Local Economy, the majority of the delegates who attended this conference were representatives of the 'Third Element'. Among the zemstvo activist minority, the leading role was played by the radical members of *Beseda* – Shakhovskoy, Prince Peter D. Dolgorukov and others. Apart from these two groups these conferences were attended by radical intellectuals from the capital who had escaped arrest. Among these the most important figure was Vladimir Korolenko.[4]

Although the exact number of circles established at this time is not known, Bogucharskiy and Shakhovskoy must have been quite successful in their efforts because, according to Milyukov, 'in spring 1902 the preparations for the publication (of *Osvobozhdeniye*) had reached such an advanced stage that I was summoned to Petrunkevich's estate, Mashuk (Tver Province), for the composition of the programmatic announcement. Besides Petrunkevich, D. I. Shakhovskoy and A. A. Kornilov took part in its composition. This announcement was published, almost without alterations, in the first (June) issue of *Osvobozhdeniye*.'[5] Milyukov's participation in the composition of the

---

[1] See *Kuskova* XVIIIa.   [2] *Belokonskiy* ibid.   [3] See *Fischer*, p. 126.
[4] See *Belokonskiy* II, pp. 85–8 and *Shakhovskoy* IV, pp. 85–6.
[5] *Milyukov* v₃, p. 117. Milyukov's evidence about the time of the meeting is corroborated by the text of the announcement. In its introductory section there is an indirect reference to the assassination of Sipyagin ('new flare-ups of terrorism as demonstrated by the assassination of *two ministers* within a year') and to peasant disturbances (*Osvobozhdeniye* (1902),

announcement (published under the title 'From the Russian Constitutionalists')[1] was apparently his first step on the path which brought him to the leadership of the Constitutional-Democratic Party (*Konstitutsionno-Demokraticheskaya Partiya*) or, in short, the Cadets, in October 1905.[2]

Unlike other leaders of the Liberation Movement, Milyukov began his oppositional activity neither because of practical work in the zemstvos nor as a result of early adherence to socialism. He became involved in it mainly as a result of his academic activity. Born in 1859 into a family which belonged to the *raznochinnaya* (i.e. non-noble)* intelligentsia,[3] Milyukov decided quite early in life to become a historian. By the time he reached his early thirties, however, he found the road to academic advancement at Moscow University, his *alma mater*, blocked by his most distinguished teacher, Vasiliy Kluchevsky. Although personal incompatibility also played a role, the main bone of contention between the two was Milyukov's interpretation of Russian history.[4] In contrast to Kluchevsky, who accepted many liberal Slavophile ideas about the uniqueness of Russia's development, Milyukov held two common nineteenth-century assumptions. He believed in progress determined by the 'iron laws' of history, and in the uniform development of all societies, i.e. he believed that all societies, despite certain local variations, were subject to the same laws of evolution. He also believed in the importance of the economic factor in history.[5] Applying his general beliefs to the particular case of Russian history, he wrote in his first major historical work, *The National Economy of Russia in the First Quarter of the XVIII Century and the Reforms of Peter the Great*, that 'the Europeanization of Russia is not a product of adoption but an inevitable consequence of inner evolution,

no. 1, p. 7, italics added). Sipyagin was assassinated on 2 April 1902 and widespread peasant disturbances occurred in the provinces of Poltava and Kharkov in March–April 1902 (see *Groman*, pp. 244–5, *Osvobozhdeniye* (1902), no. 8, pp. 120–1).

[1] See *Osvobozhdeniye*, no. 1, 18 June/1 July 1902.   [2] See below.

* Literally *raznochinnyy* meant a commoner who had not attained that rank (*chin*) in government service (whether military or civilian) which carried with it ennoblement (according to the 'table of ranks' introduced by Peter the Great in 1722 and subsequently adapted to changing circumstances by later legislation). At the same time, the *raznochinnyy* had more civil rights than the *podatnoye* (poll-tax paying) estate. This was mainly because of educational achievements. For a legal and practical definition of the term *raznochinnyy* see *Brokgaus*, vol. 26, pp. 179–80.

[3] See *Milyukov* Xa, pp. 9–11 and *Fischer*, pp. 67–8.

[4] See *Milyukov* ibid. pp. 119–20, 135–8.

[5] See *Fischer*, pp. 69–70, *Milyukov* Xa, p. 192, *Osvobozhdeniye* (1902), no. 1, p. 12 and below.

which is basically the same in Europe and in Russia, and which was only delayed (in the latter) by external conditions'.[1] The completion of this work in 1892 brought to a head the crisis in relations between Milyukov and Kluchevsky. Milyukov believed that this study, which he began to write as a Master's dissertation in 1886, fulfilled the requirements for the degree of Doctor of Philosophy. He was encouraged in this view by many senior members of the Moscow University Faculty of History and Philology. including the well-known professor Paul Vinogradoff.* Kluchevsky, however, thought differently and, on his insistence, the University awarded Milyukov only a Master's degree.[2] When this decision became known, the University of St Petersburg offered to confer a PhD degree on Milyukov for a work much smaller in scope which he had previously completed.[3] He declined the offer and, according to his memoirs, decided there and then never to write a doctoral dissertation.[4] This meant that an ordinary academic career was closed to him and although he continued to teach at Moscow University, his main interest shifted to extra-mural academic activity. It was at that time that he began to work on his *Outlines of Russian Culture (Ocherki Po Istorii Russkoy Kultury)*. Simultaneously he became involved in the adult education movement and he began to deliver extra-mural lectures on current affairs in Moscow and Nizhniy Novgorod.[5] The latter activity was not to the liking of the police and at the beginning of 1895 he was arrested, dismissed from the university and exiled by administrative order to Ryazan. His crime consisted of including in his lectures material of a 'disruptive' nature.[6]

According to Milyukov's memoirs, his arrest and banishment from Moscow seemed to him at the time not so much a punishment as a liberating development. His feeling of relief stemmed from the fact that, since his break with Kluchevsky, the atmosphere of Moscow University had suffocated him.[7] But although he was aware that a university

---

[1] *Milyukov* ibid. pp. 138–9.

* Sir Paul Vinogradoff or, according to the Russian usage, Pavel Gavrilovich Vinogradov (1854–1925) was a full professor at Moscow University from 1887. In 1901 he resigned his post in the wake of the student disturbances and the government reaction. In 1903 he was elected to the Corpus Christi chair of jurisprudence at Oxford, a position he held until his death. His best-known completed works are: *Villeinage in England, The Growth of the Manor* and *English Society in the Eleventh Century*.

[2] See *Milyukov* xa, pp. 138–42 and *Kluchevsky*, vol. 8, pp. 177–83.

[3] See *Milyukov* ibid. pp. 142, 146. [4] Ibid. p. 142.

[5] See ibid. pp. 156–61. [6] Ibid. pp. 161–5 and *Milyukov* v₅, p. 108.

[7] *Milyukov* xa, pp. 166–7.

career was closed to him, he did not plunge himself fully into politics but continued his work as a historian, in so far as conditions permitted. While staying in Ryazan, he continued to work on his *Outlines of Russian Culture*, instalments of which began to appear in the 'thick' journal, *Mir Bozhiy*. Their appearance in print brought him immediate fame and the reputation of a 'Marxist historian'.[1] Then, at the beginning of 1897, he was permitted to go abroad. He spent the next two years, first in Paris, where he enlarged his knowledge of European history, and then teaching history at the Institute of Higher Education in Sofia. When, on the insistence of the Russian envoy in Bulgaria, he was relieved of this post, he set out on a fact-finding tour of the Balkans[2] (and was to return to this region in 1904, in 1912 and again in 1913).[3] The first-hand knowledge of the area which he thus acquired greatly influenced his attitude to the 'Eastern Question', especially to the Straits problem during the First World War and during his short term of office as Minister of Foreign Affairs in the first Provisional Government.[4] Much earlier, he exploited his knowledge of Bulgarian affairs, not always wisely, in order to extract greater concessions from the government.[5]

Milyukov's term of banishment came to an end and in summer 1899 he was allowed to return to Russia and to settle in St Petersburg.[6] He returned a famous man. The publication of his historical works and especially the *Outlines* had earned him the reputation of being a first-class historian of Marxist leanings. His persecution by the authorities had won him the halo of a martyr. Immediately after his arrival in the capital he was approached by representatives of apparently all the political circles, who tried to persuade him to join them. But he turned them all down out of ideological as well as practical considerations.[7]

To begin with, Milyukov was not a Marxist, not even in the sense that the 'Legal Marxists' were at that time. His Marxist reputation was derived from his belief in progress determined by the 'iron laws' of history and from his emphasis on economic factors in his historical writings. However, neither at this nor at any other time did he believe in the theory of the class struggle and the proletariat, or in socialism.[8] The constitutional–parliamentary system of Western Europe represented, for him, the highest stage in the development of human society.

---

[1] *Milyukov* ibid. pp. 166–7, 192–3. [2] Ibid. pp. 169–88.
[3] See *Milyukov* v₁, pp. 109–10; v₂, pp. 109–19; xa, pp. 223–34; xb, pp. 117–42.
[4] See *Milyukov* xb, pp. 185–7, 336–71. [5] See ibid. xa, pp. 325–9.
[6] *Milyukov* v₃, p. 115; xa, p. 188. [7] Ibid. xa, pp. 188–9, 192–3 and below.
[8] See *Milyukov* xa, pp. 219–21.

Hence he neither could nor would join any Marxist group. Secondly, Milyukov was certainly not a populist. Apart from his anti-populist conception of history and lack of belief in socialism, he differed from the populists of various shades of opinion on the question of universal suffrage. Unlike them, he did not regard universal suffrage as an article of faith.[1] These ideological differences prevented him from joining any populist group.

Milyukov's differences with the populists and the Marxists made him a most desirable ally for the zemstvo radicals. Like them, before the Congress of Activists in the Field of Agronomic Aid he was a 'pure' radical constitutionalist without commitments to extensive social change. (He was a radical since he also believed that the Russian constitution should be adopted by an elected constituent assembly or institution and not granted from above.) This was, apparently, one of the main reasons why Petrunkevich asked Milyukov, at the end of 1899 or beginning of 1900, to edit an illegal 'liberal' newspaper, before he approached Struve. Despite his ideological proximity to the zemstvo radicals, Milyukov declined the offer and his reasons were mainly practical. He was still reluctant to plunge himself wholly into politics and believed, against all odds, that he would be able to continue with his scientific work, at least part-time.[2] But the odds against him were very heavy indeed.

While still working on his Master's dissertation, Milyukov had become acquainted with Myakotin, who was then a very promising young student of Russian history at the University of St Petersburg. Despite the difference in ages (Myakotin, born in 1867, was eight years younger than Milyukov) and in academic status (Milyukov was already a lecturer) they became very close friends.[3] When, some time later, Myakotin joined the editorial board of the 'Legal–Populist' *Russkoye Bogatstvo* he introduced Milyukov to its leading members.[4] On arrival in St Petersburg in 1899, Milyukov quite naturally found his personal friends among these people and also became especially close to Peshekhonov.[5] Although Milyukov did not join the board of *Russkoye Bogatstvo* because of ideological differences, his close friendship with Myakotin and Peshekhonov nevertheless led to some political co-operation between him and the group as a whole.[6] It was apparently

[1] See *Milyukov* V3, p. 118; Xa, pp. 235–7.
[2] See *Milyukov* V3, pp. 116–17 and Xa, p. 197 and below.
[3] See *Milyukov* Xa, p. 145.
[4] *Milyukov* ibid.
[5] See *Milyukov* V3, pp. 115–16; Xa, p. 193.
[6] Ibid., ibid.

123

on the suggestion of the *Russkoye Bogatstvo* people, as well as because of his fame as a historian with Marxist leanings and as a political martyr that, soon after his arrival, he became a member of the Writers Union.[1]

Thus, *nolens volens* Milyukov found himself more and more involved in the political activities of the radical intelligentsia in the capital. Less than a year after his return from exile he found himself back in prison. The direct cause of his arrest was a speech he delivered to a student meeting commemorating the famous radical, P. L. Lavrov,[2] who died at the end of January 1900. After a short spell of interrogation, Milyukov was released from prison and ordered to leave St Petersburg until the pronouncement of the verdict. He chose to spend the time in a little town in Finland which bordered on the outskirts of the capital.[3] A year later he was joined there by Myakotin and Annenskiy, after their expulsion from St Petersburg in the wake of the Kazan Square demonstration.

It was there that the first circle of 'Friends of Liberation' was founded. Milyukov neither joined this circle nor became a member of any other organization of the Liberation Movement until May 1905 (when, on his return to Russia from the US he was elected chairman of the foundation congress of the Union of Unions).[4] To join such an organization would have meant ever-growing involvement in practical politics and the abandonment for good of his work as a historian and publicist. Milyukov was not yet prepared for this and, between arrests and interrogations, he continued with his more or less academic activities. Thus, after serving his prison term for his speech at the Lavrov memorial meeting, he went to the US in spring 1903. There he lectured at Chicago University in the summer term. Afterwards he spent a year in Europe and immediately after the end of the 'Paris Conference of Oppositional and Revolutionary Organizations of the Russian Empire' in which he played a leading role[5] he returned to the United States via Russia for another tour of lectures and to prepare his *Russia and its Crisis* for publication.[6]

Milyukov's refusal to plunge himself fully into practical politics did not mean, however, total abstention from work for the Liberation Movement. The aims of this Movement were as close as possible to

---

[1] Ibid. Xa, pp. 188–9.　　　　　　　　　[2] Ibid. Xa, pp. 193–6; V3, pp. 115–16.
[3] *Milyukov* V3, p. 116; V5, p. 110; Xa, p. 197.
[4] See *Piotrov* (unpub.), pp. 54 ff., *Sverchkov* IV, p. 150 and below.
[5] See below.　　　　　　　　　　　　　　[6] See *Milyukov* Xa, pp. 199–252.

Milyukov's own political goals and he therefore became a frequent contributor to *Osvobozhdeniye* and participated in meetings when time permitted. As a consequence, although he did not engage in practical work, Milyukov's influence in the Liberation Movement was very great. His prominent position was derived mainly from his ability to gauge the mood of the radical–democratic intelligentsia and his capacity to reflect it clearly in writing. Thus, three times – in February 1903, in March–April 1904 and again in October of that year – his contributions to *Osvobozhdeniye*[1] brought about a change in the editorial policy of this newspaper and changed the general line of the Liberation Movement. And each time the move was to the left, i.e. towards the adoption by the Liberation Movement as a whole of a more radical position. This, in its turn, each time either increased or personified the growing influence of the radical–democratic intelligentsia inside the Liberation Movement. This end-product of Milyukov's articles was not always to his liking, since it was accompanied by greater emphasis in *Osvobozhdeniye* on social demands, including universal suffrage. But these events still lay in the future. Meanwhile, Milyukov's talent for giving written expression to the wishes of the radical–democratic intelligentsia was already discernible at the foundation stage of the Liberation Movement. This talent, his ideological proximity to the zemstvo radicals at the time and his fame were apparently responsible for the fact that only he, and no other representative of the radical–democratic intelligentsia, was invited to participate in the drafting of the announcement 'From the Russian Constitutionalists'. Since this invitation, unlike Petrunkevich's earlier offer of a newspaper editorship, did not make too many demands on his time, Milyukov accepted it. By so doing he became more and more involved in the destiny of the Liberation Movement.

The programmatic announcement 'From the Russian Constitutionalists', composed by Kornilov, Milyukov, Petrunkevich and Shakhovskoy, reflected both Milyukov's 'pure' radical constitutionalism and the belief current among the founding-fathers of the Liberation Movement that their main support would come from the zemstvo milieu. As far as Milyukov was concerned, the general style as well as the argumentation found in some key passages of this document substantiate his claim of being its chief author.[2] Thus, for example, it is hardly con-

[1] See *Osvobozhdeniye*, nos. 17, 16 Feb./1 March 1903; 19 (43), 7/20 March 1904; 21 (45), 2/15 April 1904 and 57, 2/15 October 1904. See also below.

[2] See *Milyukov* xa, p. 236.

ceivable that any of the other participants would have formulated the beliefs of the founders of the Movement thus:

Free forms of political life are as little national as are the use of the alphabet or of the printing press, steam or electricity. These are merely forms of higher culture – broad and flexible enough to contain the most varied national content. The adoption of these forms becomes necessary when public life becomes so complicated that it can no longer be contained within the framework of a more primitive public structure. When such a time arrives, when a new era of history knocks at the door, it is useless to place restraints and delays in its path. It will come just the same.[1]

Similar traces of Milyukov's pen can be found in the arguments employed by the authors of the announcement in defence of the clauses dealing with the 'constituent institution' and its election.[2] But what is more significant, the announcement also reflected the desire to cater to the zemstvo milieu.

The establishment of the 'Friends of Liberation' circles constituted the first organizational expression of the alliance between the zemstvo radicals and the radical–democratic intelligentsia. Additional supporters were needed in order to transform these circles into a political movement with the help of *Osvobozhdeniye*. The founders of the Liberation Movement were faced with the basic problem of where to find them.

The aim of the Liberation Movement – the replacement of autocracy by a constitutional–democratic regime – restricted their field of choice to the milieu from which both partners in the alliance had sprung: the 'zemstvo people' and the 'classless intelligentsia,' i.e. the 'Third Element', people engaged in liberal and technical professions and urban white-collar workers.[3] They rightly assumed that these were the only two social strata in Russia at the time which were concerned with the question of political freedom.[4] But although they shared a common interest in political freedom, these two social groups were poles apart in terms of their relative levels of political consciousness and the political aspirations of their politically conscious members.

On the whole, the zemstvo milieu was still apolitical, while the vast majority of the rank-and-file zemstvo activists were still either liberal Slavophiles or moderate constitutionalists. The intelligentsia, on the other hand, was on the whole politically minded and, apart from the

---

[1] *Osvobozhdeniye*, no. 1, (18 June/1 July 1902), p. 12.   [2] See below.
[3] For statistical data on the number and professional classification of the Russian intelligentsia at the turn of the century see *Yerman* III, pp. 9–17 ff.
[4] See above and *Kuskova: Credo, Kuskova* I, p. 151. See also *Akselrod* I, pp. 3–5, 13, 23–4, III, p. 22.

small minority which belonged to or supported the revolutionary parties,[1] the great majority of the intellectuals (especially among the 'Third Element' and the St Petersburg radical intelligentsia) were radical democrats with strong socialist–populist inclinations. Their conception of a minimum demand was the destruction of autocracy through the convening of a constituent assembly elected on the basis of universal suffrage.[2] This they regarded as the only safeguard against the encroachment of the 'bourgeoisie' on the rights of the people.

By the time of the composition of 'From the Russian Constitutionalists', however, both partners in the alliance were pinning their hopes on the zemstvo activists rather than on the more politically conscious intelligentsia. There were two good reasons for this. To begin with, after the suppression of the Writers Union and the expulsion of its leaders from St Petersburg, the radical intelligentsia remained leaderless, with no possibility of expressing themselves publicly. This left the zemstvo activists in possession of the only institution in which public (i.e. political) questions could be discussed legally. Secondly, the establishment of *Beseda*, which had taken place a year earlier, had provided the zemstvo radicals for the first time with the opportunity of exerting influence over the zemstvo milieu on a national scale.

Because of their hopes of the zemstvo activists, the authors of 'From the Russian Constitutionalists' toned down their programme. They formulated their constitutional aims so as to avoid over-antagonizing the liberal Slavophiles and did not insist on the demand that all constitutional changes be achieved 'from below', i.e. against the wishes of the Tsar. They also omitted demands for universal suffrage and social reforms. The fact that Milyukov was not committed to the latter two demands made the task easier for them. As a consequence, the programmatic announcement was less radical than that of the People's Rights Party, adopted a decade earlier, and it fell far short of the expectations of the rank-and-file members of the intelligentsia wing of the 'Friends of Liberation' circles.

'From the Russian Constitutionalists'[3] opened by explaining the need for the publication of *Osvobozhdeniye*. The aim of the newspaper, according to the authors, would be to attract 'those groups in Russian society which cannot find an outlet for their feelings of indignation –

---

[1] Kuskova calculated that the number of full-time members of the SD organizations in Russia proper in 1900 was 63. See *Kuskova* v, p. 327.
[2] See *Osvobozhdeniye* (1903), no. 17, pp. 291–2.
[3] See *Osvobozhdeniye* (1902), no. 1, pp. 7–12.

neither in class nor in revolutionary struggle. We wish to represent exclusively, and be supported by, non-class public opinion'.[1] Among these groups, the authors stated, they regarded themselves as closest to the zemstvo activists. The first task of *Osvobozhdeniye* would, therefore, consist of 'working out a programme of clearly defined political demands, on the basis of which the zemstvo group would be able to co-operate with other social groups'.[2]

Immediately afterwards, they qualified their statement on the 'clearly defined political demands'. The only definite demands they were prepared to voice at this time were that the Tsar should grant personal freedom to the population and replace the autocratic arbitrary regime with a representative form of government based on legality. To go farther than that, i.e. to define exactly 'the competence of the representative institution, its relation to the prerogative, the electoral rights of the population, the responsibility of the government, legislative initiative[3] . . . and to include demands for economic, financial, cultural and administrative reforms, labour legislation and to touch on the agrarian question'[4] seemed to the authors of the announcement too dangerous because of the negative effect it might have on the attitude of the zemstvo activists to the Liberation Movement. They hastened to add that they knew that 'in the zemstvo milieu there are already people who have answers to these questions, answers which are identical with those of the Russian intelligentsia'.[5] Nevertheless, the vast majority of zemstvo activists did not yet favour either universal suffrage or social reforms.

After thus explaining the limitations they imposed upon themselves, the authors of the announcement spelled out their main demands in detail. First they enumerated those demands which were acceptable to the vast majority of the zemstvo activists, including the liberal Slavophiles. These were the demands concerning the rights of the individual:[6]

personal freedom, guaranteed by *independent law courts*. From this principle there follows the abolition of arbitrary arrests and searches, administrative expulsions, extraordinary courts and similar procedure;

equality of all before the law, and, as a consequence, the abolition of all national, religious and estate discriminations and privileges. The application of this principle to the Russian situation would lead to several things: to the equalization of the rights of the peasantry with the rights of other estates (the abolition of corporal punishment is self-evident in this context), to the abolition of 'odious privileges'

[1] Ibid. p. 7. [2] Ibid. [3] Ibid. p. 8.
[4] Ibid. p. 10. [5] Ibid. [6] Ibid. p. 9, italics in text.

of the nobility in the fields of administration, zemstvo representation and estate landownership, and to the recognition of the right to complete freedom of religion and conscience and to the abolition of limitations in the sphere of personal and property rights of Jews and Poles;

freedom of the press, the right to publish periodicals without prior notification and deposits, the abolition of censorship and the responsibility of the press before law-courts;

freedom of assembly and association;
the right to petition.

The authors then turned to the much more sensitive question of the replacement of autocracy by a constitutional regime. They knew very well that the liberal Slavophiles were firmly opposed to constitutionalism. They also realized that on this question, the liberal Slavophiles could still count on the support of the majority of rank-and-file zemstvo activists. In order to avoid over-antagonizing them and thus losing, at least for the time being, a large number of potential supporters, the authors formulated their main constitutional aim in very cautious terms. They deliberately avoided such loaded words as 'constitution', 'parliament' or 'legislative assembly' and merely demanded the establishment of a *'non-class representative body*, to form part of a supreme sovereign permanent institution, with the rights of legislation, of approving the budget and of controlling the administration'.[1]

After thus formulating their constitutional aim the authors of the announcement turned to the trickiest problem of them all, namely the question of means. On this, they knew, the views of the vast majority of the potential supporters of the Liberation Movement in the zemstvo milieu stood in flagrant contradiction to their own and to those held by the radical–democratic intelligentsia and the zemstvo radicals. The former, including the moderate constitutionalists, still aimed at convincing the Tsar of the necessity of granting reforms from above. The latter would have nothing to do with autocracy and stood for the introduction of a fully fledged constitutional regime through the convening of a constituent assembly. This divergence of views confronted the authors of the announcement with what amounted, in reality, to an insoluble dilemma. They tried to solve it by verbal means.

The authors tried to bridge the basic difference of views by using a formula which would give minimal offence to all concerned. Thus they deliberately avoided the loaded term 'constituent assembly'.[2] For the

---

[1] *Osvobozhdeniye* ibid. p. 10, italics in original.
[2] See, for example, *Milyukov* Xa, p. 236.

above-outlined reforms to succeed, they explained, their implementation should not be left to the discredited bureaucracy but ought to be entrusted to a 'constituent institution'.[1] To make this statement as palatable as possible to the moderate constitutionalists, they hastened to add that the convening of such an institution did not imply a revolutionary change in the regime. On the contrary, their aim was to convince the sovereign of the need to call the 'constituent institution' into being and thus guarantee the preservation of legal continuity.[2] Secondly they suggested that it should be composed mainly of representatives of the zemstvos and town dumas[3] and not elected by universal suffrage. After thus trying to placate the moderates, the authors turned their attention to the radicals. They did not touch on the question of how the 'institution' should be called into being but rather concentrated their efforts on making its composition as congenial as possible to the radicals by reconciling them to the omission of the principle of universal suffrage. They did this by putting forward three arguments. To begin with (and Milyukov's knowledge of political conditions in Bulgaria as well as his non-commitment to universal suffrage were, apparently, chiefly responsible for this[4]) they explained that an institution composed of representatives of zemstvos and other existing elected bodies was preferable to one resulting from a general election under the conditions then prevailing in backward Russia. In their own words, such a composition was preferable to 'that "leap into the dark" implied by any attempt at ad hoc elections where *government pressure would be unavoidable*, and where it would be difficult to determine the mood of *social strata unaccustomed to political life*'.[5]

Secondly, they explained, the role of the 'constituent institution created by such an imperfect and unusual method would, by its very nature, be brief and temporary...the political role of the representatives of the elected local government institutions should be limited to the...working-out of a charter, (i.e. a constitution), an electoral law and constitutional guarantees'.[6]

Lastly, they reminded the radicals that the majority of those zemstvo activists who had participated in the Congress of Activists in the Field of Agronomic Aid to the Local Economy, held a year earlier, had subscribed to a democratic programme. Hence, they argued, the radicals could be sure that a 'constituent institution' composed of

---

[1] *Osvobozhdeniye* ibid. p. 12.   [2] Ibid. p. 10.
[3] Ibid. pp. 11–12.   [4] See *Milyukov* V3, p. 118.
[5] *Osvobozhdeniye* ibid. p. 11, italics added.   [6] Ibid. p. 12.

zemstvo representatives would adopt a democratic constitution which would guarantee that the next representative assembly would be elected by universal suffrage. In their own words

the most difficult and responsible question which it (the constituent institution) will have to decide will be that concerning the election law: and there is scant reason to believe that it will decide this question less democratically than was proposed in the zemstvo discussions regarding the *all-class canton and the small zemstvo unit* in the eighties and at the present time... Then their (the representatives of the zemstvos) role will be finished and they will give way to representatives of the people, *elected by a proper vote according to the (new) law*.[1]

On this note Kornilov, Milyukov, Petrunkevich and Shakhovskoy ended the announcement. Immediately afterwards it was discussed by several circles of 'Friends of Liberation' and by a 'significant conference in Moscow'[2] (undoubtedly a meeting of the constitutional members of *Beseda*, which was then holding its spring, 1902 session). After its final approval, Shakhovskoy and N. N. Lvov brought the announcement to Struve. They also took with them 100,000 roubles, and the first issue of *Ozvobozhdeniye*, containing the text of the announcement, appeared shortly afterwards.

As might have been expected, the attempt of the authors of 'From the Russian Constitutionalists' to settle the basic differences between the moderates and the radicals was doomed to failure. The liberal Slavophiles could not be persuaded to subscribe to a programme which included a constitutional clause, even though it appeared in disguise. The moderate constitutionalists could not be won over to the idea of a constituent assembly by such means as the replacement of the term 'assembly' by 'institution' or by the logically unsound assurances that its convocation was compatible with 'legal continuity'. At the same time it was impossible to induce the rank-and-file radicals to accept a 'constituent institution' which was not elected by universal suffrage merely by asking them to emulate the stand of the majority of zemstvo representatives at the Congress of Activists in the Field of Agronomic Aid. They were fully aware, as were the authors of the announcement, that at that time the majority of zemstvo activists did not accept the democratic platform of Shakhovskoy and his supporters. Hence there was no guarantee that, in the unlikely event that the Tsar convened a 'constituent institution' composed of zemstvo representatives, it would adopt a democratic constitution. For all these reasons, 'From the Rus-

---

[1] Ibid., italics added.   [2] See *Shakhovskoy* IV, p. 86.

sian Constitutionalists' became politically obsolete a few months after its publication. But at the time of its composition, things looked quite different. The response of the zemstvo activists in late spring 1902 to the public opinion campaign initiated by *Beseda* seemed to justify the decision of the founding-fathers of the Liberation Movement to pin their hopes on them.

6

The organization of public opinion

The founding-fathers of the Liberation Movement regarded public opinion as their chief weapon in their struggle against autocracy. Since the suppression of the Writers Union in March 1901 had left the zemstvos as the only public institutions in which a public opinion campaign could be launched, the project was entrusted to the zemstvo radicals. The foundation of *Beseda* and its growing domination by the constitutionalists from the beginning of 1901 created a very convenient instrument for the fulfilment of this task. Thus it was through *Beseda* that the zemstvo radicals began to organize the public opinion campaign in the zemstvo milieu.

The first plenary meeting of *Beseda* after the tumultuous events of February–March 1901 was apparently held in June of that year. Its moderate members, and the liberal Slavophiles especially, must have regarded these events with grave concern, since they provided additional proof, if such was still needed, that unless the government could be induced to grant extensive concessions in the very near future, the situation might deteriorate into a full-scale revolutionary upheaval. In the prevailing mood of the meeting it cannot have been very difficult for the zemstvo radicals to spur the circle to immediate action. It was apparently on their initiative that *Beseda* concluded its June meeting by sending a circular letter to many zemstvo activists urging them to raise general political questions at the forthcoming (winter 1901–2) session of the provincial zemstvo assemblies. This circular subsequently became known as the 'Letter from the Veteran Zemstvo Members'.[1]

---

[1] The letter is reprinted in full in *Lenin* II, vol. 6, pp. 349–55. An English translation (which is misleading in many places) is found in *Lenin* I, vol. 6, pp. 151–6. A summary of the letter and of the demands is found in *Veselovskiy* VI, p. 555. Contrary to the claims of a modern historian of Russian liberalism, this letter was not, apparently, composed at an *Osvobozhdeniye* meeting in Moscow in June 1901 (see *Fischer* p. 126), but at a *Beseda* meeting which was held there at the same time. There are at least two indicators which point to this conclusion: first, the practical demands it contained. According to E. P. Mikheyeva, the (minimum) political programme of *Beseda* as a whole included the following demands: (1) equalization of the peasants' rights with the rights of other estates; (2) removal of adminis-

133

As befitted a *Beseda* composition addressed to rank-and-file activists, considerable space was devoted to criticism of Witte's economic policies and of his anti-zemstvo campaign, and no reference was made to constitutional demands. Despite this omission, the general tone of the Letter was quite militant, and this can be seen as an indication of the growing exasperation of the moderate members of *Beseda* (especially Shipov and his followers) with government policies. This process, which had begun in the second half of the 1890s, was greatly exacerbated by the events which occurred after the Congress of Activists in the Field of Agronomic Aid.

The 'Letter from the Veteran Zemstvo Members'[1] opened with an all-out onslaught on the economic policy of the government. First, it described the insufferable plight of the peasantry, which was being ruined by '*the chronic crop failures* and the intolerable burden of taxation in the form of *land redemption payments* (and) non-assessable taxes'.[2] Then it specifically attacked the government's (i.e. Witte's) industrialization policy. Like the State Comptroller, Lobko, a short time later,[3] the authors of the Letter blamed the government's protectionist policies, which were enabling 'foreign and domestic adventurers to plunder the productive forces of our country' for the agricultural crisis and the industrial and financial recession which Russia was then undergoing.[4]

The authors next directed their fire against the government's policy of repression. They bitterly attacked the increasingly heavy yoke of censorship, and declared that in Russia 'arbitrariness, senseless and cruel, alone raises its voice authoritatively, and reigns over the boundless expanses of our ravaged, humiliated and outraged native land'.[5]

trative tutelage over the peasants and the abolition of passport restrictions; (3) an increase in the independence of the zemstvos; (4) restoration of their non-class character to the zemstvo institutions; (5) greater freedom to discuss economic questions publicly; (6) introduction of income tax (*Mikheyeva*, p. 243). These were exactly the demands put forward in the letter.

Secondly, the letter was addressed to members of zemstvo assemblies and it is now known that in 1902 zemstvo meetings were organized by *Beseda*. See *Chermenskiy* II, pp. 46, 47.

[1] See *Lenin* I, vol. 6, pp. 151–6, *Lenin* II, vol. 6, pp. 349–55.
[2] Ibid. vol. 6, p. 151, italics added. A most illuminating analysis of the contrast between the economic insignificance of the redemption payments to the state at the turn of the century and the intolerable burden they imposed on the peasants is found in *Gerschenkron* I, pp. 780–83. Gerschenkron quite rightly points out that 'the government clung to the redemption payments because their cessation would have removed the legal ties holding the *obshchina* together' (ibid. p. 781).
[3] See above.
[4] See *Lenin* II, vol. 6, pp. 349–350 and above.
[5] *Lenin* ibid. p. 350.

blies at their forthcoming sessions, if not to adopt outright constitutional resolutions, at least to include in their petitions demands for the inclusion of elected zemstvo representatives in central government institutions. Their resolution, presented by K. K. Arsenyev, was backed not only by the zemstvo radical leaders (Petrunkevich and N. N. Lvov) but also by the moderate constitutionalists (Count P. A. Geyden and A. A. Savelyev, chairman of the Nizhniy Novgorod provincial zemstvo board and chronicler of the zemstvo movement in 1904–5,[1] and others). It called upon the zemstvo assemblies to include in their petitions the demand

that the government should invite to the central state institutions dealing with bill-drafting zemstvo representatives to be elected for that purpose by the provincial zemstvo assemblies...and that these representatives should part cipate in the drafting of all bills *and not only those concerned with local affairs.*[2]

Although this resolution did not contain any constitutional demands (and did not, in fact, go further than the political programme of the liberal Slavophiles), Shipov still opposed it vehemently, on grounds of expediency. He explained that in the given conditions the government would certainly see in this resolution an attempt to change the existing regime. There could be little doubt that in its prevailing state of mind, it would reject it out of hand and the only practical result would be an increase in friction between the government and the zemstvos, a development he was constantly trying to prevent.[3] As a result of Shipov's opposition, Arsenyev's draft resolution as well as the first part of Shipov's resolution were put to the vote. And for the last time in the annals of the zemstvo movement, Shipov carried the day (by a majority of 15 to 13).[4]

Shipov's opposition even to a resolution as mild as that presented by Arsenyev and his ability to win a majority at the congress proved to be the last straw which broke the back of the 'policy of moderation'. Some

---

[1] See *Bibliography*.   [2] *Shipov* II, p. 218, italics added.   [3] Ibid.
[4] *Shipov* II, pp. 219–20. According to Shipov, F. A. Golovin and Prince Peter D. Dolgorukov voted for his resolution and against Arsenyev's. As far as Golovin was concerned, one can attribute this to the fact that as a member of the Moscow provincial zemstvo board, he felt a strong loyalty to Shipov which prevented him from voting against him. This, however, does not apply to Dolgorukov. The only explanation for his siding with Shipov at this congress that the author of this book can contemplate, lies in his unwillingness to strain relations with the liberal Slavophiles mainly for tactical reasons. It should be remembered that it was he who (in 1902) opposed a motion to declare *Osvobozhdeniye* a mouthpiece of *Beseda* (see above). It was he again who, at the end of August 1903 (four months after this congress and a month after the Schaffhausen Conference) opposed a motion to declare *Beseda* part of the future Constitutionalist Party (see *Chermensky* II, p. 46).

171

of the initiators of this policy had already come to the conclusion that it had outlived its usefulness and that as a result of the consolidation in the ranks of the radical intelligentsia some three months previously, and its growing oppositional outspokenness a change of course was demanded. The first to state this openly in the pages of *Osvobozhdeniye* was Paul Milyukov.

On his way to the United States via Western Europe,[1] Milyukov wrote an article (published in *Osvobozhdeniye* no. 17, 16 February/1 March 1903) in which he attacked Struve's editorial policy in general and his call to the liberals to organize themselves into a party in particular. He explained that 'an organization presupposes a certain amount of homogeneity of the elements which are going to compose it and the existence of a definite aim which is understood and accepted by all of them'.[2] When *Osvobozhdeniye* was established, Milyukov continued (and thus, as it were, trying to provide an excuse for his own role in the adoption of the policy of 'wooing the moderates'), these conditions had been thought to exist. But during the short period of the paper's existence, it had become clear that they had disappeared. Under the impact of the worsening political crisis a process of differentiation had commenced in the zemstvo milieu. 'Hence', he stated, 'it has become evident that *Osvobozhdeniye* caters for too wide a range of people and strata of the population to be able to express exactly the mood and opinion of each of them'.[3] Struve's main mistake, Milyukov continued, consisted in not realizing these changes in time. From Struve's writings it appeared he believed that people like Shipov, Stakhovich and Khomyakov were not yet constitutionalists but that they were going to become such. Hence his readiness to count them among the liberals. This, however, was a fallacy:

They are supporters of autocracy, albeit in its political–Slavophile utopian form, on principle and out of conviction and not by accident or because of lack of consciousness...But if the 'idealists of autocracy'...are supposed to work together with the constitutionalists for the achievement of the same goal, this goal cannot, surely, be constitutional reform.[4]

Moreover, he continued, besides the question of aims there was also the question of means. No political organization could be effective without deciding on means. If the constitutionalists had not yet made up their minds on this, then the Slavophiles had. And then, like

[1] See *Milyukov* Xa, p. 239 and above.
[2] *Osvobozhdeniye* (1903), no. 17, p. 289 (Miluykov signed his article S.S.).
[3] *Osvobozhdeniye* ibid.   [4] Ibid. p. 290.

Peshekhonov before him but with much less justification (since in the meantime it had become apparent that Shipov was not prepared to be Plehve's puppet) Milyukov attacked Shipov personally for his organization of the zemstvo 'rump conference'.[1]

We know that Shipov's political role – and whether he did it consciously or unconsciously does not matter – consisted in replacing the big Moscow congress of liberal zemstvo people by a gathering of available elements, among whom he succeeded in organizing a 'prudent majority' from whom Mr Plehve had apparently promised to seek support in his struggle against the 'imprudent minority'.[2]

Even if Plehve accepted the full programme of the liberal Slavophiles and advised Nicholas to convene a *zemskiy sobor*, its Slavophile members would 'perform the role of some kind of political protective coloration...while the reins of "strong rule" will remain firmly in Plehve's hands'.[3]

Was it possible, Milyukov asked, to include such 'liberals' in the future liberal party? His answer was positive but only on one condition – that the future liberal party be prepared to be inactive in the forthcoming political struggle. Then and only then 'could we calmly reconcile ourselves to *zemskiy sobor* as the slogan of the party and with Messrs Stakhovich and Shipov as its members'.[4] If the liberals intended to play an important role in the fight for the destruction of autocracy then they should not accept the liberal Slavophiles into their ranks. If this entailed the postponement of the establishment of the liberal party, Milyukov went on, then so be it.

There definitely exists a need to think and care about a liberal organization. But because of the current mood of the zemstvo milieu, one must proceed very carefully: it would be more than enough if at this stage it were possible to organize a *strong nucleus of the party to consist of convinced constitutionalists.* To win over immediately a whole army of unreliable and partly suspicious elements round a vague slogan would be, to our mind, a great tactical error, weakening the energy of the movement and destroying its moral significance.[5]

The fact that Milyukov had joined the ranks of the critics of the policy of 'wooing the moderates' and the growing importance of the radical intelligentsia finally convinced Struve of the futility of continuing to defend this policy on the pages of *Osvobozhdeniye.* Although he was not yet prepared to accept Milyukov's advice not to hurry with the establishment of a party and to concentrate his efforts on the

[1] See above, p. 150. [2] *Osvobozhdeniye* ibid p. 290. [3] Ibid.
[4] Ibid. [5] Ibid. p. 291, italics added.

organization of a 'constitutional nucleus' (advice followed by the leaders of the Liberation Movement a few months later[1]) yet in his reply to Milyukov Struve showed that he had changed his mind about the composition of the liberal party.

Struve began his reply to Milyukov, which appeared in the same issue of *Osvobozhdeniye* as the latter's critical article, by pointing out that by deliberately remaining silent on many points of the Programme, the authors of 'From the Russian Constitutionalists' (Milyukov included) were as guilty of moderation as he was himself.[2] But he agreed with Milyukov that during the short span of *Osvobozhdeniye's* existence two profound changes had taken place and the time had arrived to take them into account. The first was the growing disrepute of the liberal Slavophiles for which they had only themselves to blame: 'If the slogans of the Slavophiles appear to a growing number of sections of the *Russian intelligentsia* to be not only thoughtless but also suspect, it is first of all because of the political flabbiness and cowardice of those who appear as their heralds.'[3] This by itself, he explained, would have sufficed to exclude the liberal Slavophiles from the future liberal party. But there existed a more important reason for their exclusion, connected with the second change.

Struve explained that when the first issue of *Osvobozhdeniye* appeared, the founding-fathers of the Liberation Movement had believed that the zemstvo activists would become the backbone of the liberal party. Hence the toning-down of their programme. Since then the situation had changed and they now expected 'the Russian classless intelligentsia...to constitute the chief cadres of the liberal party'.[4] But if this was to be so, then the programme of the future liberal party '*must be openly and positively constitutional*[5]... This excludes the possibility of bringing into the party people who believe in the so-called Slavophile ideology.'[6] But he made it clear that the radical intelligentsia were not only constitutionalists but also democrats with strong socialist inclinations. As a consequence, two important corrections needed to be introduced into the programme of the Liberation Movement as expounded in the announcement 'From the Russian Constitutionalists'.

First, it was necessary to make the programme '*openly and positively democratic*...(Hence) it must contain *a clear declaration in favour of universal suffrage*'.[7] Such a declaration was needed because

---

[1] See below.   [2] See *Osvobozhdeniye* ibid. p. 291.   [3] Ibid., italics added.
[4] Ibid. p. 292.   [5] Ibid. p. 291, italics in text.   [6] Ibid.
[7] Ibid. pp. 291–2, italics in text.

over the period of *Osvobozhdeniye's* existence, we have become convinced that the demand for universal suffrage, the justness of which we essentially never doubted, corresponds to the political consciousness of those strata of the Russian classless intelligentsia which stand in the first ranks of the fighters for Russia's political liberation.[1]

The second correction would have to bring about a clarification of the Liberation Movement's *'attitude to social questions – the agrarian and the workers'*.[2] Struve explained that 'when political reforms are being carried out, it is impossible to avoid the question: *cui bono?* For whose benefit?'[3] This question was of special interest to the Russian classless intelligentsia 'which, because of tradition and because of its sympathies, is closely connected with the masses and their interests'.[4] Therefore, in order 'that zemstvo noblemen and representatives of the classless intelligentsia from the "Third Element" as well as peasants who have achieved political consciousness will be able to work harmoniously side by side in the ranks of the liberal party',[5] its programme should not only be democratic but should also 'include a wide and well-composed plan of social reforms'.[6]

As events were soon to show, Milyukov's and Struve's attacks on the liberal Slavophiles did not lead to their exclusion from the Liberation Movement. Nor was it yet possible, as Struve still hoped, to transform this movement into a constitutional–democratic party. Nevertheless, that Struve now abandoned the policy of 'wooing the moderates' increasingly led to *Osvobozhdeniye* becoming a mouthpiece of the radical wing of the Liberation Movement. This development corresponded to the rapid ascendency of the radical intelligentsia in the Liberation Movement and made possible the establishment of a radical–democratic nucleus (the Union of Liberation) which soon became the co-ordinating centre of the whole movement. The decision to consolidate the Liberation Movement on the above lines was reached by its leaders at the Schaffhausen Conference, held in the second half of July 1903.[7] On the eve of the conference, Struve published an article in *Osvobozhdeniye* in which he further developed his ideas on the need for the Liberation Movement to adopt a 'well-composed plan of social reforms'.

The article was ostensibly written as an analysis of 'The German Elections'[8] in June 1903 (in which the four liberal splinter parties, forming the 'progressive bloc', lost about a fifth of their seats in the

---

[1] Ibid. p. 292. [2] Ibid., italics in text. [3] Ibid. [4] Ibid. [5] Ibid.
[6] Ibid. [7] See below. [8] *Osvobozhdeniye* (1903), no. 1 (25), pp. 3–5.

Reichstag while the Social Democrats increased their strength by more than 40 per cent.)* In reality the article was essentially an exposition of his views on the 'worker and peasant questions'. Its tone reflected both the further radicalization and consolidation of the ranks of the radical intelligentsia of St Petersburg in the wake of the Kishinev pogrom and the growing annoyance of the radicals with the zemstvo activists following the constitutionalist defeat at the April 1903 zemstvo congress.

Struve began by explaining to his readers that 'the collapse of German liberalism was an inevitable consequence of the fact that, at the most critical moment of its existence, it severed its living bond with the social and political tasks of democracy...By supporting Bismarck ...German liberalism showed its political bankruptcy.'[1] The German liberals, he continued, justified their support of Bismarck by pointing to the class-character of the German SD Party. But what, Struve asked rhetorically, did its class character mean in reality? His answer echoed almost word for word the one given by the People's Rights Party a decade earlier except for his substitution of the term 'social-democracy' for 'plain' socialism.

If we start to assess its practical programme from the point of view of the social and political interests it expresses, then we will see immediately that the struggle for its achievement is simply dictated by the demands of common morality and justice. Hence the irresistible power of social-democratic principles. (But) these principles are identical with the pure ideas of liberalism, as a political system of freedom and equality...Hence, a liberalism which opposes social-democracy repudiates its own principles and adopts a class point of view in favour of privilege.[2]

Struve ended the exposition of his theory of radical–democratic liberalism with a warning and a piece of advice:

A liberalism which in our time, the time of the conscious appearance of vast popular masses on the historical scene, refrains from putting forward clear and resolute political and social-democratic demands, will fail in the task of defending the interest of social progress and will find itself lagging behind the flag. Hence, no important stream of the Russian Liberation Movement can by-pass the agrarian and workers' questions. It has to include courageously in its programme demands for serious social reform to the advantage of the peasants and the workers. It is not yet too late for the Russian liberals to adopt a correct political position – not against but *alongside and in union with social-democracy*.[3]

* In the wake of the 1903 elections, the number of 'progressive' deputies in the Reichstag decreased from 49 to 33, while the number of SD deputies increased from 56 to 81.
[1] *Osvobozhdeniye* ibid. p. 4.　　　　[2] Ibid.　　　　[3] Ibid. p. 5, italics added.

8

The formation of the Union of Liberation

The prolonged polemics in the pages of *Osvobozhaeniye* on questions of programme and organization, prepared the ground for a decision on these issues. For that purpose the founding-fathers of the Liberation Movement convened a conference 'out of the reach of the tsarist police'. It was held at Schaffhausen, a Swiss town nearby Lake Constance, on 20–22 July (2–4 August) 1903 and was attended by twenty-one people.[1] They represented between them the leadership of two out of the three main groups composing the radical–constitutionalist nucleus of the movement. (The leaders of the *Russkoye Bogatstvo* group did not participate.) The radical–democratic intelligentsia was represented by[2] N. A. Berdyayev, V. Ya. Bogucharskiy, S. N. Bulgakov, S. L. Frank, B. A. Kistyakovskiy, E. D. Kuskova, S. N. Prokopovich and P. B. Struve. (All of these had in the past belonged to the Marxist camp for shorter or longer periods.) The zemstvo radicals were represented by Prince Peter D. Dolgorukov, N. N. Kovalevskiy, N. N. Lvov, I. I. Petrunkevich, F. I. Rodichev, Prince D. I. Shakhovskoy, V. I. Vernadskiy and D. E. Zhukovskiy. Of the remaining five delegates there were three who apparently represented the academic liberal–constitutionalist circles of the two capitals, I. M. Grevs (Professor of History at St Petersburg University); S. A. Kotlyarevsky (Professor of Law at the University of Moscow); P. I. Novgorodtsev (Professor of Philosophy at the same university), and A. S. Petrunkevich (ex-Countess Panin, Petrunkevich's wife) and V V. Vodovozov.

The two main topics discussed at the Schaffhausen Conference were

[1] Since no protocol of the Conference has, apparently, survived, the main source of information on it are the writings of four of its participants: *Frank*, pp. 37–9, *Petrunkevich* II, pp. 337–9 (both give lists of participants), *Shakhovskoy* IV, pp. 105–7 and *Vodovozov* III, p. 6. See also: *Belokonskiy* II, p. 164, *Brokgaus supp.* II, p. 354, *Cherevanin* I, p. 285. Recent accounts are found in *Chermenskiy* II, pp. 51–2, *Fischer*, pp. 140–3, *Smith* (unpub.), pp. 131–2. The last two were apparently unaware of the existence of Frank's biography of Struve, hence their account is less comprehensive than the circumstances allow.

[2] The following list of participants is based on *Chermenskiy* ibid., *Frank* ibid. and *Petrunkevich* II, p. 338.

177

the organizational form which the Liberation Movement should adopt and its programme. As regards the former, Struve apparently found himself almost completely isolated in his demand that the movement should be transformed into a liberal party. Almost all the other leaders had realized by then that the existing set of common beliefs which had made possible the establishment of the 'Friends of Liberation' circles was not sufficient for the establishment of a party. Apart from the deep divisions of opinion on the 'peasant question', there were other differences which made the establishment of a party a dubious proposition.

The zemstvo radicals were divided among themselves on at least two questions: the monarchical principle and universal suffrage. N. N. Lvov was both a strong supporter of monarchy (albeit constitutional)[1] and an opponent of the principle of universal suffrage,[2] although he supported the demand for the convocation of a constituent assembly. And although the question of monarchy was not important at the time, the question of universal suffrage was cardinal because it was connected with relations with the radical–intelligentsia wing of the Liberation Movement and with the 'worker and peasant problems'.[3] All the other leaders of the zemstvo radicals, and especially Shakhovskoy, were completely committed to universal suffrage and endorsed the programme of social reforms as propagated by Struve in *Osvobozhdeniye*. They were at variance, however, with a fairly large number of leaders of the radical intelligentsia on the scope of these reforms.[4] And these differences became even more pronounced in the lower echelons of the movement among the rank-and-file followers on both sides.[5]

[1] See *Shakhovskoy* IV, pp. 86–7. For Lvov's identification see *Petrunkevich* II, p. 337.

[2] *Frank*, p. 39.

[3] It was mainly because of disagreements on these questions that Lvov left the Cadets, at the end of the first Duma and joined the 'Party of Peaceful Renovation' (*Partiya Mirnogo Obnovleniya*) which was headed by Count P. A. Geyden, D. N. Shipov, M. A. Stakhovich and Lvov himself. (See *Dan* VII, p. 196, *Shipov* II, pp. 514–16.) N. N. Lvov's 'turn to the right' may also have had something to do with the appearance of Stolypin on the political scene. They were good friends from their days together in Saratov, where Stolypin was governor and Lvov marshal of the nobility for many years.

[4] It was partly because of these differences that the St Petersburg 'Big Group' voted against the decision to establish the Cadet Party at the fourth and last congress (23–25 August 1905) of the Union of Liberation and it refused to join this party when it was established in October 1905. (See *Bez-Zaglaviya*, no. 1, p. 7, *Gessen* I pp. 212–13, *Kuskova* XIV, pp. 85–7, *Milyukov* Xa, pp. 307–8, 338–42, *Shakhovskoy* IV, pp. 163–9, *Yordanskiy*, p. 70 and below.

[5] According to Kuskova the gap between the rank-and-file supporters of the two sides was so great at the time of the establishment of the Union of Liberation that in many towns two branches of the Union existed side by side, one composed of zemstvo constitutionalists and the other of radical intellectuals. (See *Kuskova* VIII, pp. 389–90.)

Bulgakov declared, in those cases where the landowners refused to co-operate '*the state should have the right of compulsory expropriation*'.[1] The transfer of land from the nobles to the peasants, Bulgakov continued, would satisfy the latter's immediate economic needs. But it would not, in itself, guarantee the transformation of the peasantry into a 'truly democratic rural class'. In order to achieve this, the free regime would have to make the peasants owners of the land they cultivated. At the same time it would have to prohibit the accumulation of capital in the form of land acquisition. As a result, Bulgakov apparently believed, the peasantry would be transformed from the breeding-ground of *Pugachovshchina* into a bulwark of the new democratic order. Therefore, he declared, '*the political liberation of Russia must accomplish the liberation of the peasants by recognizing the principle that the right of ownership of land belongs to those who cultivate it*'.[2]

After approving the 'social clauses' of the recommended programme, the Schaffhausen Conference ended its debates and the majority of its participants hurried back to Russia. There they utilized two public gatherings (The Agricultural Congress of the Northern Region held in Yaroslavl during the second part of August and the All-Russian Husbandry Exhibition held in Kharkov in September), attended by many zemstvo activists, members of the 'Third Element' and radical intellectuals from the capital, for propagating the organizational decisions of the Schaffhausen Conference. Particularly active in this field were Peter Dolgorukov and Shakhovskoy.[3] Soon afterwards, apparently during the fourth meeting of *Beseda* in 1903, its constitutionalist members met at the home of Yu. A. Novosiltsev and on 8 November established the Union of Zemstvo Constitutionalists.[4] (Novosiltsev was a district marshal of the nobility and a member of *Beseda*. All the future meetings of this Union were also held at his home and were known at the time as the 'Novosiltsev Congresses'.)

---

[1] Ibid., italics in original.　　　　　　　　　　　　　　　[2] Ibid., italics in original.

[3] See *Belokonskiy* II, pp. 174–5, *Shakhovskoy* IV, pp. 107–8, *Tyrkova* II, pp. 119–23 and *Veselovskiy* VI, pp. 580–1. See also *Fischer*, p. 144.

[4] *Shakhovskoy* ibid. and *Veselovskiy* ibid. The assumption that the constituent congress of the Union of Zemstvo Constitutionalists was composed of the constitutionalist 'caucus' of *Beseda* is based on the following circumstantial evidence; the number of zemstvo activists who participated in the foundation congress did not exceed the thirty mark (*Shakhovskoy* ibid.), the almost exact number of constitutionalist members of *Beseda*. It was held in Moscow in late autumn (the eve of the zemstvo assembly sessions), the time and place of the fourth *Beseda* meeting of the year. All its known leaders – Prince Pavel D. Dolgorukov, Peter's twin, Count P.A. Geyden, Yu.A. Novosiltsev and A.A. Stakhovich (see: *Budberg* II, p. 70, *Chermenskiy* II, p. 52 and *Shakhovskoy* IV, p. 108) – were moderate-constitutionalist members of *Beseda*.

The aim of the new constitutionalist organization, as defined by the foundation congress, was 'to conduct a campaign in favour of the constitutionalist platform (universal suffrage and a legislative assembly) at the sessions of the zemstvo assemblies and in the all-zemstvo congresses'.[1] But the meeting was held too late in the year to enable it to intervene in the zemstvo campaign organized by the April zemstvo congress.[2] It decided, therefore, to postpone the constitutional campaign inside the zemstvo milieu to the next year and in the meantime to work for the consolidation of the newly established organization.[3]

Some of the leaders of the radical–democratic intelligentsia attended the meeting in Novosiltsev's house as observers. Together with the zemstvo radicals, they finalized there and then the arrangements for the convening of the constituent congress of the Union of Liberation.[4] It was decided to hold it in St Petersburg at the beginning of January 1904. The time and place were undoubtedly chosen because of the two mass conventions of radical intellectuals (predominantly 'Third Element') which were going to be held then in the capital: The Ninth Congress of the Pirogov Society of Russian Doctors and the Third Congress of Activists in the Field of Technical Education. The latter was particularly highly attended (more than 3,000 delegates participated) and extreme in its anti–government manifestations. It was closed by the police on the night of 4/5 January 1904 and its principal radical leaders were arrested.[5] (One of them, apparently G. A. Falbork,[6] participated in the foundation congress of the Union of Liberation.[7])

The arrival of thousands of radical intellectuals from the provinces shielded the fifty or so delegates to the foundation congress of the Union of Liberation from the watchful eye of the secret police. The congress was in session for four days (2–5 January 1904) and its participants represented 'Friends of Liberation' groups in 23 cities and towns (St Petersburg, Moscow, Chernigov, Yaroslavl, Yurev, Kharkov, Kiyev, Kostroma, Kursk, Nizhniy Novgorod, Odessa, Orel, Samara,

---

[1] *Chermenskiy* II, p. 52.

[2] Apparently more than two-thirds of zemstvo assemblies heeded its advice and inserted its two demands in their petitions (see *Belokonskiy* II, pp. 164, 177–83).

[3] See *Shakhovskoy* IV, p. 109. [4] See ibid. pp. 108–9.

[5] See *Osvobozhdeniye* (1904), no. 17 (41), pp. 309–11.

[6] Ibid. p. 311. Falbork, as well as another congress delegate who was arrested a few days later – V.I. Charnoluskiy (ibid.) – later played an important role in the Union of Unions. The lawyer P.N. Pereverzev, who was active in the defence of the victims of the Kishinev pogrom (ibid.), was arrested together with them. It was apparently his brother – V.N. Pereverzev – who was later chairman of the all-powerful Railway Union.

[7] *Shakhovskoy* IV, p. 110.

Saratov, Simferopol, Smolensk, Tambov, Tiflis, Tula, Vladimir, Vologda, Vyatka). The majority of the delegates belonged to the radical-democratic intelligentsia. Apart from Struve and Petrunkevich (who was prohibited from entering St Petersburg) all the participants in the Schaffhausen Conference were present. They, together with the *Russkoye Bogatstvo* group, played the leading role in the congress.[1]

The divisions of opinion among the radical members of the Liberation Movement were fully reflected at the congress. After approving the organizational decisions of the Schaffhausen Conference, apparently unanimously, it ran into a prolonged debate on the name of the proposed union. Many rank-and-file radical intellectuals still remembered Struve's early attempt at moderation and were opposed to the name Union of Liberation because of its resemblance to that of the journal *Osvobozhdeniye* (Liberation).[2] When the original name was eventually approved a much more important controversy arose concerning the programme.

The suggestions of the Schaffhausen Conference were opposed from two sides. N. N. Lvov and some of the rank-and-file zemstvo radicals objected to the introduction of democratic and social clauses into the programme of the Union. In their opposition to the latter they found support in an unexpected quarter: among the delegates with 'populist inclinations'[3] (the *Russkoye Bogatstvo* group and its rank-and-file supporters). These delegates, according to Shakhovskoy, wanted the Union to be a purely 'society' organization which would 'refrain from working among the workers and the peasants'.[4] There can be little doubt that the *Russkoye Bogatstvo* group's opposition to the extension of the Union's activity beyond society and hence to the 'social clauses' was caused by their objection to the 'private ownership clause' in the agrarian programme as elaborated by the Schaffhausen Conference. But while opposing this point they supported the demand for universal suffrage and political democracy. As a consequence, Lvov's opposition to the latter was overruled, though no mention was made of what apparently seemed to the majority the ultimate democratic regime – a republic.

The programme, as finally adopted by the congress, was outspoken on political questions. It demanded the replacement of autocracy by a constitutional–democratic regime, to be based on what soon became

---

[1] In the absence of minutes, *Shakhovskoy* IV, pp. 110–17, remains the only source of direct information on the foundation congress of the Union of Liberation.
[2] *Shakhovskoy* IV, p. 110.   [3] Ibid. p. 111.   [4] Ibid.

known as the 'four-tail formula': universal, equal and direct suffrage and secret ballot. It also recognized the right of the minorities to self-determination, but was very vague on social questions. It read as follows.[1]

> The first and main aim of the Union of Liberation is the political liberation of Russia. Considering political liberty in even its most minimal form as completely incompatible with the absolutist character of the Russian monarchy, the Union will seek before all else the abolition of autocracy and the establishment in Russia of a constitutional regime. In determining the concrete forms in which a constitutional regime can be realized in Russia, the Union of Liberation will make all efforts to have the political problems resolved in the spirit of extensive democracy. Above all, it recognizes as fundamentally essential that the principles of *universal equal and direct suffrage and secret ballot* be made the basis of the political reform. Putting the political demands in the forefront, the Union of Liberation recognizes as essential the definition of its attitude in principle to the social–economic problems created by life itself. In the realm of social–economic policy, the Union of Liberation will follow the same basic principle of democracy, making the direct goal of its activity the *defence of the interests of the toiling masses*.
>
> In the sphere of national questions, the Union recognizes the right to self-determination of different nationalities entering into the composition of the Russian state. In relation to Finland, the Union supports the demand for the restoration of the constitutional status (*Gosudarstvenno-Pravovoye Polozheniye*) which existed in that country until its illegal abrogation during the current reign.[2]

After approving the programme, the congress began to debate the statutes of the Union. Here again the debates were quite fierce, but when the organizers of the congress had agreed to make important changes in their draft proposal, the statutes were approved unanimously.[3] According to the final version, the Union of Liberation was to be composed of autonomous local and professional groups. The supreme organ of the Union was to be a congress composed of elected representatives of each group belonging to it. The congress was to decide on the Union's general policy and to elect its only executive body – the Council. The Council was to conduct all the general affairs of the Union between congresses. It was to summon a congress at

---

[1] Because of the paralysing effect which the outbreak of war with Japan (26/27 January 1904) exerted at first on the Liberation Movement (see below), the programme of the Union of Liberation together with the announcement about its existence was made public only ten months after its approval by the congress. See: *Listok Osvobozhdeniya*, no. 17, 19 November/2 December 1904 and *Osvobozhdeniye* (1904), no. 61 (Leader).

[2] English translation based on *Fischer*, p. 147. Italics added.

[3] *Shakhovskov* IV, p. 113.

least once a year. It had the right to co-opt new members unanimously and to enter into agreements with other parties and groups etc.[1]

Despite the radical intelligentsia's domination of the congress, the Council elected by it was chosen according to the principle of parity. Five of its ten members represented the radical–democratic intelligentsia and five the zemstvo radicals.[2] The intelligentsia contingent included: N. F. Annenskiy (who was elected vice-chairman of the Council), V. Ya. Bogucharskiy, S. N. Bulgakov, A. V. Peshekhonov and S. N. Prokopovich. The zemstvo radicals were represented by I. I. Petrunkevich (who was chairman of the Council), Prince Peter D. Dolgorukov, N. N. Kovalevskiy, N. N. Lvov and Prince D. I. Shakhovskoy. The parity between both sides was not affected by the profound personal changes in the composition of the Council which occurred immediately after the congress ended. First, the Council co-opted two additional members – a moderate zemstvo constitutionalist, I. V. Luchitskiy, and a radical intellectual, L. I. Lutugin[3] (one of the future leaders of the Union of Unions). Then, at the beginning of February 1904, Annenskiy was arrested and exiled to the provinces[4] while S. N. Bulgakov, for unknown reasons, was apparently unable to fulfil his duties as a member of the Council. The final composition of the Council of the Union of Liberation in spring 1904, was therefore, as follows:[5] zemstvo radicals and constitutionalists: I. I. Petrunkevich (chairman), Prince Peter D.

---

[1] Ibid.

[2] According to Shakhovskoy, the first council elected by the constituent congress was composed of ten members: 'Four of them were men of letters from St Petersburg, four zemstvo activists who were considered Moscow men, although only one of them lived in Moscow, one a professor from Kiyev and one a zemstvo man from Kharkov . . . One of the ten was elected in absentia, because he was prohibited from entering St Petersburg and hence could not participate in the congress.' (*Shakhovskoy* IV, p. 117.) These were later identified by name (see *B.S.E.* I, vol. 52, col. 342, *M.S.E.* vol. 8, cols 257–8). The four 'men of letters from St Petersburg' were Annenskiy, Bogucharskiy, Peshekhonov and Prokopovich (all of them had belonged in the past to the Peoples' Right Party). The four 'Moscow men' were Dolgorukov (the only one who lived in Moscow), Lvov, Shakhovskoy and Petrunkevich (the one who 'was elected in absentia') The 'professor from Kiyev' was Bulgakov, who was at the time Professor of Political Economy in the local Polytechnic (see *Brokgaus supp.* I, pp. 330–1), and the 'zemstvo man from Kharkov' was Kovalevskiy.

[3] See *Milyukov* Xa, p. 266 and *Fischer*, p. 150.

[4] The direct cause of Annenskiy's arrest was a speech which he delivered at the funeral of N.K. Mikhaylovskiy (who died on the night of 27 January 1904). After his arrest, however, charges connected with his activity as head of the 'culinary committee' were brought against him. The fact that 18 volumes of *Osvobozhdeniye* were found in his possession apparently clinched the case and he was expelled from St Petersburg. (See *Brokgaus supp.* I, p. 122, *Listok Osvobozhdeniya* (1904), no. 1, p. 4, *Osvobozhdeniye* (1904), no. 18 (42), p. 328.)

[5] See *Chermenskiy* II, p. 53 and *Kuskova* XVIIIa.

The formation of the Liberation Movement

Dolgorukov, N. N. Kovalevskiy, I. V. Luchitskiy, N. N. Lvov and Prince D. I. Shakhovskoy (apart from Luchitskiy, all zemstvo-radicals of old standing). Radical intelligentsia: V. Ya. Bogucharskiy, V. V. Khizhnyakov, E. D. Kuskova, L. I. Lutugin, A. V. Peshekhonov and S. N. Prokopovich (apart from Lutugin, all ex-members of the Peoples' Rights Party).

The maintenance of the principle of parity in the composition of the Council undoubtedly reflected the awareness on the part of the leaders of the radical intelligentsia that the zemstvo milieu was still very important for the Liberation Movement and was to remain so for a long time to come. At the same time the predominant position of the radical intellectuals was institutionalized immediately after the congress ended, when the Council decided at its first meeting to establish a 'technical group'.[1] This group consisted of Bogucharskiy, Khizhnyakov, Kuskova (who were also members of the Council of the Union), N. D. Sokolov and half a dozen or so of the lesser-known radical intellectuals of the capital.[2] At the time of its foundation the main task of the 'technical group' was to smuggle into Russia copies of *Osvobozhdeniye* and other illegal literature published by Struve. (Kuskova, who had been active in this field since *Osvobozhdeniye* began to appear,[3] and who together with Struve had established a very successful network for its transportation through Finland and distribution inside Russia,[4] became the dominant figure in that group.) But very soon afterwards it greatly expanded the scope of its political activity.

The 'technical group', together with the radical intellectual wing of the Council of the Union of Liberation, soon formed the St Petersburg branch of this organization, which became known as the 'Big Group'.[5] With the outbreak of the Russo-Japanese war and the intensification of the internal political crisis, the 'Big Group', which later formed the nucleus of the Union of Unions, became the real nerve-

[1] See *Shakhovskoy* IV, p. 117.
[2] *Milyukov* Xa, p. 266.
[3] See above and *Kuskova* VIIIa, *Tyrkova* II, pp. 131–2, 162, 164–5. For Struve's contribution to the establishment of this network see *Pipes* IIa, pp. 348–53.
[4] The organization for smuggling *Osvobozhdeniye* into Russia failed badly only once. This happened when E.N. Anichkov and Ariadna Borman (later Tyrkova-Williams) were arrested on the Russo-Finnish border carrying 400 copies of the paper. And even this was not so much a failure of the organization as of Anichkov who did not know how to behave as a 'smuggler'. (See *Tyrkova* ibid. pp. 133–69, *Osvobozhdeniye* (1904), no. 24(48), pp. 426–31; no. 25(49), pp. 449–50; no. 51, pp. 28–9; no. 52, pp. 39–41; *Pravo* (1904), no. 27, cols 1431–3, *Shakhovskoy* IV, pp. 123–5).
[5] See *Belokonskiy* II, p. 93.

centre of the Union of Liberation and hence of the Liberation Movement as a whole. But the war, which opened up these opportunities,
seemed at first to endanger the very existence cf the newly consolidated
Liberation Movement.

able substitute for the banned Union, and which was almost identical in composition with the 'Finnish circle' of 'Friends of Liberation'.[1] The main activity of this committee was the organization of literary dinners (hence its nickname) where political questions were discussed and resolutions adopted. These dinners sometimes reached the dimensions of mass banquets with 200 or more people participating,[2] and their proceedings and resolutions were regularly reported in *Osvobozhdeniye*.[3] Through their discussion of politics and adoption of resolutions, the literary dinners proved an excellent means of consolidating the ranks of the radical intelligentsia in the capital under the leadership of the 'Finnish circle'. The process was greatly accelerated by the shock of the Kishinev pogrom.

The official anti-Jewish policy of the autocratic regime, which had derived much of its strength from the anti-Semitism of the last two tsars, became particularly virulent after Plehve became Minister of the Interior. Either because he wanted to please his master or because he believed that the anti-Semitism of the illiterate masses constituted a barrier to socialist ideas, Plehve conducted a vicious anti-Jewish policy. He and the Tsar justified this policy by referring to the prominent place the Jews were occupying in the revolutionary movement.[4] Exactly a year after his nomination, Plehve's policies bore bitter fruit. On 6 April 1903 – Easter Day – the mob was given free rein in Kishinev (Bessarabia) and for two days they plundered and destroyed Jewish property and murdered any Jewish man, woman or child, they could lay their hands on. These atrocities, in which hundreds of Jews lost their lives or were badly injured, could not have taken place but for the connivance of the local authorities who did not intervene because Plehve had ordered the governor not to resort to force against the rioting mob.[5] The barbaric events shocked enlightened public opinion in Russia and gravely damaged the already tarnished image of autocracy abroad. In order to understand the magnitude of the shock, one must remember that the Kishinev pogrom occurred before the world had witnessed the horrors of Stalin's mass terror or the atrocities of the Nazi Holocaust. The first to react publicly inside Russia to the bloody events were

---

[1] See *Belokonskiy* II, p. 93, *Shakhovskoy* IV, p. 102. For the composition of the 'Finnish circle' see above.
[2] See *Shakhovskoy* ibid.
[3] See, for example, *Osvobozhdeniye* (1903), no. 19, p. 325.
[4] See, for example, *Kuropatkin* I, p. 43.
[5] See *Charques*, pp. 82–3 and *Osvobozhdeniye* (1903), no. 22, pp. 377–80; no. 24, pp. 452–3 (Gorky's article).

the radical intellectuals of St Petersburg. A fortnight after the Kishinev pogrom, on 20 April, the 'culinary committee' organized a meeting of writers and radical intellectuals, attended by more than 200 people. After discussing the barbaric events and condemning the anti-Semitic mob and the connivance of the authorities, it adopted a resolution emphasizing the close connection between these events and the existing regime and ended with the following declaration: 'The Jewish question, exactly like all the other sore questions of the current Russian reality, can be solved only by the free and independent activity of society. In this sense, the Jewish question becomes identical with the all-Russian question and only together with it can it find its radical solution.'[1] With the benefit of hindsight, one need hardly emphasize the over-simplicity of this declaration. But at the time, things looked quite different and the meeting which adopted it proved a landmark on the road to consolidation of the ranks of the St Petersburg radical intelligentsia.

Among those who participated in this meeting and signed its resolution[2] were familiar figures from the 'Finnish circle' and other 'Liberators' (Annenskiy, Bogucharskiy, Kuskova, N. K. Mikhaylovskiy, Peshekhonov, D. E. Zhukovskiy), as well as some new names, such as E. V. Anichkov (who was soon to become famous because of his trial).[3] Other signatories included people who became famous with the establishment of the Union of Unions and/or the St Petersburg Soviet in 1905: V. I. Charnoluskiy (member of the Central Bureau of the Union of Unions and of its secretariat);[4] L. I. Lutugin (member of the first Council of the Union of Liberation, organizer of the all-powerful Union of Engineers, its representative in the Central Bureau of the Union of Unions, member of its secretariat and one of the founders of the People's Socialist Party in 1906);[5] N. D. Sokolov (one of the organizers of the Union of Advocates, its representative in the Central Bureau of the Union of Unions and apparently the author of Order No. 1 in 1917);[6] D. F. Sverchkov (Bogucharskiy's nephew, one of the leaders of the important Union of Clerks and Book-keepers, its representative in the Central Bureau of the Union of Unions and one of the

[1] *Osvobozhdeniye* (1903), no. 23, p. 420.
[2] A full list of participants and signatories appears in *Osvobozhdeniye* ibid.
[3] See *Osvobozhdeniye* (1904), no. 24 (48), pp. 426–31; no. 25 (49), pp. 449–50; no. 51, pp. 28–9; no. 52, pp. 39–41. See also below.
[4] See *Kirpichnikov* I, pp. 140–1.
[5] Ibid. and *Chermenskiy* II, p. 55; *Syn Otechestva* (1905), no. 184, p. 3; *Narodno-Sotsialisticheskoye Obozreniye*, p. 16.
[6] *Kirpichnikov* ibid.; *Milyukov* Xa, p. 339; *Chamberlin* I, p. 86. See also below.

organizers of the St Petersburg Soviet);[1] and V. V. Svyatlovskiy (member of the Central Bureau of the Union of Unions, organizer and historian of the Russian trade union movement).[2]

While the 'culinary committee' was consolidating the ranks of the St Petersburg radical intelligentsia, the 'Third Element' was putting the professional conferences to good use for voicing oppositional demands.[3] The most important among these was the Teachers Congress or, according to its official title, 'Congress of Representatives of Teachers Relief Societies'. This gathering was held in Moscow on 28 December 1902 – 6 January 1903.[4] Its chairman was Prince Pavel D. Dolgorukov and the vice-chairman was his twin brother, Prince Peter D. Dolgorukov. Despite all the administration's efforts, the Congress was, from the very beginning, transformed into a prolonged oppositional rally in which the audience took an active part, booing the few conservative delegates and loudly cheering the avalanche of oppositional speakers. The radical–oppositional mood of the Congress was reflected in its decisions, which had almost nothing to do with the professional needs of teachers for the discussion of which the Congress had ostensibly been convened. The resolutions included the following demands: the abolition of corporal punishment; the establishment of the small zemstvo units; the introduction of zemstvo institutions into all parts of Russia; and the 'strengthening of the principle of self-government' (which, when translated into ordinary language, meant the establishment of a representative regime in Russia).

The consolidation of the ranks of the radical intelligentsia and its ever-growing mood of opposition soon overshadowed developments in the zemstvo milieu. Even after the public opinion campaign, the majority of zemstvo activists were still lagging far behind the intelligentsia in radicalism and were to do so until the Liberation Movement disintegrated. This fact, which was well known to the leaders of the Liberation Movement, manifested itself during the zemstvo congress of 24–25 April 1903.[5] This gathering, held in St Petersburg during a conference on fire insurance, was much smaller in scope than its May 1902 predecessor. All in all, 28 zemstvo activists from 17 provinces participated, half of them chairmen of provincial zemstvo boards.[6] It

[1] *Kirpichnikov* ibid.; *Sverchkov* I, pp. 19, 107. See also below.
[2] *Kirpichnikov* ibid. and below. [3] See *Veselovskiy* III, p. 306.
[4] A full report of the proceedings of the Congress appears in *Osvobozhdeniye* (1903), no. 19, pp. 333–5. For its importance to the Liberation Movement see *Shakhovskoy* IV, p. 99.
[5] See *Belokonskiy* II, pp. 153–64 and *Shipov* II, pp. 215–21.
[6] A full list of participants is found in *Shipov* II, pp. 219–20.

was convened not by the organizational bureau chosen by its May predecessor, but by Shipov personally,[1] who was apparently in a hurry to bring about a united zemstvo stand on the Tsar's Manifesto of 26 February 1903.[2] Although Shipov was well aware that in this document Nicholas wanted to convey to the population his determination to preserve autocracy unreformed[3] he was nevertheless prepared to find in those clauses dealing with the need to adapt the central and local administrative organs to the changed circumstances a good pretext for reopening negotiations between the zemstvos and the government. Despite all his disappointments, Shipov still clung to his policy which aimed at reconciling both sides.

On convening the Congress, Shipov made it clear that the question of the zemstvo attitude to the 'reform proposals included in the February Manifesto' would be its main topic. Since he knew that the constitutionalist contingent to the Congress intended to adopt a different attitude, he refused to take the chair in order to have a free hand in the anticipated struggle. The Congress, therefore, chose Prince D. I. Shakhovskoy as its chairman[4] and began to debate the question of the proper attitude to the February Manifesto. Shipov submitted a resolution which called upon all the zemstvo assemblies to adopt at their coming sessions identical petitions, requesting of the government: first,

that all those bills to be drafted according to the Manifesto of 26 February and concerned with local affairs, should be submitted for preliminary consideration to the provincial zemstvo assemblies.[5]

Secondly, that in the future,

when ministers invite members of zemstvo boards to participate in conferences, consultations etc., they should (*a*) send invitations to all the provincial zemstvos; (*b*) invite only people elected for that purpose; (*c*) inform the zemstvos beforehand of the topics to be discussed at the particular conference etc., so that the assemblies will be able to give their elected representatives suitable instructions.[6]

The second part of Shipov's draft resolution was acceptable to all participants in the Congress. Not so the first. The constitutionalist contingent, led by I. I. Petrunkevich, regarded the unexpected convening of the Congress as an opportunity to induce the zemstvo assem-

---

[1] *Shipov*, ibid. p. 215.
[2] The text of the Manifesto may be found, among other places, in *Pravo* (1903), no. 10, front p. and cols. 675–6.
[3] See *Shipov* II, pp. 203–5.   [4] See ibid. p. 216.   [5] Ibid. p. 218.   [6] Ibid. p. 220.

blies at their forthcoming sessions, if not to adopt outright constitutional resolutions, at least to include in their petitions demands for the inclusion of elected zemstvo representatives in central government institutions. Their resolution, presented by K. K. Arsenyev, was backed not only by the zemstvo radical leaders (Petrunkevich and N. N. Lvov) but also by the moderate constitutionalists (Count P. A. Geyden and A. A. Savelyev, chairman of the Nizhniy Novgorod provincial zemstvo board and chronicler of the zemstvo movement in 1904–5,[1] and others). It called upon the zemstvo assemblies to include in their petitions the demand

that the government should invite to the central state institutions dealing with bill-drafting zemstvo representatives to be elected for that purpose by the provincial zemstvo assemblies...and that these representatives should participate in the drafting of all bills *and not only those concerned with local affairs.*[2]

Although this resolution did not contain any constitutional demands (and did not, in fact, go further than the political programme of the liberal Slavophiles), Shipov still opposed it vehemently, on grounds of expediency. He explained that in the given conditions the government would certainly see in this resolution an attempt to change the existing regime. There could be little doubt that in its prevailing state of mind, it would reject it out of hand and the only practical result would be an increase in friction between the government and the zemstvos, a development he was constantly trying to prevent.[3] As a result of Shipov's opposition, Arsenyev's draft resolution as well as the first part of Shipov's resolution were put to the vote. And for the last time in the annals of the zemstvo movement, Shipov carried the day (by a majority of 15 to 13).[4]

Shipov's opposition even to a resolution as mild as that presented by Arsenyev and his ability to win a majority at the congress proved to be the last straw which broke the back of the 'policy of moderation'. Some

---

[1] See *Bibliography*. [2] *Shipov* II, p. 218. italics added. [3] Ibid.
[4] *Shipov* II, pp. 219–20. According to Shipov, F. A. Golovin and Prince Peter D. Dolgorukov voted for his resolution and against Arsenyev's. As far as Golovin was concerned, one can attribute this to the fact that as a member of the Moscow provincial zemstvo board, he felt a strong loyalty to Shipov which prevented him from voting against him. This, however, does not apply to Dolgorukov. The only explanation for his siding with Shipov at this congress that the author of this book can contemplate, lies in his unwillingness to strain relations with the liberal Slavophiles mainly for tactical reasons. It should be remembered that it was he who (in 1902) opposed a motion to declare *Osvobozhdeniye* a mouthpiece of *Beseda* (see above). It was he again who, at the end of August 1903 (four months after this congress and a month after the Schaffhausen Conference) opposed a motion to declare *Beseda* part of the future Constitutionalist Party (see *Chermenskiy* II, p. 46).

of the initiators of this policy had already come to the conclusion that it had outlived its usefulness and that as a result of the consolidation in the ranks of the radical intelligentsia some three months previously, and its growing oppositional outspokenness a change of course was demanded. The first to state this openly in the pages of *Osvobozhdeniye* was Paul Milyukov.

On his way to the United States via Western Europe,[1] Milyukov wrote an article (published in *Osvobozhdeniye* no. 17, 16 February/1 March 1903) in which he attacked Struve's editorial policy in general and his call to the liberals to organize themselves into a party in particular. He explained that 'an organization presupposes a certain amount of homogeneity of the elements which are going to compose it and the existence of a definite aim which is understood and accepted by all of them'.[2] When *Osvobozhdeniye* was established, Milyukov continued (and thus, as it were, trying to provide an excuse for his own role in the adoption of the policy of 'wooing the moderates'), these conditions had been thought to exist. But during the short period of the paper's existence, it had become clear that they had disappeared. Under the impact of the worsening political crisis a process of differentiation had commenced in the zemstvo milieu. 'Hence', he stated, 'it has become evident that *Osvobozhdeniye* caters for too wide a range of people and strata of the population to be able to express exactly the mood and opinion of each of them'.[3] Struve's main mistake, Milyukov continued, consisted in not realizing these changes in time. From Struve's writings it appeared he believed that people like Shipov, Stakhovich and Khomyakov were not yet constitutionalists but that they were going to become such. Hence his readiness to count them among the liberals. This, however, was a fallacy:

They are supporters of autocracy, albeit in its political–Slavophile utopian form, on principle and out of conviction and not by accident or because of lack of consciousness...But if the 'idealists of autocracy'...are supposed to work together with the constitutionalists for the achievement of the same goal, this goal cannot, surely, be constitutional reform.[4]

Moreover, he continued, besides the question of aims there was also the question of means. No political organization could be effective without deciding on means. If the constitutionalists had not yet made up their minds on this, then the Slavophiles had. And then, like

---

[1] See *Milyukov* xa, p. 239 and above.
[2] *Osvobozhdeniye* (1903), no. 17, p. 289 (Miluykov signed his article S.S.).
[3] *Osvobozhdeniye* ibid.
[4] Ibid. p. 290.

Peshekhonov before him but with much less justification (since in the meantime it had become apparent that Shipov was not prepared to be Plehve's puppet) Milyukov attacked Shipov personally for his organization of the zemstvo 'rump conference'.[1]

We know that Shipov's political role – and whether he did it consciously or unconsciously does not matter – consisted in replacing the big Moscow congress of liberal zemstvo people by a gathering of available elements, among whom he succeeded in organizing a 'prudent majority' from whom Mr Plehve had apparently promised to seek support in his struggle against the 'imprudent minority'.[2]

Even if Plehve accepted the full programme of the liberal Slavophiles and advised Nicholas to convene a *zemskiy sobor*, its Slavophile members would 'perform the role of some kind of political protective coloration...while the reins of "strong rule" will remain firmly in Plehve's hands'.[3]

Was it possible, Milyukov asked, to include such 'liberals' in the future liberal party? His answer was positive but only on one condition – that the future liberal party be prepared to be inactive in the forthcoming political struggle. Then and only then 'could we calmly reconcile ourselves to *zemskiy sobor* as the slogan of the party and with Messrs Stakhovich and Shipov as its members'.[4] If the liberals intended to play an important role in the fight for the destruction of autocracy then they should not accept the liberal Slavophiles into their ranks. If this entailed the postponement of the establishment of the liberal party, Milyukov went on, then so be it.

There definitely exists a need to think and care about a liberal organization. But because of the current mood of the zemstvo milieu, one must proceed very carefully: it would be more than enough if at this stage it were possible to organize a *strong nucleus of the party to consist of convinced constitutionalists*. To win over immediately a whole army of unreliable and partly suspicious elements round a vague slogan would be, to our mind, a great tactical error, weakening the energy of the movement and destroying its moral significance.[5]

The fact that Milyukov had joined the ranks of the critics of the policy of 'wooing the moderates' and the growing importance of the radical intelligentsia finally convinced Struve of the futility of continuing to defend this policy on the pages of *Osvobozhdeniye*. Although he was not yet prepared to accept Milyukov's advice not to hurry with the establishment of a party and to concentrate his efforts on the

[1] See above, p. 150.   [2] *Osvobozhdeniye* ibid p. 290.   [3] Ibid.
[4] Ibid.   [5] Ibid. p. 291, italics added.

organization of a 'constitutional nucleus' (advice followed by the leaders of the Liberation Movement a few months later[1]) yet in his reply to Milyukov Struve showed that he had changed his mind about the composition of the liberal party.

Struve began his reply to Milyukov, which appeared in the same issue of *Osvobozhdeniye* as the latter's critical article, by pointing out that by deliberately remaining silent on many points of the Programme, the authors of 'From the Russian Constitutionalists' (Milyukov included) were as guilty of moderation as he was himself.[2] But he agreed with Milyukov that during the short span of *Osvobozhdeniye's* existence two profound changes had taken place and the time had arrived to take them into account. The first was the growing disrepute of the liberal Slavophiles for which they had only themselves to blame: 'If the slogans of the Slavophiles appear to a growing number of sections of the *Russian intelligentsia* to be not only thoughtless but also suspect, it is first of all because of the political flabbiness and cowardice of those who appear as their heralds.'[3] This by itself, he explained, would have sufficed to exclude the liberal Slavophiles from the future liberal party. But there existed a more important reason for their exclusion, connected with the second change.

Struve explained that when the first issue of *Osvobozhdeniye* appeared, the founding-fathers of the Liberation Movement had believed that the zemstvo activists would become the backbone of the liberal party. Hence the toning-down of their programme. Since then the situation had changed and they now expected 'the Russian classless intelligentsia...to constitute the chief cadres of the liberal party'.[4] But if this was to be so, then the programme of the future liberal party '*must be openly and positively constitutional*[5]... This excludes the possibility of bringing into the party people who believe in the so-called Slavophile ideology.'[6] But he made it clear that the radical intelligentsia were not only constitutionalists but also democrats with strong socialist inclinations. As a consequence, two important corrections needed to be introduced into the programme of the Liberation Movement as expounded in the announcement 'From the Russian Constitutionalists'.

First, it was necessary to make the programme '*openly and positively democratic*...(Hence) it must contain *a clear declaration in favour of universal suffrage*'.[7] Such a declaration was needed because

---

[1] See below. [2] See *Osvobozhdeniye* ibid. p. 291. [3] Ibid., italics added.
[4] Ibid. p. 292. [5] Ibid. p. 291, italics in text. [6] Ibid.
[7] Ibid. pp. 291–2, italics in text.

over the period of *Osvobozhdeniye's* existence, we have become convinced that the demand for universal suffrage, the justness of which we essentially never doubted, corresponds to the political consciousness of those strata of the Russian classless intelligentsia which stand in the first ranks of the fighters for Russia's political liberation.[1]

The second correction would have to bring about a clarification of the Liberation Movement's '*attitude to social questions – the agrarian and the workers*'.[2] Struve explained that 'when political reforms are being carried out, it is impossible to avoid the question: *cui bono*? For whose benefit?'[3] This question was of special interest to the Russian classless intelligentsia 'which, because of tradition and because of its sympathies, is closely connected with the masses and their interests'.[4] Therefore, in order 'that zemstvo noblemen and representatives of the classless intelligentsia from the "Third Element" as well as peasants who have achieved political consciousness will be able to work harmoniously side by side in the ranks of the liberal party',[5] its programme should not only be democratic but should also 'include a wide and well-composed plan of social reforms'.[6]

As events were soon to show, Milyukov's and Struve's attacks on the liberal Slavophiles did not lead to their exclusion from the Liberation Movement. Nor was it yet possible, as Struve still hoped, to transform this movement into a constitutional–democratic party. Nevertheless, that Struve now abandoned the policy of 'wooing the moderates' increasingly led to *Osvobozhdeniye* becoming a mouthpiece of the radical wing of the Liberation Movement. This development corresponded to the rapid ascendency of the radical intelligentsia in the Liberation Movement and made possible the establishment of a radical–democratic nucleus (the Union of Liberation) which soon became the co-ordinating centre of the whole movement. The decision to consolidate the Liberation Movement on the above lines was reached by its leaders at the Schaffhausen Conference, held in the second half of July 1903.[7] On the eve of the conference, Struve published an article in *Osvobozhdeniye* in which he further developed his ideas on the need for the Liberation Movement to adopt a 'well-composed plan of social reforms'.

The article was ostensibly written as an analysis of 'The German Elections'[8] in June 1903 (in which the four liberal splinter parties, forming the 'progressive bloc', lost about a fifth of their seats in the

---

[1] Ibid. p. 292.   [2] Ibid., italics in text.   [3] Ibid.   [4] Ibid.   [5] Ibid.
[6] Ibid.   [7] See below.   [8] *Osvobozhdeniye* (1903). no. 1 (25), pp. 3–5.

Reichstag while the Social Democrats increased their strength by more than 40 per cent.)* In reality the article was essentially an exposition of his views on the 'worker and peasant questions'. Its tone reflected both the further radicalization and consolidation of the ranks of the radical intelligentsia of St Petersburg in the wake of the Kishinev pogrom and the growing annoyance of the radicals with the zemstvo activists following the constitutionalist defeat at the April 1903 zemstvo congress.

Struve began by explaining to his readers that 'the collapse of German liberalism was an inevitable consequence of the fact that, at the most critical moment of its existence, it severed its living bond with the social and political tasks of democracy...By supporting Bismarck ...German liberalism showed its political bankruptcy.'¹ The German liberals, he continued, justified their support of Bismarck by pointing to the class-character of the German SD Party. But what, Struve asked rhetorically, did its class character mean in reality? His answer echoed almost word for word the one given by the People's Rights Party a decade earlier except for his substitution of the term 'social-democracy' for 'plain' socialism.

If we start to assess its practical programme from the point of view of the social and political interests it expresses, then we will see immediately that the struggle for its achievement is simply dictated by the demands of common morality and justice. Hence the irresistible power of social-democratic principles. (But) these principles are identical with the pure ideas of liberalism, as a political system of freedom and equality...Hence, a liberalism which opposes social-democracy repudiates its own principles and adopts a class point of view in favour of privilege.²

Struve ended the exposition of his theory of radical–democratic liberalism with a warning and a piece of advice:

A liberalism which in our time, the time of the conscious appearance of vast popular masses on the historical scene, refrains from putting forward clear and resolute political and social-democratic demands, will fail in the task of defending the interest of social progress and will find itself lagging behind the flag. Hence, no important stream of the Russian Liberation Movement can by-pass the agrarian and workers' questions. It has to include courageously in its programme demands for serious social reform to the advantage of the peasants and the workers. It is not yet too late for the Russian liberals to adopt a correct political position – not against but *alongside and in union with social-democracy*.³

* In the wake of the 1903 elections, the number of 'progressive' deputies in the Reichstag decreased from 49 to 33, while the number of SD deputies increased from 56 to 81.
¹ *Osvobozhdeniye* ibid. p. 4.   ² Ibid.   ³ Ibid. p. 5, italics added.

176

8

The formation of the Union of Liberation

The prolonged polemics in the pages of *Osvobozhdeniye* on questions of programme and organization, prepared the ground for a decision on these issues. For that purpose the founding-fathers of the Liberation Movement convened a conference 'out of the reach of the tsarist police'. It was held at Schaffhausen, a Swiss town nearby Lake Constance, on 20–22 July (2–4 August) 1903 and was attended by twenty-one people.[1] They represented between them the leadership of two out of the three main groups composing the radical–constitutionalist nucleus of the movement. (The leaders of the *Russkoye Bogatstvo* group did not participate.) The radical–democratic intelligentsia was represented by[2] N. A. Berdyayev, V. Ya. Bogucharskiy, S. N. Bulgakov, S. L. Frank, B. A. Kistyakovskiy, E. D. Kuskova, S. N. Prokopovich and P. B. Struve. (All of these had in the past belonged to the Marxist camp for shorter or longer periods.) The zemstvo radicals were represented by Prince Peter D. Dolgorukov, N. N. Kovalevskiy, N. N. Lvov, I. I. Petrunkevich, F. I. Rodichev, Prince D. I. Shakhovskoy, V. I. Vernadskiy and D. E. Zhukovskiy. Of the remaining five delegates there were three who apparently represented the academic liberal–constitutionalist circles of the two capitals, I. M. Grevs (Professor of History at St Petersburg University); S. A. Kotlyarevskiy (Professor of Law at the University of Moscow); P. I. Novgorodtsev (Professor of Philosophy at the same university), and A. S. Petrunkevich (ex-Countess Panin, Petrunkevich's wife) and V. V. Vodovozov.

The two main topics discussed at the Schaffhausen Conference were

[1] Since no protocol of the Conference has, apparently, survived, the main source of information on it are the writings of four of its participants: *Frank*, pp. 77–9, *Petrunkevich* II, pp. 337–9 (both give lists of participants), *Shakhovskoy* IV, pp. 105–7 and *Vodovozov* III, p. 6. See also: *Belokonskiy* II, p. 164, *Brokgaus supp.* II, p. 354, *Cherevania* I, p. 285. Recent accounts are found in *Chermenskiy* II, pp. 51–2, *Fischer*, pp. 140–3, *Smith* (unpub.), pp. 131–2. The last two were apparently unaware of the existence of Frank's biography of Struve, hence their account is less comprehensive than the circumstances allow.

[2] The following list of participants is based on *Chermenskiy* ibid., *Frank* ibid. and *Petrunkevich* II, p. 338.

177

the organizational form which the Liberation Movement should adopt and its programme. As regards the former, Struve apparently found himself almost completely isolated in his demand that the movement should be transformed into a liberal party. Almost all the other leaders had realized by then that the existing set of common beliefs which had made possible the establishment of the 'Friends of Liberation' circles was not sufficient for the establishment of a party. Apart from the deep divisions of opinion on the 'peasant question', there were other differences which made the establishment of a party a dubious proposition.

The zemstvo radicals were divided among themselves on at least two questions: the monarchical principle and universal suffrage. N. N. Lvov was both a strong supporter of monarchy (albeit constitutional)[1] and an opponent of the principle of universal suffrage,[2] although he supported the demand for the convocation of a constituent assembly. And although the question of monarchy was not important at the time, the question of universal suffrage was cardinal because it was connected with relations with the radical–intelligentsia wing of the Liberation Movement and with the 'worker and peasant problems'.[3] All the other leaders of the zemstvo radicals, and especially Shakhovskoy, were completely committed to universal suffrage and endorsed the programme of social reforms as propagated by Struve in *Osvobozhdeniye*. They were at variance, however, with a fairly large number of leaders of the radical intelligentsia on the scope of these reforms.[4] And these differences became even more pronounced in the lower echelons of the movement among the rank-and-file followers on both sides.[5]

---

[1] See *Shakhovskoy* IV, pp. 86–7. For Lvov's identification see *Petrunkevich* II, p. 337.

[2] *Frank*, p. 39.

[3] It was mainly because of disagreements on these questions that Lvov left the Cadets, at the end of the first Duma and joined the 'Party of Peaceful Renovation' (*Partiya Mirnogo Obnovleniya*) which was headed by Count P. A. Geyden, D. N. Shipov, M. A. Stakhovich and Lvov himself. (See *Dan* VII, p. 196, *Shipov* II, pp. 514–16.) N. N. Lvov's 'turn to the right' may also have had something to do with the appearance of Stolypin on the political scene. They were good friends from their days together in Saratov, where Stolypin was governor and Lvov marshal of the nobility for many years.

[4] It was partly because of these differences that the St Petersburg 'Big Group' voted against the decision to establish the Cadet Party at the fourth and last congress (23–25 August 1905) of the Union of Liberation and it refused to join this party when it was established in October 1905. (See *Bez-Zaglaviya*, no. 1, p. 7, *Gessen* I pp. 212–13, *Kuskova* XIV, pp. 85–7, *Milyukov* Xa, pp. 307–8, 338–42, *Shakhovskoy* IV, pp. 163–9, *Yordanskiy*, p. 70 and below.

[5] According to Kuskova the gap between the rank-and-file supporters of the two sides was so great at the time of the establishment of the Union of Liberation that in many towns two branches of the Union existed side by side, one composed of zemstvo constitutionalists and the other of radical intellectuals. (See *Kuskova* VIII, pp. 389–90.)

There were also other considerations which prevented the assembled leaders from deciding on the establishment of a party at that time. It was very doubtful, to say the least, whether the moderate constitutionalists would join a party whose programme included ever part of the demands put forward by the radical intelligentsia. It was even more unlikely that the liberal Slavophiles would join such a party. And despite the growing campaign against the liberal Slavophiles in *Osvobozhdeniye* the leaders of the zemstvo radicals knew that Shipov and his supporters were still indispensable to conducting the public opinion campaign in the zemstvo milieu. And although Plehve's policies left the liberal Slavophiles little choice but to co-operate with the zemstvo radicals, the establishment of a party might have driven them away from politics altogether, as was the case with Shipov in summer 1905.[1]

For all the above reasons, the conference decided by an overwhelming majority not to try to establish a party but instead to consolidate the Liberation Movement on the following lines.[2] It decided to organize the zemstvo radicals and the radical–democratic intelligentsia into a Union of Liberation. This Union was to become the conspiratorial co-ordinating centre of the Liberation Movement and it was to create new channels of communication with the 'masses' and with the revolutionary parties. The moderate constitutionalists were to be organized into a union of zemstvo constitutionalists which was also to include the zemstvo radical members of *Beseda*. The leading positions in the Union were purposely left in the hands of the moderates (Prince Pavel D. Dolgorukov, Count P. A. Geyden, Yu. A. Novosiltsev and A. A. Stakhovich). The *Beseda* circle was to remain uncommitted (to constitutionalism). As events were soon to show, this organizational framework possessed very great advantages from the point of view of the founding-fathers of *Osvobozhdeniye*.

The continued existence of *Beseda* as a non-constitutional circle, made it possible to keep the liberal Slavophiles inside the Liberation Movement. At the same time, the establishment of the Union of Zemstvo Constitutionalists enabled the radical leaders of the Liberation Movement to by-pass Shipov and his followers and to try to directly influence the zemstvo activists in favour of supporting constitutionalist demands. (After their defeat at the April 1903 zemstvo congress, it became vitally necessary to the zemstvo radicals to by-pass Shipov.) Finally, the establishment of the Union of Liberation enabled its leaders

---

[1] See *Shipov* II, pp. 320–2.   [2] See *Shakhovskoy* IV, p. 106 ff.

to manipulate the other organizations and groups in the Liberation Movement and thus transform it in practice into an illegal radical movement.

Because of the absence of the *Russkoye Bogatstvo* group the conference was not wholly representative of the radical–democratic intelligentsia; its decisions were therefore no more than recommendations and carried no official weight. As far as organizational matters were concerned, this did not make much difference, since they were implemented almost to the letter. But this was not the case regarding its decisions on the programme of the Union of Liberation. These were implemented only so far as universal suffrage was concerned, but not as regards the social clauses and especially the 'peasant question'. But although part of the decision had no immediate practical consequences, the whole was nevertheless of the outmost importance. Beside throwing light on the state of mind of the majority of the radical leaders of the Liberation Movement at the time, it was destined to become the basis of the programme of the Cadet Party in autumn 1905.

According to Semyon Frank, the Schaffhausen Conference almost unanimously approved Struve's point of view, as expressed in *Osvobozhdeniye* from issue no. 17 onwards, that the programme must be democratic and must deal with social questions. Only N. N. Lvov raised objections to the democratic principles by saying that 'everything should be done for the people, but not always through the people'.[1] The decisions of the Conference on this topic were incorporated in Bulgakov's article 'On the Agrarian Question', published in *Osvobozhdeniye* no. 9 (33).[2] In the first part of his article, Bulgakov referred to some of Struve's statements made in the latter's 'The German Elections'. He began by alleviating some of Struve's 'fears' regarding the dangers threatening Russian liberalism if it followed the example of its German counterpart. Bulgakov explained that in Russia, unlike Western Europe, there was no connection between liberalism and the bourgeois class. Russian liberalism was therefore, according to him, democratic almost by definition[3] and he saw proof of this in the 'fact'

---

[1] *Frank*, p. 39. See also *Shakhovskoy* IV, p. 106.

[2] Bulgakov signed his article with the letter L. For his identification see *Smith* (unpub.), p. 143n. The fact that this article expressed not only its author's views but those of the Schaffhausen Conference as a whole, was made plain at the time by Struve's introductory remarks: 'The closest friends of *Osvobozhdeniye* and its editor are in complete agreement with the author of this article as regards the practical demands of the agrarian policy.' (*Osvobozhdeniye* (1903), no. 9(33), front page n.)

[3] See *Osvobozhdeniye* ibid. front page.

that 'no basic objections are raised to the principle of universal, equal and direct...suffrage.'[1] If there existed a danger to liberalism in Russia, he stated prophetically, it lurked on the left and not on the right:

Russian society, because of its fully understandable political immaturity, suffers from an opposite sin to that of its Western counterpart and – at least in theory – too easily sacrifices the interests of political liberalism, and of political freedom, on the altar of the interests of a democratic social policy.[2]

Immediately afterwards, as if frightened by his own daring, Bulgakov restated almost sentence for sentence the thesis of Bogdanovich and Struve regarding the identity of liberalism and social democracy:

Political liberalism and social–economic democracy have essentially the same content. They differ only in the means by which they strive to achieve their identical goal: the creation of a free personality, its liberation from the political and social–economic yoke...Hence, not only must liberalism never be opposed to socialism, but they must not even be separated from one another. According to their basic ideal they are identical and indivisible. (Hence) in contrast to what many people fear, socialism does not threaten liberalism. Socialism comes not to destroy but to fulfil the legacy of liberalism.[3] (Therefore) it is almost axiomatic that political liberalism and social–economic democracy, demands for political freedom and for democratic and social reforms, cannot be separated from one another in the general programme of the Russian Liberation Movement.[4]

Bulgakov (and the Schaffhausen Conference) went further than either Struve or Bogdanovich, in translating these general statements into practical demands. And from studying these demands one can deduce that by then they equated urban social economic democracy with what can best be described as a welfare state. In the countryside they aimed at establishing a pre-capitalist 'bourgeois' society, i.e. they wanted to transform the peasantry into a class of small proprietors and to permit only those who cultivated the land themselves to own it. Such a society would, according to them, be truly democratic, since it would be based on the principle of equality transferred from the political to the economic sphere.

Bulgakov expounded the Conference's views on desirable social reforms under the already familiar two headings, the 'workers question'

---

[1] Ibid. p. 156. Bulgakov, of course, exaggerated here considerably. As has been shown there were people, even among the radical leaders of the Liberation Movement, who did not subscribe to this principle (N. N. Lvov, Milyukov), not to mention its rank-and-file supporters among the zemstvo activists.

[2] *Osvobozhdeniye*, ibid.   [3] *Osvobozhdeniye* ibid.   [4] Ibid.

and the 'peasant problem'. First he dealt with the former, which became very topical by the time the Schaffhausen Conference opened its debates.

By the end of 1902 the worst phase of the economic recession in Russia was over. The beginning of the revival of business activity put an end to the docility of the workers and in November of that year a large-scale strike broke out in Rostov-on-Don,[1] the first since the beginning of 1900. In spring 1903 industrial unrest spread into other parts of the South and as was often the case in Russia at the time the pace of events was greatly accelerated by the muddleheadedness of the government.

Strikes were regarded by the tsarist regime as a form of rebellion and trade unions were prohibited by law.[2] At the same time representative organizations of employers were protected and encouraged in their activities by Witte.[3] As a result the workers began to consider the regime rather than their direct employers as their chief enemy. This state of affairs had led the Russian orthodox Marxists to declare from the first that the proletariat was the most revolutionary class in Russia. It also resulted in the appearance in Russia of what soon became known as 'police unionism', which became the catalyst of the industrial unrest in 1903.

The idea of 'police unionism' originated in the fertile mind of the head of the Moscow *okhrana* (secret police), S. V. Zubatov (hence its appellation *Zubatovshchina*[4]) who in his youth was close to revolutionary circles.[5] In Zubatov's view, there was no objective reason why the workers should oppose the existing regime. The workers, according to him, were interested only in the improvement of their economic conditions and not in abstract theories of socialism (and the appearance of the books by Bernstein and Prokopovich at the turn of the century

[1] See *Seton-Watson*, p. 564.
[2] See ibid. p. 528.
[3] Much valuable information on these organizations is to be found in *A. Yermanskiy*.
[4] For accounts in English of *Zubatovshchina*, see: Gurko, pp. 114–20, Keep, pp. 102–6, Pospielovski (unpub.), *Schapiro* I, pp. 41–2, *Schwartz* I, pp. 267–304, *Tidmarsh*. For material in Russian on this episode see *inter alia*, *Aynzaft*, pp. 38–109, *Bukhbinder* II, pp. 289–334; III, pp. 96–133, *Gots, Kuropatkin* I, pp. 81–2, *Ozerov*, esp. pp. 144–6, 195–234, *Polovtsev* I, pp. 108–9, 121–3, 127–8, 132, 135–6, *Pyontkovskiy* I, pp. 289–314; II, pp. 66–100, *Tikhomirov* V, *Von Stein* II, *Zaslavskiy* VII, *Zubatov* I, II, III. See also *Osvobozhdeniye* (1902), no. 1, p. 9; (1903), nos. 17, pp. 293–5; 18, pp. 317–19; 19, pp. 331–2; 20/21, pp. 352–3, 361–3; 22, pp. 393–4.
[5] See *Gots, Zubatov* II, pp. 74–6 and *Osvobozhdeniye* (1903), no. 22, pp. 393–4. This, incidentally, later enabled his enemies inside the government to accuse him of playing a double game. See *Polovtsev* I, pp. 121–2 and *Mednikov*, p. 203.

strengthened his beliefs).[1] Insofar as they followed the lead of the socialists, they did so only because the government sided all the time with their employers, but there was no objective reason for the government to do so. In his view, autocracy stood above all classes and hence could look after the interests of the workers in the same way as it had so far nurtured the interests of the employers.[2] If the government would realize this, and change its policy, it would deprive the revolutionary intelligentsia, the only real enemy of autocracy, of its mass support. This reasoning, as well as Zubatov's 'excellent' performance as an *okhrannik*, appealed to D. F. Trepov[3] and Grand Duke Sergius, Chief of Police and Governor-General of Moscow respectively. The resurrection of political terror and the students' street demonstrations at the turn of the century clinched the argument in his favour and they agreed to his daring plan of organizing 'police trade unions' in Moscow.[4]

Witte had been opposed to Zubatov's activity from the moment he got wind of it. But he was unable to intervene so long as Zubatov enjoyed the patronage of Grand Duke Sergius,[5] who was Nicholas II's uncle and brother-in-law.* Zubatov was able, therefore, to execute his plan and 'police trade unions' were organized in Moscow during 1901. Then, at the beginning of 1902 Zubatov, together with L. Tikhomirov, the ex-*narodovolets* who turned arch-conservative, staged an event which, under different conditions, should have finally proved the soundness of his theory. On 19 February 1902, the 51st anniversary of the liberation of the peasants, they organized a huge patriotic manifestation, which was supposed to be the people's answer to the Kazan Square demonstration. About 50,000 men women and children took part in this 'peaceful procession'[6] which, according to Tikhomirov, demonstrated to the intelligentsia the patriotism of the Russian workers.[7] But instead of finally proving the soundness of Zubatov's ideas, the manifestation turned out to be the swan-song of *Zubatovshchina* in Moscow.

The workers, as Zubatov had rightly predicted, were interested in immediate economic gains and not in abstract theories of socialism, democracy or autocracy. They disregarded the warnings of the revolu-

---

[1] See *Zubatov* I, p. 79.   [2] See *Keep*, p. 105, *Tidmarsh*, pp. 341–2, 345.
[3] *Ozerov*, pp. 144–6, *Tidmarsh*, p. 337.   [4] See *Zubatov* I.
[5] See *Polovtsev* I, pp. 108–9, 121–2.
* Sergius was married to the Tsarina's sister.
[6] See *Bukhbinder* III, p. 119, *Pyontkovskiy* I, p. 312. *Tidmarsh*, p. 338, *Tikhomirov* V, pp. 81–8, *Zubatov* II, pp. 79–80.
[7] *Tikhomirov* ibid. p. 85.

tionaries and joined his unions in their thousands (exactly as they did later when Gapon began organizing his union in St Petersburg), because they hoped thereby to improve their material conditions. But when, several days after the patriotic manifestation, Zubatov tried to satisfy their immediate demands in part, the impracticality behind the idea of 'police unionism' came to the surface. The rough tactics which the *okhrana* used at the beginning of March 1902, to compel some employers to fulfil the demands of strikers belonging to their unions, brought sharp retaliation from the employers in the form of a formal complaint to the Ministry of Finance and to the Emperor. Witte now exploited these complaints in an open attack on the whole conception of 'police unionism',[1] and succeeded in bringing about their gradual suspension in Moscow. Zubatov himself was transferred to St Petersburg.[2]

Zubatov's transfer from Moscow did not put an end to *Zubatovshchina*. On the contrary, his experiment with police manipulation of workers if not his genuine concern for their welfare, fitted neatly into Plehve's policy of ruling Russia by and through the police. Hence, despite their personal incompatability, Zubatov was given a free hand to organize 'police unions' in the west and south of Russia. But since the police lacked efficient instruments of control this ended in disaster when one of Zubatov's agents, a certain Dr Shayevich, organized a strike in Odessa in June 1903 in an atmosphere charged with industrial unrest.[3] This strike triggered off a chain-reaction and by mid-July Odessa, Baku, Batum and Tiflis were in the grip of what was almost a general strike.[4]

Plehve retaliated swiftly and harshly. He utilized all the might of the police apparatus to suppress the wave of strikes, which according to a modern historian was 'the worst which had yet afflicted tsarist Russia'.[5] He also made Zubatov pay a heavy price for his failure. He was summarily dismissed from his post on 19 August 1903 and exiled to Vladimir province.[6] But Plehve neither could nor would abandon his suicidal policy, which eventually led to 'Bloody Sunday'.

Besides contributing directly to the events of 9 January 1905 the experiment with 'police unionism' had at least four disastrous side-effects from the point of view of the tsarist regime. The abrupt manner

[1] See *Polovtsev* I, pp. 127–8.
[2] See *Keep*, p. 104, *Pyontkovskiy* I, p. 310, *Tidmarsh*, p. 339.
[3] *Tidmarsh*, pp. 339–40 [4] See *Von Laue* III, p. 256.
[5] Ibid. [6] See *Mednikov*, p. 203 and *Zubatov* II, p. 78.

in which Plehve dismissed Zubatov had a demoralizing effect on the higher echelons of the *okhrana*[1] and thus contributed to its growing inefficiency. It increased the friction between the Ministry of Finance and the Ministry of the Interior and thus added to the disarray on the government's side. It shattered the belief of many industrialists in the usefulness of autocracy as a guardian of their interests and thus prepared the ground for their oppositional stand during the first ten months of 1905.[2] Lastly, what proved most disastrous to the regime in the long run was Plehve's use of force for the suppression of the strike-wave in southern Russia. It provided additional proof to the workers that the government was their chief enemy.

The reappearance of the workers as a mighty anti-government force could not but lead to a reassessment of their role by the radical–democratic leaders of the intelligentsia who had assembled at Schaffhausen. All of them (and especially Kuskova) had become disillusioned with the proletariat as a political factor in Russia several years earlier. Their insistence on the inclusion of demands for universal suffrage and for a radical solution to the 'workers question' had till then been mainly a result of their commitment to democracy and not a consequence of a practical need. The events of summer 1903 changed their attitude to the workers and they began to look for ways and means of inducing them to support the Liberation Movement. The change in their attitude was undoubtedly responsible for the timing of Bulgakov's demand that what amounted to the 'minimum programme' of the socialist parties (an eight-hour working day, a weekly uninterrupted period of 42 hours' rest, government old-age insurance for workers etc.[3] i.e. a welfare state) 'could and should be included in the programme of Russian democratic liberalism'.[4]

After dealing with the workers, Bulgakov turned to the 'peasant problem'. He opened by dissociating the Liberation Movement from two concepts which till then had been almost sacred in the eyes of the Russian radical intelligentsia. First he criticized the Marxist solution to the peasant question (especially as exposed several years earlier by Struve and Tugan-Baranovskiy).[5] He did not believe, he wrote (and

---

[1] See *Mednikov* ibid.
[2] See *Pravo* (1905), no. 4. col. 263 (*Zapiska Moskovikikh Zavodchikov i Fabrikantov*, cols 260–5) and below.
[3] For the 'minimum programme' regarding the 'workers question' of the Russian Social-Democratic Workers Party, as adopted by its second congress (which opened three days before the Schaffhausen Conference but ended much later), see, *inter alia*, Harcave, pp. 265–7. [4] *Osvobozhdeniye* (1903), no. 9 (33), p. 154. [5] See above.

developments in Western Europe bore him out), that social progress in the countryside was identical with large-scale latifundia run on capitalistic lines and the destruction of the peasant small-holdings.[1] Then he turned against the old populist notion of the commune. He explained that with the equalization of the rights of peasants with those of members of other estates, the commune would automatically lose its compulsory legal character and would survive, if at all, only as a voluntary economic association.[2]

Afterwards he developed his own (and the Schaffhausen Conference's) programme of agrarian reform. He began by claiming that it could be implemented only after the replacement of autocracy by a free regime. The first step to be taken by such a regime would have to be the granting of full civic rights to the peasants and the abolition of the nobility's privileges, including its special bank. Immediately afterwards it would have to transform the zemstvos into truly democratic institutions by introducing small zemstvo units and by replacing the existing electoral system, based on estate representation, by a system based on universal, equal and direct suffrage.[3]

After political and legal reform had been achieved, he went on, it would be possible to deal with the most urgent economic aspects of the peasant question. Here, like Struve before him, Bulgakov explained that land-hunger was the immediate cause of the peasants' economic misery. It was true, he rightly observed, that this land-hunger was mainly a consequence of the peasants' backwardness which prevented them from cultivating their plots intensively, and not of the smallness of the plots themselves. The average plot was larger in Russia than in Western Europe. Hence, Bulgakov continued, the ultimate economic solution to the plight of the peasants lay in raising their cultural level.[4] But, he hastened to add, not only would this be a very slow process, but in some parts of Russia the size of plots was much below average and the hunger for land there was a real physical need.[5] In order to begin the task of improving the economic lot of the peasantry immediately, the new regime would not only have to change the existing economic policy completely and start a drive for the raising of the cultural level of the peasants, but would also have to bring about more equal distribution of the available land. The best way to achieve this was to induce the big land-owners to sell part of their land, directly or through intermediaries (the Peasant Bank, the state itself etc.) to the peasants. But,

---

[1] *Osvobozhdeniye* ibid.   [2] Ibid. p. 155.   [3] Ibid. pp. 155–6.
[4] *Osvobozhdeniye* ibid. p. 156.   [5] Ibid. p. 157.

The formation of the Union of Liberation

Bulgakov declared, in those cases where the landowners refused to co-operate '*the state should have the right of compulsory expropriation*'.[1] The transfer of land from the nobles to the peasants, Bulgakov continued, would satisfy the latter's immediate economic needs. But it would not, in itself, guarantee the transformation of the peasantry into a 'truly democratic rural class'. In order to achieve this, the free regime would have to make the peasants owners of the land they cultivated. At the same time it would have to prohibit the accumulation of capital in the form of land acquisition. As a result, Bulgakov apparently believed, the peasantry would be transformed from the breeding-ground of *Pugachovshchina* into a bulwark of the new democratic order. Therefore, he declared, '*the political liberation of Russia must accomplish the liberation of the peasants by recognizing the principle that the right of ownership of land belongs to those who cultivate it*'.[2]

After approving the 'social clauses' of the recommended programme, the Schaffhausen Conference ended its debates and the majority of its participants hurried back to Russia. There they utilized two public gatherings (The Agricultural Congress of the Northern Region held in Yaroslavl during the second part of August and the All-Russian Husbandry Exhibition held in Kharkov in September), attended by many zemstvo activists, members of the 'Third Element' and radical intellectuals from the capital, for propagating the organizational decisions of the Schaffhausen Conference. Particularly active in this field were Peter Dolgorukov and Shakhovskoy.[3] Soon afterwards, apparently during the fourth meeting of *Beseda* in 1903, its constitutionalist members met at the home of Yu. A. Novosiltsev and on 8 November established the Union of Zemstvo Constitutionalists.[4] (Novosiltsev was a district marshal of the nobility and a member of *Beseda*. All the future meetings of this Union were also held at his home and were known at the time as the 'Novosiltsev Congresses'.)

---

[1] Ibid., italics in original.   [2] Ibid., italics in original.

[3] See *Belokonskiy* II, pp. 174–5, *Shakhovskoy* IV, pp. 107–8, *Tyrkova* II, pp. 119–23 and *Veselovskiy* VI, pp. 580–1. See also *Fischer*, p. 144.

[4] *Shakhovskoy* ibid. and *Veselovskiy* ibid. The assumption that the constituent congress of the Union of Zemstvo Constitutionalists was composed of the constitutionalist 'caucus' of *Beseda* is based on the following circumstantial evidence; the number of zemstvo activists who participated in the foundation congress did not exceed the thirty mark (*Shakhovskoy* ibid.), the almost exact number of constitutionalist members of *Beseda*. It was held in Moscow in late autumn (the eve of the zemstvo assembly sessions), the time and place of the fourth *Beseda* meeting of the year. All its known leaders – Prince Pavel D. Dolgorukov, Peter's twin, Count P.A. Geyden, Yu.A. Novosiltsev and A.A. Stakhovich (see: *Budberg* II, p. 70, *Chermenskiy* II, p. 52 and *Shakhovskoy* IV, p. 108) – were moderate-constitutionalist members of *Beseda*.

The aim of the new constitutionalist organization, as defined by the foundation congress, was 'to conduct a campaign in favour of the constitutionalist platform (universal suffrage and a legislative assembly) at the sessions of the zemstvo assemblies and in the all-zemstvo congresses'.[1] But the meeting was held too late in the year to enable it to intervene in the zemstvo campaign organized by the April zemstvo congress.[2] It decided, therefore, to postpone the constitutional campaign inside the zemstvo milieu to the next year and in the meantime to work for the consolidation of the newly established organization.[3]

Some of the leaders of the radical–democratic intelligentsia attended the meeting in Novosiltsev's house as observers. Together with the zemstvo radicals, they finalized there and then the arrangements for the convening of the constituent congress of the Union of Liberation.[4] It was decided to hold it in St Petersburg at the beginning of January 1904. The time and place were undoubtedly chosen because of the two mass conventions of radical intellectuals (predominantly 'Third Element') which were going to be held then in the capital: The Ninth Congress of the Pirogov Society of Russian Doctors and the Third Congress of Activists in the Field of Technical Education. The latter was particularly highly attended (more than 3,000 delegates participated) and extreme in its anti-government manifestations. It was closed by the police on the night of 4/5 January 1904 and its principal radical leaders were arrested.[5] (One of them, apparently G. A. Falbork,[6] participated in the foundation congress of the Union of Liberation.[7])

The arrival of thousands of radical intellectuals from the provinces shielded the fifty or so delegates to the foundation congress of the Union of Liberation from the watchful eye of the secret police. The congress was in session for four days (2–5 January 1904) and its participants represented 'Friends of Liberation' groups in 23 cities and towns (St Petersburg, Moscow, Chernigov, Yaroslavl, Yurev, Kharkov, Kiyev, Kostroma, Kursk, Nizhniy Novgorod, Odessa, Orel, Samara,

---

[1] *Chermenskiy* II, p. 52.
[2] Apparently more than two-thirds of zemstvo assemblies heeded its advice and inserted its two demands in their petitions (see *Belokonskiy* II, pp. 164, 177–83).
[3] See *Shakhovskoy* IV, p. 109.   [4] See ibid. pp. 108–9.
[5] See *Osvobozhdeniye* (1904), no. 17 (41), pp. 309–11.
[6] Ibid. p. 311. Falbork, as well as another congress delegate who was arrested a few days later – V.I. Charnoluskiy (ibid.) – later played an important role in the Union of Unions. The lawyer P.N. Pereverzev, who was active in the defence of the victims of the Kishinev pogrom (ibid.), was arrested together with them. It was apparently his brother – V.N. Pereverzev – who was later chairman of the all-powerful Railway Union.
[7] *Shakhovskoy* IV, p. 110.

Saratov, Simferopol, Smolensk, Tambov, Tiflis, Tula, Vladimir, Vologda, Vyatka). The majority of the delegates belonged to the radical-democratic intelligentsia. Apart from Struve and Petrunkevich (who was prohibited from entering St Petersburg) all the participants in the Schaffhausen Conference were present. They, together with the *Russkoye Bogatstvo* group, played the leading role in the congress.[1]

The divisions of opinion among the radical members of the Liberation Movement were fully reflected at the congress. After approving the organizational decisions of the Schaffhausen Conference, apparently unanimously, it ran into a prolonged debate on the name of the proposed union. Many rank-and-file radical intellectuals still remembered Struve's early attempt at moderation and were opposed to the name Union of Liberation because of its resemblance to that of the journal *Osvobozhdeniye* (Liberation).[2] When the original name was eventually approved a much more important controversy arose concerning the programme.

The suggestions of the Schaffhausen Conference were opposed from two sides. N. N. Lvov and some of the rank-and-file zemstvo radicals objected to the introduction of democratic and social clauses into the programme of the Union. In their opposition to the latter they found support in an unexpected quarter: among the delegates with 'populist inclinations'[3] (the *Russkoye Bogatstvo* group and its rank-and-file supporters). These delegates, according to Shakhovskoy, wanted the Union to be a purely 'society' organization which would 'refrain from working among the workers and the peasants'.[4] There can be little doubt that the *Russkoye Bogatstvo* group's opposition to the extension of the Union's activity beyond society and hence to the 'social clauses' was caused by their objection to the 'private ownership clause' in the agrarian programme as elaborated by the Schaffhausen Conference. But while opposing this point they supported the demand for universal suffrage and political democracy. As a consequence, Lvov's opposition to the latter was overruled, though no mention was made of what apparently seemed to the majority the ultimate democratic regime – a republic.

The programme, as finally adopted by the congress, was outspoken on political questions. It demanded the replacement of autocracy by a constitutional-democratic regime, to be based on what soon became

---

[1] In the absence of minutes, *Shakhovskoy* IV, pp. 110–17, remains the only source of direct information on the foundation congress of the Union of Liberation.
[2] *Shakhovskoy* IV, p. 110.   [3] Ibid. p. 111.   [4] Ibid.

known as the 'four-tail formula': universal, equal and direct suffrage and secret ballot. It also recognized the right of the minorities to self-determination, but was very vague on social questions. It read as follows.[1]

The first and main aim of the Union of Liberation is the political liberation of Russia. Considering political liberty in even its most minimal form as completely incompatible with the absolutist character of the Russian monarchy, the Union will seek before all else the abolition of autocracy and the establishment in Russia of a constitutional regime. In determining the concrete forms in which a constitutional regime can be realized in Russia, the Union of Liberation will make all efforts to have the political problems resolved in the spirit of extensive democracy. Above all, it recognizes as fundamentally essential that the principles of *universal equal and direct suffrage and secret ballot* be made the basis of the political reform. Putting the political demands in the forefront, the Union of Liberation recognizes as essential the definition of its attitude in principle to the social–economic problems created by life itself. In the realm of social–economic policy, the Union of Liberation will follow the same basic principle of democracy, making the direct goal of its activity the *defence of the interests of the toiling masses*.

In the sphere of national questions, the Union recognizes the right to self-determination of different nationalities entering into the composition of the Russian state. In relation to Finland, the Union supports the demand for the restoration of the constitutional status (*Gosudarstvenno-Pravovoye Polozheniye*) which existed in that country until its illegal abrogation during the current reign.[2]

After approving the programme, the congress began to debate the statutes of the Union. Here again the debates were quite fierce, but when the organizers of the congress had agreed to make important changes in their draft proposal, the statutes were approved unanimously.[3] According to the final version, the Union of Liberation was to be composed of autonomous local and professional groups. The supreme organ of the Union was to be a congress composed of elected representatives of each group belonging to it. The congress was to decide on the Union's general policy and to elect its only executive body – the Council. The Council was to conduct all the general affairs of the Union between congresses. It was to summon a congress at

---

[1] Because of the paralysing effect which the outbreak of war with Japan (26/27 January 1904) exerted at first on the Liberation Movement (see below), the programme of the Union of Liberation together with the announcement about its existence was made public only ten months after its approval by the congress. See: *Listok Osvobozhdeniya*, no. 17, 19 November/2 December 1904 and *Osvobozhdeniye* (1904), no. 61 (Leader).

[2] English translation based on *Fischer*, p. 147. Italics added.

[3] *Shakhovskov* IV, p. 113.

least once a year. It had the right to co-opt new members unanimously and to enter into agreements with other parties and groups etc.[1]

Despite the radical intelligentsia's domination of the congress, the Council elected by it was chosen according to the principle of parity. Five of its ten members represented the radical–democratic intelligentsia and five the zemstvo radicals.[2] The intelligentsia contingent included: N. F. Annenskiy (who was elected vice-chairman of the Council), V. Ya. Bogucharskiy, S. N. Bulgakov, A. V. Peshekhonov and S. N. Prokopovich. The zemstvo radicals were represented by I. I. Petrunkevich (who was chairman of the Council), Prince Peter D. Dolgorukov, N. N. Kovalevskiy, N. N. Lvov and Prince D. I. Shakhovskoy. The parity between both sides was not affected by the profound personal changes in the composition of the Council which occurred immediately after the congress ended. First, the Council co-opted two additional members – a moderate zemstvo constitutionalist, I. V. Luchitskiy, and a radical intellectual, L. I. Lutugin[3] (one of the future leaders of the Union of Unions). Then, at the beginning of February 1904, Annenskiy was arrested and exiled to the provinces[4] while S. N. Bulgakov, for unknown reasons, was apparently unable to fulfil his duties as a member of the Council. The final composition of the Council of the Union of Liberation in spring 1904, was therefore, as follows:[5] zemstvo radicals and constitutionalists: I. I. Petrunkevich (chairman), Prince Peter D.

---

[1] Ibid.

[2] According to Shakhovskoy, the first council elected by the constituent congress was composed of ten members: 'Four of them were men of letters from St Petersburg, four zemstvo activists who were considered Moscow men, although only one of them lived in Moscow, one a professor from Kiyev and one a zemstvo man from Kharkov. . . . One of the ten was elected in absentia, because he was prohibited from entering St Petersburg and hence could not participate in the congress.' (*Shakhovskoy* IV, p. 117.) These were later identified by name (see *B.S.E.* I, vol. 52, col. 342, *M.S.E.* vol. 8, cols 257–8). The four 'men of letters from St Petersburg' were Annenskiy, Bogucharskiy, Peshekhonov and Prokopovich (all of them had belonged in the past to the Peoples' Right Party). The four 'Moscow men' were Dolgorukov (the only one who lived in Moscow), Lvov, Shakhovskoy and Petrunkevich (the one who 'was elected in absentia'). The 'professor from Kiyev' was Bulgakov, who was at the time Professor of Political Economy in the local Polytechnic (see *Brokgaus supp.* I, pp. 330–1), and the 'zemstvo man from Kharkov' was Kovalevskiy.

[3] See *Milyukov* xa, p. 266 and *Fischer*, p. 150.

[4] The direct cause of Annenskiy's arrest was a speech which he delivered at the funeral of N.K. Mikhaylovskiy (who died on the night of 27 January 1904). After his arrest, however, charges connected with his activity as head of the 'culinary committee' were brought against him. The fact that 18 volumes of *Osvobozhdeniye* were found in his possession apparently clinched the case and he was expelled from St Petersburg. (See *Brokgaus supp.* I, p. 122, *Listok Osvobozhdeniya* (1904), no. 1, p. 4, *Osvobozhdeniye* (1904), no. 18 (42), p. 328.)

[5] See *Chermenskiy* II, p. 53 and *Kuskova* XVIIIa.

Dolgorukov, N. N. Kovalevskiy, I. V. Luchitskiy, N. N. Lvov and Prince D. I. Shakhovskoy (apart from Luchitskiy, all zemstvo-radicals of old standing). Radical intelligentsia: V. Ya. Bogucharskiy, V. V. Khizhnyakov, E. D. Kuskova, L. I. Lutugin, A. V. Peshekhonov and S. N. Prokopovich (apart from Lutugin, all ex-members of the Peoples' Rights Party).

The maintenance of the principle of parity in the composition of the Council undoubtedly reflected the awareness on the part of the leaders of the radical intelligentsia that the zemstvo milieu was still very important for the Liberation Movement and was to remain so for a long time to come. At the same time the predominant position of the radical intellectuals was institutionalized immediately after the congress ended, when the Council decided at its first meeting to establish a 'technical group'.[1] This group consisted of Bogucharskiy, Khizhnyakov, Kuskova (who were also members of the Council of the Union), N. D. Sokolov and half a dozen or so of the lesser-known radical intellectuals of the capital.[2] At the time of its foundation the main task of the 'technical group' was to smuggle into Russia copies of *Osvobozhdeniye* and other illegal literature published by Struve. (Kuskova, who had been active in this field since *Osvobozhdeniye* began to appear,[3] and who together with Struve had established a very successful network for its transportation through Finland and distribution inside Russia,[4] became the dominant figure in that group.) But very soon afterwards it greatly expanded the scope of its political activity.

The 'technical group', together with the radical intellectual wing of the Council of the Union of Liberation, soon formed the St Petersburg branch of this organization, which became known as the 'Big Group'.[5] With the outbreak of the Russo-Japanese war and the intensification of the internal political crisis, the 'Big Group', which later formed the nucleus of the Union of Unions, became the real nerve-

---

[1] See *Shakhovskoy* IV, p. 117.

[2] *Milyukov* Xa, p. 266.

[3] See above and *Kuskova* VIIIa, *Tyrkova* II, pp. 131–2, 162, 164–5. For Struve's contribution to the establishment of this network see *Pipes* IIa, pp. 348–53.

[4] The organization for smuggling *Osvobozhdeniye* into Russia failed badly only once. This happened when E.N. Anichkov and Ariadna Borman (later Tyrkova-Williams) were arrested on the Russo-Finnish border carrying 400 copies of the paper. And even this was not so much a failure of the organization as of Anichkov who did not know how to behave as a 'smuggler'. (See *Tyrkova* ibid. pp. 133–69, *Osvobozhdeniye* (1904), no. 24(48), pp. 426–31; no. 25(49), pp. 449–50; no. 51, pp. 28–9; no. 52, pp. 39–41; *Pravo* (1904), no. 27, cols 1431–3, *Shakhovskoy* IV, pp. 123–5).

[5] See *Belokonskiy* II, p. 93.

centre of the Union of Liberation and hence of the Liberation Movement as a whole. But the war, which opened up these opportunities, seemed at first to endanger the very existence of the newly consolidated Liberation Movement.

PART THREE: WAR AND REVOLUTION

The war will distract the attention of the masses from political questions.

(Plehve to Kuropatkin. *Kuropatkin* I, p. 94)

War with Japan will be extremely unpopular in Russia. The anti-governmental party will take advantage of the war to increase sedition.

(Kuropatkin to Nicholas II. Ib.d. p. 90)

The worst thing about the war is not that it is difficult to win it but that it is dreadful to win it.

(Struve in *Osvobozhdeniye* (1904), no. 23(47), p. 410)

What will the Russian people lose if their army and navy are routed in the Far East? ...They will lose the assurance that tsarist power is indestructible...But...if their army is victorious...they will lose everything...They will lose the last hope of liberation.

(A young Russian scholar in *Osvobozhdeniye* (1904), no. 22(46), p. 399)

Marshal Oyama [C.-in-C. Japanese army] is the best ally in the struggle for the liberation of Russia.

(Opinion in *Osvobozhdeniye* (1904), no. 61, p. 186)

Down with the War! Long live the Constituent Assembly!

(Student demonstrators. *Osvobozhdeniye* (1904), no. 62, pp. 210–12)

9

Setback and recovery

The surprise attack launched by Japanese naval detachments on the Russian forces in Port Arthur on the night of 26/27 January (8/9 February) 1904, started what may be described as the most unpopular war in Russia's history. The adventurous policy of Nicholas II, which proved to be one of its direct causes, was condemned at the time not only by the revolutionary and oppositional elements in society, but also by the most responsible ministers in the government, namely Witte, Lamsdorf (Foreign Minister) and even to some extent by the War Minister, A. N. Kuropatkin, as well as by the majority of the Imperial family. Besides the 'Bezobrazov Clique', only Plehve seems to have supported the Tsar's Far-Eastern policy.[1] His main reason was, apparently, his wish to please Nicholas and to discredit Witte.[2] But in conversations with ministers, Plehve apparently expressed the opinion that 'the war would distract the attention of the masses from political questions',[3] a remark paraphrased as the quest for 'a little victorious war'.[4] As events were soon to show, instead of being victorious, the war turned out to be disastrous for Russian arms. This, together with the fact that it was conducted in an area where no vital Russian interests

---

[1] For a detailed account of Russia's policy in the Far East, which eventually embroiled it in the disastrous war with Japan, see *White*, pp. 1–131. The author of this book does not accept White's partial exoneration of Bezobrazov and his clique from their share of responsibility for the outbreak of war (ibid. pp. 38 ff). Nor does he share the view that 'however ill-conceived it might appear in the test to which it was soon subjected, it was a *well-considered* policy and not a product of hasty improvization, devised under pressure from a group of adventurers; it must be viewed, therefore, as a *national policy*' (ibid. p. 75, italics added). For the present writer's version of these events see *Galai*, pp. 87–8. For material which, in his opinion, largely refutes White's version see: *Bezobrazov* I, II, pp. 133–5, 137–46, 148–62, *Kuropatkin* I, pp. 11–12, 17–22, 30–1, 33–4, 37–50, 56–9, 61, 64–8, 76, 81, 83, 85–109, *Nicholas* IIg, pp. 41–3, 48–53, 55–6, *Polovtsev* I, pp. 87–94, 108, 134–5, 167, *Witte* III, p. 106; IV, pp. 33–42, 44–6.
[2] See *Kuropatkin* I, pp. 82–3, 101; VII, p. 25.   [3] Ibid. I, p. 94.
[4] Plehve's support of the policy which involved Russia in war with Japan was cited by the central committee of the SR Party as one of the reasons for Plehve's assassination. See *Osvobozhdeniye* (1904), no. 53, p. 64. See also ibid. no. 55, p. 83.

seemed to have been threatened, apparently accounted for its un-popularity. In the words of Struve, 'the overwhelming majority of the Russian people have no interest either in Manchuria or in Korea and Japan'.[1]

But however unpopular the war turned out to be its very outbreak confronted the recently consolidated Liberation Movement with a problem of the first magnitude. The question was what was permissible for an opposition in times of war, even when this opposition was illegal and (apart from the liberal Slavophiles) was opposed not only to the government but also to the existing regime? The different answers given to this question by the various groups composing the Liberation Movement threatened its very existence for a while. However, as was always the case with Nicholas II's government, its political ineptitude, matched this time by a display of military incompetence, not only saved the Liberation Movement from disintegration but also presented it with the best opportunity for achieving its aim – the replacement of autocracy by a constitutional regime.

Broadly speaking, the question of the attitude towards the government in time of war brought about a four-way split in the Liberation Movement. The liberal Slavophiles immediately abandoned all oppositional activity and offered unconditional support to the government. Where they were still very influential, the zemstvo assemblies, together with the town dumas, were among the first corporate bodies in the realm to express their support for the government in wartime.[2] They sent messages of goodwill to the Tsar[3] and allocated considerable sums of money for the war effort. Moreover, on Shipov's initiative, the zemstvos responded to the appeal of the head of the Russian Red Cross (Count I. I. Vorontsov-Dashkov) and established an All-Zem-stvo Organization to help the sick and wounded.[4]

It is not known how many of the moderate zemstvo constitutional-ists shared the patriotic feelings of their liberal Slavophile fellow-councillors. But almost all of them were taken aback by the upsurge of patriotism in their milieu. They were also swayed by the several patriotic demonstrations which were held in some Russian towns and cities including both capitals, immediately after the official declaration of war on Japan. Although many of the participants were apparently paid by the police for their activities during these days, there were also

---

[1] See *Osvobozhdeniye* (1904), no. 17(41), p. 302n.   [2] See *Galai*, p. 88.
[3] For the contents of these messages see *Otkliki Russkoy Zemli*.
[4] See *Galai*, p. 90 and *Shipov* II, pp. 92–6.

genuine manifestations of patriotic feeling.[1] The moderate constitutionalists feared, therefore, that unless they adopted a patriotic stand, they and the Liberation Movement as a whole might forfeit influence in their milieu. (One of them even went as far as to warn the editor of *Osvobozhdeniye* that unless his paper joined in support of the government during the war, he would suffer the fate of Herzen, who lost much influence in Russia as a result of his support of the Poles in 1863.[2]) As a consequence, they adopted a position which can be described as 'defensist'. It was defensist in the sense that without abandoning their ultimate goal and their right of criticism, they decided not to continue with active opposition to the government while Russia was at war.

Struve, who was always more sensitive to developments in the zemstvo milieu than were the other leaders of the radical intelligentsia, was greatly affected by the attitude of the moderate zemstvo constitutionalists. Moreover, unlike the majority of Russian radical intellectuals, he had always regarded the state as a positive phenomenon[3] and since his break with orthodox Marxism, patriotism and nationalism had become more and more important elements in his *Weltanschauung*. These factors should, in theory, have induced Struve to adopt a straightforward defensist position. But he was still too much of a radical, remembering the benefits Russia had derived from its defeat in the Crimea, and too critical of the whole Far-Eastern adventure[4] to be able to do so. Hence Struve opted for what may be described as an intermediary position (between defensism and defeatism). It was based on the assumption that it was possible to distinguish between the existing regime (and not only the current government and/or ruler) which was a temporary phenomenon, and the Russian state. The former should and could be attacked, while the latter must not be touched. As he soon discovered for himself, it was easier to make such a distinction in theory than in practice.

The radical intelligentsia members of the Union of Liberation, excluding Struve, as well as all the known zemstvo radical leaders, adopted what may be called as a 'defeatist' position.[5] Like the revolutionaries

---

[1] See *Galai*, p. 88.　　　　　　[2] *Osvobozhdeniye* (1904), no. 22(46), p. 400.
[3] See *Struve* IV, pp. 52–3 and above.
[4] See for example, *Osvobozhdeniye* (1904), no. 17(41), pp. 297–301.
[5] It is not known how many rank-and-file zemstvo radical members of the Union of Liberation followed the example of their leaders and how many were influenced by the 'defensism' of the moderate zemstvo constitutionalists. The latters' number could not have been negligible, because, as the composition of the Second Congress of the Union of

they not only condemned the war from the very beginning, but also believed that an unfavourable outcome would provide the opportunity they were awaiting for the achievement of their aims. Hence they demanded not the suspension, but the intensification of oppositional activity. And there were radicals among them who were already speaking in terms of 'the worse the better'.[1]

The adoption of a 'defeatist' position by the zemstvo radical leaders preserved the unity of the Council of the Union of Liberation[2] and prevented the disintegration of the Liberation Movement. The United Council, however, was unable to initiate any meaningful activity during the first months of the war because of the various stands adopted by the liberal Slavophiles, the moderate constitutionalists and Struve.

The defensism of the moderates deprived the Council of its two main political instruments in the zemstvos: *Beseda* and the Union of Zemstvo Constitutionalists. The former decided at a meeting it held on 15 February 1904 that 'during the war the tactics should be defensive and not offensive. In other words, no initiative for the achievement of new reforms should be taken.'[3] The latter held its second congress a week afterwards (on 23 February).[4] The main item on its agenda was the question of the attitude of the Union of Zemstvo Constitutionalists towards the government during the war. The viewpoint of the moderates was put forward by the marshal of the nobility of the Tambov district, V. M. Petrovo-Solovovo.[5] He declared that because of the upsurge of patriotic feelings in the country, it would be impractical to put forward constitutional demands or to ask the zemstvo assemblies to incorporate such demands in their petitions.[6] He was answered by N. N. Lvov and F. I. Rodichev on behalf of the zemstvo radicals. Lvov, who was the more moderate of the two, agreed that the war had generated patriotic feelings in the country and that, as a consequence, the

Liberation showed, the Union was numerically stagnant, throughout the first ten months of its existence (see *Shakhovskoy* IV, p. 119 and below).

[1] See *Galai*, pp. 88–9.

[2] According to Shakhovskoy only one member (presumably Luchitskiy) resigned from the Council because of the war issue (*Shakhovskoy* ibid.).

[3] *Chermenskiy* II, p. 54. Chermenskiy, who quotes this decision from the *Beseda* archives, does not indicate which constitutionalist members of the circle supported it and which opposed it. Since, however, the liberal Slavophiles were there in a small minority, it could not have been adopted without the support of a large number of moderate constitutionalists. This assumption is supported by the information available on the second congress of the Union of Zemstvo Constitutionalists.

[4] See *Shakhovskoy* IV, p. 119.   [5] See *Veselovskiy* VI, p. 224.

[6] See *Budberg* II, p. 71.

Tsar had begun to enjoy unprecedented popularity. However, he continued, constitutional reforms would only add to the Tsar's prestige, since they would dissociate him from the incompetent bureaucracy. Lvov implied that the adoption of constitutionalist decisions was really in the best interests of Tsar and country.[1]

Rodichev was much more outspoken in his attack on the moderates' position. He warned them that if they did not put forward constitutional demands then others would and their historical role would be finished: 'Gentlemen, if you refrain from saying your word in the (forthcoming sessions of the) zemstvo assemblies, it will be proclaimed by others. But by then, the historical role of the zemstvo will be reduced to zero.'[2] Neither Lvov nor Rodichev won the day and the resolution adopted by the congress expressed the point of view of the moderate constitutionalists.

The resolution, which was published as an appeal to the population,[3] opened by condemning the irresponsible policy of the government which had brought about the war, then it attacked the existing regime as the chief cause of the irresponsibility of the government, and dissociated the Union from the vulgar forms of chauvinism which had been displayed at the outbreak of war. Since the war was already a fact, its authors continued, 'to fight for Russia is now a national duty'.[4] And they merely expressed the hope that 'after the defeat of the external enemy of Russia, we will be able to help to defeat its internal enemy, arbitrary rule'.[5]

A plenary meeting of the Council of the Union of Liberation was held in St Petersburg four days earlier on 19 February.[6] Anticipating the defection of the Union of Zemstvo Constitutionalists from active opposition, it apparently decided 'to await further developments and to concentrate on organizational work in the meantime'.[7] The Council's decision to adopt a 'wait and see' policy was undoubtedly also influenced by the fear that it might lose the co-operation of *Osvobozhdeniye* as a consequence of Struve's intermediary position.

Struve revealed his position a week after the outbreak of war. In a leading article written under the impact of the outbreak of hostilities and the exaggerated reports of the 'patriotic outbursts' in Russia, Struve attacked the government and the regime for their policy which had

---

[1] *Budberg*, ibid.   [2] Ibid.
[3] The appeal was published in *Osvobozhdeniye* (1904), no. 22(46), p. 407. Extracts from it are reprinted in *Fischer*, pp. 164–5.
[4] *Osvobozhdeniye* ibid.   [5] Ibid.   [6] See *Shakhovskoy* IV, p. 118.   [7] Ibid.

'plunged the nation into this terrible misfortune'.[1] He warned them that after the war they would pay dearly for their adventurism. But, he continued, since the war was already a fact, there could be no question of not defending the fatherland. *'The Russian army has always fulfilled its duty heroically'*,[2] he stated and explained that the people (i.e. the patriotic demonstrators) were right in manifesting their support of the army. But

the sympathy for the suffering heroes should awake among the Russian people a sense of indignation against those who, by their thoughtlessness, drew them far away from their homes to occupy unnecessary lands and made them victims in a bloody war. They should always remember that the honour and greatness of Russia depend neither on the fields of Manchuria nor on the mountains of Korea or the Chinese waters.[3]

Struve's distinction between the current regime and the army which, in his view, was the embodiment of the Russian state, became even more pronounced in his celebrated 'Letter to the Students', written a few days later.[4] The students were the first organized body in Russia to publicly voice their opposition to the war. Their attitude, the fact that by then it was evident that news of the 'patriotic outbursts' in Russia were exaggerated,[5] together with the first signs of military reversals in the Far East, led Struve to emphasize the difference between his position and that of the 'defensists'. He did not advise the students to stop their anti-war manifestations. On the contrary, he explained that the general excitement and the first reversals in the Far East provided an excellent opportunity for propagating constitutional ideas in circles which until then had been immune to them. But, he continued, to be able to exploit this opportunity, the students would have to develop a real understanding of the political situation. They would have to distinguish between the current regime and the Russian state, between the government and the army. Otherwise, they would not only be unable to influence patriotically minded people, they would also be adopting a false position,[6] violating what by then already seemed to Struve the natural order of things in human society:

It is unnatural and shameful that those Russian people who aspire to become citizens of a self-governing state, harbour towards the armed forces of the nation no other

[1] *Osvobozhdeniye*, no. 17(41), 5/18 February 1904, front page ('War').
[2] Ibid., italics added.   [3] Ibid.
[4] *Listok Osvobozhdeniya*, no. 1, 11/24 February 1904.
[5] See *Osvobozhdeniye*, no. 18(42), 19 February/3 March 1904, pp. 325–8.
[6] *Listok Osvobozhdeniya* ibid.

feelings but those of fear and distrust. It is necessary as well as possible to end this unnatural state of affairs at this very moment...After all, *the army is the people in arms*, and whatever your attitude, mine or ours in principle to the war – the army is a fact of national life, the significance of which it is impossible to deny or to belittle.[1]

Only if the students were able to change their 'unnatural' attitude, Struve continued, should they join the patriotic demonstrations and capture them from within for the Liberation Movement by employing the following slogans: 'Long live the army! Long live Russia! Long live freedom! Long live free Russia!'[2]

Struve returned to this theme a week later. In an article entitled 'One Should Not Keep Silent' (*Nelzya Molchat*)[3] he explained that:

it is the moral right of those Russian people who love Russia and hate autocracy not to identify Russia and the fatherland with the tsar and autocracy. Moreover, I assume that at present it is not only a moral right but also the moral and political duty of all liberal Russians.[4]

The liberals should, therefore, combine their support of the fatherland with attacks on the government. He then referred to the dissolution of the elected Tver zemstvo and its replacement on 8 January 1904 by a bureaucratic committee, as a consequence of which Petrunkevich and his political colleagues were banished from the Tver province.[5] Struve explained to the 'patriotically minded' liberals that 'The Tver zemstvo is as important as Port Arthur and Von Plehve is more dangerous to Russia than the Japanese.'[6]

In a second article – 'The War and Patriotism'[7] – which appeared a day later, Struve demanded of the Union of Liberation that they start a compaign against the war:

The Russian public must know that the quicker the war ends, the better it will be for the country. Hence, the main task of the representatives of the Liberation Movement should consist, at present, of explaining the real causes and prospects of the war and of propagating radical political reform as the only guarantee against dangerous and foolish adventures.[8]

But neither Struve's condemnation of the war nor his insistence on the need to continue with active opposition could make his intermediary position acceptable to the 'defeatists'. And by identifying his 'ideal'

[1] Ibid. p. 2, italics added.
[2] Ibid.
[3] Ibid. no. 2, 18 February/2 March 1904.
[4] Ibid.
[5] See *Belokonskiy* II, pp. 193–5, *Osvobozhdeniye* (1904), no. 17(41), p. 312.
[6] *Listok Osvobozhdeniya* ibid.
[7] *Osvobozhdeniye*, no. 18(42), 19 February/3 March 1904, p. 319.
[8] Ibid.

Russian state with the Russian army, Struve supplied his opponents with an excellent opening for attacking him on theoretical as well as tactical grounds.

Theoretically, to try to distinguish between autocracy and the army by describing the latter as 'the people in arms' was a fallacy and was seen as such at the time. The Russian army was the main bulwark of autocracy and was known as such. It had frequently been exploited by the current rulers of Russia, as well as by their predecessors, as a police force. This was the source of the 'fear and distrust' which not only the students and revolutionaries, radicals and minorities, but also many ordinary Russian peasants and workers felt towards the army. Tactically, it was hardly worthwhile for Struve or for the students to use the slogan 'Long live the army!' at a time when the army's prestige was rapidly waning because of the military incompetence revealed after the outbreak of hostilities.[1]

Milyukov, who was then in London,[2] was the first 'defeatist' to attack Struve.[3] In his well-known 'Letter to the Editor',[4] Milyukov wrote that Struve's advice to the students to join the patriotic demonstrations under the banner of the 'four-slogan formula' was impracticable. In his opinion, the government would immediately ban all demonstrations if the demonstrators shouted the last two slogans. But even more important, Milyukov continued, to use this formula would be immoral because

although we harbour no ill feelings towards the army nevertheless we cannot deduce from the fact that 'the army is composed of the same people' that 'the people is the army'. As long as the Russian Army remains the symbolical fist of Russian impudence...we will not be able to shout 'Long live the Russian army!'[5]

The Liberation Movement, Milyukov explained, must not compromise itself by using patriotic slogans. Nor should it enter into any agreement with the government because of the war. He realized that the war complicated the issues and that the situation was difficult. But, he continued, 'this situation was not created by us and those who are responsible for its creation are not prepared even to lift a finger for the sake of securing our co-operation. They believe that they are strong enough to deal with it themselves.'[6] Under these circumstances,

---

[1] See, for example, *Shakhovskoy* IV, p. 118.   [2] See *Milyukov* Xa, pp. 216–23.
[3] For further attacks on Struve's position by the 'defeatists' see *Osvobozhdeniye* (1904), no. 22(46), pp. 398–9; no. 24(48), pp. 433–6.
[4] *Osvobozhdeniye*, no. 19(43), 7/20 March 1904 ('The War and the Russian Opposition').
[5] Ibid. p. 330.   [6] Ibid.

Milyukov stated, the Liberation Movement should return to its old slogan 'Down with autocracy'.[1]

In his reply to Milyukov, Struve admitted that his advice to the students had been given in haste and that, at any rate, it had already become impractical *'because the patriotic demonstrations had in the meantime been banned by the government itself'*.[2] (This was mainly because in many parts of the country they provoked anti-government manifestations and because the 'patriotic demonstrations' tended to get out of hand and end in riots directed against Jews, students and others. This was combined in some cases with the plunder and destruction of property.[3]) Struve also explained that he understood only too well why Milyukov and people like him were opposed to the slogan 'Long live the army!' He admitted that it had been a mistake on his part to identify the Russian state with the army. But, even if the chosen slogan had been an error, the idea which lay behind it, namely that there was an urgent need to distinguish between autocracy and the Russian state, the current rulers and the Russian nation, was not. Beside its fundamental importance, Struve continued, such a distinction was of very great tactical value to the Liberation Movement. Among its supporters there were many who adopted a 'defensist' and even a straightforward patriotic stand and, as in the case of the liberal Slavophiles a year earlier,[4] Struve did not want to count them out:

I feel the need for national solidarity. We need a common ground with those who still do not understand us. The search for such a common ground is, for me, a most vital emotional need. I believe that it is of the utmost importance to bring about a reconciliation between this need and the unswerving struggle for freedom.[5]

Less than a month later the second and last exchange between Milyukov and Struve occurred on the question of the attitude to the state in wartime.[6] Milyukov noted with satisfaction that his own 'defeatist' position was shared by the vast majority of the radical–democratic intelligentsia. Moreover, he continued, Struve had exaggerated the importance of the patriotic outburst in Russia. Even among the zemstvo activists patriotic feelings were less widespread than Struve thought and were waning all the time. But as regards those liberal patriots who stuck to their guns, they should be excluded from the Liberation Movement. Struve's quest for 'national solidarity' was, according to Milyukov, completely misplaced at this stage.

---

[1] *Osvobozhdeniye* ibid. p. 330.   [2] Ibid., italics in text.   [3] See *Galai*, p. 88.   [4] See above.
[5] *Osvobozhdeniye* ibid. p. 331.   [6] Ibid. no. 21(45), 2/15 April 1904, pp. 377–9.

Setback and recovery

Only after the achievement of political freedom will it :e possible, by a slow process, to eradicate the sorrowful heritage of centuries of ignorance and decades of struggle which prevent the normal manifestation of healthy national feelings. Till then, any quest for common ground with those who do not understand us on national questions will inevitably only result in the obscuring of our own conceptions, in confusing (our) political behaviour and in overshadowing more urgen: questions of internal policy.[1]

In his short answer to Milyukov's lengthy reply, Struve explained that he did not agree with Milyukov on the question of nationalism. But he was not prepared to press the issue any further at this time because he acknowledged that Milyukov was right as far as the factual political development was concerned.[2] The rapidly deteriorating internal situation in the Russian Empire deprived his controversy with Milyukov of much of its political importance and lent it a somewhat academic air. And in spring 1904 Struve had very little time or use for academic problems.[3]

While Milyukov and Struve were engaged in their second exchange of letters, a succession of military reversals in the Far East and the shortsightedness of Plehve's policies at home were rapidly undermining the position of the autocratic regime. The first to react to the defeats were the minorities, especially the Finns and the Poles. They were convinced that a military defeat would destroy autocracy and thus open the way for them to assert either genuine autonomy or complete independence. They, therefore, welcomed with jubilation every despatch from the front telling of a new Russian reversal. As early as 1 March 1904 a mass demonstration was held in Warsaw which proclaimed such slogans as 'Down with Tsarism!' 'Long live an independent socialist Poland!' 'Down with the war!' and 'Long live Japan'![4] The reaction in Russia proper to defeats was different. Only a small minority of the population had participated in the patriotic manifestations after the outbreak of war, but nevertheless those radicals and revolutionaries who were hoping for a Russian defeat were apparently even fewer in number. At best the 'silent' majority of the population passively hoped for a Russian victory and at worst it stayed indifferent. Their 'passive patriotism' or indifference began to turn into discontent in the second half of April 1904 when the news of the first

---

[1] Ibid. p. 378.
[2] Ibid. p. 379. For an exposition of Struve's views cn this subject after October 1905, especially as expressed in his contribution to *Vekhi*, see *Schapiro* IV, pp. 57–8, 64–6.
[3] See *Frank*, pp. 36 ff.   See *Galai*, p. 89.

Russian defeat on land (Yalu, 18 April/1 May 1904) arrived from the Far East.[1] This discontent was augmented by Plehve's renewed campaign against the zemstvos.

The readiness of the majority of the zemstvo activists to forget their grievances and co-operate with the government in wartime had no effect on Plehve. He still regarded the moderates as at least as dangerous an enemy of autocracy as the revolutionaries. He was particularly apprehensive of the activity of the All-Zemstvo Organization because 'it creates a precedent for common action by the zemstvos in other fields'.[2] On 17 April he issued a circular urging the governors of zemstvo provinces to prevent those zemstvos which had not already done so from joining the All-Zemstvo Organization.[3] Five days later, on the 22nd, he refused to approve Shipov's re-election to the chairmanship of the Moscow provincial zemstvo board.[4] Plehve explained to him that his refusal resulted from the fact that

I consider your activity harmful...in the political sense. When one speaks about political harmfulness...one usually has in mind political unreliability, conspirative revolutionary activity etc. In your case, however, this does not even arise. I consider your activity harmful in the political sense because you consistently strive for the widening of the competence and sphere of activity of the public institutions and for the establishing of an organization which will bring about a unification of the activities of zemstvo institutions in various provinces.[5]

Plehve's actions dismayed the moderate zemstvo activists and when, on 2 May 1904, representatives of the fourteen zemstvos belonging to the All-Zemstvo Organization held their first conference, they ended their self-imposed truce and renewed their attacks on the government.[6] This ended the political paralysis which had beset the Liberation Movement[7] and thus enabled the Union of Liberation and its Council to exploit to the full the rapidly increasing discontent of the population at large with the existing regime.

The defeat on the Yalu, which started the 'process of discontent' in Russia proper was soon overshadowed by a succession of even greater débâcles. Less than a month after Yalu, the Russian army was defeated at Nashau-Kinchau (13/26 May). Then on 2–3/15–16 June it was defeated at Tellisu (Vafangah). On 28 July/10 August the Japanese succeeded in preventing the Russian fleet from breaking out of Port Arthur and three days later (1/13 August) they virtually annihilated the

[1] Ibid. pp. 91–2.   [2] See *Galai*, p. 90.   [3] Ibid.   [4] See *Shipov* II, pp. 233–5.
[5] Ibid. p. 234.   [6] *Galai* ibid.   [7] See *Shakhovskoy* IV, p. 127.

Russian naval detachment in Vladivostok. On 20 August/2 September, after a fierce eight-day battle the Japanese routed a numerically superior Russian army at Lyao-Yang.

Each new defeat increased discontent in Russia proper and helped crystallize the opposition to tsarist rule in the minority provinces.[1] This, in its turn, created favourable conditions for the use of personal terror as a political weapon on an unprecedented scale. The wave of terrorist attacks which swept the vast Russian Empire in spring and summer 1904 culminated in the assassination of Bobrikov on 3 June by E. Shauman (a non-party Finnish nationalist),[2] and of Plehve on 15 July by Sazonov (a member of the SR's Fighting Organization, who was acting on its orders).[3]

The assassination of Plehve proved to be a watershed in the policies of Nicholas II. It deprived him of the main proponent in the government of the policy of firm rule without concessions to the opposition.[4] And coming so soon after the assassination of Bobrikov, it intensified the Tsar's feeling of isolation from his own administration. This can be deduced from the 15 July entry in his diary: 'In the person of good Plehve I have lost a friend and an irreplaceable Minister of the Interior ...In such a short time I have lost two such devoted servants.'[5]

Nowhere else in his rather dreary diary did Nicholas write with such affection about his assassinated subordinates and in no other case did he spend so long looking for a new minister. However, even before he chose a successor to Plehve as Minister of the Interior, his actions showed that he had almost no choice but to follow a policy aimed at appeasing some sections of public opinion. This he did on 11 August 1904, when he published a Manifesto (on the occasion of the christening of his son) and a decree (*ukaz*). They contained the first concessions

---

[1] See *Galai*, p. 91.

[2] See *Osvobozhdeniye* (1904), no. 50, p. 7; no. 51, p. 31; *Smirnov*, p. 127.

[3] Ibid. no. 53, pp. 63–4. There was a touch of 'poetic justice' in the fact that the assassination of Plehve, who prided himself on his police force and ruled only through it, was planned, prepared and supervised by the notorious Azef, who was playing a double game at the time. (See *Azef*, pp. 200, 206–8, 219–20, 227 remark (8), *Nikolayevskiy* I, pp. 72–91 and *Ratayev*, pp. 194, 204.) According to Nikolayevskiy (ibid. pp. 95–6), the *okhrana* failed to discover Azef's double game immediately after Plehve's assassination because its members hated Plehve too much to be willing to make an effort to find the people behind Sazonov. There can be little doubt that the way in which Plehve had dismissed Zubatov a year earlier contributed much to his unpopularity in *okhrana* circles. On the basis of *okhrana* behaviour after his assassination, one can safely establish that in contrast to what Plehve himself thought at the time (see *Osvobozhdeniye* (1904), no. 52, p. 46) he had made the police less efficient than they had been before.

[4] See *Galai*, p. 95.   [5] *Nicholas IIa*, p. 161.

since his accession to the throne, and included, for example, the abolition of corporal punishment, and cancellation of outstanding arrears in the redemption payments.[1] Then, a fortnight later, immediately after the Russian defeat at Lyao-Yang, Nicholas nominated Prince Svyatopolk-Mirskiy, who was known for his liberal propensities, as Minister of the Interior.[2]

Immediately after his nomination Svyatopolk-Mirskiy made two announcements. In the first, made during an interview given to a foreign correspondent in Vilna (where he was Governor General before his nomination), he declared that his policy would be based on religious tolerance (especially as far as the Jews were concerned) and decentralization, i.e. close collaboration with the zemstvos which, according to him, were excellent institutions. In his second statement, made during a speech to the departmental heads in the Ministry of the Interior, he declared his 'confidence in society'.[3] And in order to show society that he meant what he said, he started to relax the censorship of the press and also restored full rights (including the right to reside in St Petersburg), to such prominent leaders of the opposition as Annenskiy,[4] Myakotin,[5] Petrunkevich,[6] Rodichev,[7] and scores of others.

To paraphrase Tocqueville, the most dangerous moment for a bad government is when it suddenly starts to yield to public opinion. Had the tsarist regime made such concessions a few years earlier, they might have achieved their aim of conciliating the moderate elements in society. Now, however, they achieved the opposite. Not only did these concessions fall far short even of the liberal Slavophile demands, but they were also granted under the twin pressures of military defeats in the Far East and the growing discontent and intensification of the terror campaign at home. This invited new pressure on the government and inflamed public opinion even further, thus providing the Union of Liberation with its best opportunity so far for achieving its aim.

The leaders of the Liberation Movement were very quick to discern the beginnings of a change in the mood of the population in spring 1904. In commenting on the defeat on the Yalu,[8] Struve noted with

[1] See *Pravo* (1904), no. 33, cols 1640–60 and no. 35, Leader and cols 1706–8.

[2] Nicholas told Svyatopolk-Mirskiy about his nomination on 25 August 1904 (see *Nicholas IIa*, pp. 167–8) and the nomination was officially announced a day later (see *Russkiy Kalendar* 1905, p. 350).

[3] The full text of both statements may be found, among other places, in *Pravo* (1904), no. 38, cols 1858–9.

[4] *Brokgaus supp.* I, pp. 122–3.   [5] *Brokgaus supp.* II, p. 232.

[6] *Petrunkevich* II, p. 349.   [7] *Brokgaus supp.* II, p. 542.

[8] *Listok Osvobozhdeniya*, no. 7, April 26/May 9 1904.

satisfaction that the military reversals had compelled even the 'legal conservative patriotic press' (*Novoye Vremya* etc.) to hint about the need for reforms. From this he deduced that the political crisis was coming rather rapidly to a head and declared that 'through the bloody glow that hangs over the Yellow Sea we can already see the dawn of Russia's liberation'.[1] Struve's intuitive assumption was immediately confirmed by reports from *Osvobozhdeniye*'s correspondents in Russia. One of these, writing immediately after Yalu,[2] informed his readers that 'as a consequence of the military defeats it has become very easy to disseminate constitutionalist propaganda'.[3] These developments gradually led Struve to abandon his initial intermediary position, till by summer 1904 he had become to all intents and purposes a 'defeatist'. This change was fully reflected in his editorials, comments etc. in *Osvobozhdeniye* and in *Listok Osvobozhdeniya*. Their tone became more and more radical and this helped the Council of the Union of Liberation in its drive to impose the 'defeatist' point of view on all sections of the Liberation Movement.

Commenting on the Yalu defeat, Struve wrote *inter alia*, 'The worst thing about the war is not that it is difficult to win it, but that it would be dreadful to win it.'[4] In the next issue of *Osvobozhdeniye*,[5] Struve published four letters, all of which supported the 'defeatist' point of view. In the first letter 'Zemstvo Councillor U.' concluded his 'anti-patriotic' article (written before Yalu) by prophesying that 'very soon Manchurian patriotism will be replaced by real patriotism which will lead us towards our only cherished aim – the overthrow of autocracy.'[6] The second letter, signed 'Karin', demanded complete dissociation from the government.[7]

The third letter to the editor, signed X and dated 26 April 1904 (OS? NS?),[8] demanded co-ordination of the activities of all the parties and groups which were fighting autocracy. In order to achieve this, the author continued, a conference of their representatives should be held outside Russia. This conference should 'elaborate a common minimum programme and elect an all-party executive committee'. All parties sending representatives to this committee would have to undertake to disseminate its publications on equal terms with their own and to follow its instructions on tactics. The letter ended with the following post-

[1] Ibid. p. 2. [2] *Osvobozhdeniye* (1904), no. 24(48) ('Samara'), pp. 437–8.
[3] Ibid. p. 438. [4] *Osvobozhdeniye*, no. 23(47), 2/15 May 1904, p. 410.
[5] Ibid. no. 24(48) May 21/June 3, pp. 434–6. [6] Ibid. p. 434 [7] Ibid.
[8] Ibid. p. 435. The author was apparently either Zilliacus or one of his political friends, a Finnish nationalist called Leo Mechelin. See *Pipes* IIa, p. 364 and below.

script: 'It is desirable that the regional parties (Poles, Finns, Bund, Latvians, Armenians, Georgians etc.) as well as the all-Russian social-revolutionary and oppositional parties, should participate' (in the conference).

In the fourth letter, a frequent contributor to *Osvobozhdeniye* demanded that the newspaper adopt a more radical line and urged all the 'liberal patriots' (like the one who had reminded Struve of Herzen's fate) to leave the 'liberal party'.[1] A fortnight later, in a short preface to a 'defensist' article (written by Prince G. Volkonskiy)[2] Struve declared that he rejected the author's juxtaposition of the national–patriotic and the party's points of view: '*We regard the Far Eastern policy of the St Petersburg government...as basically erroneous and harmful and we believe that its speedy termination, on whatever conditions available, would be a blessing for Russia.*'[3]

Six weeks later *Osvobozhdeniye* published a long article by Milyukov (written in the Balkans, on the eve of Plehve's assassination) the content of which was whole-heartedly approved by Struve.[4] Milyukov stated that the time had arrived for the Liberation Movement to reveal the political part of its programme in full. Four months earlier, when the Movement had become paralysed by the outbreak of war, Milyukov would have been satisfied if all its groups had united around the simple slogan 'Down with autocracy'. But now, he argued, the Liberation Movement must be more specific. It must openly declare its minimal demand to be the establishment of a representative institution, elected directly by the people with full legislative powers, including supervision of the budget.[5] As for the remaining parts of the programme (e.g. the social clauses of the programme of the Union of Liberation) Milyukov hinted that these would have to be revealed later, when circumstances were more favourable.[6] Little did he know that by the time his article appeared, these circumstances would already have arrived.

The assassination of Plehve introduced an element of urgency into the deliberations of the Council of the Union of Liberation and by the end of July it had published its first appeal to the population.[7] Entitled 'The People and the War'[8] it was written in very simple language so as

[1] *Osvobozhdeniye* ibid. pp. 435–6.
[2] *Osvobozhdeniye*, no. 25(49) 2/15 June 1904, pp. 446–9.
[3] Ibid. p. 446. Italics in text.
[4] *Osvobozhdeniye*, no. 52, 19 July/1 August 1904, pp. 36–9.
[5] *Osvobozhdeniye* ibid. p. 38.   [6] Ibid. pp. 38–9.   [7] *Shakhovskoy* IV, p. 126.
[8] Reprinted in *Osvobozhdeniye* (1904), no. 57, pp. 119–20.

to enable the 'masses' to understand its message. The authors began their appeal by explaining the causes of the war, which had brought so much suffering on the Russian people. The war, they wrote, had begun because of the foolhardy policy of the Tsar and his clique of irresponsible advisers, ministers and grand dukes. If the Tsar had been surrounded, not by irresponsible and non-representative 'magnates' but by representatives of the people, he would have been unable to conduct such a policy. Then they explained that surrounding the Tsar with representatives of the people would constitute a constitutional form of government, and they enumerated the blessings which such a form of government could bestow on the people: equality of all before the law ('peasants and landowners enjoy the same rights'), freedom of travel and of expression etc. Then they stated that 'if the Russian people would demand for themselves and obtain from the Tsar a constitution,'[1] not only would they enjoy all these blessings but also

the representatives of the people would quickly calculate and satisfy the people's important needs. They would find out how, from where and on whose account to allocate to the peasants enough land and how to transfer the burden of taxes from the people to the shoulders of the rich...Under a constitution the people would be free and would live a real, good life.[2]

And they ended their appeal with the dual slogan (which caught the imagination of the public a few months later at the time of the 'banquet campaign'): 'Down with autocracy!' 'Long live the constitution!'[3]

The first organized body of the Liberation Movement (besides the Council of the Union of Liberation) to hold a meeting after Plehve's assassination and Nicholas's Manifesto of 12 August 1904 was *Beseda*, which met on the 31st of that month.[4] Prince Pavel D. Dolgorukov opened the meeting by asking the circle to change its decision of 15 February.[5] He said, *inter alia*: 'Has not the time arrived for the zemstvos to renounce official patriotism, return to the offensive and demand of the government that it end this useless war?'[6]

He was supported by Maklakov (who stated that the government itself would be grateful to anyone who helped to end the war) and by N. N. Lvov, who declared that 'there is an urgent need to end the

[1] Ibid. p. 120.   [2] Ibid.   [3] Ibid.
[4] *Chermenskiy* II, pp. 54–5 (his description is based on the *Beseda* archives). Chermenskiy does not mention any discussion of the Manifesto, but in the opinion of the present author, this must have taken place. At any rate the decisions taken at the meeting show that the concessions contained in the Manifesto fell far short of the demands of even the most moderate members of the circle.
[5] See above.   [6] *Chermenskiy*, ibid. p. 54.

useless war. The existing government, however, lacks sufficient authority to do it. Hence the zemstvos should adopt resolutions declaring that in view of the difficult situation created by the war, it is desirable that elected representatives of the country should be summoned.'[1]

The opposition to this point of view was led by Petrovo-Solovovo, who declared that peace without victory was undesirable and defended the circle's February decision. In contrast to the situation at the Second Congress of the Union of Zemstvo Constitutionalists in February, where Petrovo-Solovovo and Lvov had also opposed one another,[2] it was Lvov who carried the day this time. The final resolution adopted by the meeting called on the zemstvo assemblies to demand that representatives of the people be convened, without specifying whether they should have a decisive or only a consultative voice.[3]

If Nicholas's concession could not satisfy even the moderate *Beseda* it is hardly surprising that they only spurred on the leaders of the Union of Liberation to adopt an increasingly radical position. While analysing the 11 August Manifesto, Struve explained that its most important political concession was undoubtedly the abolition of corporal punishment. But, he continued, its importance lay not in the measure itself but in the fact that 'this measure represents a victory of public opinion over the government'.[4] Therefore, 'Russian society must not thank the autocratic regime for this "favour" but utilize it for the further struggle with autocracy[5]... The opposition, by definition, can use (favours) for one aim only – for a further onslaught'.[6] Commenting in the same issue of *Osvobozhdeniye* on the nomination of Svyatopolk-Mirskiy 'who was known as a liberal bureaucrat', Struve warned his readers to be careful not to succumb to the new temptation.[7]

Writing a month later on the same question, Milyukov could already be more specific. Commenting on Svyatopolk-Mirskiy's 'new course',[8] his 'confidence in society' speech, the amnesty granted to leading oppositionists etc., Milyukov wrote:

Svyatopolk-Mirskiy apparently intends...to return to the *status quo ante* Plehve... If this is so, then his programme differs, not only from the programmes of other parties which are fighting against autocracy but also from our own...We are not interested in tolerance limited by the bounds of the existing laws, because such (tolerance) does not exist. What we want is an open and official recognition of

---

[1] Ibid. pp. 54–5.   [2] See above.   [3] *Chermenskiy* ibid. p. 55.
[4] *Osvobozhdeniye*, no. 55, 2/15 September 1904, front page.   [5] Ibid.
[6] Ibid. p. 82.   [7] Ibid. pp. 84–5.   [8] Ibid. no. 57, 2/15 October, 1904.

complete freedom of religion and conscience, as well as freedom of the press, of meetings, unions, travel, personal immunity as well as immunity of property and dwellings...We are also not interested in the (formula of)...'locally self-governing land with an autocratic tsar at its head'...We want a formal abolition of autocracy. ...We want the Tsar to give the Russians what he gave the Bulgarians.[1]

There would be some people, he continued, who would warn against excessive demands in times of war. To this his answer was that only because the war had weakened the government had it been forced to grant concessions. Then he warned the government against the fatal error of giving too little, too late and explained that half-measures would now not suffice. *'There are no intermediary positions between autocracy and consistent constitutionalism.'*[2] This was true, he stated, not only because the constitutionalists no longer believed in the government and hence were not prepared to wait patiently for the gradual transition from autocracy to constitutionalism, but also because even if they agreed to such a policy, other parties and forces would not, and the constitutionalists would lose all influence. Moreover, although the position of the 'consistent constitutionalists' might seem too radical to the government, it was in reality already too moderate for other forces. His conclusion was that the consistent constitutionalists could not afford to compromise and must insist on the acceptance of their full programme.

We will not offer you any of our people, we will not render you any credit, we will not grant you any respite till you accept our full programme. And even then, we are not sure if we will be able to save Russia from your political dilettantism and, without shocks, lead her along the road of peaceful political development.[3]

---

[1] Ibid. front page.   [2] Ibid. p. 114, italics in text.   [3] Ibid.

10

'No enemies on the left'

Milyukov's insistence on the immediate implementation of the Union of Liberation's full political programme logically led him and the Union to seek allies on the left, among the revolutionary parties. And indeed, at about the time his article was written (or shortly before) Milyukov, Struve, Bogucharskiy and Peter Dolgorukov had participated in the 'Paris Conference', or as it was officially called, the 'Conference of Oppositional and Revolutionary Organizations of the Russian Empire'[1] which was held in Paris between 17 and 25 September (30 September – 8 October) 1904.[2]

The idea of holding such a conference became popular in oppositional and revolutionary circles in late spring/early summer 1904. The main driving force behind it was Konni Zilliacus, the leader of the Finnish Party of Active Resistance.[3] But it was only after Plehve's

[1] The main sources of information on the proceedings of the conference are *Menshchikov*, pp. 182–95 and *Listok Osvobozhdeniya*, no 17, 19 Nov./2 Dec. 1904. Cf. *Akselrod* IV, pp. 107–9, *Azef*, pp. 210, 213–15, *Belokonskiy* II, pp. 211–12, *Chernov* III, pp. 208–13 (his reminiscences on the conference are inaccurate and very disappointing), *Iskra* no. 79, pp. 1–4, *Lopukhin* IV, p. 220, *Milyukov* V₃, pp. 122–7; X*a*, pp. 241–5, *Osvobozhdeniye* (1904), no. 61, *Shakhovskoy* IV, pp. 136–7, *Smirnov*, p. 129. For treatment of this subject by a modern historian see *Fischer*, pp. 167–70, cf. *Futtrell*, p. 66 and *White*, p. 141. In his recent biography of Struve, Professor Pipes sheds some new light on the origins of the conference (see *Pipes* IIa, pp. 363–6). But this does not alter the overall picture as described on the following pages.

[2] Milyukov claimed in his memoirs that the date 30 September/8 October was OS (see *Milyukov* V₃, p. 123; X*a*, p. 242). He apparently based his claim on the fact that Ratayev's report to St Petersburg on the conference (i.e. Azef's report which he sent to Ratayev, head of the *okhrana*'s Western-European Section) was dated 9/22 October 1904 (see *Menshchikov*, p. 182). Milyukov's claim was accepted by modern historians of the period (see, for example, *Harcave*, p. 54). But in his statement to the third Duma on the 'Azef Affair', Stolypin explicitly stated that the Paris Conference was held between 17 and 24 September 1904 (see *S.O.*, 1909 Second Session, part II, meetings 37–60, col. 1427). Stolypin's statement is confirmed by Azef's two preliminary reports to Ratayev on the preparations for the conference. They carry a single date (NS) – 7 Sept. and 22 Sept. respectively (*Azef*, pp. 209–10, 213). Only Azef's reports from Russia usually carried a double date (the OS in brackets: see ibid. pp. 204, 206–7 ff.) Hence the dates 30 September–8 October must have been in accordance with the Gregorian calendar (or NS).

[3] See above and *Nikolayevskiy*, pp. 57–8, *Volkovicher*, pp. 119–22.

assassination that he produced a concrete proposal according to which representatives of all revolutionary and oppositional parties and groups in the Russian Empire should meet in Paris in order to co-ordinate their activities. As a first step towards its realization, Zilliacus envis‑ aged the election by the conference of a central bureau for dissemin‑ ating information on developments inside Russia to the outside world. He suggested that the conference make arrangements for the publica‑ tion of joint leaflets.[1] His suggestion was rejected by the RSDRP and by five SD parties among the minorities (Bund, SD Party of Poland and Lithuania, Polish Socialist Party ('Proletariat'), Latvian SD Party and the Ukrainian Revolutionary Party).[2] The reasons they gave for refusing to participate were that the SD parties would be in a minority in the proposed conference as well as in the executive bodies it was due to elect, and also that according to widespread rumours at the time (which were partly verified) the Finns and the Poles had entered into some kind of relationship with the Japanese government, which had financed the preparations for the conference.[3]

It may well be that the SD would have rejected Zilliacus's invitation even if they had not suspected the Finns and the Poles of co-operation with the enemy. Their fear of remaining in a minority would have sufficed for such a decision[4] (though Plekhanov claimed at the time that their suspicions constituted the most important reason for not partici‑ pating in the conference).[5] But even if this were so, the very fact that

[1] See *Azef*, p. 210 and *Volkovicher*, p. 119. The very strong resemblance between this plan and the one which appeared in *Osvobozhdeniye* (1904), no. 24(48) (see above), may give some room for assumption that the latter was written either by Zilliacus himself or by one of his friends. This is to some extent corroborated by Plekhanov, who told a meeting of the council of RSDRP, held at the beginning of June 1904 (about a fortnight after the appearance of the above letter), that Zilliacus had suggested to him the holding of a con‑ ference in Paris. On the other hand there is the evidence given by Martov at the same meet‑ ing, according to which similar suggestions were made at the same time by the SRs and the *Osvobozhdentsy* (members of the Union of Liberation). (See *Nikolayevskiy*, pp. 58–9.) Hence, even if the latter in *Osvobozhdeniye* was written by Zilliacus (or by Mechelin, see *Pipes* IIa, pp. 363–4), the idea of holding a conference in Paris was not alien to the leaders of the Liberation Movement. And indeed, as early as May, Struve was formally approached by the Finns regarding the possibility of holding such a congress (see *Pipes* ibid.).
[2] See *Iskra*, no. 79, 1 December 1904, p. 4.
[3] See ibid. and *Volkovicher*, pp. 119–21. Modern research on this subject has confirmed the existence of contacts between Zilliacus and the Japanese at the time of the conference (see *Futtrell*, p. 66 and *White*, p. 141 – Zilliacus himself was the first to disclose his contacts with them). However, no evidence could be found to prove that the 'Paris Conference' was actually financed by the Japanese government (a private letter from Mr Futtrell to the author of this book).
[4] See, for example, the bitter attack on the 'Paris bloc' on principle in *Iskra*, no. 79, pp. 1–3.
[5] See *Volkovicher*, p. 121.

the SDs chose these rumours as partial justification for refusal to take part in the 'Paris Conference' indicates the importance attached to them at the time. This in itself throws important light on the state of mind of the leaders of the Union of Liberation, who, in contrast to the SDs, decided to participate. (Struve particularly must have undergone a very rapid process of radicalization in summer 1904, if his patriotism did not prevent him from participating in the conference.[1]) In addition to the Union of Liberation, the Finnish Party of Active Resistance, the SRs and five other revolutionary groups accepted Zilliacus's invitation and participated in the conference. Ten organizations (including the six SD parties) did not attend.[2] As a result, the conference was much

[1] Writing many years after the events, Milyukov tried to justify his participation in the conference (for which he was attacked by his opponents inside and outside Cadet circles in exile) by claiming that at the time he had heard nothing about Zilliacus's contacts with the Japanese, though, by implication, he stated that Struve must have known about them. Secondly, he stated that there was no 'defeatist mood' at the conference and that in any case it had no practical results (see *Milyukov* V3, pp. 123–7; Xa, pp. 242–5). As far as Milyukov's second claim is concerned it is refuted by the proceedings, decisions and their influence on the events in Russia (see below). As regards his first claim, it is hardly conceivable that Struve, who must have got wind of the rumours regarding Zilliacus's contacts with the Japanese, did not tell the other members of the Union of Liberation delegation about them on their arrival in Paris.

[2] A list of the eighteen organizations invited and the eight which attended is found in *Listok Osvobozhdeniya* no. 17. A list of those attending, including names and some pseudonyms is found in *Menshchikov*, p. 185. The names of the four Union of Liberation delegates were disclosed by Stolypin on 11 Feb. 1909 during a debate at the third Duma on the 'Azef Affair'. See *S.O.* ibid; see also *Belokonskiy* II, pp. 211–12. The final list of participants was as follows:

The Party	Delegates	Pseudonyms
Armenian Revolutionary Federation	(1) Varandyan (ed. of *Droshak*)	—
Finnish Party of Active Resistance	(2) K. Zilliacus	—
	(3) A. Neovins	—
Georgian Party of Socialists–	(4) Dekanozov	—
Federalists–Revolutionaries	(5) Gabuniya	—
Latvian SD Workers Party	(6) Ossols	—
(only SD Party present)		
Polish National League	(7) S. Balicki	—
	(8) R. Dmowski	—
PPS	(9) Malinowski	Konewski
	(10) Iodko (Nazkiewicz)	Ulrich
	(11) Baron Keller-Krause	Lyusnia
SR	(12) Victor Chernov	Gordenin
	(13) Yevno Azef	Dikenskiy
Union of Liberation	(14) V.Ya. Bogucharskiy	Glebov
	(15) Prince Peter D.	
	Dolgorukov	Anisimov
	(16) P.N. Milyukov	Aleksandrov
	(17) P.B. Struve	—

less representative than intended by its organizer. Nor was it able, because of the divergent views of its participants, to agree on the establishment of a 'central bureau' for co-ordinating the activities of the parties and groups which participated. But it was nevertheless not a complete waste of time from the point of view of the anti-government forces.

Three topics dominated the discussions at Paris; the nature of the future political regime of the Russian Empire, the nationality question, and the means by which the various groups intended to conduct their struggle against autocracy. The decisions of the conference on these questions were incorporated in two documents – 'Summary of the Protocol' and a 'Declaration of Principles' (both, apparently, drafted by Milyukov).[1] They were published only seven weeks after it ended[2] because the representatives of the Union of Liberation had to present them to the congress of the Union (held four weeks later) for official approval.[3] From these documents, as well as from Azef's reports to *okhrana* headquarters,[4] it is known that – regarding the first topic – the conference declared its unanimous acceptance of two principles. First, all participants agreed that they were united in striving for the destruction of autocracy. And therefore 'the parties represented at the conference will *unite their efforts* in order to hasten the inevitable fall of absolutism, which is equally *incompatible with the realization of all the long-term diverse aims which each of these parties is trying to achieve'.*[5] Secondly, they agreed that the political regime which would replace autocracy, should be based on democratic principles. They did not specify whether it should be a monarchy or a republic. In their own words: 'The Conference, after ascertaining that all its participants are striving to establish a democratic regime in Russia, has agreed on the following formula accepted by all participating parties: that the popular representatives must be elected by universal suffrage.'[6]

The decisions of the conference on the national question[7] were much more specific and straightforward. It declared that 'all the parties represented at the conference regard the struggle against russification . . .and against the stirring up of national hatred as a task as important as the fight against the aggressive foreign policy'. They specifically called

---

1 See *Milyukov* v3, pp. 125–6; xa, pp. 244–5.
2 *Listok Osvobozhdeniya*, no. 17, 19 Nov./2 Dec. 1904.
3 See *Milyukov* ibid., ibid., *Menschikov*, p. 193, *Shakhovskoy* IV, pp. 136–7 and below.
4 See *Menshchikov*, pp. 182–95.
5 *Listok Osvobozhdeniya*, ibid. front page, italics added.
6 Ibid.   7 See ibid.

(apparently on the insistence of Zilliacus) for the 'revoking of all the measures curtailing the constitutional rights of Finland'. And they declared that 'all the parties recognize the right of each nationality to self-determination and the need to guarantee free national development by law'. As regards the means of conducting the struggle, the conference recognized the right of each of the represented parties to choose its own. This (according to the protocol) should not be an obstacle to the co-ordination of their activities.[1] And, indeed, the representatives of the Union of Liberation, while stating that they would use only 'peaceful means', informed the conference regarding their plans for the immediate future. The Union intended to organize a constitutional campaign in the zemstvos and in other 'public institutions' and it would be prepared, so they believed, to co-ordinate it with the revolutionary activity of the other parties and groups.[2]

After approving the 'Protocol' and the 'Declaration', the conference ended its deliberations. Struve remained in Paris, whence the editorial office of *Osvobozhdeniye* had been transferred from Stuttgart that summer.[3] Milyukov, Bogucharskiy and Dolgorukov hurried back to Russia where the Council of the Union of Liberation was then holding a series of most important meetings.[4] (The fact that they were not arrested on arrival was a sign of the growing weakness of the government, which all along knew from Azef's reports about their activities in Paris. Milyukov stayed in St Petersburg only a few days and then left for the United States.[5])

From the point of view of Zilliacus, though not for the Union of Liberation delegates, the conference must have been a disappointment. As far as the latter were concerned, its outcome must have justified the policy of 'no enemies on the left'. The contacts which they established there with the SRs (especially Victor Chernov) proved of great value during the 'banquet campaign' which was launched soon afterwards, and the establishment of the intelligentsia unions, which later amalgamated in the Union of Unions. In contrast to the SDs, the SRs neither tried to disrupt the former nor to hinder the development of the latter. On the contrary, in many cases they actively co-operated with the 'Liberators' in both enterprises.

It is quite possible that a certain amount of co-operation between the two sides would have taken place even without the Paris Conference

---

[1] Ibid. [2] *Menshchikov*, p. 194.
[3] The main reason for Struve's move was police harrassment (see *Pipes* IIa, pp. 356–7).
[4] See *Shakhovskoy* IV, pp. 130–2. [5] See *Milyukov* V3, pp. 127–31; Xa, pp. 246–7.

because of the ideological affinity between the *Russkoye Bogatstvo* group, its many rank-and-file followers and the SRs. Another factor was the close personal ties which must have existed at the time not only between Chernov and the *Russkoye Bogatstvo* people,[1] but also between him and the other ex-members of the People's Rights Party who were on the board of the Council of the Union of Liberation (Bogucharskiy, Khizhnyakov, Kuskova and Prokopovich).

But had it not been for the 'Paris Conference', it would have been quite unthinkable for the zemstvo constitutionalist wing of the Union of Liberation to co-operate with the SRs to the extent it subsequently did, especially in Moscow. There, apparently as a direct consequence of the Paris Conference, the local branch of the Union of Liberation made an attempt to organize an 'oppositional bloc'. On the initiative of V. Maklakov, the secretary of *Beseda* and future 'right-wing' Cadet, representatives of the Moscow branch of the Union of Liberation and of the SD and SR local committees held an 'official' conference in mid-December 1904. This conference failed to establish such a bloc because the SD refused to collaborate with 'bourgeois elements'.[2] It succeeded, however, in establishing a working partnership between the Moscow branch of the Union of Liberation and the local SRs.

The satisfaction of the Union of Liberation delegates with the out-come of the Paris Conference was reflected in an article by Struve, published shortly after it ended. He wrote it in direct response to an article by Professor Prince E. N. Trubetskoy (brother of the future first elected rector of Moscow University, S. N. Trubetskoy, and moderate constitutionalist member of *Beseda*)[3] published in *Pravo* on 26 September 1904 and entitled 'The War and the Bureaucracy'. Trubetskoy's article was very outspoken in its criticism of the govern-ment though, out of considerations for censorship, he used the term 'bureaucracy' for 'autocracy'[4] and 'national regeneration' instead of 'constitution'. Moreover, his article proved to be a turning-point in the annals of the Russian press,[5] for it opened the anti-government press campaign which was to transform the Russian press for a while into one of the freest presses in the world! Being himself a moderate, he was

[1] See *Chernov* II, III, pp. 237–61.
[2] See *Chermenskiy* II, pp. 58–9, *Mitskevich* III, pp. 221–2.
[3] See above. In 1906 he joined the moderate Party of Peaceful Renovation (*Partiya Mirnogo Obnovleniya*) which was headed by D.N. Shipov, M.A. Stakhovich, Count P.A. Geyden and N.N. Lvov (see *Shipov* II, pp. 512–15).
[4] This was standard usage in the legal press at the time. See *Gessen* I, p. 179.
[5] See *Shakhovskoy* IV, p. 128.

opposed to revolution as much as to autocracy. He appealed to the government to introduce far-reaching reforms from above in order to enable society to share in the process of governing Russia and thus prevent an upheaval from below.

Trubetskoy pointed out that the political monopoly which 'bureaucracy' had enjoyed for so long had brought only disaster to Russia. Internally it had resulted in a 'monopoly' of the extreme parties over the hearts and minds of the population. Externally it had brought about the disastrous war with Japan.[1] But, he continued, if the government would go beyond the policies pronounced by Svyatopolk-Mirskiy, it might still be possible to prevent the final catastrophe. If the government would give society its proper share in the running of the state, 'then we will not need to be afraid *either of the internal or of the external enemy*. And the Tsar, after surrounding himself by the Land (*Zemlya*) will achieve glory, greatness and strength.'[2]

It would have been unthinkable for such an article to appear in a legal newspaper before the appointment of Svyatopolk-Mirskiy, nor would it have aroused much criticism on the part of Struve if Trubetskoy had somehow managed to publish it legally after the outbreak of war but before the Paris Conference. By the time it appeared in print, however, the Union of Liberation had already entered into a formal alliance with those 'extremist parties' which Trubetskoy feared, and Struve was quick to disclose the new facts of life to him. In so doing, he restated in *Osvobozhdeniye* for the first time since the outbreak of war his theoretical formulation of the policy of 'no enemies on the left'.[3]

In an 'Open Letter to Professor Prince E. N. Trubetskoy', published in *Osvobozhdeniye* on 14(27) October 1904, Struve pointed out that he had explained to his readers from the outset that the liberals must regard the revolutionary parties not as enemies but as allies. The reason for this, he continued, was that

as long as the stronghold of autocracy has not been destroyed, anyone who is fighting against it represents, not 'a grave danger' but a great blessing...[4] In Russia there is no internal enemy apart from autocracy...Solidarity between all our oppositional forces...constitutes the first commandment of a sensible political struggle.[5]

And he ended his attack on Trubetskoy by proclaiming the old–new

---

[1] See *Pravo* (1904), no. 39, cols 1874–5.   [2] Ibid. col. 1875, italics added.
[3] For Struve's pre-war announcements on this subject see above pp. 162–3.
[4] *Osvobozhdeniye* (1904), no. 58, p. 136.   [5] Ibid. p. 137.

battle-cry of the Union of Liberation: 'There is only one internal enemy in Russia and its name is – autocracy.'[1]

Meanwhile, even before the Paris Conference ended, those members of the Council of the Union of Liberation who remained in Russia started preparations for the Second Congress of the Union. The proposed agenda of this congress was discussed at two meetings of the Council, held on 20 September, and 8 October.[2] There can be little doubt that the second meeting was the decisive one because of the participation of Bogucharskiy, Milyukov and Dolgorukov, who informed the Council of the outcome of the Paris Conference.

The zemstvo radicals first reported their success in persuading *Beseda* to adopt a resolution calling on the zemstvo assemblies to demand the convocation of representatives of the people.[3] Then they turned to the various steps they had taken to ensure that these demands should be constitutional, i.e. that the representatives of the people should have a decisive and not a consultative voice. The main step in this direction was Shipov's agreement to co-operate in the convocation of a zemstvo congress where, they believed, the constitutionalists would be able to achieve a majority.[4] They suggested, therefore, that the zemstvo-constitutionalist wing of the Union of Liberation should play the leading role in the forthcoming zemstvo campaign.

The representatives of the radical–democratic intelligentsia on the Council then suggested the organization of 'banquets'. This had been the traditional means of struggle of the St Petersburg radical intelligentsia since the beginning of the century and now that Annenskiy and Myakotin had returned to the capital, there was good reason to believe that a 'banquet campaign' might prove a great success. Both suggestions were approved by the Council which submitted them, together with the resolutions of the 'Paris Conference', to the Second Congress of the Union of Liberation for final sanction.

This congress met in St Petersburg between 20 and 22 October 1904.[5] Like the foundation congress, it was composed of fifty delegates, who represented the same provincial branches[6] (and who, one strongly suspects, were mostly the same people). The numerical stagnation thus revealed undoubtedly reflected the Union's political paralysis

[1] Ibid.
[3] See above.
[5] The main source of information on the Second Congress of the Union of Liberation is *Shakhovskoy* IV, pp. 133–6. See also: *Belokonskiy* II, pp. 210–11, *Cherevanin* II, p. 149 and *Fischer*, pp. 175–7.
[6] See *Shakhovskoy* ibid. p. 133.

[2] See *Shakhovskoy* IV, pp. 130–2.
[4] See *Shakhovskoy* IV, pp. 131–2 and below.

during the first months of the war. The decisions of the Second Congress, however, as well as the atmosphere of exaltation which prevailed throughout its debates, were an expression of the newly acquired confidence of its leaders and rank-and-file members, who believed that they were finally standing at the gates of their 'new Jerusalem'. And indeed, they could now survey the political panorama in Russia like the Creator after the Creation and pronounce it good.

The autocratic government which, only a few months earlier, had seemed as strong and immovable as a rock, was beginning to crumble before their eyes. The relaxation of censorship provisions had resulted in a growing flood of criticism of the government and demands for peace and reforms were intensifying daily.[1] The ministers were at a complete loss, caught as they were between the twin pressures of the growing clamour for peace and reforms in Russia proper, disorders in the minority provinces[2] and incessant defeats in the Far East on the one hand and Nicholas II's notorious opposition to any political change which might infringe on his autocratic powers on the other. The leaders of the Union of Liberation needed no better indication of the weakness of the government than the invitation extended at the end of September or beginning of October by Svyatopolk-Mirskiy to the doyen of zemstvo-radical constitutionalism, I. I. Petrunkevich, to come and discuss the general situation with him.[3] The state of public opinion, the weakness of the government and the Tsar's stubbornness, all seemed to them to justify the policy of 'no enemies on the left'. This policy was aimed at bringing as much pressure as possible, and as quickly as was feasible, to bear on the government in order to bring it to its knees in the shortest possible time.

The congress therefore approved the decisions of the Paris Conference and agreed, apparently unanimously, on the publication of the two documents which summed up its results. But, on the insistence of the radical intelligentsia delegates, it instructed the Council to publish, together with the above two documents, an announcement of the existence of the Union of Liberation as well as of its programme.[4] They probably insisted on this because, in contrast to the two documents approved by the Paris Conference (which did not include any social clauses and demanded only 'universal suffrage') the programme of the Union included the 'four-tail formula' ('Universal, equal and direct suffrage and secret ballot') as well as a 'declaration of intent' in the social

---

[1] See *Shakhovskoy* ibid. pp. 128–9 and *Galai*, pp. 96, 98.   [2] *Galai* ibid.
[3] See *Petrunkevich* II, p. 349.   [4] See *Shakhovskoy* IV, pp. 134–7.

field.[1] Then the Council presented its three-point plan of action to the congress. It demanded: that members of the Union take an active part in the forthcoming zemstvo congress; that the Union instruct the zemstvo constitutionalists to raise constitutional demands at the forthcoming zemstvo assemblies; that the Union organize public banquets in as many cities as possible on 20 November 1904 (the fortieth anniversary of the judicial reforms).[2]

The congress approved this plan but added a fourth point which became of cardinal importance a few weeks later. This was that the Union of Liberation should

> begin a propaganda campaign for the formation of unions of advocates, professors, writers and other members of the liberal professions, for the organization by them of congresses which would elect permanent bureaux and for the amalgamation of these bureaux...into a single Union of Unions.[3]

The idea of forming such unions was not itself a new one and in the words of Shakhovskoy 'it fitted in the best possible way into the (Liberators') general line of activity'.[4] And, indeed, as early as November 1903, *Osvobozhdeniye* had published an article entitled 'The Liberation Tasks of the Russian Intelligentsia',[5] which, but for some practical changes, had anticipated the above decision and the way in which it was implemented during the 'banquet campaign' and early in 1905. The author of this article (who, according to Struve, did not belong at the time to the Liberation Movement but whose basic ideas he welcomed

[1] See *Milyukov* Xa, p. 245 and *Iskra*, no. 79, pp. 1–4. For the contents of the two documents and the programme of the Union of Liberation see *Listok Osvobozhdeniya* no. 17 and above.

[2] *Shakhovskoy* ibid. pp. 131–2.

[3] *Shakhovskoy* IV, p. 132. According to *Belokonskiy* II, pp. 210–11 and *Cherevanin* II, p. 149, this point was included in the original plan presented to the congress by the Council and it was approved by it. Shakhovskoy, on the other hand, stated explicitly that the plan of action as approved by the congress did not include this point, but that it was added later by the Council. And indeed, if this point was formulated as quoted by Shakhovskoy, it could not have been accepted by the Union of Liberation before summer 1905 because it included a reference to the 'Bureau of Congresses of Zemstvo and Town Activists' (*Shakhovskoy* ibid.). But the 'town activists' were not organized until June 1905 (see *Belokonskiy* II, p. 288n. and *Syn Otechestva* (1905), no. 105, p. 5, col. 4) and they joined the zemstvo congresses and their 'bureaux' only in July of that year (see *Belokonskiy* ibid. p. 292). On the basis of the available material (the composition of the first elected bureaux of the various unions etc.) there can be little doubt that either the congress itself or the Council of the Union of Liberation immediately after its re-election decided to launch the intelligentsia unions (see below).

[4] *Shakhovskoy* ibid. p. 132.

[5] *Osvobozhdeniye*, no. 11 (35), 12/25 November 1903, pp. 187–9.

nevertheless) explained that in order to make the struggle of the intelligentsia against autocracy more efficient,

all the professional zemstvo people ('Third Element') – physicians, teachers, agronomists, veterinary surgeons, statisticians, technicians... of each district should unite and form a district committee of struggle for liberation... These district committees will be joined by all those professional people of the towns who sympathize with the course... The activity of the district committees will have to be co-ordinated by provincial committees, which will be manned by representatives of the former. The provincial committees must be in close unity among themselves and will have to act in accordance with a common plan.[1]

The outbreak of war and its paralyzing initial effect on the Liberation Movement prevented these proposals from being implemented at the time. But the seed which was sown in November 1903 began to bear fruit a year later, in the wake of the November 1904 zemstvo congress.

The zemstvo radicals were the first to implement the tactical decisions of the Second Congress of the Union of Liberation. More than a month before the congress met, they began to prepare the ground for a zemstvo congress, which eventually met in St Petersburg on 6 November 1904. In order to ensure a constitutionalist majority, they employed the following tactics.[2] A week after *Beseda*'s meeting of 31 August,[3] F. A. Golovin, the new chairman of the Moscow provincial zemstvo board,[4] convened the 'organizational bureau', which had been elected by the May 1902 zemstvo congress, but had never convened.[5] When it assembled on 8 September 1904, it was composed[6] of: five zemstvo radicals (F. F. Kokoshkin, I. I. Petrunkevich, Prince D. I. Shakhovskoy, V. I. Vernadskiy and V. E. Yakushkin); six prominent moderate constitutionalists (F. A. Golovin, Prince G. E. Lvov,* R. A. Pisarev, N. F. Richter,† A. A. Saveleyev‡ and V. D. Von Derviz§); five rank-and-file

[1] Ibid. p. 188.
[2] The proceedings and resolutions of the November 1904 zemstvo congress as well as the political manoeuvring which secured a constitutional majority in it are described and reprinted, *inter alia*, in *Belokonskiy* II, pp. 212–36, *Budberg* II, *Listok Osvobozhdeniya* (1904), no. 18, *Shipov* II, pp. 240–85, *Vtoroy Syezd Zemskikh Deyateley* and *Zemskiy Syezd*. See also *Chermensky* II, p. 55, *Fischer*, pp. 177–88, *Gutovskiy* I, p. 38, *Iskra*, nos. 77–8, *Kokoshkin*, pp. 213–16, *Martov*, pp. 394–5, *Milyukov* IV, pp. 40–2, *Osvobozhdeniye* (1904), no. 60, p. 183; no. 61, pp. 195–6, *Petrunkevich* II, pp. 356–9, *Pipes* IIa, pp. 367–70 and *Veselovskiy* III, pp. 311–12.   [3] See above.   [4] *Shipov* II, p. 237.
[5] See ibid. p. 213 and above.   [6] *Shipov* ibid. and pp. 241–3, 256.
* Chairman of the Tula provincial zemstvo board (see *Vtoroy Syezd Zemskikh Deyateley*) and future chairman of the provisional government.
† Chairman of the Moscow district zemstvo board (ibid.).
‡ Chairman of the N. Novgorod provincial zemstvo board.
§ Chairman of the suppressed Tver provincial zemstvo board (ibid.).

moderate constitutionalists and D. N. Shipov, who was soon to hand over the chairmanship of the 'bureau' to Yakushkin.[1]

At this meeting the 'bureau' unanimously resolved to convoke a congress of 'representatives of provincial zemstvo boards and zemstvo activists' on 6 November in Moscow.[2] It also unanimously agreed on a four-point agenda to be presented for discussion at the congress. The first three items on the agenda dealt with zemstvo grievances, while the fourth point, undoubtedly echoing the decision of *Beseda* a week earlier, proposed that the congress discuss 'needs arising from the War'.[3] A week after the bureau adopted this resolution, Svyatopolk-Mirskiy delivered his famous speech of 'Confidence in Society'.[4] The radicals regarded it as a further manifestation of the government's weakness, which spurred them to adopt a more and more radical position, but Shipov saw it as the first ray of hope of achieving his ultimate aim – the bridging of the gulf between government and society.[5] Hence, when the bureau re-assembled in the second half of September, a confrontation between the two sides became unavoidable.

At the opening of this meeting, the zemstvo radicals submitted an entirely new agenda, the main item of which was a discussion of 'the desirable changes in the political conditions prevailing in Russia'.[6] When a vote was taken and Shipov discovered that he was alone in his opposition to the 'desirable changes' clause (knowing that it implied a constitution), he threatened to resign from the bureau and not to participate in the proposed congress.[7] His co-operation, however, was still indispensable to the holding of the congress.[8] Therefore, in order to prevent his resignation, the radicals suggested the appointment of a committee of three – Yakushkin (chairman), Kokoshkin and Shipov – to define the 'desirable changes'. Shipov agreed to this suggestion, probably assuming that his participation would prevent first the organizational bureau and then the congress from adopting constitutional demands.[9]

The last-minute agreement with Shipov must have greatly relieved

<hr>

[1] See *Shipov* II, p. 243.
[2] Ibid. p. 241.
[3] See *Shipov* ibid.
[4] Ibid.
[5] See *Shipov* ibid. pp. 241–2.
[6] Ibid. p. 242.
[7] Ibid. pp. 242–3.
[8] See *Petrunkevich* II, pp. 356–7.
[9] *Shipov* II, p. 243.

the radicals, who were now able to inform the Council of the Union of Liberation, at its meeting of 8 October 1904, that the zemstvo congress would certainly take place.[1] Their elaborate plans were almost spoiled at the last moment by the new Minister of the Interior, who learned of the decision to hold a congress. Svyatopolk-Mirskiy requested and received the Tsar's permission to hold a congress of chairmen of provincial zemstvo boards in St Petersburg. When he discovered that rank-and-file zemstvo activists had also participated in the May Congress, he agreed that they too could participate.[2]

Svyatopolk-Mirskiy's intention of transforming the zemstvo congress into an official gathering, and thus limiting the scope of its agenda and the number of its participants, ran contrary to the plans and wishes of the radicals and the moderate constitutionalists. Hence, while the organizational bureau gave Shipov permission to enter into negotiations with Svyatopolk-Mirskiy,[3] it continued to implement its original plans and thus ensured the withdrawal of the Tsar's permission. It made only one 'concession' – it agreed to transfer the location of the congress from Moscow to St Petersburg.[4]

On 16 October the bureau sent invitations to 95 prominent zemstvo activists to participate in the congress.[5] Since only 52 activists, including 16 chairmen of provincial zemstvo boards, had participated in the May 1902 congress,[6] the decision to invite 95 people meant a rejection of Svyatopolk-Mirskiy's numerical limitation. (Even if all the chairmen of the provincial zemstvo boards had attended the May 1902 congress, the total number of participants would have been only 70.*) The bureau met again on 29 October for the approval of the 'desirable changes' clause. The final draft of this clause ('clause six' of the proposed agenda) urged the delegates to discuss 'the general conditions which have an adverse impact on the proper development of our zemstvo and state life and the desirable means to bring about their removal'.[7] The same meeting of the bureau also decided that I. I. Petrunkevich and G. E. Lvov should accompany Shipov during the final stage of the negotiations with Svyatopolk-Mirskiy.[8]

After learning of these developments, Svyatopolk-Mirskiy informed the delegation that it would be impossible for him to obtain the Tsar's permission to hold a zemstvo congress thus composed. At the same

---

[1] See *Shakhovskoy* IV, pp. 130–1 and above. [2] *Shipov*, ibid. pp. 243–5.
[3] Ibid. [4] Ibid. p. 246. [5] Ibid. [6] Ibid. pp. 160–1.
* Zemstvo institutions existed in only 34 provinces. [7] *Shipov* II, p. 256.
[8] For a detailed account of this phase of the negotiations see ibid. pp. 255–8.

time, however, he told them that the police would not prevent the holding of the congress if it took the form of a 'private meeting'.[1] Had it not been for Shipov, who headed the delegation, Svyatopolk-Mirskiy would almost certainly not have given his undertaking not to interfere with the holding of a 'private' congress. Moreover, he gave this guarantee on the understanding that the congress would debate the agenda shown to him by Shipov and the two other members of the delegation. Although this agenda included one point (clause six) to which Svyatopolk-Mirskiy personally objected, the absence of any specific constitutional demand and the fact that all other points dealt with zemstvo grievances, enabled him to give the above undertaking. However, neither he nor Shipov suspected at the time that the zemstvo radicals were using them as mere pawns in a complicated game. While Shipov was negotiating with Svyatopolk-Mirskiy on behalf of the delegation, the radicals on the board of the bureau changed the proposed agenda completely and introduced a veiled constitutional clause.

In mid-October the leaders of the Union of Zemstvo Constitutionalists, acting on the initiative of the radicals, sent invitations to its members to assemble on 2 November in Moscow. The sixty or so delegates from 29 provinces who arrived on the fixed date,[2] made up the Third Congress of the Union of Zemstvo Constitutionalists (2–3 November 1904). During its opening session the Congress was informed by Petrunkevich and Prince Lvov of the outcome of the negotiations with Svyatopolk-Mirskiy. Then Yakushkin presented to the congress a draft agenda for the forthcoming zemstvo congress which was considerably different from the one approved by the organizational bureau on 29 October. This document included a veiled constitutional clause and, apparently in order to soften the blow, Shipov was invited to Novosiltsev's house (where all the congresses of the Union of Zemstvo Constitutionalists were held) to discuss it.

Although Shipov does not say so in his memoirs,[3] the realization that he had been deceived must have been a terrible shock. At any rate, he again threatened that if the constitutional clause were not removed, he would not attend the congress. Since his services were still indispensable to the radicals, they agreed to a compromise, which was acceptable to Shipov, namely that the clause in dispute (no. 9 in the agenda as debated in Novosiltsev's house and no. 10 in the resolution as approved by the zemstvo congress), should be presented in two versions, one

[1] See *Budberg* II, pp. 72–3.   [2] Ibid.   [3] See *Shipov* II, p. 266.

sponsored by the constitutionalists and the other by Shipov. This clause reads as follows:[1]

In order to create and preserve an always active and close contact and unity of the State with society...the following is absolutely essential:

Constitutionalists	Shipov
the regular participation of representatives of the people in a distinct elected institution in carrying out legislative functions, in fixing the state budget of income and expenditure and supervizing the legality of the administration's actions.	the proper participation in legislation of representatives of the people in a distinct elected institution.

Although there was a strong minority which favoured a demand for the convocation of a constituent assembly,[2] the Congress of the Union of Zemstvo Constitutionalists approved this compromise. Afterwards it decided that its members should exert their influence to induce the zemstvo assemblies to adopt, at their forthcoming sessions, resolutions based on the constitutionalist version of the approved agenda. On this note the congress ended its deliberations and the great majority of its delegates left for St Petersburg to participate in the zemstvo congress.[3]

By convoking the Third Congress of the Union of Zemstvo Constitutionalists at the beginning of November, the radicals ensured a majority for constitutionalist decisions at the zemstvo congress. This majority was not at first sufficiently great.[4] Hence, on their initiative, the organizational bureau invited S. A. Muromtsev and eleven other 'prominent zemstvo activists'* to participate in the congress immedi-

---

[1] Original, *inter alia*, in *Shipov*, ibid. pp. 264–5. English translation based on *Fischer*, p. 187.

[2] See *Budberg* II, pp. 73–4.

[3] According to Baron Budberg, only sixteen of the participants of the 'Third Congress of the Union of Zemstvo Constitutionalists', were invited to participate in the zemstvo congress (see *Budberg* II, p. 74). His assertion, however, does not make sense. In *Beseda* alone there were more than thirty constitutionalists, all of whom were members of the Union of Zemstvo Constitutionalists, and almost all *Beseda* members participated in the zemstvo congress. (For a full list of participants, see *Vtoroy Syezd Zemskikh Deyateley* and *Zemskiy Syezed*, pp. 22–5.) And indeed, according to Shipov, all those who were present at the meeting in Novosiltsev's house, later participated in the zemstvo congress (see *Shipov* II, p. 266).

[4] See *Milyukov* IV, p. 41.

* Although Muromtsev was a well-known constitutionalist (see above), he was not active in zemstvo affairs till November 1904 (see *Kokoshkin*, pp. 205 ff.). Hence, the invitation to him to participate in the congress as a 'prominent zemstvo activist' did not exactly correspond to the facts.

ately after its opening.[1] After they joined the congress, its approval of the 'constitutionalist clause' became a foregone conclusion.

The 'Second' Zemstvo Congress* opened in St Petersburg on 6 November 1904 by electing D. N. Shipov as its chairman. This was done more as a recognition of his services to the zemstvo movement in the past, than as a reflection of his influence in the present. The election of the other officers corresponded more to the actual distribution of power in the Congress: I. I. Petrunkevich and Prince G. E. Lvov (who was a moderate constitutionalist) were elected vice-chairmen and F. F. Kokoshkin (radical) and three moderate constitutionalists (the most prominent among whom was F. A. Golovin) were elected secretaries.[2]

After electing its officers the congress began to debate the agenda and approved the 'constitutional clause' (point 10) by a 71 to 27 majority.[3] But, immediately afterwards, the constitutionalist majority was in danger of disintegrating as a consequence of the opposition of the rank-and-file zemstvo radicals to the last clause of the agenda (point 11), namely the suggestion that the outlined reforms be granted from above. This clause read as follows:

In view of the importance and difficulty of external and internal conditions being experienced by Russia, the Private Conference expresses the hope that the supreme authority will call together freely elected representatives of the people, in order to guide our fatherland with their collaboration to a new path of State development and to the establishment of principles of law and interaction between the State and the People.[4]

The spokesmen of the opposition demanded instead that the resolutions of the congress be submitted for approval to a constituent assembly, elected on the basis of the 'four-tail' (*chetyrekhvostka*) formula (universal, equal and direct suffrage and secret ballot) which should be assembled without delay.[5]

This demand was unacceptable to the moderate constitutionalists. Count P. A. Geyden, their chief spokesman at the congress, had already explained at one of its first sessions that he wanted a constitu-

[1] See *Shipov* II, p. 246n. and *Kokoshkin*, pp. 213–14.
* It was dubbed 'second' at the time in order to distinguish it and the May 1902 congress from the 'Shipov Congresses' of 1896, 1898 and of April 1903. This distinction, however, seems to be superficial and arbitrary.
[2] *Shipov* ibid. p. 259 and *Fischer*, p. 181.
[3] See *Shipov* ibid. p. 269, *Vtoroy Syezd Zemskikh Deyateley* etc.
[4] English translation based on *Fischer*, p. 188. Original found, *inter alia* in *Shipov* II, 265.
[5] See *Budberg* II, p. 86.

tion granted from above, in order to prevent a revolution from below.[1] No wonder, therefore, that the demand of the rank-and-file radicals provoked him to deliver a strong speech in support of clause 11 and of D. N. Shipov's proposal that the congress should elect a delegation to present its resolutions to Svyatopolk-Mirskiy.[2]

A final showdown between the two sides was prevented by the intervention of the radical leaders. They and their counterparts in the Council of the Union of Liberation knew all the time that the majority of the moderate constitutionalists would not subscribe to a demand for the convocation of a constituent assembly. Moreover, this demand was superfluous as far as their main aim, the opening of a public opinion campaign, was concerned. They rightly believed that this aim could be served well enough by the congress's adoption of the moderate constitutionalist programme. To achieve this aim, they were even prepared not to mention the very word 'constitution', though everyone knew what 'clause 10' meant. They were, however, very careful from the beginning to explain to their supporters that their 'moderation' was merely tactical.

Thus, Petrunkevich stated at one of the first sessions of the Congress that:

although it is said, and it may be true, that the greater part of educated Russia supports us, nevertheless we must not forget that we constitute only a private gathering. The right to express the thoughts of the people belongs not to us, but to the people themselves. (By stating this) we are not raising the question of the need to convoke a constituent assembly, but merely ascertaining the principle that the right to determine the question of reforming the existing regime, belongs to the people together with the government.[3]

In other words, Petrunkevich tried to explain to his followers that they should not raise the demand for the convocation of a constituent assembly, because the zemstvo congress was unrepresentative. At the same time he also tried to placate the moderates by referring to the 'people and the government' as the sovereign entity of Russia. The rank-and-file radicals were not impressed by this self-contradictory argument and it was left to N. N. Lvov to try and convince them during the debate on clause 11.

In a strong speech Lvov explained that (in contrast to Geyden) he was afraid neither of the demand for the convocation of a constituent assembly, nor of a revolution. But he stated that neither the zemstvo

---

[1] See *Shipov* II, p. 260.   [2] See ibid. pp. 275–6 and *Budberg* II, p. 87.
[3] *Shipov* II, p. 260.

activists nor the people had the power to compel the government to convoke a constituent assembly. He therefore asked the rank-and-file radicals to withdraw their demand in the name of *realpolitik*. Lvov's arguments convinced the left wing and the congress approved clause 11 almost unanimously.[1]

After thus finally approving the draft resolution, as presented by Yakushkin on behalf of the organizational bureau, the congress quickly disposed of the remaining items on the agenda. First it elected a delegation to present its resolutions to Svyatopolk-Mirskiy.[2] Then it laid down the rules for electing delegates to future congresses. According to these rules, each zemstvo province was to be represented at all-zemstvo congresses by the elected members of all provincial zemstvo boards (their number varied between 5 in the provinces of the capitals and 3 in all others) and by four elected representatives of the provincial assemblies.[3] Afterwards it elected a new 'organizational bureau' under the chairmanship of F. A. Golovin.[4] Finally, it adopted a resolution which urged all the local zemstvo assemblies to incorporate the decisions of the congress in the petitions they were bound to adopt at their forthcoming sessions.[5] The congress was closed by Prince Peter D. Dolgorukov, who, in a very emotional speech, appealed to the government to grant complete amnesty to all political 'offenders'.[6]

---

[1] See *Budberg* II, p. 86, *Shipov* II, pp. 274–5. See also *Fischer*, p. 188.

[2] According to *Shipov* II, pp. 277–81 (who is the main source on the delegation and on the subsequent developments in connection with it), the delegation elected by the congress for presenting its resolutions to Svyatopolk-Mirskiy was composed of D. N. Shipov, I. I. Petrunkevich and Prince G. E. Lvov (chairman and vice-chairmen of the congress), Count P. A. Geyden and M. V. Rodzyanko (chairman of the Yaroslavl provincial zemstvo board and future chairman of the fourth Duma). Svyatopolk-Mirskiy refused to receive it but was prepared to see Shipov, who presented him with a copy of the resolutions. During their conversation, Svyatopolk-Mirskiy asked for a memorandum on their 'theoretical basis'. This memorandum was drafted by the following people: M. V. Chelnokov, Prince P. D. Dolgorukov (Pavel? Peter?), F. A. Golovin, F. F. Kokoshkin, Prince G. E. Lvov, N. N. Lvov, I. I. Petrunkevich, R. A. Pisarev, Prince D. I. Shakhovskoy, D. N. Shipov, Prince S. N. Trubetskoy, V. I. Vernadskiy, N. N. Khmelyev, N. F. Richter and V. E. Yakushkin. The final draft of the memorandum was composed by Trubetskoy, who presented it, together with Shipov, to Svyatopolk-Mirskiy on 29 November 1904. By that time, however, the moderate demands included in the memorandum no longer corresponded to the wishes of a great part of society as expressed during the 'banquet campaign', which was then in full swing. (The memorandum is reprinted in full in *Shipov* II, pp. 581–7.)

[3] See *Shipov* II, p. 277. For a different version see *Belokonskiy* II, p. 236.

[4] See *Petrunkevich* II, p. 366.   [5] See *Shipov* II, p. 277.   [6] See *Budberg* II, pp. 87–8.

11

Unleashing the Revolution

The 'Second' Zemstvo Congress proved an even greater success than the leaders of the Union of Liberation had hoped. The protracted negotiations with Svyatopolk-Mirskiy lent it greater political importance than it would otherwise have had, and this was augmented in the eyes of the public by the last-minute decision of the Minister to prohibit any reporting of its proceedings in the legal press.[1] (While in session it received 42 cables of support from public institutions and various groups.[2]) Not only the friends but also the Social-Democratic opponents of the Liberation Movement regarded the congress as a political event of the first magnitude, and both friends and foes used almost identical words in describing it. Struve wrote in *Osvobozhdeniye* that the congress was 'an event of paramount historical importance',[3] and he was echoed by the editors of *Iskra*, who wrote in a leading article on 'The Results of the Zemstvo Parliament',[4] that 'the decisions of the Zemstvo Congress have acquired the significance of a political event of paramount importance'.[5]

The success of the congress enabled the Council to tackle without delay the two tactical points decided on at the Union of Liberation's Second Congress, namely the launching of the 'banquet campaign' and the establishment of intelligentsia unions. By so doing the Council put into motion the political events of November 1904 – December 1905, commonly known as the 'First Russian Revolution'.* On the evening that the 'Second' Zemstvo Congress ended its deliberations, its delegates were invited to a mass-banquet organized in their honour

[1] See, for example, *Iskra* nos. 77, 78 (leading articles).
[2] See *Shipov* II, p. 260n. These are reprinted in *Zemskiy Syezd*, pp. 25–30.
[3] *Osvobozhdeniye* (1904), no. 60, p. 183.
[4] *Iskra*, no. 78, front page.   [5] Ibid.
* This was not a revolution in the proper sense of the word since the autocratic government was not overthrown, though for long periods of time it was unable to enforce the existing laws. One of the main reasons for the regime's ability to withstand the storm was the support extended to it by the army, which by and large remained loyal to the Tsar throughout this period.

by the Union of Liberation. The chairman of the banquet was V. G. Korolenko, who had become sole editor of *Russkoye Bogatstvo* after Mikhaylovskiy's death in January 1904* and it was attended by the cream of the capital's radical intelligentsia.[1] It was followed by similar banquets, and as a consequence the 'banquet campaign' was inaugurated about a fortnight earlier than planned.[2] The organization of these gatherings followed a simple pattern: the organizers (in St Petersburg the 'Big Group' and particularly the editors of *Russkoye Bogatstvo*,[3] and in the provinces supporters of the Union of Liberation or, where these existed, its local branches[4]) provided the halls, the chairmen, the speakers and the draft resolutions, which were always approved. At first these draft resolutions contained 'moderate' demands, i.e. demands for personal freedom (immunity etc.), freedom of assembly and association, freedom of the press etc.[5] But as the intelligentsia responded to these slogans with a fervour which surprised even the most optimistic of the Union of Liberation's leaders,[6] the latter soon raised their stakes. As a result the 'banquet campaign' went a good deal further than the 'Second' Zemstvo Congress and subsequent zemstvo meetings as regards its resolutions. By 20 November (originally planned as the date for inaugurating the campaign), these were closely reflecting the programme of the Union of Liberation.

In Moscow, St Petersburg,[7] Samara,[8] Kaluga, Rostov-on-Don[9] and many other towns all over Russia,[10] the banquets adopted resolutions

* Mikhaylovskiy died on the night of 27/28 January.

[1] See *Shakhovskoy* IV, p. 141.

[2] It should have started on 20 November. See above.

[3] For the composition of the 'Big Group' and the involvement of the *Russkoye Bogatstvo* people in banquets see above.

[4] The Union of Liberation had branches in twenty-one provincial towns at the time. See above.

[5] See, for example, the banquet in Saratov held on 5 November 1904, on the eve of the 'Second' Zemstvo Congress (*Pravo* (1904), no. 46, cols 3202–3). To the best of the author's knowledge, this was the first meeting of the 'banquet campaign'. But because it was held in the provinces, its impact was initially smaller than that of the banquet held in honour of the delegates to the 'Second' Zemstvo Congress.

[6] See, for example, *Gessen* I, pp. 184, 186.

[7] See *Fischer*, pp. 192–5. Fischer failed to distinguish between the resolutions of the zemstvo congress and the zemstvo assemblies which followed it and the radical demands found in the resolutions of the intelligentsia banquets.

[8] See *Syn Otechestva* no. 12, 29 November/12 December 1904.

[9] For a summary of the proceedings and the decisions of the banquets in Kaluga and Rostov-on-Don see *Osvobozhdeniye* (1905), no. 63, pp. 227–8.

[10] A summary of the proceedings and resolutions of thirty-nine banquets is found in *Cherevanin* II, pp. 149–63. As a critic of the Liberation Movement from the left, Cherevanin minimized the radicalism of the decisions.

calling for the convocation of a constituent assembly elected on the basis of the 'four-tail' (*chetyrekhvostka*) formula. Some also incorporated a demand for the immediate ending of the war (this becoming almost universal after the fall of Port Arthur),[1] while others approved demands which went even further than the programme of the Union of Liberation. Thus, for example, the central banquet held in St Petersburg on 20 November adopted a resolution which called not only for the convocation of a constituent assembly elected on the basis of the 'four-tail' formula, but also for the introduction of 'ministerial responsibility to the assembly of popular representatives'.[2]

The 'banquet campaign' created an enormous sensation, since such demands had never before been publicly voiced in Russia. Nor had the legal press ever been so free to report and comment on them. The oppositionally inclined *Pravo* and other liberal newspapers became increasingly bold in their attacks on the government, while a host of new dailies and weeklies were established in the wake of Svyatopolk-Mirskiy's relaxation of censorship regulations.[3] The most important of these new papers were *Nasha Zhizn* (Our Life), *Nashi Dni* (Our Time) and *Syn Otechestva* (Son of the Fatherland). Together with *Pravo* they soon overshadowed *Osvobozhdeniye* as mouthpieces of the Liberation Movement.[4] The general excitement generated by the banquets and the press's increasing boldness was used by the Council of the Union of Liberation for the launching of the intelligentsia unions. The first to be established was the 'All-Russian Union of Engineers and Technicians', which was later to play an important part in the organization of the general strike of October 1905. It originated in two mass-banquets of engineers which were held simultaneously in Moscow and St Petersburg on 5 December 1904.[5]

---

[1] See below.

[2] Quoted in *Fischer*, p. 194. This demand was left out of the programme of the Union of Liberation precisely because many rank-and-file members and even leaders (N. N. Lvov for example) of the zemstvo radicals, as well as the more moderate supporters of the Union of Liberation in the towns (professors etc.) were opposed to it either on principle or for tactical reasons. The leaders of the Liberation Movement, however, found a theoretical justification for this omission (as well as for the omission of specific social demands) by emphasising the need to give the constituent assembly a free rein to decide on the shape of the future regime.

[3] One of the results of the freedom of the press during 1904–5 was the appearance of a large number of satirical publications, some of them of high standard. See, for example, *Botsyanovskiy*.

[4] See *Akselrod* IV, p. 137, *Bukhbinder* I, pp. 312, 314, 318–19, *Pavlov* I, pp. 47–8, *Pipes* IIa, p. 375 and *Shakhovskoy* IV, p. 138.

[5] An account of the proceedings and decisions of the Moscow banquet is found, *inter alia*,

Both these gatherings were attended not only by working (or teaching) engineers but also by various captains of industry, high-ranking officers etc. who happened to possess engineering diplomas. The presence of the latter apparently inhibited the drafters of the resolutions to some extent, and they refrained from raising the demand for the convocation of a constituent assembly based on the 'four-tail' formula,[1] though they found a reasonable equivalent for it. The resolution of the Moscow banquet called on the government to:

grant complete personal immunity and freedom of assembly, association, speech and the press; abrogate the extraordinary State-Protection Statute (*Polozheniye ob Usilennoy Okhrane*)...and grant complete amnesty to all people sentenced or exiled by administrative orders for political crimes; replace the existing bureaucratic regime by a representative form of government; convene representatives of the people to elaborate the basis of the new regime.[2]

The St Petersburg banquet adopted a similar resolution, calling on the government 'to convene representatives of the people immediately for the promulgation of new fundamental laws'.[3] In the organizational field it went even further. The organizers, L. I. Lutugin and S. D. Kirpichnikov[4] (who was also chairman), proposed the election of a committee for the organization of an Engineers Union. Their suggestion was approved and the gathering elected a committee of three, chaired by Kirpichnikov and with the participation of Lutugin. This committee contacted the Moscow engineers and about a month later the 'bureau' of the 'All-Russian Union of Engineers and Technicians' came into being under the leadership of Lutugin and Kirpichnikov.[5]

Lutugin was also involved in the organization of another union in that same month. In his capacity as professor at the St Petersburg *Gornyy Institut* he organized the 'Academic Union' in the last week of December[6] together with V. I. Vernadskiy, I. M. Grevs and others. The

in *Elektricheskaya Energiya* (1905), no. 1, p. 41. An account of the proceedings and decisions of the St Petersburg meeting is found, *inter alia*, in *Kirpichnikov* I, pp. 136–7; II, pp. 137, 152, *Osvobozhdeniye* (1904), no. 62, p. 214. Cf. *Galai*, p. 97.

[1] See *Cherevanin* II, pp. 173–5.   [2] *Elektricheskaya Energiya*, ibid.
[3] *Osvobozhdeniye* (1904), no. 62, p. 214.
[4] Lutugin was a member of the Council of the Union of liberation (see above). Kirpichnikov was, apparently, a newcomer to the Liberation Movement. Both were professors at the St Petersburg *Gornyy Institut*, and both played a very important role in the organization of the intelligentsia unions and later in the Union of Unions. They were the only leaders of the Union of Unions who were members of its central bureau without interruption for as long as it existed. (See *Kirpichnikov* I, pp. 139 ff.)   [5] Ibid. pp. 136 ff.
[6] See *Cherevanin* II, pp. 177–8, *Kirpichnikov* ibid. pp. 139–40; II, pp. 137, 153–4 and *Sputnik*, pp. 57 ff.

basis of its political programme was a memorandum composed by Vernadskiy and signed by 342 professors and lecturers at universities and institutes of higher education (the 'Vernadskiy memorandum'), which was published in the press immediately after 'Bloody Sunday'.[1]

A third intelligentsia union, the 'All-Russian Union of Medical Personnel' also began to take shape during December. A banquet of 270 physicians, held in St Petersburg on 18 December 1904, adopted a resolution which included the demand for a constituent assembly elected according to the 'four-tail formula'.[2] The same people met again on 6 January, 1905 when they decided to establish a 'Union of Medical Personnel' and elected an 'organizational bureau' for that purpose.[3]

While their elders were attending banquets and joining unions, the students began to stage a series of mass meetings (*skhodki*) which usually culminated in the adoption of resolutions calling for the immediate end of the war and for a constituent assembly elected on the 'four-tail' principle. Before the inauguration of the 'banquet campaign' such meetings were held in Russia proper mainly in the capitals, but they subsequently spread to the provinces, and were replaced in the capitals by street demonstrations. Such demonstrations had become almost daily occurrences in the minority provinces, especially in Poland, the Baltic region and the Caucasus, where a strike movement also began which paralyzed the Baku oilfields for most of December.[4] These events were, however, soon overshadowed by developments in the working-class quarters of the capital.

By autumn, 1904, the St Petersburg 'Assembly of Russian Factory Workers', an offshoot of the Zubatov movement, had begun to gain considerable influence among the workers. Under the leadership of the charismatic Father Gapon, who was assisted by a group of self-educated workers of socialistic inclinations, it rapidly became radicalized.[5] Since the Social-Democrats of both factions (Bolshevik and Menshevik) refused to have anything to do with Gapon or his organization till early January 1905,[6] its leaders contacted the St Petersburg branch of

[1] It is found, *inter alia*, in *Pravo* (1905), no. 3, cols. 180–2.
[2] The resolution is found in *Osvobozhdeniye* (1904), no. 63, pp. 226–7.
[3] See *Kirpichnikov* II, pp. 155–6.
[4] For developments among the students and in the minority provinces in the last months of 1904 see *Galai*, pp. 97–9. Cf. *Seton-Watson*, pp. 607–12 and *Schwarz* I, pp. 301–14.
[5] For accounts in English of Gapon's organization see, *inter alia*, *Harcave*, pp. 39–40, 65–70, *Keep*, pp. 154–8 and *Schwarz* I, pp. 58–9, 271–8, 281–4. For a partial list of Russian-language publications on this subject, see *Keep* p. 155n.
[6] See *Keep*, pp. 156–7, *Schwarz* ibid. pp. 59–70 and *Karelin*, pp. 115–16.

the Union of Liberation. By late November, if not before, a working relationship had been established between Gapon and his associates on the one hand, and Bogucharskiy, Khizhnyakov, Kuskova and Proko-povich, representing the 'Big Group' on the other. The latter kept Gapon's inner circle informed on political developments and on the aims of the Union of Liberation, and also provided them with news-papers, especially *Nasha Zhizn* and *Nashi Dni*, which were distributed to the local branches of the Assembly.[1] These apparently were the channel by which the excitement of society reached the workers. The news of the surrender of Port Arthur to the Japanese on 20 December 1904 (2 January 1905)[2] added fuel to their growing discontent, and just at this time four members of Gapon's organization were dismissed from their jobs at the Putilov metallurgical works. In the charged atmosphere of St Petersburg, this dismissal triggered off a strike in the Putilov factory. From there it spread like wildfire to other enterprises, and by the first week of January 1905 almost all the factory workers in the capital were on strike.[3]

Confronted with what was rapidly developing into a revolutionary situation the government could not decide on a consistent policy. Svyatopolk-Mirskiy insisted on additional concessions and forced the Tsar's hand by tendering his resignation on 21 November 1904. (It was refused.)[4] He submitted a plan for reforms which included a sug-gestion aimed at pacifying the moderate elements of society: the introduction of representatives of the provincial zemstvo assemblies and of the dumas of the big towns into the State Council.[5] Before agreeing to this concession, Nicholas asked Witte's opinion on its compatibility with autocracy. As in his notorious secret memorandum, although now apparently for different reasons, Witte replied that the introduction of representatives of zemstvos and town dumas into the State Council would be the first step towards the establishment of a constitutional regime in Russia. If the Tsar contemplated granting a constitution, only then should he retain this concession. Nicholas, as Witte had correctly predicted, struck it out on the spot,[6] and Svyato-

[1] See *Gapon* I, pp. 78–81, 101–2, 129, *Gimer*, p. 11, *Karelin*, pp. 110–11, 115–16, *Pavlov* I, pp. 47–8; II, pp. 91–2, *Varnashev*, pp. 194–5, 198, 201, 203. Cf. *Bukhbinder* I, pp. 312, 314–15, 319, *L. Gurevich*, p. 202, *Kuskova* XV, no. 9, p. 377, *Nevskiy* I, p. 134; VI, pp. 20–4, 24–9, 33–5, *Presnyakov*, p. 32n., *Shilov*, pp. 22–39. See also *D.i.M.* I, no. 87.
[2] See *Seton-Watson*, pp. 593–5.   [3] See *Harcave*, pp. 68–79, *Keep*, pp. 153, 155–6.
[4] See *Chermenskiy* II, p. 57, *K. K. Romanov* I, pp. 97–8 and *Nicholas* IIa, p. 183.
[5] *Chermenskiy* ibid.
[6] See *Nicholas* ibid. p. 186, *Romanov* ibid. p. 102, *Shipov* II, p. 290 and *Witte* VIII, p. 274. There can be little doubt that, in contrast to his motives for writing his memorandum in

polk-Mirskiy's reform programme was thus to a large degree diluted. The Decree to the Ruling Senate of 12 December 1904,[1] which incorporated the final programme of reforms, therefore included modest and mainly non-political concessions. In it the Tsar promised to curtail the use and the scope of the emergency laws and to safeguard the rule of law; to grant more powers and more autonomy to the zemstvos; to provide government insurance for factory workers; to introduce a policy of religious tolerance to end religious discrimination not based on law and to abolish all unnecessary restrictions on the press 'so as to enable it to fulfil its task of truthfully expressing prudent desires for the good of Russia'.

It is highly doubtful, to say the least, whether a promise to bring representatives of zemstvos and town dumas into the State Council could have prevented the rapid deterioration of the internal situation. But, in any case, the fact that the 12 December Decree did not contain such a promise destroyed any chance of success it might have had. The Tsar's intentions were revealed in their true light when, two days after publication of the Decree, a government announcement[2] appeared, condemning as unlawful the zemstvo congress, other gatherings and demonstrations being held all over Russia, and the papers reporting them. Those taking part in these demonstrations were, according to the announcement, 'unconsciously acting not for the good of the fatherland but for its enemies'. The government would punish them in accordance with the law, especially those government employees among them. The zemstvo assemblies, town dumas and other corporative institutions 'must not deal with or consider matters which are not within their legal competence' and the press should help to soothe over-excited public opinion. The publication of such threats at a time when what in reality amounted to freedom of speech, press, assembly, demonstration and strikes had already been established in Russia 'without preliminary permission' (*Yavochnym Poryadkom*) served only to further inflame public opinion.

By the end of December the government had realized that its policy

1898, this time his wish to return to power rather than questions of policy prompted Witte to give his Mephistophelian advice (see *Gessen* I, pp. 186–8). In the opinion of the author, the turning point in Witte's attitude to power and politics was his dismissal on 15 August 1903. From then on he was interested in one thing only – return to power. (See, for example, his pleading with Kuropatkin at the end of December 1903 to ask the Tsar to nominate him again as Minister of Finance 'in case war broke out' – *Kuropatkin* I, p. 99.) When he regained power in October 1905 his main interest lay in retaining it.

[1] The full text of the decree is found, *inter alia*, in *Pravo* (1904), no. 51, cols 3511–14.
[2] For the full text of the announcement, see ibid. cols 3515–76.

of partial concessions combined with threats had misfired. Then, at the beginning of January 1905 it suddenly learned that the striking workers of St Petersburg were being urged by Gapon to stage a peaceful procession to the Winter Palace in order to present to the Tsar a petition reflecting the demands of the Union of Liberation.[1] As a result the government panicked and ordered troops into the capital.[2] The 'Big Group' realized what was at stake and tried to dissuade Gapon from holding the procession on Sunday, 9 January 1905. When he refused the Group convened a meeting on the premises of *Syn Otechestva* late in the evening on 8 January and elected a delegation of ten people. It was composed of one worker, D. V. Kuzin, and nine intellectuals, at least five of whom were members or active supporters of the Union of Liberation: N. F. Annenskiy, K. K. Arsenyev, I. V. Gessen, V. A. Myakotin and A. V. Peshekhonov (who was also a member of the Council of the Union). The other four were M. Gorky, N. I. Kareyev, E. I. Kedin and V. I. Semevskiy.[3] This delegation called on Witte and Svyatopolk-Mirskiy at midnight hoping to persuade them to try change the order to the troops and prevent them from firing on the peaceful procession. The mission, as might have been expected, failed,[4] and the crowds of peaceful demonstrators were received not by their 'Little Father' but by volleys of bullets, fired by his faithful soldiers. The number of demonstrators killed and wounded on that fateful day (which went down in history as 'Bloody Sunday') apparently reached the thousand mark.[5]

Under different circumstances this massacre might have frightened the urban population into docile silence and thus restored 'law and order'. But at a time when the Russian army was suffering defeat after

---

[1] On the eve of the procession to the Winter Palace, two different versions of a petition were apparently circulating. One included mainly economic demands and the other mainly political ones. Both, however, included the demand for the convocation of a constituent assembly. (See *Galai*, p. 101, *Shilov*.) The final draft which Gapon intended to present to Nicholas was the more political (see *Presnyakov*, p. 23n.). It was, apparently, composed by Kuskova and Prokopovich. (See *Nevskiy* I, p. 134, cf. *Kuskova* xv, no. 9 p. 377.)

[2] For the disarray on the government side on the eve of 'Bloody Sunday', see *Bukhbinder* I, pp. 332–5, *Chizhov* I, II, III, *Kokovtsev* III, *B. A. Remanov* I, p. 41, *Falk* and *E. Vuich*.

[3] See *Gessen* I, pp. 191–3 and *L. Gurevich*, pp. 213–15.

[4] Ibid., ibid. Cf. *Harcave*, pp. 81–8.

[5] The exact number of casualties is not known. The government claimed that 96 people were killed and 333 wounded, 32 of them mortally (see *Pravo* (1905), no. 3, col. 180). According to rumours circulated at the time, the number of dead and wounded reached the 5,000 mark (see *Harcave*, p. 93n. and *Schwarz* I, p. 5fn). A Soviet historian who studied the various figures, came to the conclusion that all in all about 200 people were killed and 800 wounded. (See *Nevskiy* VI, p. 56, cf. *Schwarz* ibid.)

defeat on the fields of Manchuria, its victory over unarmed workers in the streets of St Petersburg could neither enhance its reputation and that of the regime nor put fear into the hearts of the people. On the contrary, the massacre was correctly assessed at the time as a thoughtless and barbaric deed executed on the orders of a frightened government, and aroused in the population hatred and contempt for the regime in general and for Nicholas II in particular. (He was immediately dubbed 'The People's Executioner' by Struve.[1]) Reaction to the bloody events did not amount to a 'revolution' (as many revolutionary and oppositional leaders hoped at the time[2]) nor did it usher in the revolutionary outbursts of 1904–5 (as is maintained by official Soviet historiography,[3] though not by some better Soviet historians who have successfully side-stepped the issue[4]). But it did intensify discontent throughout the Russian Empire. It also attracted to oppositional activity new strata of the urban population such as the business community, which until then had been extremely loyal to the government.

The reaction to 'Bloody Sunday' was particularly violent in the minority provinces. Numerous strikes and demonstrations were held in Poland, in Finland, in the Baltic region and in the Caucasus, where Baku (for the second time) and Tiflis were paralysed by them. In Russia proper the students went on strike and the universities were closed down, to reopen only in September. They were joined by workers who downed tools in many towns and cities in January and part of February. The SRs stepped up their terror campaign, which culminated in the assassination of Grand Duke Sergius, the Tsar's uncle, on 4 February. Then, at the end of January, the industrialists joined the general clamour for political freedom, including the freedom to establish trade unions, as the only way out of the impasse created by the disastrous war and by the internal policies of the government. The tragic events of 9 January had also inflicted heavy damage on the image and standing of autocracy abroad. Under these circumstances, Nicholas had little choice but to agree to further concessions.[5]

He first tried to placate the workers. On the advice of D. F. Trepov, who was appointed Governor-General of St Petersburg on the day after 'Bloody Sunday', the Tsar granted an audience to a deputation of

[1] See *Osvobozhdeniye*, no. 64, 12(25) January 1905 (*Palach Naroda*).
[2] See, for example, Struve's reaction in ibid. (*Revolyutsiya v Rossii*).
[3] See, for example, *D.i.M.*I, p. xiv.
[4] See, for example, *Chermenskiy*, pp. 3–51ff.
[5] See *Galai*, pp. 101–2, *Keep*, pp. 158–60, *Chermenskiy*, pp. 52–4 and *Narodnoye Khozyaystvo* (1905), kn.1, pp. 195–201.

'loyal workers' on 19 January.[1] This in itself was an unprecedented act but the favourable impression this gesture was supposed to make on Russian workers was spoiled, to a large extent, by the Tsar's concluding remarks to the deputation. After assuring them that he would do everything in his power to improve the living conditions of the workers and would ensure that their requests could be expressed legally, he blurted out as he was leaving the room: 'I forgive you.'[2] This was astoundingly tactless on the part of the 'Executioner', and thus the only positive outcome of the visit was the early release of several workers arrested on 'Bloody Sunday'.[3]

The Tsar's two other attempts to placate the workers were no more successful. On 24 January the then Minister of Finance, V. U. Kokovtsev, asked the industrialists to respond to some of the economic demands of the workers. The replies of the various associations of industrialists which flooded in during the coming weeks rejected his request, the main argument being that the background of the workers' strikes was political rather than economic. Therefore the government should first of all respond to the political demands of the population and grant them political freedom, and only then would it be possible to contemplate ways of improving their economic situation.[4] On 29 January Nicholas appointed the senator N. V. Shidlovsky as chairman of a committee appointed to 'investigate the reasons for the discontent of the workers in St Petersburg and its environs and to recommend measures for the prevention of such discontent in the future'.[5] The innovation in the operation of this committee lay in the fact that it was to hear the evidence of *elected representatives* of workers from the entire St Petersburg area; regulations for their election were published on 7 February.[6] The Social-Democrats, who had 'missed the bus' on 9 January, now fully exploited the opportunity presented to them, and most of the representatives elected hearkened to their instructions to utilize the committee as a platform for anti-government propaganda. The government was obliged to formally announce the ending of 'Shidlovskiy's experiment' on 20 February.[7]

[1] See *K.A.* vol. xx (1927), pp. 240–2. Trepov was undoubtedly influenced in giving this advice by his past connection with Zubatov. See above.

[2] The full text of the very short speech is found, *inter alia,* in *Pravo* (1905), no. 3, col. 176. Cf. *Schwarz* I, pp. 80–1.   [3] See *K.A.* vol. LXIII (1935), p. 58.

[4] See *K.L.* no. 1(12) (1925), pp. 49–56, cf. *Chermenskiy,* pp. 52–4, *Sputnik,* pp. 114–15.

[5] See *Sputnik,* p. 109.

[6] See *Pravo* (1905), no. 6, cols. 435–6, italics added. For a full account in English of the Shidlovskiy Commission episode see *Schwarz* ibid. pp. 86–128, cf. *Keep,* pp. 175–6.

[7] See *Pravo* (1905), no. 8, col. 605.

When it became clear to the Tsar that attempts to clear the atmosphere through partial reforms would not meet with immediate success, and that most of his ministers and military commanders in the Far East, as well as Wilhelm II who was then his close confidante, supported far-reaching political reforms,[1] he was obliged to give in. But as in the case of the measures of 12 and 14 December, he did so with such bad grace that the new concessions only led to renewed pressure on the government. On 18 February three documents were published simultaneously: a rescript to the newly appointed Minister of the Interior, A. G. Bulygin, a decree (*ukaz*) to the Ruling Senate and a manifesto.[2] The rescript promised to call 'worthy representatives of the people to participate in the preliminary consideration and elaboration of proposed laws', to be based on the promises of reform made by Nicholas on 12 December 1904. So as to make this procedure compatible with the 'immovable basic laws of the Empire' (i.e. the autocratic power of the Emperor) 'a special conference under the chairmanship of Bulygin' was to be established 'to study ways and means'.[3] In other words, the rescript promised to include representatives of the people in a consultative capacity in the making of laws.

Thus the Tsar was obliged to agree to those reforms which he had opposed so vehemently only two months before. But although his promise constituted a departure from the past, it still fell far short of fulfilling the demand for a constituent assembly, which had now become the order of the day in oppositional circles. The decree which accompanied the rescript enabled the opposition to voice their demands legally. It promised to make it easier for all 'subjects with good intentions' to offer advice on necessary reforms, and ordered the Council of Ministers to receive all communications on this subject from individuals and corporate bodies.[4]

In contrast to the two above documents, the manifesto was a straightforward reactionary document which could be and was interpreted as a call for civil war.[5] It called on 'all true Russians...men of good intentions from all estates and ranks, everyone in his place and his estate'[6]

[1] See *Galai*, p. 102, *Chermenskiy*, pp. 54–8.
[2] The full text of the three documents is found, *inter alia*, in *Pravo* (1905), no. 7, cols. 471–6.
[3] *Galai*, p. 103.   [4] *Galai* ibid.
[5] And, indeed, it was at the time of the publication of the Manifesto that the press first began to refer to the Black Hundreds and their activities. See, for example, *Pravo* (1905), no. 8, cols 607–9.
[6] These words were introduced into the Manifesto on Pobedonostsev's advice. See *Pobedonostsev* I, p. 204.

to rally round the Tsar to defend the fatherland from external enemies and protect 'true autocracy' from internal sedition.[1] And as if to add insult to injury, it described the disastrous war as being fought 'for the glory and honour of Russia and for the domination of the Pacific Ocean'. Exactly one week after these words appeared in print, the Russian army suffered a crushing defeat at Mukden.[2]

As in November 1904, renewed pressure on the government following these three documents and the military defeat, was directed in Russia proper by the Liberation Movement. The SDs were unable to repeat their success with the Shidlovskiy commission until October. The number of strikes declined steadily from the beginning of February and by the end of March industrial production had returned almost to normal.[3] In the minority provinces the picture was different. There, social and national grievances were intermingled and the workers fully supported the local revolutionaries. Clashes with the police and the army became more and more frequent and in some of the provinces the rebellious mood began to spread from the towns to the countryside.[4]

But although the leading position which the Liberation Movement now held among the oppositional forces resembled that of November–early January, the Movement itself had changed considerably since then. Its activities were no longer directed and co-ordinated by one centre – the Council of the Union of Liberation. For this there was, first of all, a practical reason. All members of the intelligentsia wing of the Council, with the exception of Lutugin, were arrested on the morrow of 'Bloody Sunday'.[5] Peshekhonov was arrested together with seven other members of the delegation to Witte and Svyatopolk-Mirskiy.[6] (The two members who escaped were Arsenyev and Gorky; the latter slipped away in disguise.) They were arrested because the police apparently believed that the ten-man delegation was intended to become a 'provisional government'.[7] In the same period Boguchar-skiy, Khizhnyakov, Kuskova and Prokopovich were arrested for their contacts with Gapon[8] (all of them were released about a month later). Thus the Union of Liberation was left without leadership in St Petersburg at a time when events were so stormy that even if the Council members had not been arrested, it is doubtful whether they could have influenced them.[9] But even when there was a certain lull in

[1] *Galai* ibid.   [2] Ibid. p. 104   [3] See *Keep*, pp. 158–9.   [4] Ibid. pp. 159–60.
[5] See *Shakhovskoy* IV, p. 145. For the personal composition of the Council of the Union of Liberation see above. pp. 191–2.
[6] See above.   [7] See L. *Gurevich*, pp. 214–15 and *Gessen* I, p. 193.
[8] See *D.i.M.* I, no. 87, p. 161.   [9] See *Shakhovskoy* IV, p. 146.

the situation in March and opposition to the regime in Russia proper was once again concentrated in society, which followed the slogans of the Liberation Movement, the Council of the Union of Liberation no longer fulfilled a guiding and co-ordinating role. This was mainly because the events of January 1905 had imposed very great strain on the Liberation Movement which was, in reality, a coalition of various groups held together by the desire to achieve one common aim. In consequence a rift began to develop between the zemstvo constitutionalists and their allies in the liberal professions (mainly the academic world) and the St Petersburg radical intelligentsia and their allies in the 'Third Element'. Furthermore, within each of these heterogeneous groups, differences came to light which grew sharper with time.

While they still adhered to the policy of 'no enemies on the left', the zemstvo radical leaders and rank-and-file members were in favour of continuing the struggle against the autocratic regime mainly through the Liberation Movement's traditional means – the organization of public opinion. They therefore continued to work chiefly through the zemstvo movement, which they captured from Shipov in November 1904. The radical intelligentsia, on the other hand, was increasingly prepared to use extra-parliamentary means, especially strikes, and, immediately after 'Bloody Sunday', even political terror.[1] They became more closely involved in the organization of intelligentsia unions and in trying to capture the working class for the cause of democracy. The radical intellectuals were encouraged in this by the incorporation of the demands of the Union of Liberation into Gapon's petition. They did not try to discover to what extent these demands represented the views of the ordinary workers, and to what extent they had been imposed on them by Gapon's charismatic leadership. Nor did they pause to study the lessons of the 'Shidlovskiy committee' which inferred that, when aroused, the workers might follow not the Liberators but the more extreme SDs. The fact that after February the SDs did not repeat their initial success until the autumn was, apparently, the main reason why the St Petersburg radical intelligentsia was unable to read the writing on the wall.

By the end of March the rift between the two wings of the Union of Liberation was so wide that its Third Congress, held on 25–28 of that month, in Moscow, was unable to agree on a binding programme.[2]

---

[1] See *Azef*, pp. 219–20.

[2] For the proceedings of the congress and the non-binding programme it adopted in the end see *Shakhovskoy* IV, pp. 151–6. The full programme in English may be found in *Harcave*, pp. 273–9. Cf. *Milyukov* Xa, pp. 266–7.

Since the very brief programme adopted at the First Congress[1] no longer served the needs of the Union, it decided in the end to replace it with a non-binding manifesto. This included the by then customary demand for the convocation of a constituent assembly elected by universal (male and female), direct and equal suffrage and secret ballot; a government responsible to the legislature; the equal status of all citizens before the law; the granting of full personal freedom etc. It also included some radical demands in the social sphere, such as the gradual abolition of all indirect taxes (including redemption payments) and their replacement by progressive income-tax. It demanded that the amount of land available to the peasants be increased, if necessary through the confiscation of private land with compensation. The manifesto also insisted on the need for gradual introduction of the eight-hour working day and the establishment of what amounted to a welfare state. But it was renowned for its omissions rather than its demands. Because of the participation of the *Russkoye Bogatstvo* people the congress could not decide on the question of peasant ownership of land. It also avoided touching on such hotly debated topics as the right of all minorities to self-determination (speaking of 'cultural self-determination' instead), the final form of the future regime, i.e. constitutional monarchy or republic, unilateral or bilateral legislative chamber etc. Even with all these omissions, the congress only succeeded in approving the above-described 'substitute' rather than a concrete and binding programme.

But despite the growing estrangement of the two wings of the Union of Liberation, personal ties of friendship etc. prevented an open split in the Union's ranks until August 1905. The occasional meetings of its Council enabled the leaders and the rank-and-file members to keep in touch politically and thus exercise greater pressure on the government. But by then it was not the Union of Liberation but one of its offspring, the All-Russian Unions, which was setting the pace for the opposition.

The establishment of intelligentsia unions commenced in December 1904, and continued gradually throughout January and February of 1905. At the beginning of March it gathered momentum and by May there were already fourteen unions which became organized in a Union of Unions. In the process one of the newly established unions took in not only members of the intelligentsia but also workers.[2] The

---

[1] See above.

[2] Despite the fact that the various all-Russia unions and the Union of Unions played a very important role in 1905, they are still awaiting their chronicler. The archives of the

turning-point in the campaign for launching these unions came with the decree of 18 February which endowed such organizations with semi-legal status.

Besides the three All-Russian Unions mentioned above (Engineers and Technicians, Academic, Medical Personnel) the following eleven unions were established during this period: (1) *Agronomists and Statisticians*: Membership came mainly from the 'Third Element'; the union was therefore very radical in its political demands and inclined towards socialism of the populist brand in its social programme.[1] (2) *Pharmaceutical Assistants*: Unlike the other unions, this was mainly a professional association which conducted a strike campaign against the employers throughout most of 1905.[2] (3) *Clerks and Book-keepers*: Despite its very prosaic name, one of the most radical and important unions. Its chief organizer was S. N. Prokopovich and among its leaders were many SDs, including Sverchkov, Voytinskiy and others. It had branches in more than seventeen cities and towns, including St Petersburg (about 2,500 members), Moscow (about 5,000), Rostov-on-Don (about 1,700) and Kiyev (about 1,500) and was one of the few unions whose representatives were allowed to join the St Petersburg Soviet in October.[3] (4) *Equal Rights for Jews*: Its centre was in Vilna.[4] (5) *Journalists and Writers*: One of the most reputable unions from the point of view of leadership. It included many future Cadet leaders, such as P. N. Milyukov, who returned to Russia at the beginning of April,[5] I. V. Gessen and M. M. Vinaver as well as almost the entire

Union of Unions are located in *Tsentralnyy Gosudarstvennyy Arkhiv Oktyabrskoy Revolyutsii*, F. 518 (see *Chermenskiy*, p. 446). This material was inaccessible to the present author. The story of the activities of these unions as told below is based, therefore, entirely on published sources, which are abundant. The most important among them are the newspapers and periodicals of the time, including those published by various professional bodies. Besides these, the most important sources are: *Cherevanin* II, pp. 170–202; *D.i.M.* II, III, IV, *Kirpichnikov* I, II, III, IV, *Pereverzev* and *Sverchkov* IV. Cf. *Glinskiy* V, pp. 260–5, 598–619, *Milyukov* V7, Xa, pp. 285–301, *Petrunkevich* II, pp. 393–4, 398–402, *Sverchkov* II, pp. 105–9, 116, 119–20 and *Chermenskiy*, pp. 97–100.

[1] For the establishment, activities and programme of this union, see *Pravo* (1905), no. 7, col. 528; no. 15, cols 1198–9, *Syn Otechestva* (1905), no. 170, p. 3, col. 5. See also *Belokonskiy* II, pp. 269–71, *Maslov* IV, p. 111, *Sputnik*, p. 160 and *Sverchkov* IV, p. 149.

[2] See *Bez-Zaglaviya*, no. 4, pp. 150–1, *Farmatsevticheskiy Vestnik*, 13 March 1905 (no. 10), p. 120, *Syn Otechestva* (1905), nos. 175, 177–8, 180, 182–3, 186, 188–9, 193. See also *D.i.M.* II, no. 357, p. 438; III, no. 428, p. 597 and *Milonov* I, p. 68.

[3] See *Pravo* (1905), no. 12, cols 926–7 and *Syn Otechestva* (1905) nos. 68, p. 2; 175, p. 2; 186, p. 3; 191, p. 4. Cf. *Glinskiy* V, p. 251, *Kats*, p. 42, *Kirpichnikov* II, p. 137, *Milonov* I, pp. 52–3, 79–80 and *Sverchkov* II, pp. 105–7; IV, p. 149.

[4] See *Pravo* (1905), no. 10, cols 737–40; no. 14, col. 1142, *Kirpichnikov* II pp. 156–7 and *Zalevskiy* II, pp. 318–24.

[5] See *Milyukov* V5, p. 111; Xa, p. 262.

board of *Russkoye Bogatstvo*: N. F. Annenskiy, V. A. Myakotin, V. G. Korolenko and others. But because of the growing rift between the two wings of the Union of Liberation and because of the existence of a strong contingent of outright revolutionarily inclined socialists among its members, this Union as a body was unable to play an important role in the Union of Unions,[1] though its individual leaders achieved considerable influence in that organization. (6) *Lawyers*: Among the leaders were, once again, I. V. Gessen and M. M. Vinaver as well as F. I. Rodichev and V. A. Maklakov, all future Cadet leaders. Vinaver in particular became famous in summer 1905 because of the government's decision to bring him to trial for membership in the Union, and make his trial a test-case. The total membership of this Union reached the 2,500 mark and it had branches in eleven cities and towns. The most important of these were in Moscow (600 members), St Petersburg (350), Vilna and Warsaw (300 each) and Kiyev, Kharkov and Odessa (about 200 each).[2]

The other five unions established at the same time were: (7) *Government, Municipal and Zemstvo Employees*, with about 600 members in St Petersburg alone.[3] (8) *Teachers*: Like the Union of Agronomists, to a large extent dominated by the 'Third Element', i.e. by radical intellectuals with populist inclinations. It also had a strong Bolshevik contingent, led by N. A. Rozhkov and I. I. Skvortsov-Stepanov. The Bolsheviks, who were extremely hostile to the whole idea of intelligentsia unions, tried to transform this union into a professional organization and, when they failed, they left it. At the peak of its power this union had a membership of about 7,500.[4] (9) *Veterinary Surgeons*: Like the previous union, predominantly 'Third Element', but much smaller in size and less influential.[5] (10) *Zemstvo Activists*: This was the Union of Zemstvo Constitutionalists under a different name. Its establishment enabled the leaders of the zemstvo radicals and the moderate constitu-

---

[1] See *Pravo* (1905), no. 15, cols 1221–7; 17, cols 1381–6. Cf. *Belokonskiy* II, p. 268, *Cherevanin* II, pp. 175–7 and *Sputnik*, pp. 157–8.

[2] See *Pravo* (1905), no. 9, col. 685 and *Syn Otechestva* (1905), nos. 14, p. 3; 16, p. 3; 17, p. 3; 97, p. 3; 105, p. 3; 119, p. 3; 183, p. 3; and 199, p. 2. Cf. *Cherevanin* II, pp. 171–2, 182, 185, *Kirpichnikov* II, p. 137 and *Sputnik*, p. 156.

[3] See *Osvobozhdeniye* (1905), no. 73, p. 392 and *Syn Otechestva* (1905), no. 82, pp. 1–2. Cf. *Belekonskiy* II, p. 271, *Cherevanin* II, p. 179 and *Sputnik*, p. 160.

[4] *Osvobozhdeniye* (1905), no. 74, pp. 413–15, *Pravo* (1905), no. 12, cols 922–4; 17, col. 1393, *Syn Otechestva* nos 26–7, 56, 60, 184–5. Cf. *Belonskiy* II, p. 268, *Mitskevich* III, pp. 342–3, *Kirpichnikov* II, pp. 137, 154–5.

[5] See *Pravo* (1905), nos 14, cols 1105–6; 17, col. 1432; 21, cols 1757–8 and *Veterinarnoye Obozreniye* (1905), no. 7. Cf. *Cherevanin* II, p. 179 and *Sputnik*, p. 160.

tionalists (I. I. Petrunkevich, Prince D. I. Shakhovskoy, Prince Peter Dolgorukov, Yu. A. Novosiltsev and others) to participate in the foundation congress of the Union of Unions. But shortly afterwards, the zemstvo people left that organization because of its rapidly increasing radicalization.[1] (11) *Railway Workers and Employees*: This was the biggest and most important of all the unions. Its size was a result of there being workers among its members, while its influence was derived from its ability to paralyze the main means of communication in the whole Empire.[2] Its very establishment represented a victory for those members of the intelligentsia wing of the Union of Liberation who believed it was possible to draw the workers into the struggle against autocracy on the basis of a radical–democratic platform.

Apart from the Pharmaceutical Assistants, all the All-Russian Unions engaged mainly in political rather than professional activity. At that stage their activity was confined to drafting petitions and proclamations calling for an end to the war, and the convening of a constituent assembly, elected on the basis of the 'four-tail formula'. (Some unions added to this formula the already well-known appendix: 'without regard to sex, religion and nationality'.) But two unions – the All-Russian Union of Railway Workers and Employees and the All-Russian Union of Engineers and Technicians – went much further in their definition of the means by which these aims could be achieved. At the end of April both unions decided to try to organize a general political strike as the best means of forcing the tsarist regime to capitulate.[3]

By the beginning of May the process of consolidating the fourteen All-Russian Unions had progressed sufficiently for the organizers to establish a co-ordinating centre, the Union of Unions. Representatives of the various unions assembled in Moscow on 8 May, and constituted the foundation congress of the Union of Unions.[4] They elected P. N. Milyukov as chairman, and after two days of debates agreed on a common programme and statutes. The programme reflected the content of the programmes of the individual unions, and its main demand

[1] See *Pravo* (1905), no. 19, col. 1618, *Kirpichnikov* I, pp. 139–40 and *Sverchkov* IV, pp. 150–1 and below.

[2] See *Pravo* (1905), no. 17, cols 1397–9, *Syn Otechestva* (1905), nos. 60, 78, *Pereverzev*, *Cherevanin* II, pp. 178, 191–4, 201–2, *Kirpichnikov* II, p. 137, *Maslov* IV, p. 111, *Sputnik*, pp. 159–60 and below.

[3] See *Pravo* (1905), no. 17, cols 1393–9; no. 20 cols 1666–74.

[4] For the composition and decisions of the congress see, *inter alia*, *Pravo* (1905), nos. 19, col. 1618; 20, cols 1664–5, *Cherevanin* II, pp. 170–83, *Kirpichnikov* I, pp. 139–41 and *Sverchkov* IV, pp. 150–1.

Unleashing the Revolution

consisted of the 'four-tail formula'. The statute declared the Union of Unions to be a 'roof organization' in which the individual unions would enjoy very wide autonomy. After accepting both documents the congress elected a central bureau and a secretariat. The first bureau consisted of 28 members (two from each union), the most important of whom were Lutugin, Bogucharskiy, N. D. Sokolov, Annenskiy, Milyukov, Vinaver, Rodichev, Sverchkov and V. V. Svyatlovskiy. But the real power lay in the hands of the secretariat of five people, the leading role being played by Lutugin and Kirpichnikov.

The formation of the Union of Unions brought to a head the controversy between the radical intelligentsia wing of the Union of Liberation and the SDs (especially the Bolsheviks). The latter took an increasingly apprehensive view of the leading role the All-Russian Unions were playing in the anti-tsarist movement, a role which, according to the 'hegemony theory',[1] belonged to the SDs. Immediately after the foundation congress of the Union of Unions, they announced their decision to leave the various unions and not to co-operate with the central co-ordinating body.[2] But their decision made very little impact at the time. The All-Russian Unions continued to grow rapidly and to acquire more and more political influence, and many rank-and-file SDs disregarded their leaders' instructions and continued to participate in the work of the unions (Sverchkov, for example). The apprehension of the Bolsheviks (and of many Mensheviks) increased when they discovered that some members of the 'Big Group' had invaded what they regarded as their own exclusive field of activity, namely workers' professional trade unions. S. N. Prokopovich was particularly active in the organization of these trade unions. Together with several other 'left-wing liberators' who apparently joined the 'Big Group' in spring 1905 (V. V. Svyatlovskiy and G. S. Khrustalev-Nosar, the future chairman of the St Petersburg Soviet etc.) he helped to establish the Printers Union in St Petersburg (which closely collaborated with the All-Russian Union of Clerks and Book-keepers), the Union of Textile Workers and many others. The organization of these unions continued throughout the summer and on 6–7 October an all-Russian conference of representatives of the existing trade unions was held in Moscow. Prokopovich, Svyatlovskiy and Khrustalev-Nosar played the leading role in this conference. The initiative for the establishment of a soviet

---

[1] See above.
[2] See, for example, N. A. Rozhkov's article in *Syn Otechestva*, no. 73 (12 May 1905). Cf. *Mitskevich* III, pp. 349–50.

during the October general strike apparently originated in the St Petersburg branches of some of these unions.[1]

While the 'Big Group' was forging its links with the 'masses', the zemstvo radicals and their allies were busy consolidating their hold on the zemstvo movement. The organizational bureau elected by the November 1904 zemstvo congress convened a new congress for this purpose, which was held in Moscow on 22–26 April 1905.[2] About 150 delegates attended, the overwhelming majority of them already fully-fledged constitutionalists. (The number of Shipov's supporters was reduced from 27 in November to 17.) By a vast majority the congress decided to call upon the government to convene representatives of the people elected by universal and equal suffrage and secret ballot. By a smaller majority (71 to 51) it also decided that elections should be direct, that the first elected representative body should be unicameral (subsequent ones to be bicameral) and that its main task should be 'not so much legislation on individual questions as the establishment of a legal order in the state (constitution)'.[3] In other words the zemstvo congress added its voice, though in oblique language, to those of the Union of Liberation and the All-Russian Unions which demanded the convocation of a constituent assembly elected on the basis of the 'four-tail formula'.

The day before the congress ended, the censor released for circulation a pamphlet written by Shipov and some of his liberal Slavophile friends, in which they restated their opposition to a Western-type constitution and to universal suffrage. They suggested instead the transformation of the State Council into an elected body (elected by the zemstvos and town dumas) with consultative powers.[4] This proposal was totally incompatible with the decisions of the zemstvo congress, and during its closing stages Shipov, N. A. Khomyakov, M. A. Stakhovich, M. V. Rodzyanko and eleven other delegates announced their withdrawal from the all-zemstvo movement. On that day it was generally believed that the split in the ranks of the zemstvo activists was final. In reality, however, things turned out differently and this split was postponed for a month by the Tsushima disaster.

[1] See *Kats*, pp. 42, 67–9, *Kuskova* XV, no. 10, pp. 408–9, *Milonov* I, pp. 114–28, *Bez-Zaglaviya*, no. 14, pp. 56–60. Cf. *Schwarz* I, pp. 315–19.
[2] For the April zemstvo congress see, *inter alia*, *Belokonskiy* II, pp. 276–82, *Chermenskiy*, pp. 64–6, *Milyukov* V$_6$, pp. 128–30; XA, pp. 274–6, *Shipov* II, pp. 310–13, *Veselovskiy* IV, p. 12, *Osvobozhdeniye* (1905), no. 69/70, pp. 330–1 and *Smith* (unpub.), pp. 336–42.
[3] Quoted in *Smith* ibid. p. 338.   [4] See *Shipov* I.

12

Defeat in victory

On 19 May (1 June) 1905 Nicholas II received full details of the unprecedented Russian naval catastrophe in the Tsushima Straits.[1] After a voyage of nearly eight months, fraught with disaster from the first (on the night of 8/21 October 1904 the Russian Baltic fleet had opened fire on English fishing boats near Dogger Bank in the belief that they were Japanese, thus bringing relations with Britain to breaking-point), almost the entire Russian fleet had been annihilated by the Japanese in a matter of a few hours on 14/27 May. This spelled the end of the Tsar's hope that he might succeed in winning the war.[2] He now bowed to the inevitable and accepted offers of mediation from Wilhelm II and Theodore Roosevelt. The supreme war council he held on 24 May decided almost unanimously that the war should be ended,[3] since 'the re-establishment of internal order is much more important than victory over the external enemy'.[4] But subsequent negotiations, conducted at first in secrecy, progressed at a very slow pace and when peace was eventually concluded on 23 August (5 September) 1905, it was too late to prevent the revolutionary process from reaching its peak.

As might have been expected, public opinion reacted violently to the news of the Tsushima disaster. Zemstvo assemblies, town dumas and other public organizations, as well as the vast majority of the press, called for immediate peace and the convening of elected representatives of the people in order to conclude a peace settlement.[5] At the same time, almost all the All-Russian Unions joined the revolutionary parties in advocating the summoning of a constituent assembly in 'revolutionary fashion'. These divergent demands, which reflected the growing

[1] See *Nicholas IIa*, p. 201.
[2] See ibid. pp. 167–8, 177, *Nicholas IIh*, pp. 63–5, 67–72, 85n., 93, 102–5, cf. *Charques*, pp. 100, 117, *Seton-Watson*, p. 596 and *Hough* I.
[3] See *Konets Russko-Yaponskoy Voyny, Kuropatkia* IV, pp 88–9.   [4] *Konets*, p. 201.
[5] See, for example, *Pravo* (1905), no. 21, front p. and cols 1721–2, 1763–4, 1769–70 and *Syn Otechestva* (1905), no. 78, pp. 82–8.

estrangement of the two wings of the Liberation Movement, found full expression in the decisions of the emergency congresses of the zemstvo organization and of the Union of Unions, both of which were held in Moscow on 24–26 May 1905.

The zemstvo conference which, because of its composition, was known at the time as the 'Coalition Congress'[1] was the largest zemstvo assembly ever held. It was attended by about 300 delegates, representing the zemstvo constitutionalist majority, many town dumas (for the first time) and provincial assemblies of the nobility. It was also attended by the liberal Slavophile minority, who had agreed to participate under the impact and shock of the Tsushima disaster. But Shipov and his political associates laid down certain conditions before agreeing to attend, namely that the congress should refrain from adopting resolutions containing straightforward constitutional demands and the 'four-tail' formula. As a result the decisions of this gathering were more moderate than those of its April predecessor. Its main demand was that the Tsar should 'convene properly elected representatives of the people to decide, *together with the Emperor*, the issues of war and peace and the future legal order in Russia'.[2] The congress also elected a deputation, under the chairmanship of Prince S. N. Trubetskoy, which presented its resolutions to Nicholas II on 6 June.[3]

The moderation of the decisions of the 'Coalition Congress', and especially the deputation to the Tsar, drew considerable criticism from the radical intelligentsia. At the same time the resolutions were regarded as over-radical by Shipov and his colleagues. He was particularly opposed to the assumption implicit in the central demand, that the representatives of the people would have rights equal to those of the Tsar. As a result of this difference of opinion, the split in the ranks of the zemstvo activists, which had been checked for a time by the Tsushima catastrophe, became final after the congress ended. This was the last zemstvo congress which Shipov, who had initiated these gatherings, attended.[4]

The second (or emergency) congress of the Union of Unions was smaller in scope than the zemstvo gathering, but its resolutions were

---

[1] For the proceedings and decisions of the 'Coalition Congress' see, *inter alia, Belokonskiy* II, pp. 286–92, *Chermenskiy*, pp. 68–71, *Osvobozhdeniye* (1905) nos. 72, pp. 365–6; 74, pp. 403–8, *Petrunkevich* II, pp. 374–81, *Shipov* II, pp. 313–20, *Smith* (unpub.), pp. 366–9 and *Veselovskiy* IV, pp. 12–13.
[2] *Osvobozhdeniye* (1905), no. 72, p. 366, italics added.
[3] Trubetskoy's speech delivered on this occasion may be found in *S. Trubetskoy*, pp. 7–13.
[4] See *Shipov* II, p. 320.

of greater importance at the time.[1] Milyukov again presided, and the congress was attended by 70 delegates, representing fourteen All-Russian Unions, though not the same fourteen which had participated in the foundation congress. Two of the unions which had participated in the previous meeting – the Academic and the Union of Zemstvo Activists – did not attend this time. The main reason for their abstention was the rapid radicalization of the Union of Unions, though the latter had a formal excuse for non-participation – the simultaneous session of the 'Coalition Congress'. Their place was taken by representatives of two newly-established unions: the All-Russian Union for Equal Rights for Women[2] and the All-Russian Peasants Union. (Despite the title of the latter, it had hardly any peasant members. It was really an extension of the Union of Agronomists and Statisticians, and its objective was to attract the peasants to the anti-government struggle on the basis of the agrarian programme of *Russkoye Bogatstvo* and the SRs, namely the nationalization of the land by a decision of the Constituent Assembly.[3]) After two days of debates, the emergency congress adopted a resolution which, in contrast to that of the zemstvo congress, was addressed not to the Tsar but to 'all the Russian people, societies and organizations'. It called upon them to convene 'in revolutionary fashion' a constituent assembly 'which will put an end, as quickly as possible, to the war and to the existing regime'.[4]

This resolution was framed by Milyukov, and its composition symbolized the zenith of his influence in the Union of Unions, though this was much less than it may have appeared at the time. Soon afterwards a new issue raised its head, which proved to be the direct cause of the final split between the two wings of the Union of Liberation. Milyukov sided, on this question, with the zemstvo radicals (to whom he had always been closest, ideologically speaking, in the Liberation Movement) and their allies (the Academic and Zemstvo Activists Unions, which for all practical purposes had already left the Union of Unions; the majority of the Unions of Lawyers, Equal Rights for Jews, Equal

---

[1] For the composition, proceedings and decisions of the emergency congress of the Union of Unions see *Osvobozhdeniye* (1905), no. 72, p. 367, *Syn Otechestva* (1905), no. 87, *Kirpichnikov* II, p. 144, *Milyukov* v₇, pp. 144–6; Xa, pp. 290–2 and *Sverchkov* IV, pp. 152–3.

[2] For the foundation and activities of this union see, *inter alia*, *Pravo* (1905), nos. 12, cols 928–9; 17, cols 1399–1401; 18, col. 1504; 21, col. 1753 and *Tyrkova* III, pp. 185 ff.

[3] For the organization, composition and aims of this union, see, *inter alia*, *Bez-Zaglaviya* (1906), no. 10, pp. 391–3, *Syn Otechestva* (1905), nos 170, p. 3; 180, p. 3, *Glinskiy* IV, pp. 260–1, *Maslov* III, pp. 236 ff.; IV, p. 121 and *D.i.M.* III, nos. 10n, pp. 843–4; 16, pp. 40–1; 19, p. 55; IV, no. 16, pp. 51–76. For the *Russkoye Bogatstvo* agrarian programme see above and *Chernov* III, pp. 239–40.   [4] Quoted in *Galai*, p. 107.

Rights for Women; part of the Union of Journalists and Writers, and members of some other unions). As a result, he found himself in a minority in the Union of Unions and soon left it altogether.

The issue which brought about the final break-up of the Union of Liberation was provided by the conclusions of the 'Bulygin Conference', which had been established by the 18 February rescript. The main outlines of its proposals – the formation of a consultative assembly (State Duma), elected by restricted franchise (Jews to be totally excluded) and indirect ballot – became common knowledge immediately after Tsushima.[1] Such an assembly was naturally unacceptable to all sections of the Liberation Movement, except for the liberal Slavophiles. But there is no indication that Bulygin's proposals were even mentioned at the emergency congresses of the zemstvo people and of the Union of Unions. Both meetings were preoccupied with the naval disaster, and this was reflected in their resolutions. By the beginning of June, however, the shock had waned and as a consequence, these proposals began to assume increasing importance.

While rejecting Bulygin's proposals on principle the zemstvo radicals and their allies were nevertheless prepared to participate in the elections to the Duma, with the aim of transforming it into a legislature. They believed that the first task of such a legislative assembly would be to change the electoral law in accordance with the 'four-tail' formula.[2] This attitude towards the Bulygin proposals ostensibly fitted in with their tendency to regard public opinion campaigns as the chief means of struggle. But in reality the adoption of such a policy at the time was bound to weaken rather than strengthen the public opinion campaign. They were fully aware that the radical intelligentsia shared the revolutionary belief that no compromise should be made with the existing regime, and themselves adhered to this view till the end of April (Milyukov, at least, holding it till the end of May). Thus, the reasons behind their decision to participate in the elections to the 'Bulygin Duma' were no longer mainly tactical but went deeper. They were connected with the dawning doubts of the zemstvo radicals and their allies as to the wisdom of the policy of 'no enemies on the left'. This must have been a painful reassessment for people like Struve, Milyukov and especially Petrunkevich, who had formulated this same policy in 1878, and was not undertaken lightly but rather forced upon them by the expansion of the revolutionary process.

[1] See *Pravo*, 22 May 1905 (no. 20), col. 1691, *Syn Otechestva*, 24 May 1905 (no. 83), cf. bid. no. 97 (*Khronika*). [2] See below.

Defeat in victory

The zemstvo radicals were apparently drawn to abandon the policy of 'no enemies on the left' by a series of events which occurred in late spring and early summer 1905, though these did not affect their commitment to political democracy and progressive social legislation. In the minority provinces armed demonstrations and uprisings had been the order of the day for some time, and now a new wave of strikes commenced in Russia proper in the wake of Tsushima. It culminated in an almost general strike accompanied by street clashes in Odessa in mid-June. The situation there was aggravated by the outbreak of a mutiny on the battleship *Potemkin* (itself a delayed reaction to the naval disaster). By 17 June the number of those killed in Odessa alone during the few days of street fighting had reached the 2,000 mark. The number of wounded was much higher and the damage to property was incalculable.[1] This was violence on an unprecedented scale even for the Russia of 1905. Despite their bold phrases about bloody revolution and their endorsement of political terror, people like Milyukov, Petrunkevich, Shakhovskoy and Struve were not basically men of violence, and the events in Odessa and elsewhere affected them profoundly. Their apprehension increased as a result of two other threats which, if they had materialized, would have led to violence on an even larger scale. The third congress of RSDRP (Bolsheviks), held in London in April 1905, declared that the preparation of an all-Russian armed uprising was the order of the day for party activists in Russia.[2] At the same time, the SRs, together with those All-Russian Unions which were dominated by the 'Third Element', were beginning a propaganda campaign in the countryside which could have resulted in a Pugachov-style jacquerie.[3] To some of the leaders of the zemstvo radicals and their associates, the former threat seemed the most imminent at the time.[4] But the majority rightly believed the latter to constitute the greater danger.

Pugachovschina presented a two-fold threat. It endangered not only the existing regime and the property of landowners (Petrunkevich had been ready to sacrifice this on behalf of the people since 1878, and the majority of the zemstvo radicals had adopted this view later) but also the whole fabric of Russian civilized society. (Developments in 1917 were to prove this assessment correct.) Secondly, and this was regarded

[1] See *Harcave*, pp. 152–8.
[2] See *Izveshcheniye*, pp. 3–6. That this decision was taken seriously at the time can be seen from the remarks of *Osvobozhdenets* in *Osvobozhdeniye* (1905), no. 74, pp. 398–402.
[3] See *Petrunkevich* II, pp. 397–402 and *Harcave*, pp. 171–3.
[4] See, for example, *Osvobozhdeniye* ibid.

as a more imminent danger in summer 1905, the first signs of unrest in the countryside drastically changed the mood of the nobility. The majority of the noble landowners, who had withdrawn their support from the government because of its economic policies, now forgot all their grievances and rallied to its rescue. The preservation of autocracy seemed to them the best means of preventing a social upheaval and of defending their estate privileges.

The first signs of a reactionary backlash by the nobility appeared in early spring[1] but only began to pose what looked like a real threat in May. Two noble reactionary organizations were established in that month: the All-Russian Union of Landowners was organized on 14 May (Tsushima day) in Saratov and the much more influential Union of the United Nobility, under the leadership of Count A. A. Bobrinskiy, was founded in St Petersburg on the 22nd. Both unions declared the preservation of autocracy, orthodoxy and private property to be their main aim.[2] These developments threatened to deprive the zemstvo radicals and the moderate constitutionalists of their social basis. There was also a danger that the increasing violence of the Black Hundreds* against the intelligentsia and the minorities (especially the Jews),[3] combined with these developments, might tempt Nicholas II to abandon his policy of concessions and return to his old reactionary methods. As it turned out, the zemstvo radical fear of such a regression was somewhat premature, though very real.

In abandoning the policy of 'no enemies on the left' these radicals hoped to achieve a two-fold aim: first, to make it more difficult for the revolutionaries to stage a nationwide armed uprising and/or unleash a *Pugachovshchina*; secondly, by decreasing the threat from the left, to diminish the provocation to the right, thus making a reactionary move by the government less likely. It seemed to them that their participation in the elections to the 'Bulygin Duma' would have a similar effect. They believed that by agreeing to the establishment of an elected consultative assembly, the Tsar had reached his Rubicon. They hoped that, by playing along with him, they could induce him to cross it and launch Russia on a path which might eventually lead to the adoption of a fully-fledged constitutional–democratic regime. Their announcement of

---

[1] See *Veselovskiy* IV, pp. 4–7.   [2] See *Levitskiy*, pp. 386–8.

* Black Hundreds (*Chernyye Sotni*) was a term generally used at the time to describe the bands of strong-arm supporters of autocracy. Though they lacked official status, they enjoyed the support of the authorities, especially at the local level.

[3] See *Harcave*, pp. 150–1, *Seton-Watson*, p. 611 and above p. 242n.

willingness to participate in the elections served to inform all those concerned that the policy of 'no enemies on the left' was no longer in force. This reasoning was fully reflected in the way in which some of their leaders, writing in the daily papers, defended the decision to participate in the elections. V. D. Kuzmin-Karavayev, then one of the leaders of the moderate constitutionalists, in an article written at the beginning of June, appealed to all oppositional groups and individuals 'who were striving to abolish autocracy by peaceful and not by revolutionary means'. He begged them not to cling to the 'four-tail' formula and not to boycott the elections, lest they 'deliver the fatherland into the hands either of all-destroying reaction or of a *Pugachovshchina*'.[1] Two months later Milyukov expressed similar views, though from a different angle, in commenting on the Manifesto of 6 August, which formally established the State Duma and promised elections by the end of the year (the only marked improvement in the final version of the 'Bulygin Duma' was the enfranchisement of the Jews).[2] He wrote, *inter alia*: 'Today we have reached the other shore...A return to the past is impossible...Today "people's representation" was born in Russia, and this fact cannot be obscured by attacks from either the *right* or the *left*.'[3] In years to come, Milyukov was to bitterly regret his early optimism. But at the time it was shared by the majority of zemstvo radicals and their associates, who endorsed the 'new course'. This amounted to a search for the 'middle ground' in politics, at least as far as tactics and means were concerned.

The question of participation in the elections to the 'Bulygin Duma' was the main topic at the congress of representatives of zemstvos and town dumas held on 6–8 July in Moscow.[4] (A. I. Guchkov, the future leader of the Octobrists, made his political debut at this congress.) The majority favoured participation in the elections with the aim of transforming the Duma into a 'truly representative legislative assembly'. But since the government had not yet officially announced its intention to establish a Duma, the congress thought it expedient to postpone its

[1] *Syn Otechestva*, 10 (23) June 1905 (no. 98), p. 2.
[2] The full text of the Manifesto may be found, *inter alia*, in *Sputnik*, pp. 247–9. For the lengthy deliberations held in Peterhof on 19–26 July 1905, at the end of which the final version of the Manifesto was approved, see, *inter alia*, *Petergofskoye Soveshchaniye*, *Portsmut* I, pp. 24, 27, 32–3, *Milyukov* xa, pp. 298–9, cf. *Harcave*, pp. 161–2 and *Chermenskiy*, pp. 105–8.
[3] *Syn Otechestva*, 7(20) August 1905 (no. 147), 'O Gosudarstvennoy Dume', italics added.
[4] For the composition, proceedings and decisions of the congress see *Belokonskiy* II, pp. 292–334, *Smith* (unpub.), pp. 382–9, 420–7, 435, *Osvobozhdeniye* (1905), no. 76, pp. 447–60, cf. *N. Astrov* III, pp. 307–11, *Chermenskiy*, pp. 90–5 and *Milyukov* xa, pp. 294–6.

final decision on this question till the government announcement was made.

The Fifth Congress of the Union of Zemstvo Constitutionalists, which opened just after the zemstvo congress closed (9–10 July)[1], was less inhibited by such formalities. It elected a committee of twenty for the purpose of establishing contact with 'like-minded groups' so as to set up a temporary bureau of a zemstvo constitutionalist party to participate in the forthcoming elections. The committee applied itself diligently to its task, and immediately after publication of the 6 August Manifesto, it issued a list of 91 candidates for the elections. The most important among them were: Prince P. (Pavel?) D. Dolgorukov, F. A. Golovin, S. A. Muromtsev, F. F. Kokoshkin, N. N. Kovalevskiy, F. I. Rodichev, I. I. Petrunkevich, V. D. Kuzmin-Karavayev, V. I. Vernadskiy, Count P. A. Geyden and Prince M. V. Golitsyn.[2] Publication of this list turned out to be somewhat premature. A new upsurge of the revolutionary activity swept away the 'Bulygin Duma' together with many other government projects. When the elections were eventually held, many of those original candidates (including Geyden and Golitsyn) appeared on a different ticket from the zemstvo radicals and their allies in the academic world and the liberal professions. But the committee did not work in vain. Its activity helped lay the organizational foundation for the launching of the Constitutional-Democratic Party two months later.

The decision of the zemstvo radicals to break with the left and participate in the elections infuriated the 'Big Group' and its supporters in the Union of Unions. They particularly resented Milyukov's sudden change of heart and did not mince words in expressing their feelings. The showdown between the two sides began at the third congress of the Union of Unions at the beginning of July and ended about two months later at the fourth and last congress of the Union of Liberation.

For security reasons, the congress of the Union of Unions was held on 1–3 July in Terioki, a well-known Finnish resort on the outskirts of St Petersburg.[3] In contrast to the two previous congresses, Milyukov

---

[1] See *Osvobozhdeniye*, no. 75, pp. 434–5; 78/79, cf. *Belokonskiy* II, pp. 346–8, *Chermenskiy*, pp. 100–5, *Milyukov* Xa, pp. 296–8 and *Smith* (unpub.), pp. 398–403, 439.

[2] *Syn Otechestva* (1905), no. 153, p. 2 contains the complete list.

[3] Published information on this congress is found mainly in *Chermenskiy*, p. 100 (based on the archives of the Union of Unions), *Cherevanin* II, pp. 185–6, *Kirpichnikov* II, pp. 146–7, *Milyukov* v₇, pp. 146–7; Xa, pp. 292–3, *Smith* (unpub.), pp. 381–2, *Sputnik*, p. 13, *Sverchkov* II, p. 111; IV, p. 156. Milyukov's claim that he did not participate (*Milyukov* ibid., ibid.) is not sustained by the other evidence.

was not elected chairman this time, and this in itself was a sign of his fall from grace. The main debate centred on the question of the 'Bulygin Duma', and Milyukov tabled a motion calling for participation in the forthcoming elections. N. D. Sokolov, who spoke on behalf of the majority of the central bureau, opposed this suggestion and submitted a draft resolution calling for the boycotting of these elections. After a prolonged and heated debate, Sokolov won with a two-thirds majority (43 against 20 with 2 abstentions). The final resolution of the congress affirmed the unswerving loyalty of the Union of Unions to the 'four-tail' formula and forbade its members participation either actively or passively in the elections.[1]

Immediately after the congress, Milyukov began to organize the minority into a more cohesive unit, but was unable to continue this activity for long. Simultaneously with the 6 August Manifesto, a government announcement was published, officially revoking the decree of 18 February. This removed the semi-legal sanction from the non-violent political activity then going on in Russia.[2] Less than twenty-four hours later, the police raided Milyukov's place of residence where he was conferring with his supporters in the central bureau of the Union of Unions. All those present were arrested, and although they were released about a month later,[3] Milyukov did not resume his activity in the Union of Unions. And thus the police unwittingly played into the hands of the extremists once again. Now that Milyukov and his principal supporters were in prison, the central bodies of the Union of Unions were able to stop arguing about the 'Bulygin Duma' and to devote all their time to what had become their chief preoccupation – the organization of a general political strike. Taking their cue from the All-Russian Unions of Railwaymen and Engineers[4] they established a special committee for preparation of such a strike at the beginning of June.[5] But it was only in mid-August that the committee found its hands full. Since by then the Union of Unions could rely on the active support of some 50,000 members (the number soared to 100,000 in autumn), without taking into account those members affiliated to the Union of Railwaymen,[6] its activities soon attained crucial importance.

Unlike the situation at the third congress of the Union of Unions, the zemstvo radicals succeeded in mustering a majority at the Union of

---

[1] *Chermenskiy* ibid. [2] See *Syn Otechestva* (1905), no. 150 (Leader) and above.
[3] See *Milyukov* v₇, pp. 148–9; xa, pp. 300–1 and *Sverchkov* II, p. 112; IV, pp. 156–7.
[4] See above. [5] See *Syn Otechestva* (1905), no. 98, p. 4.
[6] See *Kirpichnikov* I, p. 140.

Liberation's fourth and last congress, held in Moscow on 23–24 August.[1] Participation in the forthcoming elections was decided upon, with the aim of transforming the Duma into a legislative assembly and changing the electoral laws in accordance with the 'four-tail' formula. Since only an open party could participate in the election campaign, the congress decided to dissolve the conspiratorial Union of Liberation. Its members were asked to join other like-minded groups, i.e. the moderate zemstvo constitutionalists and their like, to form together a Constitutional-Democratic Party. The programme of the new party was to be based on the non-binding programme adopted at the third congress of the Union.[2] The congress ended its deliberations by electing a committee of forty which was to combine with the committee of twenty (elected by the Fifth Congress of the Union of Zemstvo Constitutionalists) in a temporary central committee for the future party. Its main task was to prepare the foundation congress of the party, to be held in October.

Ostensibly the zemstvo radicals had won a great victory at the congress, but this was not really so. The 'Big Group' refused to join the new party and although it had been outnumbered at the congress, it still enjoyed a large following in the country. As a result, the social basis of the Cadets (as the members of the new party were soon nicknamed by Annenskiy)[3] was considerably narrowed. The 'Big Group's' opposition to the planned party became public knowledge immediately after the congress ended. In a long article, published on 2 September, Peshekhonov bitterly attacked his former political comrades and personal friends ('Milyukov and Co.') for their intention to participate in the elections to the 'Bulygin Duma' and for their break with the left. He warned them that the time had not yet arrived in Russia to steer a middle course in politics. In adopting their position, he explained, the Cadets were cutting themselves off from their most ardent supporters. (i.e. the radical intelligentsia) and were in danger of finding themselves between two firing lines[4] (i.e. the government and the revolutionaries). By the time these words appeared in print their truth was already being demonstrated, and the Cadets escaped some of the worst consequences of their policy only by joining the all-out onslaught on autocracy at the last minute in October.

[1] The main sources of information on the congress are *Osvobozhdeniye* (1905), nos. 77, p. 475; 78/79, pp. 487–8 and *Shakhovskoy* IV, pp. 164–9, cf. *Chermenskiy*, pp. 111–13.
[2] See above. [3] See *Gessen* I, p. 205.
[4] See *Syn Otechestva*, no. 171 (front page), cf. *Kuskova* XIV, pp. 85–7, *Martynov*, p. 9 and *Yordanskiy*, p. 70.

Defeat in victory

As so often occurs in a revolutionary situation, the threat from the right, which appeared so formidable in summer 1905, suddenly evaporated and gave way to a new upsurge of anti-government feeling. The turning-point proved to be the granting of autonomy to the universities on 27 August 1905.[1] The Tsar and his advisers were encouraged by the emergence of what appeared to be a strong pro-autocratic movement, by the favourable reaction of a sizeable section of society to the 'Bulygin Duma' and by the signing of the peace treaty with Japan on 23 August. They apparently reached the conclusion that the regime had weathered the storm and the country was returning to normal. It was apparently on D. F. Trepov's advice that Nicholas decided to accelerate this process by reopening the universities at the beginning of the new academic year and granting them academic freedom.[2] He could not have made a graver mistake.

At a series of mass meetings (*skhodki*) held during the first half of September in almost all the universities of the Empire, the students decided to utilize the new freedoms granted to them in order to transform the universities into 'islands of liberty' where all sections of the population (except for the reactionaries) could hold political meetings with impunity.[3] This idea apparently originated with the Mensheviks[4] and the Cadets were at first opposed to it.[5] S. N. Trubetskoy, the newly elected rector, even closed Moscow University for a week in the second half of September in order to prevent outsiders from roaming its halls.[6] But the opposition was soon overcome and the universities, especially in the two capitals, were transformed into focal points of the anti-tsarist movement. Tens of thousands of workers, radical intellectuals and even 'law-abiding citizens' gathered there every evening and listened to inflammatory speeches delivered by members of the revolutionary parties and of the Union of Unions. Their impact was immediately reflected in a new wave of economic strikes, culminating in the printers' strike in Moscow, which began on 23 September and lasted for a week, during which no newspapers appeared in the city. The strike ended only when the employers agreed to all the workers'

---

[1] For the 'temporary regulations' which established this autonomy see, *inter alia*, *Sputnik*, p. 70 and *Pravo* (1905), no. 35, cols 2870–1.
[2] See *Witte* VIII, p. 446.
[3] See *Syn Otechestva* (1905), nos. 172, p. 2; 176, p. 4; 177, p. 5; 179, front page; 182, pp. 2–3; 183, p. 2; and 189, p. 3.
[4] See *Keep*, pp. 216–17.
[5] See Struve's article in *Osvobozhdeniye* (1905), no. 78/79, pp. 495–8.
[6] See *Syn Otechestva* (1905), nos. 191, p. 3; 194, p. 2, 199, p. 3.

261

demands.[1] By then the atmosphere was charged with mounting discontent. Street demonstrations and clashes with the police were common occurrences and, what was more important, the railway workers were beginning to show signs of restlessness.[2]

Russia was more dependent than any other European country at that time on the smooth functioning of its railways. This was especially true of the Trans-Siberian line which provided the only means of communication with the army in Manchuria. Its importance did not diminish with the conclusion of peace. On the contrary, as a result of the upsurge of revolutionary pressure in European Russia, the survival of autocracy became almost entirely dependent on the speedy return of loyal troops from the Far East. The Ministry of Transport therefore spared no effort throughout 1905 to placate the railwaymen. In the spring, it was the first government department to introduce the nine-hour working day in all its enterprises.[3] Since about two-thirds of Russia's railways were state-owned,[4] this was an important step towards the improvement of working conditions. The railways therefore, functioned more or less smoothly throughout the summer, and with the appearance of the first signs of renewed industrial unrest in early autumn, the Ministry of Transport tried to repeat its earlier success. On the invitation of Khilkov, the Minister of Transport, elected representatives of the railwaymen assembled in St Petersburg to discuss revising the regulations concerning pension and savings funds.[5] This was a vital welfare problem, and Khilkov undoubtedly hoped that concessions on this point would pacify the railwaymen. He was soon proved wrong. The delegates arrived in a rebellious mood and, on the instructions of the Railwaymen's Union, which was dominated by intellectuals, they refused to discuss economics and raised general political questions. This led to a head-on collision with officials of the Ministry, and by the beginning of October rumours were circulating that the police were planning to arrest the delegates.

These rumours provided the signal for which the All-Russian Union of Railwaymen had been waiting since April, and the Union of Unions since June. On the initiative of the local branch of the former, a railway

---

[1] See ibid. nos. 195, front page; 196, p. 3; 198, p. 3; 199, p. 3, cf. *Keep*, pp. 218–20.
[2] See *Syn Otechestva* (1905), nos. 195, front page; 198 p. 3; and 199, p. 3.
[3] See Aleksandrov's article in ibid. no. 79.
[4] See *Seton-Watson*, p. 660.
[5] The story of this conference, as outlined below, is based mainly on *Syn Otechestva*, nos. 190, p. 3; 191, p. 2; 192, p. 3; 194, p. 3; 196, p. 2 and 199, p. 2. Cf. *Glinskiy* IV, pp. 614–15, *Prokopovich* IX, pp. 19–21, *Sverchkov* II, pp. 116–17 and *Keep*, p. 220.

strike began in Moscow on 7 October.[1] A day later the whole Moscow network was paralyzed and the strike spread like wildfire to other regions. On the same day the Union of Unions instructed its members to join the railwaymen and began to organize strike committees all over Russia.[2] The response of the All-Russian Unions and of the urban population as a whole was overwhelming. It looked as if all sections of the urban population of the Empire – the minorities, the intelligentsia, manual and white-collar workers, and their employers (who continued to pay them during the October general strike),[3] most of the merchants and others – had decided once and for all to put an end to autocracy by joining the strike. On 15 October, when the strike became truly widespread, it looked as if Struve's earlier dream of toppling the regime through the efforts of the 'whole nation' was about to come true. But this was not so.

Lacking sufficient army units to crush a popular movement of such dimensions, Nicholas II had no choice but to accept Witte's programme. This plan aimed at gaining breathing-space for autocracy by granting further concessions to placate the more moderate elements in the opposition. These concessions were contained in the Imperial Manifesto of 17 October.[4] The most important were the promises to grant personal freedoms, to extend the franchise beyond that granted in the 6 August Manifesto and to bestow legislative powers on the State Duma. These promises fell far short of the expectations not only of the revolutionaries and the Union of Unions but even of the Cadets, who were then holding their foundation congress in Moscow. On the eve of the general strike they had been very sceptical about its outcome. But they were all, and especially Milyukov, soon intoxicated with success, and returned for a while to the axiom that nothing less than the immediate convocation of a constituent assembly on the basis of

---

[1] See *D.i.M.* II, nos. 138, 140–2, 144, 147, 332, *Prokopovich* ibid. pp. 21–2, *Pereverzev*, pp. 50–1 and *Mitskevich* III, pp. 390–4.

[2] For the crucial role the Union of Unions played at the beginning of the October general strike see L. A-Va in *Byloye*, no. 13 (1910), pp. 25–33, *Akselrod* IV. pp. 136–7, 140, 146, *Cherevanin* II, pp. 194–5, *Kirpichnikov* I, pp. 142–3; II, pp. 148–9, *Mitskevich* III, pp. 394–8, *Pereverzev*, pp. 51–2, *Tyrkova* II, p. 209, *Trotsky* IV. pp. 160–1, *Sverchkov* V, pp. 40–1 and *D.i.M.* II, nos. 284, 287–92, 301, 351, 355–7, 359, 361, 367, 369–70, *D.i.M.* III, no. 16 (pp. 37–51).

[3] See *Berlin*, pp. 234–5.

[4] An English translation of the Manifesto is found *inter alia*, in *Harcave*, pp. 195–6. For the considerations which led Nicholas, after prolonged consultations, to sign the Manifesto, see *Mosolov* pp. 131–47, *Nicholas II*a, pp. 221–3, *Polovtsev* II, pp. 77–9, 83–4, *K. K. Romanov* II, pp. 137–44, *Shipov* II, pp. 341–2, *Witte* IX, pp. 1–24 and *D.i.M.* II, nos. 141 (pp. 213–14), 348–9, 352.

the 'four-tail' formula could satisfy them. Milyukov especially took offence at the fact that the magic word 'constitution' had not been pronounced.[1] The omission was, of course, not accidental. Nicholas had no intention of becoming a constitutional monarch and the publication of the Manifesto was aimed at furthering his own aims. Unlike the revolutionaries, the Union of Unions and the Cadets, the majority of the urban population of Russia proper regarded the Manifesto as a great victory, and went back to work. Thus, the general strike was over before the most important objectives of both wings of the Union of Liberation could be realized. The tsarist government thus gained a breathing-space and was able to rush back from the Far East sufficient loyal troops to make doubly sure that these objectives would not be fulfilled at that time. The defeat of both wings of the Union was much greater than many of their leaders then knew. In the fight with autocracy they merely lost a battle, but in the struggle to win the Russian people over to the cause of political freedom and democracy they lost a war.

Even before the strike ended it had become apparent in St Petersburg and later in other industrial centres in Russia proper that the workers' interest in political liberty was rapidly waning. Kuskova had rightly predicted in 1898 that the workers were mainly interested in improving their economic lot, though because of the stormy events commencing with the strike wave in the South in summer 1903 she forgot this. In autumn 1905 the workers tried to achieve their aim, i.e. the immediate introduction of an eight-hour working-day, by 'direct-action' tactics. The employers retaliated by resorting to lock-outs on a large scale. The bitter economic class-warfare thus engendered brought about the isolation of the proletariat, which made the government's counter-offensive easier to start.

The 'Big Group' and its supporters in the Union of Unions regarded these developments with growing consternation, but because of the SDs were powerless to prevent them. The latter were prepared to support the workers' most extreme economic demands as well as their syndicalistic tactics and as a result, they captured the leadership of the proletariat from the Union of Unions. Nowhere was this process more rapid and clearer than in St Petersburg. There the Union of Unions helped to launch a council (*soviet*) of workers' deputies during the October general strike, and Khrustalev-Nosar, one of its supporters,

---

[1] See *Chermenskiy*, pp. 133–5, *Maklakov*, vol. III, pp. 442–50 and *Milyukov*, V9, pp. 121–8; V10 pp. 128–31; X*a*, pp. 306–14, 324–9.

Defeat in victory

was even elected chairman of this body. But no sooner had the Soviet been established than the local Mensheviks, headed by Trotsky, became its true leaders and almost all the local branches of the Union of Unions were excluded from it. (The three exceptions were the Unions of Railwaymen, Clerks and Book-keepers, and Pharmaceutical Assistants.[1]) The disappointment of the ex-SD members of the 'Big Group' with the workers was matched by the disillusionment of the *Russkoye Bogatstvo* people with the peasants. In Russia proper the latter did not begin to respond to the exhortations of the Peasant Union and other 'Third Element' unions on a large scale until November.[2] But by then the peasant disturbances, instead of helping the opposition, played into the hands of the government. Their immediate result was to hasten and strengthen the reactionary backlash of the nobility.

Deprived of the workers' support and unable to rally the peasants, the Union of Unions lost most of its influence immediately after the end of the October general political strike. As a result the 'Big Group' divided back into its two main components. The ex-'Economists', Kuskova and Prokopovich, together with Bogucharskiy, Khizhnyakov and some less-known people, started to publish a periodical in January 1906 appropriately named *Bez-Zaglaviya* ('Without a Title'). During its short lifetime,[3] it tried to revive the Union of Liberation, but this was an impossible task. The *Russkoye Bogatstvo* group (Annenskiy, Korolenko, Myakotin, Peshekhonov, Lutugin and their followers) co-operated for a while with the SRs, especially on the editorial board of *Syn Otechestva* (Son of the Fatherland). But since they were opposed to terror as advocated by the SRs at their foundation congress in January 1906, they established a splinter party of their own. It was named the People's Socialist Party (*Narodno-Sotsialisticheskaya Partiya*), and was able to despatch fourteen deputies to the second Duma.[4] (It did not achieve such success again until 1917.)

At first it looked as if the Cadets had encountered greater success than their former allies in the Union of Liberation. Under the leader-

[1] For the origins, leadership, composition and activities of the St Petersburg Soviet see, *inter alia*: *D.i.M.* III, no. 16, pp. 47–9, *Cherevanin* II, pp. 197–201, *Gliaskiy* V, pp. 250–8, *Gutovskiy* I, pp. 88–110, *Kantarovich*, pp. 117–45, *Spunik*, pp. 120–4, *Kirpichnikov* I, pp. 142ff, *Sverchkov* II, pp. 122–7; v. Cf. *Keep*, pp. 228–42.
[2] See *Harcave*, pp. 148, 170–3, 185.
[3] It existed for less than five months (24 January–14 May) and during this period sixteen numbers appeared. (See *Bibliography*.) It was later replaced by the daily *Tovarishch* (Comrade). See *Martynov*, p. 14.
[4] See *Chernov* III, pp. 237–49, 259–61, *Peshekhonov* v. VII, and *Maslov* IV, pp. 109, 113–14, 151–8, cf. *Seton-Watson*, pp. 618–19.

265

ship of Milyukov (who was by then already well known in the English-speaking countries too) and such well-known political figures as Petrunkevich, Rodichev, Shakhovskoy, the Dolgorukov twins, V. A. Maklakov, V. D. Nabokov and many others[1] they soon made a name for the party in the country. After their initial intoxication with their taste of success in October, they returned to reality and to the policy of searching for the 'middle ground'. They plunged enthusiastically into the campaign for elections to the legislative Duma and were handsomely rewarded. They became the largest single faction in the Duma (179 deputies out of a total of some 480) and actually dominated it. But, as events were soon to show, their victory proved, to a very large extent, a hollow triumph.

For one thing, their great success at the polls was due, at least in part, to the fact that the SRs, the SDs (with the exception of the Georgians) and the more extreme parties of the minorities, boycotted the elections. When these latter parties participated in the elections to the second Duma, the Cadets suffered a sizeable defeat.[2] Secondly, their attempt to steer a 'middle course' in politics with regard to tactics so as to ensure the realization of Union of Liberation aims, proved a failure. Not only the revolutionaries but also the tsarist government were mainly relying on force, and this fact of life could not be altered by the Cadet's treatment of the Duma as a kind of Russian House of Commons. Thirdly, and this was most important from the point of view of future developments, the idea of the Duma – the representative form of government – so dear to the Cadets and their former allies in the Union of Liberation, did not take root in the population as a whole. It is true that there was a high participation rate in the elections. But when the Duma was forcibly dissolved on 9 July 1906, barely two months after its official inauguration, not a stir was felt in the country. The people's reaction to the call to stop paying taxes, issued by a meeting of 200 Duma delegates (including 120 Cadets) in Vyborg the day after the dissolution,[3] did not differ greatly from that of the Germans in 1862–3 to the exhortations of the progressives during the constitutional crisis in Prussia. In both cases the call for passive resistance on behalf of the rights of the representative institution evoked no response.

---

[1] The list of the thirty members of the first elected central committee of the Constitutional-Democratic Party can be found, *inter alia*, in *Martynov*, pp. 15–16.
[2] See *Seton-Watson*, p. 626.
[3] See ibid. pp. 623–5. Cf. *Milyukov* xa, pp. 401–7.

The position of the Cadets was further weakened by developments in the zemstvo milieu. The reactionary backlash of the nobility, which gathered momentum in autumn 1905, deprived the Cadets of all influence in the zemstvos by the end of 1906.[1] Since they lost the support of the radical intelligentsia in 1905 and were unable to gain the support of the business community (which mainly joined the Octobrists), because of their devotion to a radical political and social programme, the cadets turned into a party of intellectuals engaged in the liberal professions and academic work, and of radical noblemen who lost all influence in their milieu. There were certain advantages to this composition. Being free of the need to represent interests, it became a party which represented the ideal of political freedom, and to a certain extent, of social justice, in its pure and abstract form. The trouble was, of course, that the pure ideal of political liberty and individual freedom did not mean much to the half-starved and wholly-ignorant masses who, to some extent because of government policy, believed that only violence could prove effective. In a situation in which government, people and privileged classes each regarded violence as the sole arbiter in political matters, the Cadet Party had but a slender chance of success.

The participation of a large number of Russian radical intellectuals in the Liberation Movement helps explain its commitment to democracy and social justice. But it does not account for the Movement's unique composition nor for the readiness of its noble members to support a radical–democratic programme. In order to understand these phenomena, we must return to the dichotomy which characterized Russian government policy in the period under review, and take into account the peculiar features of the industrialization campaign of the 1890s, conducted under Witte's guidance.

[1] The magnitude of the reactionary backlash in the zemstvo milieu is illustrated in the following figures:

Political affiliation of chairmen of provincial zemstvo boards

The Party	Before winter 1906/7 elections	After elections
Cadets	15	1
Progressionists	6	3
Octobrists	13	19
Right-wing	—	11
Total	34	34

(Source: *Dan* VII, p. 208)

The abstention of the newly formed bourgeoisie from any oppositional activity throughout most of the existence of the Liberation
Movement was largely a consequence of Witte's economic policies. In
order to achieve the extremely high rate of industrial expansion attained
in the 1890s, Witte did everything in his power to encourage the indi-
genous and foreign business communities. Vyshnegradskiy's tariff
system which, in 1891, had turned Russia into the most protectionist
country in the world, was greatly expanded. The rouble was put on a
gold standard basis, and no direct taxes were imposed on income. The
government also safeguarded the profits of industrialists and railway
builders by paying out direct subsidies, by making cheap loans available, by fixing internal transport tariffs in their favour and by purchas-
ing their goods and services on a guaranteed profit basis. Since the
government, besides being a direct investor, was also the chief customer
of heavy industry and railways, the profit-guaranteeing policy was of
very great importance to industrialists and railway-owners. Moreover,
while strikes and trade unions were prohibited by law, the business
community was not only permitted, but actually encouraged to establish
representative bodies which acted as powerful pressure groups on the
government. It is, therefore, not surprising that businessmen were, on
the whole, satisfied with government policies and did not join the ranks
of the opposition till the beginning of 1905.

The goodwill of the business community and the rapid pace of
industrialization were obtained at a heavy political cost to autocracy.
Not only did Witte's policies swell the ranks of the intelligentsia, create
an urban working class and produce an explosive situation in the
countryside by reducing the peasantry to total misery, but they also
alienated the nobility. This estate, according to the official pronouncements of Alexander III, was supposed to constitute the social bulwark
of autocracy. But there was a glaring contrast between the exalted and
privileged social position of the nobility during Alexander's reign, and
its continuous economic decline, manifested in the loss of about one-
third of its privately owned land in the period 1877–1905.

Not all the nobility's economic ailments were caused by the government. Witte could hardly be blamed for its lack of business initiative
or for the drastic drop in the world price of grain, which began in the
mid-1870s and reached rock-bottom in the mid-1890s. Nevertheless,
his tariff and monetary policy greatly aggravated its economic plight.
Having failed, despite the support of a powerful noble clique at court,
to change Witte's policies, the nobility became more and more alien-

ated from the government. As a result most nobles temporarily lost interest in politics, while an ever-growing minority chose the path of active opposition to the government. This, in the conditions then prevailing in Russia (and unchanged to this day), was synonymous with opposition to the regime. By the beginning of the twentieth century this expanding minority had become more and more radical, mainly thanks to the interplay of three factors. The first of these was the existence of a radical fringe (the zemstvo radicals) inside the nobility.

The Russian nobility (especially before the emancipation of the serfs) was much more dependent on autocracy than were its Western counterparts on absolutism. This fact did not prevent individuals and groups of nobles from agitating or trying to overthrow the existing political and social order. Radishchev and the Decembrists, Herzen, Bakunin and a large proportion of the participants in the 'going to the people' movement, as well as many members of the People's Will Party (*Narodnaya Volya*) were nobles by origin. But these nobles differed from the radical fringe in the ranks of the nobility on one vital point: by becoming radicals or revolutionaries, they ceased to be nobles and joined what became known in the 1860s as the intelligentsia. In consequence they forfeited their influence in their own milieu. Since they failed to gain the confidence of the people, i.e. the peasants, for whose sakes they had chosen this path in the first place, they and the movements to which they belonged were unable to create a social basis for the struggle against the regime. Hence, although they achieved national and international renown, especially in the eyes of subsequent generations of revolutionaries, they failed to achieve any of their aims. In contrast to them, the radical fringe consolidated in the ranks of the nobility in the late 1870s did not lose its social identity. This was because it utilized the newly established institutions of elective local government – the zemstvos – for its own purposes.

By exploiting the zemstvos as their main field of activity, the zemstvo radicals were able to maintain contact with the great non-radical majority of zemstvo councillors of noble origin, and even to influence them to some extent. Through them they maintained constant contact with the nobility as a whole. When a rapidly expanding section of the nobility chose the path of active opposition at the turn of the century, they found a convenient organizational instrument in the zemstvos. As this opposition came more and more to resent government policies, it tended rather to follow the leadership of Petrunkevich and his group.

Thus the latter were able to transform the zemstvos (which were created partly because of administrative necessity and partly in order to safeguard autocracy from the political consequences of the emancipation of the serfs) into one of the main organizational weapons of the radical opposition. But however great the influence of the zemstvo radicals, they could not have succeeded so rapidly in persuading an important section of the nobility to support a political programme which ultimately threatened their own vital interests were it not for the other two factors – the ultra-conservative stand of the Tsar's administration on political and social questions, and the disastrous war with Japan.

The dichotomy between the government's dynamic economic policy and its ultra-conservative attitude to political and social questions created the danger of a social upheaval. This could have been prevented by the modification and adaptation of the regime to changing conditions through the introduction of reforms from above. Since all hopes of bringing about such a development were dashed by Nicholas's determination to preserve autocracy untouched, more and more oppositionally inclined nobles began to regard the abolition of the existing regime as the only means of preventing a bloody social revolution. The outbreak of the war with Japan in January 1904 (for which the Tsar was rightly held personally responsible) greatly increased this threat. In consequence, many nobles who would otherwise not have dreamt of joining the Liberation Movement, turned against the government, hoping to forestall the danger by bringing about the speedy end of the war and of autocracy.

The war presented the Liberation Movement with its greatest opportunity to achieve its aims, and its leaders lost no time in seizing on it. The Social-Democrats were engrossed in inter-faction fighting, and had adopted a very hostile attitude to the existing workers organizations (which were of the 'Zubatov' type). The Bolsheviks were extremely reluctant, to say the least, to co-operate with non-social-democratic groups. The SRs were concentrating their efforts upon conducting a personal terror campaign and on agitation in rural areas. All these factors were instrumental in enabling the Liberation Movement to achieve supremacy among the forces fighting autocracy. That the Liberation Movement did not become a party contributed to the same end. By remaining a loosely organized movement, it allowed the moderate zemstvo activists to belong to the same overall organizational framework as the radicals. This was greatly to the advantage of the latter. While they were busy forging alliances with the revolutionaries and establishing lines of communication with the 'masses', i.e. mainly the workers of St Petersburg and the peasants, the moderates, through their contacts with the higher echelons of the bureaucracy, were helping to undermine belief in autocracy's continued right to exist. Furthermore, as the growing unrest in the country began to affect the industrial workers who, especially in the capital, were showing signs of supporting the aims of the Liberation Movement, the newly formed bourgeoisie began to turn against the existing regime in the hope that the abolition of autocracy and conclusion of peace would put an end to the industrial disturbances.

But as the revolutionary process deepened in the wake of 'Bloody Sunday', the advantages which the Liberation Movement derived from being a loosely organized political body began to turn into disadvantages. As the strains and stresses became greater, the Movement found it impossible to preserve its unity. The first to leave were the liberal Slavophiles, who believed that the reforms extracted from the government by spring 1905 could suffice to bridge the gulf which had, until then, separated autocracy and society. Then, with the appearance of the first signs of *Pugachovshchina*, the nobility began to desert the Liberation Movement en masse and to rally to the support of the autocratic regime. Finally, in the wake of the publication of the government proposals to establish an elective all-Russian consultative assembly, there came the final split in the Movement. The zemstvo radicals and the more moderate radical intellectuals (and especially the academics among them) were frightened by the spectre of bloodshed on an unprecedented scale likely to result from the growing reliance of both revolutionaries and supporters of autocracy on violence. As a result they abandoned the policy of 'no enemies on the left' and began to organize a party which could work for the realization of the aims of the Liberation Movement by non-violent means, i.e. by participation in the elections to the proposed consultative Duma in order to transform it into a fully-fledged parliament. As developments were soon to show, this was an unattainable aim under the conditions then prevailing in Russia.

The majority of the radical intelligentsia, on the other hand, were intoxicated rather than frightened by the deepening revolutionary process. Through the Union of Unions and some of its affiliated trade unions, they were instrumental in bringing about the culmination of this process in the October general political strike. Although this strike forced Nicholas II to publish his famous manifesto, autocracy, though

271

modified, survived the crisis. At the same time the several components into which the Liberation Movement had by then disintegrated, forfeited a considerable part of their influence on events for a long time to come.

Appendix A: The origins of *Beseda*

The foundation stage of *Beseda* is still to a great extent shrouded in mystery. As far as the date of foundation is concerned, one can dismiss as a memory-lapse Maklakov's claim that *Beseda* was founded at the beginning of the 1890s (see *Maklakov*, vol. II, p. 291). All other sources, with the exception of Shipov, give 1899 as the year of foundation. (See: *Belokonskiy* II, p. 80, *Chermenskiy* II, p. 44, *Mikheyeva*, p. 241, *Shakhovskoy* IV, p. 103.) According to Shipov's testimony, the circle was established at the end of 1900. He himself, however, writes about preliminary discussions which took place at the end of 1899 and beginning of 1900 (*Shipov* II, pp. 134–5, 152).

Taking into account Shipov's vagueness about dates and the statements of Chermenskiy and Mikheyeva that *Beseda* did not begin to discuss political questions before summer 1900, the present author has arrived at the conclusion that although it is probable that *Beseda* was established at the end of 1899, it did not begin to function regularly (nor was it given its name) until summer 1900.

As in the case of the foundation-date, the sources differ on the identity of the founders. According to Belokonskiy, *Beseda* was founded by the princely brothers Pavel and Peter Dolgorukov (*Belokonskiy*, ibid.). Chermenskiy adds the name of D. N. Shipov (*Chermenskiy*, ibid.), while Shakhovskoy claims that *Beseda* was founded by six zemstvo activists, five of whom were marshals of the nobility. (*Shakhovskoy* ibid.). The present writer has taken certain clues into account:

(*a*) If Shakhovskoy is right, then either Shipov or Peter Dolgorukov, but not both of them, could have been among the founders since neither were marshals of the nobility.

(*b*) Apart from Belokonskiy, all other sources name Shipov as one of the founders.

(*c*) Shipov's list does not include Peter Dolgorukov.

(*d*) According to the available evidence, Pavel Dolgorukov was less radical than his brother (see, for example, *Gessen* I, p. 165), and hence was more likely to have been approached by Shipov.

(*e*) Chermenskiy does not indicate that his statement is based on evidence he found in the archives.

(*f*) The fuller list given by Chermenskiy on the same page apparently applies to a later stage in the development of *Beseda*.

On the basis of the avilable evidence, the conclusion is that Shipov's list is the most reliable and represents the actual membership of *Beseda* in summer 1900.

Appendix B: A bibliographical note on the writings of Kuskova and Prokopovich in the years 1898–9

If it were not for their adversaries, little or nothing would be known about the exact content of Kuskova's and Prokopovich's criticism of orthodox Marxism. At the time they expressed their views orally or in letters, only one of which was intended for publication. (This, incidentally, explains to a large degree the lapses in style as well as some of the inconsistencies in their writings of this period.) Four of their critical writings have survived in print. They are:

(*a*) a private letter from Kuskova to Akselrod, apparently written in the second half of March or beginning of April 1898, and published by Plekhanov in *Vademecum*, pp. 17–21.[1] The authorship and approximate date can be established on the basis of the following information:

authorship – according to Plekhanov the letter was written by M.M.[2] This was Kuskova's pseudonym at the time, and she herself stated explicitly in her early memoirs that she wrote the letter.[3] Hence, despite the fact that the grammatical composition indicates a male author, it was apparently written by Kuskova and not Prokopovich;

the date – according to Plekhanov it was written in spring 1898.[4] On the basis of the available evidence it is possible to be more precise and state that it was written between the middle of March and the beginning of April. It could not have been written before 13 March (see above p. 81n.) nor after 5 April, since between 6 and 26 April Kuskova was in Zurich. At the end of her stay, relations between her and the Liberation of Labour Group had deteriorated to such an extent that it would have been unthinkable for her to have written such a letter.[5]

(*b*) A lengthy reply by Prokopovich to a pamphlet written by Akselrod.[6] This reply was not, apparently, completed before the end of May 1898.[7] This was the only composition Prokopovich wrote for publication at that time. However, he withheld its publication, apparently on the advice of Kopelson-Grishin; Akselrod wanted to publish it against the author's wishes and Zasulich's intervention prevented him from doing so.[8] Two years later Plekhanov published it in *Vademecum*, pp. 37–60.[9]

(*c*) Four letters from Kuskova to 'Timofey' (Ts. Kopelson-Grishin). Found in *Kuskova* I.[10] They were apparently written some time between the end of April and

---

[1] See *Kuskova* II.
[3] See *Kuskova* V, p. 326, *Masanov*, vol. II, pp. 147–8.
[5] See *Perepiska*, vol. II, pp. 13–20.
[6] *K Voprosu o Sovremennykh Zadachakh* (*Akselrod* III).
[7] See *Perepiska*, vol. II, pp. 9–10, 37–8, *Gruppa* VI, p. 210.
[8] *Perepiska* ibid. pp. 42–3.   [9] See *Prokopovich*.

[2] *Vademecum*, p. x.
[4] *Vademecum*, p. x.

[10] See *Bibliography*.

the end of June 1898, when Kuskova decided to return to Russia. The approximate date of the letters can be established on the basis of the following information: in her first letter Kuskova told Grishin about her negotiations with Plekhanov and Akselrod and about her and Prokopovich's undertaking to present them with the latter's reply to Akselrod's pamphlet a month later. She also told him about their declaration that they would leave the Union if it were not published.[1] This statement was made on 24 or 25 April 1898.[2] In her fourth and last letter Kuskova reproached Grishin for holding a personal meeting with Plekhanov in Geneva.[3] This meeting took place at the end of May 1898.[4]

From her fourth letter it is possible to learn that she was going to leave Berlin for Russia very soon after writing it and that she was afraid of being arrested on the border like one of her friends who had gone to Russia straight from Brussels a few days earlier.[5]

(d) *Credo*.[6]

[1] *Kuskova* I, pp. 154–5.　　　　　　[2] See *Perepiska*, vol. II, pp. 9, 11, 13.
[3] *Kuskova* I, pp. 159, 161.　　[4] See *Perepiska* ibid. pp. 35, 37.　　[5] *Kuskova* ibid. p. 163.
[6] For the story behind *Credo* see *Kuskova* V, pp. 324–6, *Lenin* III, vol. I, pp. 664–5 and *Schapiro* I, pp. 34–5.

Appendix C: Note on sources on the formation
of the Liberation Movement

In the absence of archival material [if Prince D.I. Shakhovskoy, one of the founding-fathers of the Liberation Movement, is to be believed, such material never existed (see *Shakhovskoy* IV, p. 81); Professor Pipes seems to believe that such an archive existed but may have perished (see *Pipes* IIa, p. 308n.)], the main source on the history of the formative stage of the Liberation Movement is provided by the memoirs and early recollections of its principal participants. Among these the most important are: *Belokonskiy* II, pp. 92–4 and *Shakhovskoy* IV, pp. 85–7. The former obtained his information from V. Ya. Bogucharskiy ('a well-known writer who accompanied Struve during his negotiations with the editors of *Iskra* in Europe') and the latter wrote the only existing history of the Union of Liberation. Besides these two sources, valuable information is also found in the following: *Kuskova* V, pp. 325–6; VIII, pp. 383–4; IXc; XI, pp. 368–70; XVIIIa (one must exercise caution with these memoirs since she often contradicts herself); *Maklakov* I, pp. 142–4; *Milyukov* V3, pp. 116–17; *Petrunkevich* II, pp. 336–7 (Petrunkevich's memory failed him with regard to dates: meetings which took place in 1901 he placed in 1902, and 1902 meetings are dated in 1903); and *Rodichev* IV, pp. 322–3. Valuable new information on the formative stage of the Liberation Movement is found in *Chermenskiy* II, p. 50 and *Mikheyeva*, p. 243. More valuable material may be located in Struve's private archives (see above), although Prof. R. Pipes doubts this (letter to the author of this book, dated 3 May 1967). Rodichev's memoirs aside, English-language accounts of these developments are found in *Fischer*, pp. 125–6 and *Smith* (unpub.), pp. 42–54.

Bibliography

A. *Unpublished sources*
B. *Collections of published sources*
C. *Encyclopaedias and guides*
D. *Newspapers and periodicals*
E. *Books, pamphlets and articles*

A. UNPUBLISHED SOURCES

Galai S., 'The Liberation Movement and Its Role in the First Russian Revolution'. PhD thesis, London University, 1967.

Hutchinson J. F., 'The Octobrists in Russian Politics, 1905–1917'. PhD thesis, London University, 1966.

Keep J. L. H., 'Development of the S.D. in Russia, 1898–1907'. PhD thesis, London University, 1954.

Morse M., 'The Political Career of P. N. Milyukov, 1905–1917'. PhD thesis, University of Wisconsin, 1950.

Piotrov F. L., 'P. Milyukov and the Constitutional-Democratic Party'. PhD thesis, Nuffield College, Oxford, 1962.

Pospielovski D., 'The Legal Trade Union Movement in Russia – The Police Socialism, 1898–1903'. M. Phil. London University, June 1967.

Smith N., 'The Constitutional-Democratic Movement in Russia, 1902–1906'. PhD thesis, University of Illinois, 1958.

Tokmakoff G. B., 'A Political Evaluation of Stolypin'. PhD thesis, London University, 1963.

Zagorin B. L., 'The Political Thought of P. B. Struve, 1870–1917'. PhD thesis, University of Illinois, 1957.

B. COLLECTIONS OF PUBLISHED SOURCES

(*A.R.R.*) *Arkhiv Russkoy Revolyutsii*, ed. I. V. Gessen, 22 vols (Berlin 1921–47).

Byloye (London – Spb – Paris – Petrograd/Leningrad 1900–26),
    nos. 1–6, 1900–4, London,
    nos. 1–12 ⎰
    nos. 1–10 ⎱ 1906–7, Spb,

nos. 7–14, 1908–12, Paris,

nos. 1–35, 1917–26, Petrograd/Leningrad.

Dela i Dni-Istoricheskiy Zhurnal, 3 vols (Petrograd 1920–2).

(*D.i.M.*) *Revolyutsiya 1905–1907gg v Rossii. Dokumenty i Materialy*, ed. A. M. Pankratova and others (Moscow 1955–). (Enumeration of volumes added.)

vol. I, *Nachalo Pervoy Russkoy Revolyutsii : Yanvar-Mart 1905* (1955).

(*D.i.M.* I)

vol. III, *Vserossiyskaya Politicheskaya Stachka v Oktyabre 1905g*, book 1 (1955).

(*D.i.M.* II)

vol IV, *Vysshiy Podyem Revolyutsii : Noyabr-Dekabr 1905g*, part 1 (1955).

(*D.i.M.* III)

vol. V, *Vtoroy Period Revolyutsii, 1906–1907*,

part I, Jan.–April 1906, book 1 (1957),   (*D.i.M.* IV)

part II, May–Sept. 1906, book 1 (1961),   (*D.i.M.* V)

part III, Oct.–Dec. 1906 (1963),   (*D.i.M.* VI)

part IV, Jan.–June 1907, book 1 (1963).   (*D.i.M.* VII)

(*G.D.*) *Gosudarstvennaya Duma. Sistematicheskiy svod Uzakoneniy i Rasporazheniy Pravitelstva*, comp. A. Khlebnikov (Spb 1906).

Golos Minuvshago (Moscow 1913–23, Paris 1926–8).

Istoriko-Revolyutsionnyy Byuletin, 3 vols (Moscow 1922).

Istoriko-Revolyutsionnyy Sbornik, 3 vols (Moscow–Petrograd (Leningrad) 1924–6).

(*K.A.*) *Krasnyy Arkhiv*, 106 vols (Moscow 1923–41).

(*K.i.S.*) *Katorga i Ssylka*, 116 vols (Moscow, Petrograd/Leningrad 1921–35).

(*K.L.*) *Krasnaya Letopis* (Petersburg/Leningrad–Moscow 1922–36).

Letopis Revolyutsii, izd. Z. I. Grzhebina, kn. 1 (Berlin–Petrograd–Moscow 1923).

(*Letopis Revolyutsii* I)

Letopis Revolyutsii, izd. Z. I. Grzhebina, nos. 1–14 (Berlin–Petrograd–Moscow 1922–4).   (*Letopis Revolyutsii* II)

Minuvshiye Gody, nos. 1–12 (Spb 1908).

Na Chuzhoy Storone, nos. 1–13 (Berlin–Prague 1923–5).

Nasha Strana, no. 1 (Spb 1907).

(*P.R.*) *Proletarskaya Revolyutsiya* (Moscow–Petrograd/Leningrad 1921–41).

(*P.S.Z.* II) *Polnoye Sobraniye Zakonov, Sobraniye 2-e* (12 Dec. 1825 – Feb. 1881, Spb).

(*P.S.Z.* III) *Polnoye Sobraniye Zakonov, Sobraniye 3-e* (1 March 1881 – 31 July 1907, Spb).

(*S.O.*) *Gosudarstvennaya Duma. Stenograficheskiye Otchety* (Spb 1906–16).

C. ENCYCLOPAEDIAS AND GUIDES

Bibliografiya Periodicheskikh Izdaniy Rossii 1901–1916gg, 4 vols (Leningrad 1958–61).

Bibliography

(*Brokgaus*) *Entsiklopedicheskiy Slovar*, ed. Prof. I E. Andreyevskiy, publ. F. A. Brokgaus and I. A. Efron (Spb 1893–1904).

(*Brokgaus supp.*) *Entsiklopedicheskiy Slovar : Supplementary Vols I-II* (Spb 1906–7).

(*B.S.E.* I) *Bolshaya Sovetskaya Entsiklopediya* (Moscow 1926–47).

(*B.S.E.* II) *Bolshaya Sovetskaya Entsiklopediya*, 2-ye izd. (Moscow 1949–57).

Deyateli Revolyutsionnogo Dvizheniya v Rossii, publ. O-vo Byvshikh Politicheskikh Katorzhan*...vols I–V (Moscow 1927–33).

Dossik J. J., *Doctoral Research on Russia and the Soviet Union* (N.Y. 1960).

Dumesnil A., *Catalogue méthodique du fonds Russe: de la Bibliothèque de la Guerre* (Paris 1932).

(*Granat*) *Entsiklopedicheskiy Slovar Tovarishchestva Bratya A.i I. Granat'*, 7th edn, ed. Prof. M. M. Kovalevskiy, S. A. Muromtsev and K. A. Timiryazev (Moscow 1910–38).

Horecky P. L., *Russia and the Soviet Union, a Bibliographical Guide to Western Language Publications* (University of Chicago Press 1965).

Lichnyye Arkhivnyye Fondy v Gosudarstvennykh Arkhivnykh Khranilishchakh v SSSR, 2 vols (Moscow 1962–3).

Masanov I. F., *Slovar Psevdonimov Russkikh Pisateley, Uchennykh i Obshchestvennykh Deyateley*, 4 vols (Moscow 1956–60).

Materialy Dlya Biograficheskogo Slovarya Sotsial-demokratov, vyp. I (A–D), (Moscow–Petrograd 1923).

Mezer A. V., *Slovarnyy Ukazetel Po Knigovedeniyu*, 3 vols (Moscow, Leningrad 1931–4).

(*M.S.E.*) *Malaya Sovetskaya Entsiklopediya*, vols 1–12 (Moscow 1931–2).

Pervaya Russkaya Revolyutsiya-Ukazatel Literatury, ed. G. K. Derman, Kommunisticheskaya Akademiya (Moscow 1930).

Russkiy Kalendar (Spb 1872–1916).

Shapiro D. M., *A Selected Bibliography of Works in English on Russian History, 1801–1917* (Oxford 1962).

Ukazatel Knig Po Istorii i Obshchestvennykh Voprosakh (Spb 1909).

Ukazatel Zhurnalnoy Literatury, comp. N. A. Ulyanov (Moscow 1911 (1912)).

Voltsenberg O. E., *Bibliograficheskiy Putevoditel Po Revolyutsii 1905g* (Leningrad 1925).

Yevreyskaya Entsiklopediya, 16 vols (Spb 1912–14).

Yezhegodnik (Statisticheskiy...) (Spb 1905–12).

D. NEWSPAPERS AND PERIODICALS

Bankovaya i Torgovaya Gazeta	(Spb 1902–16)
Beseda	(Spb 1903–8)
Bez-Zaglaviya nos. 1–16	(Spb 1906)
Birzhevyye Vedomosti	(Spb 1904–7)
Chelovecheskaya Zhizn nos. 1–12	(Spb 1905)

Bibliography

Elektricheskaya Energiya	(Moscow 1902–5)
Elektrichestvo	(Spb 1880–1916)
Farmatsevt	(Moscow 1893–1907)
Farmatsevticheskiy Vestnik	(Moscow 1897–1906)
Farmatsevticheskiy Zhurnal	(Spb 1864–1917)
Gornozavodskoy Listok	(Kharkov 1888–1909)
Iskra nos. 1–112	(Munich, Geneva... 1900–5)
Istoricheskiy Vestnik vols 1–149/50	(Spb 1880–1917)
Izvestiya Moskovskogo Soveta R.D. nos. 1–6	(Moscow 7–12 December 1905)
Izvestiya O-va Grazhdanskikh Inzhinerov	(Spb 1895–1908)
Izvestiya Soveta R.D. nos. 1–10	(Spb 1905)
Kontorshchik nos. 7–8	(Spb 1906)
Listok Osvobozhdeniya nos. 1–26	(Stuttgart-Paris 1904–5)
Moskovskiya Vedomosti	(Moscow 1756–1917)
Narodnoye Khozyaystvo	(Spb 1900–5)
Nasha Zhizn	(Spb 1904–5)
Nashi Dni	(Spb 1904–5)
Nauka i Zhizn	(Spb 1904–6)
Novoye Vremya	(Spb 1891–1917)
Obrazovaniye nos. 1–79	(Spb 1892–1909)
Osvobozhdeniye nos. 1–79	(Stuttgart-Paris 1902–5)
Otkliki Sovremennosti nos. 1–5	(Spb 1906)
Pravda	(Moscow 1904–6)
Pravo	(Spb 1898–1917)
Revolyutsionnaya Rossiya nos. 3–77	(Geneva-Paris 1902–5)
Rus	(Spb 1903–8)
Russkiy Arkhiv	(Moscow 1863–1917)
Russkiy Meditsinskiy Vestnik	(Spb 1899–1905)
Russkoye Bogatstvo	(Spb 1892–1918)
Syn Otechestva	(Spb 1904–5)
Trudy Volnogo Ekonomicheskogo O-va	(Spb 1765–1915)
Vestnik Fabrichnogo Zakonodatelstva	(Spb 1905)
Vestnik Obshchestvennoy Veterinarii	(Spb 1889–1917)
Vestnik Uchiteley	(Spb 1906)
Vestnik Vospitaniya	(Moscow 1890–1917)
Vestnik Vserossiyskogo Soyuza Uchiteley	(Spb 1905)
Vestnik Yevropy	(Spb 1866–1917)
Veterinarnoye Obozreniye	(Moscow 1899–1917)
Voprosy Zhizni nos. 1–12	(Spb 1905)
Zapiski Russkogo Tekhnicheskogo O-va	(Spb 1867–1917)
Zheleznodrozhnoye Delo	(Spb 1882–1917)
Zhurnal O-va Russkikh Vrachey	(Moscow 1895–1908)
Zhurnal Zasedaniy Soveta Imperatorskogo Spb. Universiteta	(Spb 1869–1916)

Bibliography

E. BOOKS, PAMPHLETS AND SELECTED ARTICLES

A-Va L., 'Vremennoye Pravitelstvo', *Byloye*, no. 13 (1910), pp. 25–33.
Abramovich D. I., *Pisma Russkikh Pisateley K A. S. Suvorinu* (Leningrad 1927).
    (*Abramovich*)
Abramson V., *Osnovnyye Nachala Novogo Polozheniya o Vyborakh V Gosudarstve-nnuyu Dumu 3.VI. 1907* (Melitopol 1907).   (*Abramson*)
Achkasov A., *Poveyalo Vesnoy* (Moscow 1905).   (*Achkasov*)
Adams A. E. (ed.), *Imperial Russia After 1861* (Boston 1965).   (*Adams* I)
    'The Character of Pestel's Thought', *The American Slavic and East European Review*, XII (1953), pp. 153–61.   (*Adams* II)
Aivazov I. G., *Religioznoye Obnovleniye Nashikh Dney* (Moscow 1910). (*Aivazov*)
Akimov V., *Materialy Dlya Kharakteristiki Razvitiya RSDRP* (Geneva 1904).
    (*Akimov*)
Akselrod P. B., *Istoricheskoye Polozheniye i Vzaimnoye Otnosheniye Liberalnoy i Sotsialisticheskoy Demokratii v Rossii* (Geneva 1898).   (*Akselrod* I)
Iz Arkhiva P. B. Akselroda. Materialy po Istorii Russkogo Revolyutsionnogo Dvizheniya, vol. II (Berlin 1924).   (*Akselrod* II)
K Voprosu O Sovremennykh Zadachakh i Taktike Russkikh S.D. (Geneva 1898).
    (*Akselrod* III)
Pisma P. B. Akselroda i Yu. O. Martova, 1901–1916. Materialy po Istorii Russkogo Revolyutsionnogo Dvizheniya, vol. I (Berlin 1924).   (*Akselrod* IV)
Pismo v Redaktsiyu Rabochego Dela (Geneva 1899).   (*Akselrod* V)
Rozhdeniye Burzhuaznoy Demokratii (Zurich 1902).   (*Akselrod* VI)
    (See also *Gruppa 'Osvobozhdeniye Truda', Ob Agitatsii, Plekhanov*)
Aleksandrov M. S., 'Gruppa Narodovoltsev (1891–1894)', *Byloye*, no. 11 (1906),
    pp. 1–27.   (*Aleksandrov*)
Aleksinskiy G. A., *Modern Russia* (London 1913).   (*Aleksinskiy*)
Alektorov A. E., *Inorodtsy v Rossii* (Spb 1906).   (*Alektorov*)
Alisov P., *Volnoye Slovo* (London 1881).   (*Alisov*)
Almazov P., *Nasha Revolyutsiya* (Kiyev 1908).   (*Almazov*)
Alzona E., *Some French Contemporary Opinions of the Russian Revolution of 1905* (Columbia University 1922).   (*Alzona*)
Amburger E., *Geschichte Der Behoerdenorganization Russlands von Peter Dem Grossen Bis 1917* (Leiden 1966).   (*Amburger*)
Angarskiy N., *Legalnyy Marksism*, vyp.I, *1876–1897* (Moscow 1925).   (*Angarskiy*)
Annenskaya A., 'Iz Proshlykh Let. Vospominaniya O N. F. Annenskom', *Russkoye Bogatstvo* (1913),
    no. 1, pp. 53–81,   (*Annenskaya* I)
    no. 2, pp. 36–65.   (*Annenskaya* II)
Anweiler O., *Die Rätebewegung in Russland, 1905–1922* (Leiden 1958). (*Anweiler*)
Aptekman O. V., 'Partiya Norodnogo Prava. Vospominaniya', *Byloye*, no. 7 (1907),
    pp. 177–206.   (*Aptekman*)

Bibliography

Argunov A., 'Iz Proshlogo Partii S. R.', *Byloye*, no. 10 (1907), pp. 94–112.
(*Argunov*)
Arkhiv Istorii Truda v Rossii, nos. 1–10, 3 vols (Petrograd 1921–2).
Armiya v Pervoy Revolyutsii (Moscow–Leningrad 1927).
Aronson G., 'E. D. Kuskova, Portret Obshchestvennogo Deyatelya', *Novyy Zhurnal*, xxxvii (1954), pp. 236–56. (*Aronson* I)
'Liberalism i Samoderzhaviye', *Novoye Russkoye Slovo* (N.y. 6 August 1945).
(*Aronson* II)
Revolyutsionnaya Yunnost. Vospominaniya. Inter-University project of the history of the Menshevik movement. (*Aronson* III)
Rossiya Nakanune Revolyutsii (N.Y. 1962). (*Aronson* IV)
Arskiy P. A. (comp.), *1905g. Literaturno-Istoricheskiy Sbornik* (Leningrad 1925).
(*Arskiy*)
Astrov N. I., *S. A. Muromtsev v Moskovskoy Gorodskoy Dume.* In *S.A.* pp. 158–79.
(*N. Astrov* I)
Pamyati Pogibshikh (Paris 1929). (*N. Astrov* II)
Vospominaniya (Paris 1940). (*N. Astrov* III)
Astrov N. I., Kokoshkin F. F. *Zakonodatelnyye Proyekty Partii Narodnoy Svobody* (Spb 1907). (*N. Astrov* IV)
Astrov V. (ed.), *An Illustrated History of the Russian Revolution*, vol. 1 (London 1928). (*V. Astrov*)
Avidonov N., '9-go Yanvarya 1905g. i Synod', *Byloye*, no. 1 (1925), pp. 46–50.
(*Avidonov* I)
'Gapon v Dukhovnoy Akademii', ibid. pp. 51–7. (*Avidonov* II)
Avinov M. N., 'Glavnyye Cherty v Istorii Zakonodatelstva o Zemskikh Uchrezh-deniyakh'. In *Yubileynyy Sbornik*, pp. 1–34. (*Avinov*)
Aynzaft S., *Zubatovshchina i Gaponovshchina* (Moscow 1925). (*Aynzaft*)
Azef E., 'Doneseniya E. Azefa', *Byloye*, no. 1 (1917), pp. 196–228. (*Azef*)
B.I.D., *Sbornik Program Politicheskikh Partiy* (Moscow 1906). (*B.I.D.*)
Badmayev P. A., *Za Kulisami Tsarisma* (Leningrad 1925). (*Badmayev*)
Balabanov M., *Ocherk Istorii Revolyutsionnogo Dvizheniya v Rossii* (Moscow 1925).
(*Balabanov* I).
Ot 1905g K 1917g. Massovoye Rabocheye Dvizheniye (Moscow-Leningrad 1927).
(*Balabanov* II)
'Promyshlennost Rossii v Nachale xx Veka', *O.D.* vol. I, pp. 39–87.
(*Balabanov* III)
'Promyshlennost v 1904–1907gg', *O.D.* vol. IV, part I, pp. 33–135.
(*Balabanov* IV)
Balabanova A., *My Life as a Rebel* (London 1938). (*Balabanova*)
Baring M., *A Year in Russia* (London 1907). (*Baring*)
Baron S. H., *Plekhanov – The Father of Russian Marxism* (London 1963). (*Baron* I)
'The First Decade of Russian Marxism', *American Slavic and East European Review*, xiv (1955), pp. 315–30. (*Baron* II)

Bibliography

Beloff M., 'The Russian Nobility'. In Goodwin, A. (ed.), *The European Nobility in the Eighteenth Century* (London 1967), pp. 172–89. (*Beloff*)

Belokonskiy I. P., *Samoupravleniye i Zemstvo* (R/N Donu 1905). (*Belokonskiy* I) *Zemskoye Dvizheniye*, 2nd edn (Moscow 1914). (*Belokonskiy* II)

Belskiy T., 'Kriticheskiye Sotsialisty i Politika Bloka'. In *Itogi i Perspektivy*, pp. 198–210. (*Belskiy*)

Benkerdorf P. K., *Last Days at Tsarskoye Selo* (London 1927). (*Benkerdorf*)

Berdyayev N. A., 'Dnevnik Publitsista', *Voprosy Zhizni*, no 4/5, pp. 320–34. (*Berdyayev*)

Berlin P. A., *Ruskaya Burzhuaziya* (Moscow 1922). (*Berlin*)

Bernstein E., *Evolutionary Socialism* (London 1909). (*Bernstein*)

(Bezobrazov A. M.), 'Bezobrazovskiy Kruzhok Letom 1904g', *K.A.* XVII (1926), pp. 70–80. (*Bezobrazov* I)

'Pisma Bezobrazova i Abazy k Nikolayu'. In *Russko-Yaponskaya Voyna*, pp. 135–62. (*Bezobrazov* II)

Biblioteka Zhizni, nos. 6–8, 10–13 (London 1902).

Billington J. H., *N. K. Mikhaylovsky and Russian Populism* (O.U.P. 1958). (*Billington*)

Bing E. J. (ed.), *The Letters of Tsar Nicholas and Empress Marie* (London 1937). (*Bing*)

Blackstock P. W., and Hoselitz B. F. (ed.), *The Russian Menace to Europe* (Free Press, Ill. 1952). (*Blackstock*)

Blum J., *Lord and Peasant in Russia*, 4th imp. (Atheneum N.Y. 1967). (*Blum*)

Bogolepov M., 'Gosudarstvennoye Khozyaystvo i Finansovaya Politika Pravitelstva', *O.D.* vol. I, pp. 151–80. (*Bogolepov*)

Bogucharskiy V. Ya., *Iz Istorii Politicheskoy Borby v 70 kh i 80-kh gg XIX veka* (Moscow 1912) (*Bogucharskiy* I)

'Zemskiy Soyuz Konsta 70-kh i Nachala 80-kh gg'. In *Yubileynyy Sbornik*, pp. 233–59. (*Bogucharskiy* II)

Bogutskaya L. V., *Bolsheviki i Armiya v 1905–1907gg* (Leningrad 1929). (*Bogutskaya* I)

Moskovskiye Bolsheviki v Stachechnykh Boyakh 1905g (Moscow 1948). (*Bogutskaya* II)

Ocherki Po Istorii Vooruzhennykh Vostaniy v Revolyutsi 1905–1907gg (Moscow 1956). (*Bogutskaya* III)

Botsyanovskiy V. L. i Gollerbakh E., *Russkaya Satira Pervoy Revolyutsii* (Leningrad 1925). (*Botsyanovskiy*)

Boyovich M. N., *Chleny Gosudarstvennoy Dumy. Pervyy Sozyv* (Moscow 1906). (*Boyovich* I)

Chleny Gosudarstvennoy Dumy. Tretiy Sozyv (Moscow 1908). (*Boyovich* II)

Bryukhatov L. D., 'Znacheniye Tretyego Elemta v Zhizni Zemstva'. In *Yubileynyy Sbornik*, pp. 186–205. (*Bryukhatov*)

Buchanan Sir G., *My Mission to Russia*, 2 vols (London 1923). (*Buchanan* I, II)

283

Bibliography

Budberg R. Yu. Baron, 'Iz Vospominaniy Uchastnika Zemskikh Syezdov', *Minuv-shiye Gody*, no. 1 (1908), pp. 220–43.   (*Budberg* I)
'Syezd Zemskikh Deyateley 6–9 Noyabrya 1904g. v Peterburge', *Byloye*, no. 3 (1907), pp. 70–92.   (*Budberg* II)
Bukhbinder N. A., 'K Istorii Sobraniya Russkikh Fabrichno-Zavodskikh Rabochikh St. Peterburga', *K.L.* no. 1 (1922), pp. 299–335.   (*Bukhbinder* I)
'O Zubatovshchine', ibid. no. 2/3 (1922), pp. 289–334.   (*Bukhbinder* II)
'Zubatovshchina v Moskve', *K.i.S.* no. 14 (1925), pp. 96–133.   (*Bukhbinder* III)
Bulgakov S. N., *Avtobiograficheskiye Zametki* (Paris 1949).   (*Bulgakov* I)
Ot Marksisma k Idealismu (Spb 1903).   (*Bulgakov* II)
Burenin N., 'Rabota s L. B. Po Podgotovke k Vooruzhennomu Vostaniyu'. In L. B. Krasin ('Nikitich'), *Gody Podpolya. Sbornik Vospominaniy* (etc.), pp. 236–43.   (*Burenin*)
Burtsev V. L., *Borba Za Svobnuyu Rossiyu* (Berlin 1923).   (*Burtsev*)
Buryshkin P. A., *Moskva Kupecheskaya* (N.Y. 1954).   (*Buryshkin*)
Bystyranskiy V., *Lenin i 1905g* (Leningrad 1925).   (*Bystyranskiy*)
Byykov P. M., 'Posledniye Dni Poslednego Tsarya', *A.R.R.* vol. XVII, pp. 305–16.   (*Byykov*)
Chamberlin W. H., *The Russian Revolution*, vols. I–II, paperbound (N.Y. 1965).   (*Chamberlin* I, II)
(Charnoluskiy V. I.), Ivanovich V., *Rossiyskiya Partii, Soyuzy i Ligi* (Spb 1906).   (*Charnoluskiy*)
Charnoluskiy V. I., *Sotsialism i Narodnoye Obrazovaniye* (Spb 1907).   (*Charnoluskiy* I)
Voprosy Narodnogo Obrazovaniye Na Pervom Obshchezemskom Syezde (Spb 1912).   (*Charnoluskiy* II)
Charques R., *The Twilight of Imperial Russia*, paperback (O.U.P. 1965).   (*Charques*)
Cherevanin (F. A. Lipkin), 'Dvizheniye Intelligentsii', *O.D.*
vol. I, pp. 259–90,   (*Cherevanin* I)
vol. II, part II, pp. 146–202.   (*Cherevanin* II)
Chermenskiy E. D., *Burzhuaziya i Tsarism v Pervoy Russkoy Revolyutsii*, 2-e izd. (Moscow 1970).   (*Chermenskiy*)
'Russkaya Burzhuaziya Osenyu 1905g', *Voprosy Istorii*, no. 6 (1966), pp. 56–72.   (*Chermenskiy* I)
'Zemsko-Liberalnoye Dvizheniye Nakanune Revolyutsii 1905–1907g', *Istoriya SSSR*, no. 5 (1965), pp. 41–60.   (*Chermenskiy* II)
Cherniavsky M., *Tsar and People, Studies in Russian Myth* (Yale U.P. 1961).   (*Cherniavsky*)
Chernomordik S. I. (ed.), *Put k Oktyabryu. Sbornik Statey, Vospominaniy i Dokumentov*, vyp. I–IV (Moscow-Leningrad 1923–6).   (*Chernomordik* I)
Pyatyy God (Moscow 1925).   (*Chernomordik* II)
(Chernov V. M.), 'K istorii partii Narodnago Prava', *K.A.* no. 1 (1922), pp. 282–8.   (*Chernov*)

Bibliography

Chernov V. M., *K Voprosu o Vykupe Zemli* (Spb 1906).   (*Chernov* I)
'Ot Revolyutsionnoy Rossii k Synu Otechestva', *Letopis Revolyutsii*, vol. I, pp.
66–98.   (*Chernov* II)
Pered Burey (N.Y. 1953).   (*Chernov* III)
'Zapiski S. R.', *Letopis Revolyutsii*, tom. II, kn. 1 [Berlin 1922).   (*Chernov* IV)
(Chizhov S.) Doklady, 'Fullonu i D. F. Trepovu', *K.L.* no. 2(13) (1925), pp. 46–7.
          (*Chizhov* I)
'Ministerstvu Finansov', *K.L.* no. 6 (1929), pp. 26–44.   (*Chizhov* II)
'Ministru Vnutrennych Del i Finansov', *K.A.* XI/XII (1925), pp. 23–5. (*Chizhov* III)
Chleny Pervoy Gosudarstvennoy Dumy (Moscow 1906).
Chleny Vtoroy Gosudarstvennoy Dumy (Spb 1907).
(Dan F. I.), Danilov F. 'Obshchaya Politika Pravitelstva i Gosudarstvennyy Stroy
k Nachalu XX veka', *O.D.* vol. I pp. 422–82.   (*Dan*)
Dan F. I., *Iz Istorii Rabochego Dvizheniya i S.D. v Rossii 1900–1904 gg* (Spb 1906).
          (*Dan* I)
'Obshchaya Politika Pravitelstva', *O.D.* vol. IV,
    part I, pp. 279–392,   (*Dan* II)
    part II, pp. 1–148.   (*Dan* III)
'K Otsenke perezhytykh Sobytiy (O Role burzhuazii)', *Otkliki Sovremennosti*, no.
11.   (*Dan* IV)
'Ocherk Politicheskoy Evolyutsii Burzhuazrykh Elementcv Gorodskogo
Naseleniya', *O.D.* vol. II, part II, pp. 101–45.   (*Dan* V)
Proiskhozdeniye Bolshevizma (N.Y. 1946).   (*Dan* VI)
Dan F. I., i Cherevanin N., 'Soyuz 17-go Oktyabra', *O.L.* vol. III, pp. 161–224.
          (*Dan* VII)
Davatts V. Kh., *Pravda o Struve* (Belgrad 1934).   (*Davatts*)
Dazdrastvuyet Narodnaya Volya, Sbornik Statey (Paris 1907).
Debogoriy-Mokriyevich V., *Vospominaniya*, vyp. III (Paris 1895).   (*Debogoriy*)
Decle L., *The New Russia* (London 1906).   (*Decle*)
(Dedyulin), 'Doklad D. F. Trepovu', *K.L.* no. 1 (1922), pp. 37–45.   (*Dedyulin*)
Demochkin N. N., 'Pod Flagom Menshevitskikh Idey. Zametki o sovremennoy
burzhuaznoy istoriografii Sovetov 1905g', *Istorya SSSR* no. 5 (1966), pp.
164–82.   (*Demochkin*)
Deutscher I., *The Prophet Armed: Trotsky 1879–1921* (O.U.P. 1954). (*Deutscher*)
Deych L. G., *G. V. Plekhanov* (Moscow 1922).   (*Deych* I)
Rol Yevreyev v Russkom Revolyutsionnom Dvizherii, vol.I (Berlin 1923). (*Deych* II)
Za Polveka (Moscow–Berlin 1922–3).   (*Deych* III)
(See also *Gruppa 'Osvobozhdeniye Truda'*)
Dillon E. J., *The Eclipse of Russia* (London–Toronto–Paris 1918).   (*Dillon*)
'Doklad Dept. Politsii ob Imperatorskom Volnom Ekonomicheskam Obshchestve',
Osvobozhdeniye, book 1, pp. 58–65.   (*Doklad* I)
'Doklad Kommissii…Prisyazhnykh Poverennykh Po Povodu Sobytiy 9–11
Yanvary, *K.L.* no. 1 (1922), pp. 137–60.   (*Doklad* II)

Bibliography

'Dokladnaya zapiska o protivopravitelstvennykh soobshchestvakh ne stol vrednykh', *Byloye*, no. 4 (1906), pp. 304–16. (*Dokladnaya Zapiska*)

'Doklady Ofitserov o 9-om Yanvare', *K.A.* XI/XII (1925), pp. 444–8.
(*Doklady Ofitserov*)

Dolgorukov Pavel D., Prince and Petrunkevich I.I. (ed.), *Agrarnyy Vopros, Sbornik Statey* (Moscow 1905). (*Pavel Dolgorukov*)
(See also *Politicheskiy Stroy..., Voprosy Gosudarstvennogo Khozyaystva...*)

Dolgorukov Peter D., Prince, 'Pamyati Grafna P. A. Geydena', *Byloye*, no. 8 (1907), pp. 300–7. (*Peter Dolgorukov*)
(See also *Melkaya Zemskaya Yedinitsa*)

Dragomanov M. P., 'Vospominaniye o Peregovorakh Dobrovolnoy Okhrany i Ispolkoma R.S.R.P. v 1882 godu', *Byloye*, no. 13 (1910), pp. 34–43. (*Dragomanov*)

Dubrovsky S. M., *Krestyanskoye Dvizheniye v Revolyutsii 1905–1907gg* (Moscow 1956). (*Dubrovsky* I)

Dubrovsky S. M., i Grabe B., *Agrarnoye Dvizheniye v 1905–1907gg*, 1905g Materialy Dokumenty Pod Obshchey Red. M. N. Pokrovskogo vol. 1 (Moscow-Leningrad 1925). (*Dubrovsky* II)

'Krestyanskoye Dvizheniye Nakanune Revolyutsii 1905g'.
In Pokrovsky M. N. (ed.), *1905g. Istoryia Revolyutsionnogo Dvizheniya...*, vol. 1, pp. 233–392. (*Dubrovsky* III)

Elkin B., 'Attempts to Revive Freemasonry in Russia', *The Slavonic and East European Review*, XLIV (1966), pp. 453–72. (*Elkin* I)

'The Russian Intelligentsia on the Eve of the Revolution'. In Pipes R., *The Russian Intelligentsia*. (*Elkin* II)

Emmons T., *The Russian Landed Gentry and the Peasant Emancipation of 1861* (C.U.P. 1968). (*Emmons*)

Faleyev N. I., 'Rossiya Pod Okhranoy', *Byloye*, no. 10 (1907), pp. 1–43. (*Faleyev*)

Finland: *Manifesto of 3(15) February 1899 on Finland*. (*Finland*)

Finlandskaya Okraina v Sostave Russkogo Gosudarstva (Spb. 1906).

Finnish Reform Bill of 1906, The (Helsingfors 1906).

Firsov N. N., 'Pobedonostsev', *Byloye*, no. 25 (1924), pp. 247–70. (*Firsov*)

Fischer G., *Russian Liberalism. From Gentry to Intelligentsia*, Harvard University Russian Research Center, Study no. 30 (Harvard U.P. 1958). (*Fischer*)

Florinsky M. T., *Russia: A History and an Interpretation*, 2 vols (N.Y. 1955).
(*Florinsky*)

'Foreign Diplomats on the 1905 Revolution', *K.A.* XVI (1926), pp. 220–4; LII (1932), pp. 151–8.

Frank S. L., *Biografiya P. B. Struve* (N.Y. 1956). (*Frank*)

Frankel J., ' "Economism": A Heresy Exploited', *Slavic Review*, XXII (1963), pp. 263–84. (*Frankel*)

Futrell M., *Northern Underground* (London 1963). (*Futrell*)

Galai S., 'The Impact of War on the Russian Liberals in 1904–5', *Government and Opposition*, no. 1 (1965), pp. 85–109. (*Galai*)

Bibliography

Gapon G., *Istoriya Moyey Zhizni* (Berlin 1925).   (*Gapon* I)
(Gapon G.), 'Pismo K Durnovu', *K.A.* IX (1925), pp. 294–7.   (*Gapon* II)
'Zapiska Gapona, Podannaya im Direktoru Dept. Politsii
Lopukhinu v Oktyabre 1903g', *Byloye*, no. 1 (29) (1925), pp. 33–45.
         (*Gapon* III)
Garvi P. A., *Vospominaniya Sotsial Demokrata* (N.Y. 1945).   (*Garvi*)
'Gazeta Dept. Politsii', *Byloye* (1908),
  no. 7, pp. 104–18,   (*Gazeta* I)
  no. 8, pp. 45–54.   (*Gazeta* II)
Gazetnyy Mir (Spb 1913).
Georgiyevskiy A. I., *Materialy Po Istorii Studencheskego Divzheniya v Rossii* (Spb
  1906).   (*Georgiyevskiy*)
Gerschenkron A., 'Agrarian Policies and Industrialization: Russia 1861–1917'. *The
Cambridge Economic History of Europe*, vol. VI, part II, ch. VIII.
         (*Gerschenkron* I)
Economic Backwardness in Historical Perspective (Harvard U.P. 1962).
         (*Gerschenkron* II)
'The Rate of Industrial Growth in Russia Since 1885', *Journal of Economic
History*, supp. 7 (1947), pp. 144–74.   (*Gerschenkron* III)
Gerye V. I., *Pervaya Gosudarstvennaya Duma* (Moscow 1906).   (*Gerye* I)
Vtoraya Gosudarstvennaya Duma (Moscow 1907).   (*Gerye* II)
Gessen I. V., 'V Dvukh Vekakh', *A.R.R.* vol. XXII (Berlin 1937).   (*Gessen* I)
Gessen I. V., i Kaminka A. I., *Konstitutsionnoye Gosudarstvo* (Spb 1905). (*Gessen* II)
Getzler I., *Martov. A Political Biography of a Russian S.D.* (C.U.P. 1967). (*Getzler*)
Gilin N., 'Mestnoye Samoupravleniye V God Revzlyutsii'. In *Itogi i perspektivy*,
  pp. 173–97.   (*Gilin*)
Gilliard P., *Thirteen Years at the Russian Court* (London 1928).   (*Gilliard*)
Gimer D., '9-go Yanvarya 1905g v Peterburge, Vospominaniya', *Byloye*, no. 1
  (1925), pp. 3–14.   (*Gimer*)
G.L.I. (Glinsky B. B.), 'Begstvo Gapona', *Istoricheskiy Vestnik*, vol. 103 (1906), pp.
  546–67.   (*Glinskiy*)
Glinskiy B. B., 'K Voprosu O Titule Samoderzhets', ibid. vol. 131 (1913), pp.
  567–603.   (*Glinskiy* I)
'Pervyy Zhenskiy Syezd', ibid. vol. 115 (1909), pp. 384–407. (*Glinskiy* II)
'Razvenchennyya Geroi Revolyutsii 1905g. Khrustalev Nosar', ibid. vol. 132
  (1913), pp. 984–1010,   (*Glinskiy* III)
  vol. 133, pp. 233–65, 598–629, 998–1039,   (*Glinskiy* IV)
  vol. 134, pp. 231–69, 631–65, 1085–1115.   (*Glinskiy* V)
'Graf S. Yu Witte', ibid. vol. 140 (1915), pp. 232–79, 573–89, (*Glinskiy* VI)
  vol. 141, pp. 204–33, 520–53, 893–906,   (*Glinskiy* VII)
  vol. 142, pp. 592–609, 893–907.   (*Glinskiy* VIII)
(Goldenberg I. P.) I. G., 'Gapon i Yego Gazeta', *Istoricheskiy Vestnik* vol. 128
  (1912), pp. 923–32.   (*Goldenberg*)

Bibliography

Goldman L. I. (ed.), *Politicheskiye Protsesy v Rossii 1901–1917* (Moscow 1932).
(*Goldman*)

Goldsmith R. W., 'The Economic Growth of Tsarist Russia, 1860–1913', *Economic Development and Cultural Change* (Chicago), vol. IX, no. 3 (April 1961), pp. 441–75. (*Goldsmith*)

Goldstein M. L., *Pechat Pered Sudom* (Spb 1906). (*Goldstein*)

Golubev V., *Rol Zemstva v Obshchestvennom Dvizhenii* (Rostov N/D 1905). (*Golubev*)

Gordon M., *Workers Before and After Lenin* (N.Y. 1941). (*Gordon*)

Gorev B. I., 'Apoliticheskiya i Antiparlyamentskiya Gruppy', *O.D.* vol. III, pp. 473–534. (*Gorev*)

Gorin P., *Ocherki Po Istorii S.R.D. v 1905g* (Moscow 1925). (*Gorin*)

Gorky A. M., i Korolenko V. G., *Perepiska. Statyi. Vyskazyvaniya* (Moscow 1957).
(*Gorky*)

Gots M., 'S.V. Zubatov', *Byloye*, no. 9 (1906), pp. 63–8. (*Gots*)

Gr-y S., *Kadety vo Vtoroy Dume* (Spb 1907).

Gredeskul N. A., 'Pervaya Duma i Yeya Predsedatel', *S.A.* pp. 309–32. (*Gredeskul*)

Gribovskiy V. M., 'Zagadochnyye Dokumenty Gapona', *Istoricheskiy Vestnik*, vol. 127 (1912), pp. 949–61. (*Gribovskiy*)

Grinevich V., 'Ocherki Razvitiya Professionalnogo Dvizheniya V g. S.-Peterburge', *Obrazovaniye* (1906),

no. 8, pp. 209–26, (*Grinevich* I)

no. 9, pp. 226–55. (*Grinevich* II)

no. 11, pp. 109–28. (*Grinevich* III)

(Groman V. G.) Gorn Vl., 'Krestyanskoye Dvizhenye do 1905g', *O.D.* vol. I, pp. 230–58. (*Groman*)

Groman V., 'O Ponimanii Sovremennogo Momenta'. In *Voprosy Momenta*.
(*Groman* I)

Gruppa 'Osvobozhdeniye Truda', 'Iz Arkhivov G. V. Plekhanova, V. I. Zasulich i L. G. Deycha. Pod. red L. G. Deycha', *Sborniki* I–VI (Moscow-Leningrad 1924–8).
(*Gruppa* I–VI)

Gurevich L., 'Narodnoye Dvizheniye v Peterburge 9-go Yanvarya 1905g', *Byloye*, no. 1 (1906), pp. 200–29. (*L. Gurevich*)

Gurevich V., 'Vserossiyskiy krestyanskiy Syezd i Pervaya Koalitsiya', *Letopis Revolyutsii* I, pp. 176–96. (*V. Gurevich*)

Gurko V. I. *Features and Figures of the Past: Government and Opinion in the Reign of Nicholas II* (Stanford U.P. – O.U.P. 1939) (*Gurko*)

Gusyatnikov P. S., *Nazreniye Revolyutsionnogo Krizisa v Rossii v Nachale XX Veka* (Moscow 1959). (*Gusyatnikov*)

(Gutovskiy V. A.) Mayevskiy Yev., 'Obshchaya Kartina Dvizheniya', *O.D.* vol. II, part I, pp. 34–184. (*Gutovskiy*)

Haimson L. H., *The Russian Marxists and the Origins of Bolshevism*, Harvard University Russian Research Center, Study no. 19 (Harvard U.P. 1955).
(*Haimson*)

Bibliography

Harcave S., *First Blood. The Russian Revolution of 1905* (London 1965). (*Harcave*)
Henderson W. D., *The Industrial Revolution on the Continent. Germany, France, and Russia, 1800–1914* (London 1961). (*Henderson*)
Hough R., *The Fleet that Had to Die* (London 1958). (*Hough* i)
The Potemkin Mutiny (London 1960). (*Hough* ii)
Imperatorskiy-Moskovskiy Universitet Doklad...O Prichinakh Studencheskikh Volneniy. Osvobozhdeniye publication (Stuttgart 1904).
Institut Marksisma-Leninisma, *Bolsheviki vo Glave Vserossiyskoy Politicheskoy Stachki v Oktyabre 1905g*, Sbornik dokumentov i materialov pod redaktsiyey P. Kostugova i Drugikh (Moscow 1955). (*Institut Marksisma-Leninisma* i)
Listovki Bolshevitskikh Organisatsiy v Pervoy Russkoy Revolyutsii 1905–7gg. (Moscow 1956). (*Institut Marksisma-Leninisma* ii)
Intelligentsiya v Rossii, Sbornik Statey (Spb 1910).
Istoriya Odnogo Soyuza (Moscow 1907).
Itogi i Perspektivy, Sbornik Statey (Moscow 1906).
Ivanov L. M., *Revolyutsiya 1905–1907gg v Natsionalnykh Rayonakh Rossii* (Moscow 1955). (*Ivanov*)
Ivanov-Razumnik V. R., *Chto Takoye Intelligentsiya?* (Berlin 1920)
(*Ivanov-Razumnik* i)
Istoriya Russkoy Obshchestvennoy Mysli, 4th edn (Spb 1914),
vol. i, (*Ivanov-Razumnik* ii)
vol. ii. (*Ivanov-Razumnik* iii)
The Memoirs of Ivanov-Razumnik transl. and ed. P. S. Squire (C.U.P. 1965).
(*Ivanov-Razumnik* iv)
Ivanovich S. (Portugeise V. L.), *A. N. Potresov, Opyt Kulturno-Psikhologicheskogo Portreta* (Paris 1938). (*Ivanovich*)
Ivanovich V. (see Charnoluskiy).
'Iz obzora vazhneyshikh doznaniy po delam o gosudarstvennykh prestupleniyakh za 1894g.', *Byloye*, no. 5 (1907), pp. 228–52. (*Iz obzora*)
Izgoyev A. S., *Russkoye Obshchestvo i Revolyutsiya*, Sbornik Statey (Moscow 1910).
(*Izgoyev*)
Izveshcheniye o Tretyem Syezde, Izdaniye Ts. K. (Geneva 1903). (*Izveshcheniye*)
(Izvolskiy A. P.), *Recollections of a Foreign Minister*. Memoirs of Alexander Izvolsky, ed. and transl. C. L. Seeger (London (?) 1920). (*Izvolskiy*)
'K Istorii Manifesta 17-go Oktyabrya. Sekretnaya perepiska', *Byloye*, no. 14 (1919), pp. 108–11.
'Kadety v 1905–1906gg', *K.A.*
xlvi (1931), pp. 38–68. (*Kadety* i)
xlvii/xlviii (1931), pp. 112–39. (*Kadety* ii)
Kaminka A. L., i Nabokov N. D., *Vtoraya Gosudarstvennaya Duma* (Spb 1907).
(*Kaminka*)
(See also *Gessen*)
Kanatchikov S. I., *Iz Istorii Moyego Bytya* (Moscow 1932). (*Kanatchikov*)

Bibliography

Kantarovich V. A., 'Khrustalev Nosar', *Byloye*, no. 4 (32) (1925), pp. 117–53.
(*Kantarovich*)
Kantor R. Ya., 'Pisma K. P. Pobedonostseva K gr. Ignatyevu', *Byloye*, no. 27/28
(1925), pp. 50–89. (*Kantor*)
Karabchevskiy N. P., *Chto Glaza Moi Videli*, vol. II (Berlin 1921).
(*Karabchevskiy*)
Karavayev V. F., 'Zemskiye Smety i Rasklady'. In *Yubileynyy Sbornik*, pp. 155–79.
(*Karavayev*)
Karelin A. E., 'Devyatoye Yanvarya i Gapon', *K.L.* no. 1 (1922), pp. 107–17.
(*Karelin*)
Karelina V., 'Leonid Borisovich – Propagandist i Organisator Rabochikh Kryzhkov'.
In L. B. Krasin ('Nikitich'), *Gody Podpolya*, pp. 86–92. (*Karelina*)
Karpov N., *Krestyanskoye Dvizheniye V Revolyutsii 1905g. Po Dokumentam* (Lenin-
grad 1925). (*Karpov*)
Karpovich M., *Imperial Russia, 1801–1917* (N.Y. 1932). (*Karpovich* I)
'Komentarii 1905g.', *Novyy Zhurnal*, XLIII (1955), pp. 234–47 (*Karpovich* II)
(Katin-Yartsev V.), 'Pervyye Shagi', *Byloye*, no. 9, (1907), pp. 134–52.
(*Katin-Yartsev*)
Katin-Yartsev V., 'Teni Proshlogo', *Byloye*, no. 25 (1924), pp. 101–18.
(*Katin-Yartsev* I)
Katkov G., *Russia 1917. The February Revolution* (London 1967). (*Katkov*)
Kats A., Milonov Yu., *Professionalnoye Dvizheniye* (Moscow–Leningrad 1926).
(*Kats*)
Kaufman A. A., 'Zemskaya Statistika'. In *Yubileynyy Sbornik*, pp. 260–91.
(*Kaufman*)
Kaufman A. E., 'Cherty iz Zhizni Grafa S. Yu. Witte', *Istoricheskiy Vestnik*, vol.
140 (1915), pp. 220–37. (*Kaufman* I)
Kaun A., *Maxim Gorky and His Russia* (N.Y. 1932). (*Kaun* I)
'Maxim Gorky in the Revolution of 1905', *Slavonic and East European Review*,
IX (1930–1), pp. 133–48. (*Kaun* II)
Keep J. L. H., *The Rise of Social Democracy in Russia* (O.U.P. 1963). (*Keep*)
Kennan G., *Posledneye Zayavleniye Russkikh Liberalov* (Rostov N/D 1916).
(*Kennan*)
Khizhnyakov V. M., *Vospominaniya Zemskogo Deyatelya* (Petrograd 1916).
(*Khizhnyakov*)
Kindersley R., *The First Russian Revisionists. A Study of Legal Marxism in Russia*
(Oxford 1962). (*Kindersley*)
King V., 'The Liberal Movement in Russia, 1905–1915', *Slavonic and East
European Review*, XIV (1935) pp. 124–37. (*King*)
Kirilov V. S. *Bolsheviki Vo Glabe Massovykh Politicheskikh Stachek 1905–1907*
(Moscow 1961). (*Kirilov*)
Kirpichnikov S. D., 'L. I. Lutugin i Soyuz Soyuzov', *Byloye*, no. 6 (34) (1925),
pp. 134–46. (*Kirpichnikov* I)

Bibliography

K(irpichnikov) S. D., 'Profsoyuzy i Obyedineniye ikh ∇ Soyuz-Soyuzov'. In *Sputnik Izbiratelya*, pp. 135–57. (*Kirpichnikov* II)
Soyuz Soyuzov (Spb 1906). (*Kirpichnikov* III)
Vserossiyskiy Soyuz Inzhinerov i Tekhnikov (Spb 1906). (*Kirpichnikov* IV)
Kiryanov Yu. L., Lebedev K. M., i Simonova M. S., 'Problemy Istorii Revolyutsii 1905–1907gg. V. Rossii', *Istoriya SSSR*, no. 3 (1966), pp. 213–17. (*Kiryanov*)
Kirzhnits A. D., *1905: Yevreyskoye Rabocheye Dvizheniye* (Moscow–Leningrad 1928). (*Kirzhnits*)
Kizevetter A. A., *Mestnoye Samoupravleniye v Rossii* (Moscow 1910). (*Kizevetter* I)
Na Rubezhe Dvukh Stoletiy (Praga 1929). (*Kizevetter* II)
'Ocherk Manifesta 17-go Oktyabrya', *Russkiye Vedomosti*, no. 233 (17 October 1915). (*Kizevetter* III)
(ed.), *Pamyati V. A. Goltseva, Statyi, Vospominaniya, Pisma* (Moscow 1910).
(*Kizevetter : Pamyati Goltseva*)
'Politicheskaya Deyatelnost S. A. Muromtseva Do Gosudarstvennoy Dumy'. In *S.A.* pp. 91–115. (*Kizevetter* IV)
Kleynbort L., 'M. I. Gurevich – "Kharkovetz" ', *Byloye*, no 16 (1921), pp. 86–107. (*Kleynbort*)
Klimov P. I., *Revolyutsionnaya Deyatelnost Rabochikh v Derevne v 1905–1907 gg* (Moscow 1960). (*Klimov*)
Klochkov M., *Zemskiye Sobory v Starine* (Spb 1905) (*Klochkov*)
Kluchevsky V. O., *Sochineniya*, 8 vols (Moscow 1956–9). (*Kluchevsky*)
Kluge E. E., *Die Russische Revolutionäre Presse in der Zweiten Hälfe des Neunzehnten Jahrhunderts, 1855–1905* (Zurich 1948). (*Kluge*)
Klyachko L. M., *Povesti Proshlogo* (Leningrad 1929). (*Klyachko* I)
Za Kulisami Starogo Rezhima, vol. I (Leningrad 1926). (*Klyachko* II)
Kobyakov R., 'Gapon i Okhrannoye Otdeleniye Do 1905g', *Byloye*, no. 1 (29) (1925), pp. 28–45. (*Kobyakov*)
Kokhan L., *Russia in Revolution* (London 1966). (*Kokhan*)
Kokhmanskiy P. V., *Moskva v Dekabre 1905g* (Moscow 1906). (*Kokhmanskiy*)
Kokoshkin F. F., 'Muromtsev i Zemskiye Syezdy'. In *S.A.* pp. 205–50 (*Kokoshkin*)
Kokovtsev V. M., *Iz Moyego Proshlogo. Vospominaniya*, 2 vols (Paris 1933), vol. I, (*Kokovtsev* I)
vol. II. (*Kokovtsev* II)
(Kokovtsev V. M.) *Doklady Tsaryu, K.A.* XI/XII (1925), pp. 3–22. (*Kokovtsev* III)
Out of My Past. The Memoirs of Count Kokovtsev, ed. H. H. Fisher, transl. L. Matveev (London 1935). (*Kokovtsev* IV)
'Telegramy k S. Yu. Witte', *K.A.* VI (1924), pp 37–40 (*Kokovtsev* V)
Kollontay A., 'Obshchestvennoye Dvizheniye v Finlandii', *O.D.* vol. IV, part II, pp. 247–300. (*Kollontay*)
Kolokolnikov P., *Proefssionalnoye Dvizheniye v Rossii*, 2nd edn (Petrograd 1917).
(*Kolokolnikov* I)

Bibliography

i Rapoport S. (comp.), *1905–1907gg. v Professionalnom Divzhenii*, i i ii, Vserossiy-
skaya Konferentsiya Profsoyuzov, Izd. V.L.S.P.S. (Moscow 1925).
(*Kolokolnikov* ii)
Koltsov D. (B. A. Ginsburg), 'Rabochiye v 1890–1904gg', *O.D.* vol. i, pp. 183–229.
(*Koltsov*)
Kon F. Ya., *Istoriya Revolyutsionnogo Dvizheniya v Rossii* (Kharkov 1929).
(*Kon* i)
Sorok Let Pod Znamenem Revolyutsii, Vospominaniya (Moscow-Petrograd 1923).
(*Kon* ii)
Vospominaniya (Moscow 1921). (*Kon* iii)
Kon F. Ya., Pleskov V. A., i Chuzhek N. F., *V Tsarskoy Kazarme, Soldaty i
Matrosy v Pervoy Revolyutsii* (Moscow 1929). (*Kon* iv)
'Konets Russko-Yaponskoy Voyny', *K.A.* xxviii (1928), pp. 182–204.
Kornilov A., *Modern Russian History* (N.Y. 1917). (*Kornilov* i)
Obshchestvennoye Dvizheniye Pri Aleksandre II, Istoricheskiye Ocherki (Moscow
1909). (*Kornilov* ii)
Ocherki Po Istorii Obshchestvennogo Dvizheniya i Krestyanskogo dela v Rossii (Spb
1905). (*Kornilov* iii)
Korolenko Vl. G., *Pisma P. S. Ivanovskoy* (Moscow 1930). (*Korolenko* i)
Sobraniye Sochineniy, vols 6–7, 10 (Moscow 1924–6),
vol. 6, (*Korolenko* ii)
vol. 7, (*Korolenko* iii)
vol. 10. (*Korolenko* iv)
V Golodnyy God, 2nd edn (Spb 1894). (*Korolenko* v)
(Korostovets I. Ya.), 'Dnevnik', *Byloye* (1918),
no. 1, pp. 177–220, (*Korostovets* i)
no. 2, pp. 110–46, (*Korostovets* ii)
no. 3, pp. 58–85, (*Korostovets* iii)
no. 6, pp. 153–82. (*Korostovets* iv)
Korostovets J. J., *Pre War Diplomacy. The Russo-Japanese Problem. Treaty signed
at Portsmouth, USA* (London 1920). (*Korostovets* v)
Kostomarov G. D., *Moskovskiy Sovet v 1905g* (Moscow 1955). (*Kostomarov* i)
Moskva v Trekh Revolyutsiyakh (Moscow 1959). (*Kostomarov* ii)
1905g V Moskve (Moscow 1955). (*Kostomarov* iii)
Kostomarov, G. D., Simonenko V., i Drezni A., *Iz Istorii Moskovskogo Vooru-
zhennogo Vostaniya. Materialy i Dokumenty* (Moscow 1930). (*Kostomarov* iv)
Kovalevskiy M. M., *Russian Political Institutions to the Present Time* (Chicago 1902).
(*Kovalevskiy*)
Kozmin B., 'K Istorii Razoblacheniya Azefa', *K.i.S.* no. 32, (1927), pp. 102–8.
(*Kozmin*)
(Krasin L. B. [Nikitich]), *Gody Podpolya, Sbornik Vospominaniy Statey i Doku-
mentov*. Sostavlen Kruzhkom Druzey Krasina Pod redaktsiyey M. N. Lyadova
i S. M. Posner (Moscow–Leningrad 1928). (*Krasin*)

Bibliography

Krasnyy Petrograd (Petrograd 1921).

Krivosheyna E., *Peterburgskiy Sovet Rabochikh Deputatov v 1905g.* (Moscow 1926).
    (*Krivosheyna*)

Kropatkin P. A., 'Pisma K V. M. Burtsevu', *Na Chuzhoy Storone*, VI (1924), pp.
119–55.
    (*Kropatkin*)

(Kryzhanovskiy S. E.), *Vospominaniya. Iz Bumag S. E. Kryzhanovskogo, Poslednyago Gosudarstvennogo Sekretarya Rossiyskoy Imperii* [Berlin 1938(?)].
    (*Kryzhanovskiy*)

Kulchycki L. (Mezowetski), *Istoriya Russkogo Revolyutsionnogo Dvizheniya*, vol. I
(Spb 1908).
    (*Kulchycki*)

Kurlov P. G., *Gibel Imperatorskoy Rossii* (Berlin 1923).
    (*Kurlov* I)

Konets Russkogo Tsarisma (Moscow-Petrograd 1923).
    (*Kurlov* II)

(Kuropatkin A. N.), 'Dnevnik', *K.A.*

    II (1922), pp. 5–117,
    (*Kuropatkin* I)

    V (1924), pp. 82–101,
    (*Kuropatkin* II)

    VII (1924), pp. 55–69,
    (*Kuropatkin* III)

    VIII (1925), pp. 70–100,
    (*Kuropatkin* IV)

    LXVIII (1935), pp. 65–96,
    (*Kuropatkin* V)

    LXIX/LXX (1935), pp. 101–26.
    (*Kuropatkin* VI)

'Prolog Manchurskoy Tragedii', *Russko-Yaponskaya Voyna*, pp. 5–53.
    (*Kuropatkin* VII)

(See also Witte S. Yu.)

(Kuskova E. D.), 'Credo', *Vademecum*, pp. 1–6.
    (*Kuskova: Credo*)

'Pisma Timofeyu'. In I. Tatarov, 'Materialy k istorii pervogo syezda', *P.R.* no. 3
(74) (1928), pp. 154–63.
    (*Kuskova* I)

'Pismo K Akselrodu', *Vademecum*, pp. 17–27.
    (*Kuskova* II)

M. M. *Son Pod Pervoye Maya*, 2nd edn (Spb 1905).
    (*Kuskova* III)

M. M. *Stachki Lzhi* (Zheneva 1898).
    (*Kuskova* IV)

Kuskova E. D. (review of) Dan F., 'Iz Istorii Revolyutsionnogo Dvizheniya i Sotsial Demokratii v Rossi' [autobiographical remarks], *Byloye*, no. 10 (1906),
pp. 320–31.
    (*Kuskova* V)

'Davno Minuvsheye', *Novyy Zhurnal*,
    (*Kuskova* VI)

    XLV (1956), pp. 149–80,
    (*Kuskova* VIa)

    XLVII (1956), pp. 154–76,
    (*Kuskova* VIb)

    XLVIII (1957), pp. 139–62,
    (*Kuskova* VIc)

    XLIX (1957), pp. 145–70,
    (*Kuskova* VId)

    L (1957), pp. 173–97,
    (*Kuskova* VIe)

    LI (1957), pp. 147–72,
    (*Kuskova* VIf)

    LIV (1958), pp. 117–47.
    (*Kuskova* VIg)

'K Voprosam Taktiki', *Bez-Zaglaviya*, no. 11, pp. 455–65.
    (*Kuskova* VII)

'Kren Nalevo', *Sovremennyya Zapiski*, XLIV (1930), pp. 366–95.
    (*Kuskova* VIII)

'Nadpolye i Podpolye Marksisma', *Novoye Russkoye Slovo* (N.Y.),
    (*Kuskova* IX)

    23 July 1954,
    (*Kuskova* IXa)

24 July 1954, (*Kuskova* IXb)
26 July 1954. (*Kuskova* IXc)
'O Staroy Vere', *Sovremennyya Zapiski*, LXV (1937), pp. 393-400. (*Kuskova* X)
'Ob Utopiyakh, Realnostyakh i Zagadkakh', ibid. XXVI (1925), pp. 359-77.
(*Kuskova* XI)
'Obezkrylennyy Sokol (Gorky)', ibid. XXXVI (1928), pp. 305-45. (*Kuskova* XII)
'Otkrytki', ibid. XXV (1925), pp. 416-40. (*Kuskova* XIII)
'Otvet Na Vopros "Kto my" ', *Bez-Zaglaviya*, no. 3, pp. 81-9. (*Kuskova* XIV)
'Pechat', ibid. nos. 1, 5, 7-16. (*Kuskova* XV)
'Pestryye Kartiny', *Sovremennyya Zapiski*, XII (1922), pp. 138-63.
(*Kuskova* XVI)
'Tragediya M. Gorkogo', *Novyy Zhurnal*, XXXVIII (1954), pp. 224-45.
(*Kuskova* XVII)
'Zigzagi Pamyati', *Novoye Russkoye Slovo*, (*Kuskova* XVIII)
 17 July 1952, (*Kuskova* XVIIIa)
 18 July 1952. (*Kuskova* XVIIIb)
Kuzmin-Karavayev V. D., *Iz Epokhi Osvoboditalnogo Dvizheniya* (Spb 1907).
(*Kuzmin-Karavayev* I)
Zemstvo i Derevnya (Spb 1904). (*Kuzmin-Karavayev* II)
(Lamsdorf V. N.), 'Dnevnik', *K.A.* III (1931), pp. 3-37. (*Lamsdorf*)
Lang D. M., *The First Russian Radical – Alexander Radishchev, 1749-1802* (London
 1959). (*Lang*)
Lazarevskiy N. I., *Russkoye Gosudarstvennoye Pravo*, tom. I,
Konstitutsionnoye Pravo (Spb 1913). (*Lazarevskiy* I)
Zakony o Vyborakh v Gosudarstvennuyu Dumu (Spb 1906). (*Lazarevskiy* II)
'Zemskoye Izbiratelnoye Pravo'. In *Yubileynyy Sbornik*, pp. 50-75.
(*Lazarevskiy* III)
Lebedev N. M., 'Revolyutsiya 1905-1907gg. v Rossii i yeya mezhdunarodnoye
znacheniye', *Novaya i Noveyshaya Istoriya*, no. 2 (1966), pp. 173-5.
(*N. Lebedev*)
Lebedev P., 'Krasnyye Dni v Novgorode, Vospominaniya', *Byloye*, no. 5 (1907),
pp. 124-48. (*P. Lebedev*)
Lenin V. I., *Collected Works* (Moscow 1960–). (*Lenin* I)
Polnoye Sobraniye Sochineniy, izd. 5-e (Moscow 1958–). (*Lenin* II)
Sobraniye Sochineniy (Moscow 1922-8). (*Lenin* III)
Leninskiy Sbornik, vol. V (Moscow-Leningrad 1924). (*Leninskiy Sbornik*)
Lenskiy Z. (Stentsel Z. S.), 'Natsionalnoye Dvizheniye', *O.D.* vol. I, pp. 349-71.
(*Lenskiy*)
Leontovitsch V., *Geschichte des Liberalismus in Russland* (Frankfurt A/Main 1957).
(*Leontovitsch*)
Lepeshinskiy P. N., *Na Povorote, Ot Kontsa 80-kh gg. k 1905g* (Petrograd 1922).
(*Lepeshinskiy*)
Levitskiy V., 'Pravyya Partii', *O.D.* vol. III, pp. 347-469. (*Levitskiy*)

Bibliography

Libanov G. M., *Studencheskoye Dvizheniye 1899g.*, Russian Free Press Fund
(London 1901). (*Libanov*)
Liberaly i Sotsialisty (Zheneva 1904).
(Linevich N. P.), 'Dnevnik'. In *Russko-Yaponskaya Voyna*, pp. 57-129.
(*Linevich* I)
'Pisma', *Byloye*, no. 4 (32) (1925), pp. 108-16. (*Linevich* II)
Listki Zhizni, nos. 1-12 (London 1902).
Logacheva-Piletskaya M., 'Soyuz Borby Za Osvobozhdeniye Rabochego Klassa',
Byloye, no. 3 (31) (1925), pp. 93-107. (*Logacheva*)
Lopukhin A. A., *Iz Itogov Sluzhebnogo Opyta* (Moscow 1907). (*Lopukhin* I)
Otryvki Iz Vospominaniy (Moscow 1923). (*Lopukhin* II)
(Lopukhin A. A.), 'Doklady Ministru Vnutrennykh Del ot Nachala Fevralya
1905g', *K.L.* no. 1 (1922), pp. 331-5. (*Lopukhin* III)
'Obvinitelnyy Akt...Ob A. A. Lopukhine', *Byloye*, no. 9/10 (1909), pp. 218-36.
(*Lopukhin* IV)
'Zapiska A. A. Lopukhina o Razvitii Revolyutsionnogo Dvizheniya v Rossi',
Byloye, no. 9/10 (1909), pp. 74-8. (*Lopukhin* V)
Lositskiy A. E., *Izbiratelnaya Sistema Gosudarstvennoy Dumy* (Spb 1906).
(*Lositskiy*)
Lukashevich S., 'The Holy Brotherhood', *American Slavic and East European
Review*, XVIII (1959), pp. 491-509. (*Lukashevich*)
Lunts M. G., *Sbornik Statey. Iz Istorii Fabrichnogo Zakonostatelstva, Fabrichnoy
Inspektsii i Rabochego Dvizheniya v Rossii* (Moscow 1909). (*Lunts*)
Lyadov M. (Mendelshtam), 'Kak voznikla Moskovskaya rabochaya organizatsiya'.
In Mitskevich S.I., *Na zare rabochego dvizheniya v Moskve*, pp. 42-96.
(*Lyadov*)
Lyashchenko P. I., *Istoriya Narodnogo Khozyaystva SSSR*, 3 vols (Moscow 1956),
vol. II. (*Lyashchenko* I)
'Ekonomicheskiye Predposylki 1917 g'. In *Agrarnaya Revolyutsya*, vol. II
(Moscow 1928), pp. 19-61. (*Lyaschenko* II)
Ocherki Agrarnoy Evolyutsii, vol. I (Spb 1908). (*Lyashchenko* III)
(Lyubimov D. N.), 'Otryvki iz Vospominaniy', *Istoricheskiy Arkhiv*, no. 6 (1962),
pp. 63-84. (*Lyubimov*)
M.I.K. 'Voyennaya Spyshka', *Istoricheskiy Vestnik*, vol. 115 (1909), pp. 612-29.
M-Ko N. M., *Gruzino Armyanskiya Pretenzii i Zakavkazkaya Revolyutsiya* (Kiyev
1906). (*M-Ko*)
Maklakov V. A., *Vlast i Obshchestvennost Na Zakate Staroy Rossii*, 3 vols (Paris
1936). (*Maklakov* I-III)
Malia M., 'What is the Intelligentsia?' In Pipes R., *The Russian Intelligentsia*.
(*Malia*)
Malyantovich P. N., i Muravyev N. K., *Zakony o Politicheskikh i bshchestvennykh
prestupleniyakh* (Spb 1910). (*Malyantovich*)
Mannheim K., *Ideology and Utopia* (N.Y. 1940). (*Mannheim*)

Bibliography

Manuilov A. A., *Ocherki po Krestyankomu Voprosu* (Moscow 1904–5).
(*Manuilov* I)
Pozemelnyy Vopros v Rossii (Moscow 1905). (*Manuilov* II)
(Martov Yu. O), 'Yegorov A, Zarozhdeniye Politicheskikh Partiy'. In *O.D.* vol. I,
pp. 372–421. (*Martov*)
Martov (Yu. O.), *Istoriya Rossiyskov Sotsial-Demokratii* (Moscow-Petrograd 1923).
(*Martov* I)
'Iz Neopublikovannykh Vospominaniy', *Leninskiy Sbornik*, vol. IV, pp. 49–61.
(*Martov* II)
'Zapiski Sotsial-Demokrata', kn. I, *Letopis' Revolyutsii*, vol. II, no. 4.
(*Martov* III)
(See also Akselrod P. B.)
Martynov A. (Piker A. S.), 'Kadetskaya Partiya', *O.D.* vol. III, pp. 1–85.
(*Martynov*)
Marx K. and Engels F., *Selected Works*, vols I–II (London 1950). (*Marx* I, II)
Maslov P. P., *Agrarnyy Vopros v Rossii*, 2 vols (Spb),
vol. I, 2nd edn (1905), (*Maslov* I)
vol. II (1908). (*Maslov* II)
'Krestyanskoye Dvizheniye, *O.D.* vol. II, part II, pp. 203–82. (*Maslov* III)
'Narodnicheskiya Partii', ibid. vol. III, pp. 89–158. (*Maslov* IV)
'Razvitiye Zemledeliya i Polozheniye Krestyan do Nachala XX veka', ibid. vol. I,
pp. 1–38. (*Maslov* V)
Materialy k Istorii Russkoy Konter-Revolyutsii, vol. I *Pogromy* (Spb 1908).
(*Materialy* I)
Materialy k Istorii Yevreyskogo Rabochego Dvizheniya (Spb 1906). (*Materialy* II)
Materialy po Istorii Agrarnoy Revolyutsii v Rossii (Moscow 1928). (*Materialy* III)
Materialy po Istorii Professionalnogo Dvizheniya v Rossii, Vserossiyskiy Tsentralnyy
Sovet Profsoyuzov, Komissiya po Izucheniyu Professionalnogo Dvizheniya v
Rossii. Sborniki I–IV (Moscow 1924–5). (*Materialy* IV, 1–4)
Materialy po Rabochemu Voprosu, vyp. I, II (Stuttgart 1902–3). (*Materialy* V, 1–2)
Materialy po Universitetskomu Voprosu s Predisloviyem P. B. Struve, vyp. I, II
(Stuttgart 1902–1904). (*Materialy* VI, 1–2)
Materialy po Vyrabotke Russkoy Konstitutsii, Izd. red. *Osvobozhdeniye* (Paris 1905).
(*Materialy* VII)
Mavor J., *An Economic History of Russia*, 2nd edn, 2 vols (London 1925).
(*Mavor* I, 1–2)
The Russian Revolution (London 1928). (*Mavor* II)
Mayevskiy E. (see *Gutovskiy V. A.*).
Mazour A. A., *The First Russian Revolution. 1825* (Stanford U.P. 1961). (*Mazour*)
Mazurenko S. 'Syezd Krestyan (V Saratove)', *Byloye*, no. 7 (1908), pp. 35–9.
(*Mazurenko*)
(Mednikov E. P.), 'Pisma Spiridovichu', *K.A.* XVII (1926) pp. 192–219.
(*Mednikov*)

Bibliography

Melgunov S. P., *Nikolay II – Materialy Dlya Kharakteristiki Lichnosti i Tsarstvo-vaniya* (Moscow 1917). (*Melgunov*)
Melkaya Zemskaya Yedinitsa, Izd. kn. Petra. D. Dolgorukova i kn. D. I. Shakhov-skogo Pri Uchastii redaktsii gazety *Pravo*, vyp. I–II (Spb 1903).
Mendel A. P., *Dilemmas of Progress in Tsarist Russia: Legal Marxism and Legal Populism*, Harvard University Russian Research Center, Study no. 43 (Harvard U.P. 1961). (*Mendel*)
Menshchikov L. P., *Russkiy Politicheskiy Sysk Zagranitsey* (Paris 1914).
(*Menshchikov*)
Mikheyeva E. P., 'Neskolko dopolneniy k istorii Besedy', *Istoriya SSSR*, no. 2 (1966), pp. 241–3. (*Mikheyeva*)
Milonov Yu., *Kak Voznikli Profsoyuzy v Rossii* (Moscow–Leningrad 1926).
(*Milonov* I)
'Milstein E., i Livshits V.', *Istoriya i praktika Rossiyskogo Professionalnogo Dvizheniya* (Moscow 1925). (*Milonov* II)
Milovidov A., 'Dokumenty o Smerti Gapona', *K.L.* no. 2 (13) (1925), pp. 244–6.
(*Milovidov* I)
'Dva Dokumenta ob Ubiystve Gapona', *Byloye.* no. 1 (29) (1925), pp. 63–5.
(*Milovidov* II)
'Neizvestnyye Proklamatsii o 9–om Yanvare', ibid. pp. 58–61. (*Milovidov* III)
Milyukov P. N., *God Borby* (Spb 1907). (*Milyukov* I)
Iz Istorii Russkoy Intelligentsii. Sbornik Statey i Etyudov, 2nd edn (Spb 1903).
(*Milyukov* II)
'Liberalism, Radicalism i Revolyutsiya', *Sovremennyya Zapiski.* LVII (1935), pp. 285–313. (*Milyukov* III)
'S.A. Muromstev. Biograficheskiy Ocherk'. In *S.A.* pp. 1–52. (*Milyukov* IV)
'Rokovyye Gody', *Russkiye Zapiski* (Paris-Shanghai), (*Milyukov* V, 1–13)
    1938: April, pp. 109–18,
    May, pp. 109–10,
    June, pp. 115–31,
    July, pp. 126–36,
    August/Sept., pp. 108–24,
    Oct., pp. 128–38,
    Nov., pp. 135–49,
    Dec., pp. 116–23,
    1939: Jan., pp. 117–28,
    Feb., pp. 120–34,
    March, pp. 101–12,
    April, pp. 127–39,
    May, pp. 106–20.
Russia and Its Crisis (Chicago 1906). (*Milyukov* VI)
'Sud Nad Kadetskim Liberalismom', *Sovremennyya Zapiski*, XLI (1930), pp. 347–71. (*Milyukov* VII)

Bibliography

Tri Popytiki, K Istorii Russkogo Lzhe-Konstitutsionalisma (Paris 1921).
                                                            (Milyukov VIII)
(ed.), M. M. *Vinaver i Russkaya Obshchestvennost Nachala XX Veka* (Paris 1937).
                                                          (Milyukov IX)
Vospominaniya, 2 vols (N.Y. 1955).   *(Milyukov* X, *a–b*)
Mintslov S. R., '14 Mesyatsev Svobody Pechati', *Byloye*, no. 3 (1907), pp. 123–48.
                                                            (Mintslov)
Mirnyy S. (see Shakhovskoy D. I.).
Mitskevich S. I. (ed.), *Albom Revolyutsionnoy Satiry 1905–1906gg* (Moscow 1906).
                                                         (Mitskevich I)
    Na Zare Rabochego Dvizheniya v Moskve (Moscow 1932).   *(Mitskevich* II)
Revolyutsionnaya Moskva (Moscow 1940).   *(Mitskevich* III)
Mogilyanskiy M., *Pervaya Gosudarstvennaya Duma* (Spb 1907).   *(Mogilyanskiy* I)
'V Devyanostyye Gody, Vospominaniya', *Byloye* (1924), no. 23, pp. 132–61.
                                                (Mogilyanskiy II)
Ibid. no. 24, pp. 96–139.   *(Mogilyanskiy* III)
Molodezh i Revolyutsiya (1860–1905) (Leningrad 1925).
'Moskovskiy Universitet v Oktyabrskiye dni 1905g', *K.A.* LXXIV (1936), pp. 195–204.
Moskovskoye Vooruzhennoye Vostaniye Po Dannym Obvinitelnykh Aktov i Sudebnykh Protokolov, vyp. 1 (Moscow 1906).
Moskva v Trekh Revolyutsiyakh (Moscow 1955).
Mosolov A. A., *Pri Dvore Imperatora (Nikolaya II)* (Riga 1937).   *(Mosolov)*
Mukhanov A. A. (see Nabokov V. D.).
(Muravyev N. V.), *Revolyutsionnoye Dvizheniye v Rossii v Dokladakh Muravyova* (Spb 1907).   *(Muravyev)*
Myakotin V. A., 'Lenin', *The Slavonic and East European Review*, II (1923–4), pp. 465–86.   *(Myakotin* I)
'O Narodno Sotsialisticheskoy Partii'. In *Narodno Sotsialisticheskoye Obozreniye* pp. 3–10.   *(Myakotin* II)
N.N., 'Posledniye Minuty Gapona', *Byloye*, no. 11/12 (1909), pp. 116–22.
Na Barikadakh...1905g. K.P.S.S., Moskovskiy Gorodskoy Komitet (Moscow 1955).
Nabokov V. D., 'Pyat let Nazad', *Russkaya Mysl*, no. 11 (1910), pp. 195–8.
                                                    (Nabokov I)
Nabokov V. D., i Mukhanov A. A., *Pervaya Gosudarstvennaya Duma* (Spb 1907).
                                                    (Nabokov II)
Naida S. F., *Revolyutsionnoye Dvizheniye v Tsarskom Flote 1905–1917* (Moscow 1948).   *(Naida* I)
Voyenyye Moryaki v Period Pervoy Russkoy Revolyutsii (Moscow 1955).
                                                    (Naida II)
Narodno-Sotsialisticheskoye Obozreniye, vyp. I–II (Spb 1906).
Narodnoye Delo, Sbornik (Paris 1909–12).

Bibliography

Naumov A. N., *Iz Utselevshikh Vospominaniy, 1868–1917* (N.Y. 1954–5). (*Naumov*)
Nestroyev G., *Iz Dnevnika Maksimalista* (Paris 1910). (*Nestroyev*)
Neurozhay i Golod v Rossii, 1905–1906 (Spb 1906).
Nevinson H. W., *The Dawn in Russia* (London-N.Y. 1906). (*Nevinson*)
Nevskiy V. I., *Rabocheye Dvizheniye v Yanvarskiye Dni 1905g* (Moscow 1930).
                  (*Nevskiy* I)
(ed.), *Sovetskaya Pechat i Literatura o Sovetakh* (Moscow-Leningrad 1925).
                  (*Nevskiy* II)
Sovety i Vooruzhennyya Vostaniya v 1905g. (Moscow 1932). (*Nevskiy* III)
'Sovety v 1905g'. In M. N. Pokrovskiy (ed.), *1905g. Istoriya Revolyutsionnogo Dvizheniya v Otdelnykh Ocherkakh*, vol. III, part I, pp. 4–72. (*Nevskiy* IV)
'Vybory v Komissiyu Shidlovskogo', *Arkhiv Istorii Truda v Rossii*, no. 3 (1922), pp. 78–90. (*Nevskiy* V)
'Yanvarskiye Dni v Peterburge', *K.L.* vol. I, no. 2/3 (1922), pp. 13–74.
                  (*Nevskiy* VI)
'Yanvarskiye Dni v Provintsii', ibid. vol. II (1922),
 no. 4, pp. 52–132, (*Nevskiy* VII)
 no. 5, pp. 85–114. (*Nevskiy* VIII)
'Zabastovka na Putilovskom Zavode'. In Pankratova A. M., *Stachechnoye Dvizheniye*, pp. 37–53. (*Nevskiy* IX)
Nevskiy Sbornik, vyp. II (Spb 1907).
(Nicholas II) *Dnevnik Imperatora Nikolaya II, 1890–1906* (Berlin 1923).
                  (*Nicholas* IIa)
'Nikolay II v 1905g. Iz Zapisnoy Knizkhi Arkhivista', *K.A.* XI/XII (1925), pp. 433–42. (*Nicholas* II b–c)
Perepiska Nikolaya i Aleksandry Romanovykh, vols III–V (Moscow-Petrograd-Leningrad 1923–7). (*Nicholas* IId)
'Perepiska Nikolaya i Aleksandry Romanovykh', *K.A.* IV (1923), pp. 159–221.
                  (*Nicholas* IIe)
'Perepiska Nikolaya i Aleksandry Romanovykh', *Byloye*, no 23 (1924), pp. 243–82. (*Nicholas* IIf)
'Perepiska Vilgelma II i Nikolaya II, 1904–1907', *Byloye*, no. 1 (1917), pp. 103–43. (*Nicholas* IIg)
Perepiska Vilgelma II s Nikolayem II, 1894–1914 (Moscow 1923).
                  (*Nicholas* IIh)
Pisma Imperatritsy Aleksandry Fedorovny k Nikolayu II (Berlin 1922).
                  (*Nicholas* IIi)
Polnoye Sobraniye Rechey, 1894–1906 (Spb 1906). (*Nicholas* IIj)
'Tobolskiy Dnevnik', *A.R.R.* vol. XVII, pp. 301–4. (*Nicholas* IIk)
Nikitin K., i Stepanov M., *Deyatelnost II-oy Dumy* (Spb 1906). (*Nikitin*)
N(ikolayevskiy) B. (I.), 'RSDRP O Soglasheniyakh S Oppositsionnymi i Revolyut-sionnymi Partiyami v 1904g', *K.i.S.* no. 32 (1927), pp. 57–72 (*Nikolayevskiy*)
Nikolayevskiy B. I., *Azeff. The Russian Judas* (London 1934). (*Nikolayevskiy* I)

Bibliography

A. N. Potresov – Opyt Literaturno-Politicheskoy Biografii'. In (A. N. Potresov)
Posmertnyy Sbornik Proizvedemiy, pp. 9–90. (*Nikolayevskiy* II)
'P. B. Struve, 1870–1944', *Novyy Zhurnal*, X (1945) pp. 306–28.
(*Nikolayevskiy* III)
Nikolayev A. A., *Teoriya i Prakitika Kooperativnogo Dvizheniya* (Moscow 1908–9).
(*Nikolayev*)
Noveyshiya Preobrazovniya Russkogo Gosudarstvennogo stroya (Spb 1906).
Novgorodtsev P. I., *Ob Obshchestvennom Ideale*, 3rd edn (Berlin 1921 (31 ?)).
(*Novgorodtsev*)
Novik I. D., *Moskovskiye Zemskiye Sobory* (Moscow 1905). (*Novik*)
Novikov N. M., *Ot Moskvy do Nyu Yorka* (N.Y. 1952). (*Novikov*)
Nuzhdy Derevni, Sbornik Statey, Izdaniye N. N. Lvova i A. A. Stakhovicha (Spb 1904).
O Minuvshem, Istoricheskiy Sbornik (Spb 1909).
Ob Agitatsii, s(predisloviyem i) Poslesloviyem P. Akselroda (Geneva 1896).
Obninskiy V., *Novyy Stroy* (Moscow 1911). (*Obninskiy* I)
Polgoda Russkoy Revolyutsii, Letopis Russkoy Revolyutsii, vol. III, part II (Moscow 1907). (*Obninskiy* II)
(Obolenskiy N. D., Prince), 'K Istorii Manifesta 17-go Oktyabrya. Zapiska Kn. N. Obolenskogo', *A.R.R.* vol. II, pp. 8–13. (*N. Obolenskiy*)
Obolenskiy V. A. (Prince), *Ocherki Minuvshego* (Belgrad 1931). (*V. Obolenskiy*)
Obshchestvennoye Dvizheniye v Rossii v Nachale XX-go Veka, Pod. red. L. Martova, P. Maslova i A. Potresova, 4 vols (Spb 1909–14). (*O.D.*)
Oldenburg, S. S., *Gosudar Imperator Nikolay II* (Berlin 1922). (*Oldenburg* I)
Tsarstvovaniye Imperatora Nikolaya II, vols I–II (Belgrad, Munich 1939–49).
(*Oldenburg* II)
(Orlov V. [Prince]), 'Iz Dnevnika Kn. Orlova. 1905g', *Byloye*, no. 14 (1919), pp. 54–7. (*V. Orlov*)
Orlov, V. I., *1905g. Bolshevitskiye Proklamatsii i Listovki po Moskve* (Moscow 1926). (*V. I. Orlov*)
Osnovnoy Gosudarstvennyy Zakon Rossiyskoy Imperii, Izdaniye redaktsii *Osvobo-zhdeniye* (Paris 1905).
Osvobozhdeniye. Sborniki, kn. 1–2 (Stuttgart–Paris 1903–4).
Ot K. D. Partii (Spring 1906).
Otkliki Russkoy Zemli na Tsarskoye Slovo o Voyne S Yaponiyey, M.V.D. (Spb 1904).
'Otvet Redaktsii Rabochego Dela na Pismo P. Akselroda'. In *Vademecum*, pp. 37–60.
Otvet Redaktsii Rabochego Dela na Pismo Akselroda i Vademecum G. Plekhanova (Geneva 1900). (*Otvet Redaktsii R.D.*)
Ovsyaniko-Kulikovskiy D. N., *Istoriya Russkoy Intelligenstii, Sobraniye Sochineniy*, vol. VII, part III (Spb 1914). (*Ovsyaniko*)
Ovsyanikov N. (ed.), *Dekabrskoye Vostaniye v Moskve* (Moscow 1922).
(*Ovsyanikov* I)
(ed.), *Na Zare Rabochego Dvizheniya v Moskve* (Moscow 1919). (*Ovsyanikov* II)

Bibliography

Ozerov I. Kh., *Politika po Rabochemu Voprosu v Rossii za Posledniye Gody* (Moscow 1906). *(Ozerov)*

Padeniye Tsarskogo Rezhima, ed. P. E. Shchegolev, vols I–IV (Moscow–Leningrad 1924–6).

Pakharnayev, A. I., *Obzor Deystvuyeshchego Svoda Zakonov* (Spb 1909).

Paléologue, M., *An Ambassador's Memoirs*, 3 vols (London 1923–5),

  vol. I, *(Paléologue I)*

  vol. II, *(Paléologue II)*

  vol. III. *(Paléologue III)*

Pankratov V. S., 'S Tsarem v Tobolske', *Byloye* (1924), no. 25, pp. 195–222.

  (Pankratov I)

  ibid. no. 26, pp. 207–21. *(Pankratov II)*

Pankratova A. M., *Istoriya Profsoyuznogo Dvizheniya v SSSR*,

  vol. I (Moscow–Leningrad 1954). *(Pankratova I)*

Pervaya Russkaya Revolyutsiya (Moscow 1957). *(Pankratova II)*

(ed.), *Pervaya Russkaya Revolyutsiya i Mezhdunarodnoye Rabocheye Dvizheniye*,

  vol. I (Moscow 1955), *(Pankratova III)*

  vol. II (Moscow 1956). *(Pankratova IV)*

'Rabochiy Klass i Rabocheye Dvizheniye na Kanune Revolyutsii 1905g'. In M. N. Pokrovskiy, *1905g. Istoriya Revolyutsionnogo Dvizheniya v Otdelnykh Ocherkakh*, vol. I, pp. 393–504. *(Pankratova V)*

(ed.), *Stachechnoye Dvizheniye. 1905g. Materialy i Dokumenty Pod Obshchey Redaktsiyey* M. N. Pokrovskogo (Moscow–Leningrad 1925). *(Pankratova VI)*

Pankratova A. M., i Kostomarov G. D. (ed.), *Ocherki po Istorii SSSR. Pervaya Russkaya Burzhuazno-Demokraticheskaya Revolyutsiya 1905–1907gg* (Moscow 1955). *(Pankratova VII)*

(See also *D.i.M.*)

Paozerskiy M., 'Synod v Borbe s Revolyutsiyey', *K.A.* VI (XXV) (1927), pp. 198–201. *(Paozerskiy)*

Pares B., *My Russian Memoirs* (London 1931). *(Pares I)*

Russia and Reform (London 1937). *(Pares II)*

The Fall of the Russian Monarchy (N.Y. 1939). *(Pares III)*

Parvus (Gelfand A.), *Nastoyashcheye Polozheniye i Vidy Budushchego* (pamphlet, Spb(?) 1906). *(Parvus I)*

Rossiya i Revolyutsiya (Spb 1906). *(Parvus II)*

'Voyna i Revolyutsiya', *Iskra* (1904), nos. 59, 6x, 79; (1905), no. 82.

  (Parvus III a–d)

Pasmanik D. S., *Revolyutsionnyye Gody v Krymu* (Paris 1926). *(Pasmanik I)*

Russkaya Revolyutsiya i Yevreystvo (Paris 1933). *(Pasmanik II)*

Pavlov I., 'Iz Vospominaniy o Rabochem Soyuze I Svyashchenike Gapone', *Minuvshiye Gody* (1908),

  no. 3, pp. 22–57, *(Pavlov I)*

  no. 4, pp. 79–107. *(Pavlov II)*

Bibliography

Pavlovich M. (Veltman M. L.), *Vneshnyaya Politikia i Russko-Yaponskaya Voyna* (Spb 1909). (*Pavlovich*)
Perepiska G. V. Plekhanova i P. B. Akselroda, ed. Berlin P. A., Voytinsky V. S., Nikolayevskiy B. I. (Moscow 1925), vols I–II. (*Perepiska* I–II)
Pereverzev V. N., 'Pervyy Vserossiyskiy Zheleznodorozhnyy Soyuz', *Byloye*, no. 4 (32) (1925), pp. 36–69. (*Pereverzev*)
Perris G. H., *Russia in Revolution* (London 1905). (*Perris*)
Pervyy Syezd Partii Narodnoy Svobody (Spb 1905).
Pervyye Narodnyye Predstaviteli. Biografii i Portrety (Spb 1907).
Peshekhonov A. V., 'Iz Vospominaniy', *Na Chuzhoy Storone* (1923),
    I, pp. 255–319, (*Peshekhonov* I)
    II, pp. 200–20. (*Peshekhonov* II)
    K Voprosu ob Intelligentsii (Spb 1906). (*Peshekhonov* III)
    Na Ocherednyye Temy (Spb 1904). (*Peshekhonov* IV)
    Nakanune (Spb 1906). (*Peshekhonov* V)
    'Pochemu My togda Ushli', *Russkoye Bogatstvo* (1917), XI/XII (Nov./Dec.), pp. 327–50. (*Peshekhonov* VI/VII)
    Zemelnyye Nuzhdy Derevni (Spb 1905). (*Peshekhonov* VIII)
Peterburzhets (Takhtarev K. M.), *Ocherk Peterburgskogo Rabochego Dvizheniya 90-kh gg*, Biblioteka Zhizni no 13 (London 1902). (*Peterburzhets*)
Petergofskoye Soveshchaniye o Proyekte Gosudarstvennoy Dumy (Berlin 1905).
Petrov N. P., 'Gapon i Witte', *Byloye*, no. 1 (29) (1925), pp. 15–27. (*Petrov* I)
Pravada o Gapone (Spb 1906). (*Petrov* II)
Petrunkevich I. I., *Intelligentsiya v Rossii* (Spb 1910), pp. iii–xv. (*Petrunkevich* I)
'Iz Zapisok Obshchestvennogo Deyatelya', *A.R.R.* vol. XXI (Berlin 1934).
(*Petrunkevich* II)
'O Russkoy Intelligentsii'. In Pasmanik D. S., *Revolyutsionnyye Gody*, pp. 195–201. (*Petrunkevich* III)
'Pamyati V. A. Goltseva (Stranichki iz Lichnykh Vospominaniy)'. In *Kizevetter: Pamyati Goltseva*, pp. 98–112. (*Petrunkevich* IV)
Piontkowski S., *Kratkiy Ocherk Rabochego Dvizheniya v Rossii, 1870–1914* (Leningrad 1925). (*Piontkowski*)
Pipes R., 'Karamzin's Conception of Monarchy', *Harvard Slavic Studies*, vol. 4 (1957), pp. 35–58. (*Pipes a*)
(ed. and transl.), *Karamzin's Memoir on Ancient and Modern Russia*, Harvard University Russian Research Center, Study no. 33 (Harvard U.P. 1959).
(*Pipes b*)
'Russian Marxism and its Populist Background', *The Russian Review* (October 1960), pp. 316–37. (*Pipes* I)
Social Democracy and the St. Petersburg Labor Movement, 1885–1897, Harvard University Russian Research Center, Study no. 46 (Harvard U.P. 1963). (*Pipes* II)
Struve: Liberal on the Left, 1870–1905, Harvard University Russian Research Center, Study no. 64 (Harvard U.P. 1970). (*Pipes* IIa)

Bibliography

(ed.), *The Russian Intelligentsia* (Columbia U.P. 1961). (*Pipes* III)
'The Russian Intelligentsia', *Daedalus* (Summer 1960), pp. 487–502. (*Pipes* IV)
'Max Weber and Russia', *World Politics*, VII (April 1955), pp. 371–401. (*Pipes* V)
Plamenatz J. P., *German Marxism and Russian Communism* (London 1954).
(*Plamenatz*)
(Plehve V. K.), 'Pismo K A. A. Kireyevu', *K.A.* XVIII (1926), pp. 20:–3. (*Plehve*)
Plekhanov G. V., *Dnevnik S. D. G. V. Plekhanova*, nos. 1–16 (Geneva 1905–11).
(*Plekhanov : Dnevnik*)
Sochineniya, vols XI–XII (Moscow-Petrograd 1924). (*Plekhanov : Sochineniya*)
(See also *Gruppa 'Osvobozhdeniye Truda', Perepiska G. V. Plekhanova i P. B.
Akselroda, Vademecum*)
(Pobedonostsev K. P.), 'Iz Chernykh Bumag K. P Pobedonostseva', *K.A.* XVIII
(1926), pp. 203–7. (*Pobedonostsev* I)
Pisma Pobedonostseva K Aleksandru III, vol. I (Moscow 1925). (*Pobedonostsev* II)
K. P. Pobedonostsev i ego Korrespondenty, Novum Regnum, Trudy Gosudarstven-
nogo Rumyantsovskogo Muzeya (Moscow 1923),
vyp. II, tom. I, polutom 1-y, vol. I, (*Pobedonostsev* III)
vyp. III, tom. I, polutom 2-y, vol. II. (*Pobedonostsev* IV)
(See also Witte S. Yu: *Perepiska S. Yu. Witte i K. P. Pobedonostseva*)
Pogromy v Rossii po Ofitsyalnym Dokumentam (Berlin 1908).
Pokrovskiy M. N., *Russkaya Istoriya v Samon Szhatom Ocherke* (Moscow 1920).
(*Pokrovskiy* I)
(ed.), *1905g. Istoriya Revolyutsionnogo Dvizheniya V Otdelnykh Ocherkakh*, 3 vols
(Moscow-Leningrad 1925–7). (*Pokrovskiy* II)
Polner T. I., *Obshchezemskaya Organizatsiya na Dalnem Vostoke* (Moscow 1908).
(*Polner* I)
Zhiznenyy Put Kn. Lvova (Paris 1932). (*Polner* II)
(Polovtsev A. A.), 'Dnevnik', *K.A.*,
vol. III (1923), pp. 76–172, (*Polovtsev* I)
vol. IV (1923), pp. 63–128, (*Polovtsev* II)
vol. XLVI (1931), pp. 110–32. (*Polovtsev* III)
Portal R., 'The Industrialisation of Russia', *The Cambridge Economic History of
Europe*, vol. VI, part II, ch IX. (*Portal*)
'Portsmut', *K.A.* (1924),
vol. VI, pp. 3–27, (*Portsmut* I)
vol. VII, pp. 3–31. (*Portsmut* II)
Posle Voyny, Voyenno-Obshchestvennyy Sbornik (Spb 1906, 1907).
(Potresov A. N.), *Posmertnyy Sbornik Proizvedeniy* (Paris 1937). (*Potresov*)
Potresov A. N., *Etyudy o Russkoy Intelligentsii* (Spb 1906). (*Potresov* I)
'Evolyutsiya Obshchestvenno-Politicheskoy Mysli v Predrevolyutsionnuyu
Epokhu', *O.D.* vol. I, pp. 538–640. (*Potresov* II)
Potresov A. N., i Nikolayevski B. I., *S.D. Dvizheniye v Rossii, Materialy* (Moscow
1928). (*Potresov* III)

303

Bibliography

Pozner S. M., *1905g. Boyevaya Gruppa pri Ts.K.R.S.D.R.P.* (*b*) (Moscow-Leningrad 1927). (*Pozner*)

Presnyakov A. E., '1905-y god', *Byloye*, no. 4(32) (1925), pp. 3–35. (*Presnyakov*)

Programa Periodicheskogo Organa S.R.S.D. '*Rabocheye Delo*' (Geneva 1899).

Programy Partiy (Spb 1906).

(Prokopovich S. N.), 'Otvet na Broshuru Akselroda: "K Voprosu o Sovremennykh Zadachach" ', *Vademecum*, pp. 37–60. (*Prokopovich*)

'Pismo K Kopelzonu'. In I. Tatarov, 'Materialy K istorii Pervogo syezda', *P.R.* no. 3(74) (1928), pp. 163–4. (*Prokopovich Ia*)

Prokopovich S. N., 'Agrarnoye Dvizheniye Osenyu 1905g', *Bez-Zaglaviya*, no. 7, pp. 256–64. (*Prokopovich Ib*)

Agraranyy Vopros i Agrarnoye Dvizheniye (Rostov N/Donu 1905).

                                            (*Prokopovich II*)

'Dekabrskoye Vostaniye', *Bez-Zaglaviya*,

    no. 2, pp. 51–9, (*Prokopovich III*)

    no. 3, pp. 97–106. (*Prokopovich IV*)

'Formy i Rezultaty Agrarnogo Dvizheniya v 1906g', *Byloye*, no. 1 (1907), pp. 155–77. (*Prokopovich V*)

K Rabochemu Voprosu v Rossii (Spb 1905). (*Prokopovich VI*)

Kooperativnoye Dvizheniye v Rossii (Moscow 1913). (*Prokopovich VII*)

Mestnyye Lyudi o Nuzhdakh Rossii (Spb 1904). (*Prokopovich VIII*)

'Oktyabrskaya Zabastovka', *Bez-Zaglaviya*, no. 1, pp. 17–27. (*Prokopovich IX*)

'Organizatsiya Rabochikh Partiy', ibid. no. 12, pp. 482–92. (*Prokopovich X*)

Rabocheye Dvizheniye na Zapade (Spb 1899). (*Prokopovich XI*)

Sbornik Statey (Paris 1956). (*Prokopovich XII*)

Soyuzy Rabochikh i Ikh Zadachi (Spb 1905). (*Prokopovich XIII*)

Proletaryat v Revolyutsii 1905–1907gg. Komunisticheskaya Akademiya, (Moscow–Leningrad 1930).

Protokoly Pervogo Syezda Partii S.R. (Paris 1906). (*Protokoly I*)

Protokoly Pervogo Syezda Partii S.R., Dobavleniye (Moscow 1906). (*Protokoly II*)

Protopopov D., *Ocherk Deyatelnosti Spb. Gorodskoy Gruppy Partii Narodnoy Svobody* (Spb 1908). (*Protopopov*)

Protses Soveta R. D. (Spb 1906).

'Proyekt Manifesta o Sobytiyakh 9-go Yanvarya', *K.A.* vol. XI/XII (1925), pp. 27–37.

Putnam G., 'P. B. Struve's View of the Russian Revolution of 1905', *The Slavonic and East European Review*, XLV (1967), pp. 457–73. (*Putnam*)

Pyatnitskiy I. A., *Vospominaniya 1896–1917* (Leningrad 1925–6). (*Pyatnitskiy*)

Pyontkovskiy S., 'Novoye o Zubatovshchine', *K.A.* I (1922), pp. 289–314. (*Pyontkovskiy I*)

'Zubatovshchina i Sotsial-demokratiya. Arkhivnyye Materialy', *K.i.S.* no. 8 (1924), pp. 66–100. (*Pyontkovskiy II*)

Rabochiy Vospros v Komissii V. M. Kokovtseva v 1905g, ed. Romanov B. A. (Moscow 1926).

Bibliography

Rabochiy Yezhegodnik, kn. 1 (Spb 1906).

Radin B., *Pervyy Sovet R.D.* (Spb 1906).   (*Radin*)

Radishchev A. N., *Puteshestviye iz Peterburga v Morevu* (Moscow 1961).
    (*Radishchev*)

Radkey O. H., 'Chernov and Agrarian Populism Before 1918': in *Simmons*, pp. 63–80.   (*Radkey* I)

The Agrarian Foes of Bolshevism (N.Y. 1958).   (*Radkey* II)

The Sickle Under the Hammer (N.Y. 1963).   (*Radkey* III)

Raeff M., *Michael Speransky* (The Hague 1957).   (*Raeff* I)

Origins of the Russian Intelligentsia. The Eighteenth-Century Nobility (N.Y. 1960).
    (*Raeff* II)

(ed.), *Plans for Political Reform in Imperial Russia. 1730–1905* (N.Y. 1966).
    (*Raeff* III)

The Decembrist Movement (N.Y. 1966).   (*Raeff* IV)

Rashin A. G., *Formirovaniye Rabochego Klassa v Rossii* (Moscow 1958).   (*Rashin* I)

Naseleniye Rossii Za Sto Let, 1811–1913 (Moscow 1957).   (*Rashin* II)

(Ratayev L.), 'Yevno Azef (Istoriya yego predatelstva. Delo Plehve)', *Byloye*, no. 2(24) (1917), pp. 191–210.   (*Ratayev*)

(Rediger A. F.) Zapiski A. F., 'Redigera', *K.A.*

    XLV (1931), pp. 86–111,   (*Rediger* I)

    LX (1933), pp. 92–133.   (*Rediger* II)

Revolyutsionnaya Molodezh v Peterburge, 1897–1917 (Leningrad 1926).

Revolyutsiya 1905g i Samoderzhaviye, Podgotovil k Pechati V. P. Semennikov (Moscow-Leningrad 1928).

Robinson G. T., *Rural Russia Under the Old Regime* (N.Y 1932).   (*Robinson*)

Rodichev F. I., 'Avtobiografiya', *Vozrozhdeniye*, no. 31 (Paris 1954).   (*Rodichev* I)

'Iz Vospominaniy', *Posledniye Novosti* (Paris 10 May 1931).   (*Rodichev* II)

'The Liberal Movement in Russia', *The Slavonic and East European Review*, II (1923/4), pp. 1–13, 249–62.   (*Rodichev* III)

'The Veteran of Russian Liberalism: Ivan Petrunkevich', ibid. VII (1928/29), pp. 317–26.   (*Rodichev* IV)

Romanov B. A., 'K Kharakteristike Gapona', *K.L.* no. 2(13) (1925), pp. 37–40
    (*B. A. Romanov* I)

Rossiya v Manchzhurii 1892–1906 (Leningrad 1928).   (*B. A. Romanov* II)

(Romanov K. K.), 'Dnevnik', *K.A.* (1931),

    XLIII, pp. 92–115,   (*K. K. Romanov* I)

    XLIV, pp. 126–51,   (*K. K. Romanov* II)

    XLV, pp. 112–29.   (*K. K. Romanov* III)

Rossiya i Yevrei, Otechestvennoye Obyedineniye Russkikh Yevreyev Zagranitsey (Berlin 1924).

Rozenberg V. A., *Iz Istorii Russkoy Pechati* (Praga 1924).   (*Rozenberg* I)

Rozenberg V. A., i Yakushkin V. E., *Russkaya Pechat i Tsensura* (Moscow 1905).
    (*Rozenberg* II)

Bibliography

Rozenblyum K. I., *O Pervoy Rossiyskoy Revolyutsii 1905g* (Leningrad 1930).
(*Rozenblyum* I)
Voyennyye Organizatsii Bolshevikov 1905–1907gg (Moscow-Leningrad 1931).
(*Rozenblyum* II)
Rozhkov N. A., *Ocherk Istorii Truda v Rossii* (Moscow-Leningrad 1924).
(*Rozhkov* I–II)
O Formakh Narodnogo Predstavitelstva (Spb 1905). (*Rozhkov* III)
Proiskhozhdeniye Samoderzhaviya v Rossii (Moscow 1906). (*Rozhkov* IV)
Russkaya Istoriya v Sravnitelno-Istoricheskom Osveshchenii (Moscow-Leningrad
1925). (*Rozhkov* V)
Rudnev V. V., *Gorky – Revolyutsioner* (Moscow-Leningrad 1929). (*Rudnev* I)
Krestyanskoye Dvizheniye v Nachale XX Veka (Moscow 1929). (*Rudnev* II)
Rumyantsev P., *Osvoboditelnoye Dvizheniye i Gosudarstvennaya Duma* (Spb 1906).
(*Rumyantsev*)
Russian Revolutionary Tracts (Geneva 1901–3).
Russian Tracts (Geneva 1900–3).
Russkaya Intelligentsiya i Krestyanstvo (Moscow 1904).
Russkiya Politicheskiya Partii (Tver 1907).
Russkiya Vedomosti, 1863–1913. Sbornik Statey (Moscow 1913).
'Russko-Germanskiy Dogovor 1905g, Zaklyuchennyy v Bjorko', *K.A.* V (1924), pp.
5–49.
Russko-Yaponskaya Voyna, Izd. Tsentrarkhiva (Leningrad 1925).
Russo-Finnish Conflict. The Russian Case (London 1910).
Rutenberg P., 'Delo Gapona', *Byloye*, no. 11/12 (1909), pp. 29–115. (*Rutenberg* I)
ibid. no. 2 (1917), pp. 6–67 [first part of ibid.]. (*Rutenberg* II)
Ubiystvo Gapona (Leningrad 1925). (*Rutenberg* III)
Ryazanov A. I., 'Vospominaniya'. In Mitskevich S. I. *Na Zare Rabochego Dvizhen-
iya v Moskve*, pp. 124–39. (*A. Ryazanov*)
Ryazanov N. (Goldenbakh D. B). *G. V. Plekhanov i Gruppa 'Osvoboghdeniye
Truda'*, 3-ye izd (Petrograd 1918). (*N. Ryazanov*)
Ryechi Po Pogromnym Delam (Kiyev 1908).
S.A. Muromtsev. Sbornik Statey (Moscow 1911). (*S.A.*)
S.K.D. (see *K*(*irpichnikov*) S. D.).
Sadikov P. A., 'Obshchestvo "Svyashchennoy Druzhiny" ', *K.A.* XXI (1927), pp.
200–17. (*Sadikov*)
Samoderzhaviye i Zemstvo, Konfidentsialnaya Zapiska, Ministra Finansov S Pred-
isloviyen P. B. Struve (Stuttgart 1901). (*Samoderzhaviye i Zemstvo* I)
ibid. 2nd edn (Stuttgart 1903). (*Samoderzhaviye i Zemstvo* II)
Samoylov F. N., *Vospominaniya*, chast I (Moscow 1922). (*Samoylov*)
Sankt-Peterburgskiy Politekhnicheskiy Institut, Sbornik no. 2 (Paris-N.Y. 1958).
Sankt-Peterburgskiy Politekhnicheskiy Institut, Yubileynyy Sbornik (Paris 1952).
Sarolea C., *The French Revolution and the Russian Revolution* (Edinburgh 1906).
(*Sarolea*)

Bibliography

Savelyev A. A., 'Na Zare Osvoboditelnogo Dvizheniya', *Golos Miruvshago*, no. 1 (1914), pp. 159–80. *(Savelyev)*

Savich G. G., *Novyy Gosudarstvennyy Stroy Rossii* (Spb 1907). *(Savich)*

Savinkov B., *Memoirs of a Terrorist* (N.Y. 1931). *(Savinkov)*

Schapiro L. B., *Rationalism and Nationalism in Russian Nineteenth Century Political Thought* (Yale U.P. 1967). *(Schapiro)*

The Communist Party of the Soviet Union (London 1966). *(Schapiro I)*

'The Pre-revolutionary Intelligentsia and the Legal Order'. In Pipes R. (ed.), *The Russian Intelligentsia*, pp. 19–30. *(Schapiro II)*

'The Role of the Jews in the Russian Revolutionary Movement', *Slavonic and East European Review*, XL (1961), pp. 148–67. *(Schapiro III)*

'The Vekhi Group and the Mystique of Revolution', ibid. XXXIV (1955), pp. 56–76. *(Schapiro IV)*

Schwartz S. M., 'Populism and Early Russian Marxism on Ways of Economic Development of Russia'. In *Simmons*, pp. 40–62. *(Schwartz)*

The Russian Revolution of 1905 (University of Chicago Press 1967). *(Schwartz I)*

Sef S. E., *Burzhuaziya v 1905g* (Moscow 1922). *(Sef)*

Semennikov V. P., *Revolyutsiya 1905g i Samoderzhaviye* (Moscow 1928). *(Semennikov)*

Semenov E. P., *The Russian Government and the Massacres* (London 1907). *(Semenov)*

Sementkovskiy R. I., *Sovremennaya Rossiya v Dni Revolyutsii* (Spb 1911). *(Sementkovskiy)*

Semevskiy V. I., Dolgorukov P. D. (Prince), i Tolstoy S. L., *Krestyanskiy Vopros v Rossii* (Spb 1905). *(Semevskiy)*

Seton-Watson H., *The Russian Empire 1801–1917* (Oxford 1967). *(Seton-Watson)*

(Shakhovskoy D. I.), 'Mirnyy', *Addresy Zemstv 1894–1895 i ikh Politicheskaya Programa* (Geneva 1896). *(Shakhovskoy)*

Shakhovskoy D. I. (Prince), 'Avtobiografiya'. In *Russkiya Vedomosti 1863–1913. Sbornik*, part II, pp. 196–200. *(Shakhovskoy I)*

'Politicheskiya Techeniya v Russkom Zemstve'. In *Yubileynyy Sbornik*, pp. 437–67. *(Shakhovskoy II)*

'Rabota v Zemstve', *S.A.* pp. 180–204. *(Shakhovskoy III)*

'Soyuz Osvobozhdeniya'. *Zarnitsy. Literaturno-Politicheskiy Sbornik*, no. 2, part II (Spb 1909), pp. 81–171. *(Shakhovskoy IV)*

Shcheglov V. G., *Gosudarstvennyy Sovet v Rossii* (Moscow 1904). *(Shcheglov)*

Shchegolev P. E., *Okhranniki i Avantyuristy* (Moscow 1930). *(Shchegolev)*

Shchepkin N. N., *Zemskaya i Gorodskaya Rossiya o Narodnom Predstavitelstve* (Rostov N/Donu 1907). *(Shchepkin)*

Shebalov A. V., 'Gr. S. Yu. Witte i Nikolay II', *Byloye*, no. 4 (32) (1925), p. 107. *(Shebalov)*

(Shebeko V. N.), 'Doklady Tsaryu. Vilgelm II o Russko-Yaponskoy Voyne', *K. A.* IX (1925), pp. 56–65. *(Shebeko)*

Bibliography

Shebunin A., 'Graf Witte i Russkoye Samoderzhaviye', *K.L.* no. 7 (1923), pp. 178–98. *(Shebunin)*

Shestakov A. V., *Krestyanskaya Revolyutsiya 1905–1907gg v Rossii* (Moscow 1926). *(Shestakov)*

Shidlovskiy S. I., *Vospominaniya 1861–1922* (Berlin 1923). *(Shidlovskiy)*

Shilov A., 'K Dokumentalnoy Istorii Petitsii 9-go Yanvarya 1905g', *K.L.* no. 2(13) (1925), pp. 19–36. *(Shilov)*

Shipov D. N., *K Mneniyu Menshistva* (Moscow 1905). *(Shipov I)*

Vospominaniya i Dumy o Perezhitom (Moscow 1918). *(Shipov II)*

Shtiglits A. N., *Narod i Vlast v Rossii Po Ucheniyu Slavyanofilov* (Spb 1907). *(Shtiglits)*

Shub D., *Lenin* (N.Y. 1948). *(Shub)*

Shulgin V. V., *Dni* (*Vospominaniya*) (Belgrad 1925). *(Shulgin)*

Simbirskiy N., *Pravda o Gapone i 9-om Yanvare* (Spb 1906). *(Simbirskiy)*

Simmons E. J. (ed.), *Continuity and Change in Russian and Soviet Thought* (Harvard U.P. 1955). *(Simmons)*

Sivkov K. V., 'Gorodskaya Burzhuaziya 10 let Tomu Nazad', *Golos Minuvshago*, no. 12 (1915), pp. 76–106. *(Sivkov)*

Sizov M. I., 'Moi Vstrechi s Gaponom', *Istoricheskiy Vestnik*, vol. 127 (1912), pp. 543–82. *(Sizov)*

Slepkov A., *Revolyutsiya 1905–1907gg.* (Moscow-Leningrad 1925). *(Slepkov)*

(Smelskiy V. N.), 'Svyashchennaya Druzhina (Iz dnevnika yeya Chlena)', *Golos Minuvshago*, nos. 1–5/6 (1916). *(Smelskiy I–V)*

Smirnov V. M., 'Revolyutsionnaya Rabota v Finlandii', *P.R.* no. 1(48) (1926), pp. 119–57. *(Smirnov)*

Sobraniye Polnoye Podrobnykh Program Russkikh i Polskikh Partiy (Vilna 1906).

Sokolov N., *Ubiystvo Tsarskoy Semyi* (Berlin 1925). *(Sokolov)*

Soldaty i Matrosy v Pervoy Revolyutsii. O-vo Byvshikh Politkatorzhan (Moscow 1929).

Somov S. I. (Peskin), 'Iz Istorii S. D. Dvizheniya v Peterburge v 1905 g (Po Lichnym Vospominaniyam)', *Byloye* (1907),

no. 4, pp. 22–55, *(Somov I)*

no. 5, pp. 152–78. *(Somov II)*

Sotsial-Revolyutsionnaya Partiya – A Manifesto (Spb 1906).

Sotsial-Revolyutsionnaya Partiya – Political Tracts (various places 1902–14).

Spector I., *The First Russian Revolution. Its Impact on Asia* (N.Y. 1962). *(Spector)*

Speransky M. M., *Proyekty i Zapiski* (Moscow-Leningrad 1961). *(Speransky)*

Spiridovich A. I., *Zapiski Zhandarma* (Kharkov 1926). *(Spiridovich)*

Sputnik Izbiratelya na 1906g (Spb 1906). *(Sputnik)*

Staryy Zhurnalist (Orsher O. L.), *Literaturnyy put do Revolyutsionnogo Zhurnalista* (Moscow-Leningrad 1930).

Stasova E. D., *Stranitsy Zhizni i Borby* (Moscow 1960). *(Stasova)*

Stepnyak (S. M. Kravchinskiy), *Nihilism as it is* (London 1895). *(Stepnyak)*

Bibliography

(Stolypin P. A.), 'K Istorii Agrarnoy Reformy Stolyṛina. Vṣepodanṇeyshiy Otchet
Saratovskogo Gubernatora P. Stolypina za 1904ʂ', *K.A* xvii (1926), pp. 81–8.
(Stolypin)
Strelskiy P., *Novaya Sekta V Ryadakh Sotsialistov* (Moscow 1907). *(Strelskiy* i)
Partii i Revolyutsiya 1905g (Spb 1906). *(Strelskiy* ii)
(Struve P. B.), *Manifest RSDRP* (Geneva 1903). *(Struve)*
'Otkrytoye Pismo Nikolayu II', *Za Sto Let*, pp. 264–7. *(Struve* i)
Struve P. B., 'M. V. Chelnokov i D. N. Shipov, Glava iz Moikh Vospominaniy',
Novy Zhurnal, xxii (1949) pp. 240–5. *(Struve* ii)
Kishinevskiy Pogrom (Stuttgart 1903). *(Struve* iii)
Kriticheskiye Zametki k Voprosu ob Ekonomicheskom. Razvitii Rcssii (Spb 1894).
(Struve iv)
'My Contacts and Conflicts with Lenin', *Slavoṛic and East European Review*,
xii (1933/4), pp. 573–95, *(Struve* v)
xiii (1934/5), pp. 66–84. *(Struve* vi)
'My Contacts with Rodichev', ibid. xii (1933/ᴢ), pp. 347–67. *(Struve* vii)
Na Raznyya Temy (Spb 1902). *(Struve* viii)
*Patriotka. Politika, Kultura, Religiya, Sotsialisṃa. Sborṇik Statṛy Za Pyat Let
(1905–1910)* (Spb 1911). *(Struve* ix)
(See also *Listok Osvobozhdeniya, Osvobbozhdeṇiye, Sṃmoderzḷaviye i Zemstvo*)
(Suvorin A. S.), *Dnevnik A. S. Suvorina* (Moscᴢw-Petrograd 1923). *(Suvorin)*
Svatikov S. G., *Sozyv Narodnykh Predstavitẹley* (Rostov N/Donu 1905).
(Svatikov)
Sverchkov D. F., *Kerenskiy*, 2nd edn (Leningrad 1927ᵔ. *(Sverchkov* i)
Na Zare Revlyutsii, 3rd edn (Leningrad 192ʂᵔ. *(Sverchkov* ii)
G. S. Nosar-Kirustalev (Leningrad 1925). *(Sverchkov* iii)
'Soyuz Soyuzov', *K.L.* no. 3 (1925), pp. 14ᴄ–62. *(Sverchkov* iv)
'Spb Sovet R. D. Po Dannyam Okhrannogᴢ Otdeleniya', *Byloye*, no. 8 (1908),
pp. 40–4. *(Sverchkov* v)
Svyatlovskiy V. V., 'Na Zare Rossiyskoy S. D Epokhṣ Kruzhḳovskchiny i Gruppa
Brusneva', *Byloye*, no. 19 (1922), pp. 13ᴄ–60. *(Svyatlovskiy* i)
Professionalnoye Dvizheniye v Rossii (Spb 1907). *(Svyatlovskiy* ii)
Professionalnyye Rabochiye Soyuzy, 3e izd. (Spb 1908). *(Svyatlovskiy* iii)
*Sovremennoye Zakonodatelstvo o Professionainykh
Rabochikh Soyuzakh* (Spb 1907). *(Svyatlovskiy* iv)
*Ukazatel Literatury po Professionalnomu Rabochemᴣ
Dvizheniyu* (Spb 1907). *(Svyatlovskiy* v)
'Syezd Krestyanskogo Soyuza v Moskve', *Byloye*, no. 7 (1908), pp. 111–12.
Tagantsev N. S., *Perezhitoye* (Petrograd 1919). *(Tagantsev)*
Takhotsky L. (see Trotsky L.).
Takhtarev K. M. (see Peterburzhets).
Takhtarev N., 'Lenin i S. D. Dvizheniye', *Byloye*, no. 24 (1924), pp. 3–28.
(Takhtarev)

Bibliography

Tidmarsh K., 'The Zubatov Idea', *American Slavic and East European Review*, XIX (1960), pp. 335–46. *(Tidmarsh)*

(Tikhomirov L.), '25 Let Nazad. Iz Dnevnika L. Tikhomirova', *K.A.* (1930),
vol. XXXVIII, pp. 20–69, *(Tikhomirov I)*
vol. XXXIX, pp. 47–75, *(Tikhomirov II)*
vol. XL, pp. 59–96, *(Tikhomirov III)*
vol. XLI/XLII, pp. 103–47. *(Tikhomirov IV)*

'Znacheniye 19-go Fevralya 1902g. Dlya Moskovskikh Rabochikh i Proyekt Ustava Obshchestva Rabochikh Mekhanicheskogo Proizvodstva goroda Moskvy', *Byloye*, no. 14 (1912), pp. 81–91. *(Tikhomirov V)*

Tikhonov T. I., *Yevreyskiy Vopros v Rossii i v Sibirii* (Spb 1906). *(Tikhonov I)*

Zemstvo v Rossii i Na Okrainakh (Spb 1907). *(Tikhonov II)*

Timonich A. A., *Russkiye Satiro-Yumoristicheskiye Zhurnaly 1905–1907gg* (Moscow 1930). *(Timonich)*

Totomyants V., 'Zhurnal "Nachalo" i Provokator Gurevich', *Novyy Zhurnal*, XLIII (1955), pp. 264–6. *(Totomyants)*

Treadgold D. W., 'The Constitutional Democrats and the Russian Liberal Tradition', *The American Slavic and East European Review*, X (1951), pp. 85–94. *(Treadgold I)*

Lenin and His Rivals: The Struggle for Russia's Future, 1898–1906 (London 1955). *(Treadgold II)*

(Trepov D. F.), 'Iz Bumag D. F. Trepova v 1905g. Iz Zapisnoy Knizhki Arkhivista', *K.A.* XI/XII (1925), pp. 448–66. *(Trepov I)*

'K Istorii Manifesta 17-go Oktyabrya', *Byloye*, no. 14, (1919), pp. 108–11. *(Trepov II)*

(Trotsky L.), Takhotsky L., *Gospodin P. Struve v Politike*, (Spb 1906). *(Trotsky)*

Trotsky L. D., 'Avtobiograficheskaya Zametka', *P.R.* no. 3 (1921), pp. 244–9.
(Trotsky I)

Itogi i Perspektivy (Dvizhushchiye Sily Revolyutsii) (Moscow, 1919). *(Trotsky II)*

Moya Zhizn, Opyt Avtobiografii, vol. I (Berlin 1930). *(Trotsky III)*

Nasha Revolyutsiya (Spb 1907). *(Trotsky IV)*

Sochineniya, vol. I (Moscow-Leningrad 1926). *(Trotsky V)*

1905g, 3rd edn (Moscow-Leningrad 1925). *(Trotsky VI)*

Trubetskaya O. N., *Kn. S. N. Trubetskoy. Vospominaniya Sestry* (N.Y. 1953). *(Trubetskaya)*

Trubetskoy E. (Prince), *Dva Zverya* (Moscow 1918). *(E. Trubetskoy)*

(Trubetskoy S. N. (Prince)), *Kn. S. N. Trubetskoy. Pervyy Borets za Pravdu i Svobody Russkogo Naroda. V Otzyvakh* (Spb 1905). *(S. Trubetskoy)*

Trudy Pervogo Vserossiyskogo Zhenskogo Syezda, 10–16. XII. 1908 (Spb 1909).

'Tsarskiy Listok', *Byloye*, no. 7 (1908), pp. 95–103.

Tsederbaum S., 'Po Povodu Statyi S. I. Somova', ibid. no. 9 (1907), pp. 296–8. *(S. Tsederbaum)*

Bibliography

Tsederbaum V. O. (Levitskiy), *Za Chetvert Veka* (*1892–1917*), vol. I, parts I–II (Moscow-Leningrad 1926, 1927). (*V. Tsederbaum*)

Tuck R. L., 'Paul Milyukov and Negotiations for a Duma Ministry, 1906', *The American Slavic and East European Review*, x (1951), pp. 117–29. (*Tuck*)

Turninskiy M., 'Kak My Isdavali Gazetu', *Istoricheskiy Vestnik*, vol. 115 (1909), pp. 206–21. (*Turninskiy*)

Tyrkova (Williams) A. V., *Anna Pavlovna Filozofova i Yeya Vremya, Sbornik Pamyati A. P. Filosofovoy*, vol. I (Petrograd 1915). (*Tyrkova* I)

Na Putyakh K Svobode (N.Y. 1952). (*Tyrkova* II)

'Pervyy Zhenskiy Syezd', *Zarnitsky*, no. 2, part II (1906), pp. 172–209.
(*Tyrkova* III)

'F. I. Rodichev (1854–1933)', *Novyy Zhurnal*, xxxviii (1954), pp. 207–23.
(*Tyrkova* IV)

'Russian Liberalism', *The Russian Review*, x (1951), pp. 3–14. (*Tyrkova* V)

1905g Armiya v Pervoy Revolyutsii (Moscow-Leningrad 1927).

1905g Bolshevitskiye Proklamatsii i Listovki (Moscow-Leningrad 1926).

1905g v Ocherkakh i Vospominaniyakh. Sbornik Zhurnala Katorga i Ssylka (Moscow 1927).

1905g v Peterburge (Moscow-Leningrad 1925).

Universitet i Politika (Spb 1906).

Urusov S. D. (Prince), *Zapiski Gubernatora: Kishinev 1903–1904* (Berlin 1907).
(*Urusov*)

(Ushakov), 'Vospominaniya. Iz Zapisnoy Knizhki Arkhivista. K Istorii Manifesta 17-go Oktyabrya', *K.A.* IV (1923), pp. 411–17. (*Ushakov*)

Vademecum (Geneva 1900).

Valentinov N., 'Tragediya G. V. Plekhanova'. *Novyy Zhurnal*, xx (1948), pp. 270–93. (*Valentinov* I)

Vstrechi S Leninym (N.Y. 1953). (*Valentinov* II)

Valk S., 'Peterburgskoye Gradonachalstvo i 9-ye Yanvarya', *K.L.* no. 1 (1922), pp. 37–46. (*Valk*)

(Vannovskiy P. S.), *Doklad Vannovskogo po Povodu Studencheskikh Besporyadkov*. Izd 'Rabochaya Znamen' (Geneva? 1900). (*Vannovskiy* I)

Reforma Generala Vannovskogo, Tipografiya Partii S.R., 2nd edn (Geneva? 1902).
(*Vannovskiy* II)

Varnashev N., 'Ot Nachala do Kontsa s Gaponovskoy Organizatsiyey', *Istoriko-Revolyutsionnyy Sbornik*, vol. I, pp. 177–208. (*Varnashev*)

Varshavskiy S., *Zhizn i Trudy Pervoy Gosudarstvennoy Dumy* (Moscow 1907).
(*Varshavskiy*)

Vasilev A. I., *The Okhrana* (London 1930). (*Vasilev*)

Vasilyev A. A., i Kudryavtsev V. A., *Krestyanskiye Nakazy Samarskoy Gubernii* (Samara 1906). (*Vasilyev*)

Vasilyev-Yuzhin M. I., *Moskovskiy S.R.D. v 1905g* (Moscow 1925).
(*Vasilyev-Yuzhin* I)

311

Bibliography

V Ogne Pervoy Revolyutsii (Moscow 1955).   (*Vasilyev-Yuzhin* II)
Vekhi. Sbornik Statey o Russkoy Intelligentsii, 2nd edn (Moscow 1909).   (*Vekhi*)
Velikhov L., *Sravnitelnaya Tablitsa Russkikh Politicheskikh Partiy* (Spb 1906).
        (*Velikhov*)
Venturi F., *Roots of Revolution* (London 1960).   (*Venturi*)
Vernadskiy G. V., *A History of Russia*, 4th edn (Yale U.P. 1954).   (*Vernadskiy*)
Veselovskiy B. B., 'Detsentralisatsiya Upravleniya i Zadachi Zemstva'. In *Yubileynyy*
  Sbornik, pp. 35–49.   (*Veselovskiy* II)
Dvizheniye Zemlevladeltsev. In *O.D.*
    vol. I, pp 291–312,   (*Veselovskiy* III)
    vol. II, part II, pp. 1–29.   (*Veselovskiy* IV)
    Istoriya Zemstva, vols I–IV:
    vols I–II (Spb 1909),   (*Veselovskiy* Va–b)
    vol. III (Spb 1911),   (*Veselovskiy* VI)
    vol. IV (Spb 1911).   (*Veselovskiy* VII)
Krestyanskiy Vopros i Krestyanskoye Dvizheniye v Rossii (Spb 1907).
        (*Veselovskiy* VIII)
Vetlugin G., 'S. Yu. Witte i Dekabrskoye Vostaniye v Moskve', *Byloye*, no. 6(34)
  (1925), pp. 225–6.   (*Vetlugin*)
Vinaver M. M., *Kadety i Yevreyskiy Vopros* (Spb 1907).   (*Vinaver* I)
Konflikty v Pervoy Dume (Spb 1907).   (*Vinaver* II)
Nedavnoye-Vospominaniya (Paris 1928).   (*Vinaver* III)
Vinogradov P., 'Thoughts and Reminiscences of D. N. Shipov', *Slavonic and East*
  European Review, II (1923/4), pp. 641–4.   (*Vinogradov*)
Vinokurov A., 'O Vozniknovenii Moskovskoy Partiynoy Organizatsii'. In Mitske-
  vich S.I., *Na Zare Rabochego Dvizheniya v Moskve*, pp. 29–39.   (*Vinokurov*)
Vishnyak M. V., *Dan proshlomu* (N.Y. 1954).   (*Vishnyak* I)
Sovremmennyya Zapiski. Vospominaniya Redaktora (Ind. U.P. 1957). (*Vishnyak* II)
Uchreditelnoye Sobraniye (Paris 1932).   (*Vishnyak* III)
Vodovozov V. V., *Kak Proizoshli Vybory v Gosudarstvennuyu Dumu Po Zakonu*
  3.VI.1907 (Spb 1907).   (*Vodovozov* I)
Proportsionalnyye Vybory Ili Predstavitelstvo
  Menshistva (Spb 1905).   (*Vodovozov* II)
Sbornik Program Politicheskikh Partiy v Rossii
  (Spb 1905–6), vyp. 1–5.   (*Vodovozov* III–VII)
Volkovicher I., 'Partiya i Russko-Yaponskaya Voyna', *P.R.* no. 12(35) (1924), pp.
  113–23.   (*Volkovicher*)
Von Laue T. H., 'Count Witte and the Russian Revolution of 1905,' *American*
  Slavic and East European Review, XVIII (1958), pp. 25–46.   (*Von Laue* I)
'The Fate of Capitalism in Russia. The Narodnik Version', ibid. XIII (1954), pp.
  11–28.   (*Von Laue* II)
Sergius Witte and the Industrialization of Russia (Columbia U.P. 1963).
        (*Von Laue* III)

Bibliography

Von Stein F., 'Khodinskaya Katastrofa', *Istoricheski y vestnik*, vol. 118 (1909), pp.
473–506.   (*Von Stein* I)
'Neudachnnyy Opyt', ibid. vol. 129 (1912), pp. 223–55.   (*Von Stein* II)
'Osvoboditelnoye Dvizheniye', ibid. vol. 134 (1913), pp. 1064–87.
                                                                           (*Von Stein* III)
Voprosy Gosudarstvennogo Khozyaystva i Byudzhetnogo Prava, Izd. Petrunkevicha
   i Dolgorukova (Spb 1907).
Voprosy Momenta (Moscow 1906).
Voytinskiy Vl., 'Gody Pobed i Porazheniy. Kn. 1-ya, 1905-yy god', *Letopis Revolyut-
sii*, vol. II, no. 8 (Berlin 1923).   (*Voytinskiy*)
Vserossiyskiy Ofitserskiy Soyuz (Spb 1907).
Vtoroy Delegatskiy Syezd K. D. Partii (Spb 1906).
Vtoroy Syezd Zemskikh Deyateley, 6–9, Noyabrya 1904g (Spb 1905).
(Vuich E. I.), 'Doklady Vuicha Ministru Yustitsii', *K.A.* LXVIII (1935), pp. 39–64.
                                                                           (*E. Vuich*)
(Vuich N. I.), 'Zapiska k Istorii Manifesta 17-go Oktyabrya', *A.R.F.* vol. II, pp. 5–8.
                                                                           (*N. Vuich*)
*Vysochayshe Utverzhdennoye 3 June, 1906, Polozheniye o Vyborakh v Gosudarstven-
nuyu Dumu* (Spb 1907).
Vysochayshiy Manifest 11 Augusta 1904g. (Spb 1904).
Walkin J., 'The Attitude of the Tsarist Government Towards the Labour Problem',
   American Slavic and East European Review, XIII (1954), pp. 163–87. (*Walkin* I)
The Rise of Democracy in Pre-Revolutionary Russia (London 1963).   (*Walkin* II)
Weber Max, 'Zur Lage der Burgerlichen Demokratie in Russland', *Archiv für
   Sozialwissenschaft und Sozialpolitik*, XXII (neue folge IV) (1906), pp. 234–353.
                                                                           (*Weber*)
Weeks A. L., *The First Bolshevik, A Political Biography of Peter Tkachev* (N.Y.
   U.P. 1968).   (*Weeks*)
Wesselitsky G. de, 'The Russian Revolution', *Sociological Papers*, III (1907) pp.
   303–17.   (*Wesselitsky*)
White, J. A., *The Diplomacy of the Russo-Japanese War* (Princeton U.P. 1964).
                                                                           (*White*)
(Witte S. Yu.), 'Iz Arkhiva S. Yu. Witte', *K.A.* XI/XII (1925), pp. 107–43.
                                                                           (*Witte* I)
'Perepiska S. Yu. Witte i A. N. Kuropatkina', *K.A.* XIX (1926), pp. 68–82. (*Witte* II)
'Perepiska S. Yu. Witte i K. P. Pobedonostseva', *K.A.* XXX (1928), pp. 89–116.
                                                                           (*Witte* III)
'Pisma S. Yu. Witte k D. S. Sipyaginu', *K.A.* XVIII (1926), pp. 30–48. (*Witte* IV)
'S. Yu. Witte o Sanovnikakh Nikolaya II, *Byloye*, no. 18 (1922), pp. 164–210.
                                                                           (*Witte* V)
'S. Yu. Witte v Borbe s Revolyutsiyey', *Byloye*, no. 9 (1918), pp. 3–10. (*Witte* VI)
Witte S. Yu., *Po Povodu Neprelozhnosti Zakonov Gosudarstvennoy Zhizni* (Spb 1914).
                                                                           (*Witte* VII)

313

Bibliography

Vospominaniya, vols. I–II (Moscow-Petrograd 1923),
vol. I, (*Witte* VIII)
vol. II. (*Witte* IX)
Vynuzhdennyya Razyasneniya Po Povodu Otcheta General-Adyutanta Kuropatkina o Voyne S Yaponeiyy (Moscow 1911). (*Witte* X)
Zapiska Po Krestyanskomy Delu (Spb 1905). (*Witte* XI)
(See also *Samoderzhaviye i Zemstvo*)
Wolfe B. B., *Strange Communists I Have known* (N.Y. 1965). (*Wolfe* I)
Three Who Made a Revolution (N.Y. 1948). (*Wolfe* II)
Yakovlenko N. N., *Vooruzhennyya Vostaniya v Dekabre* 1905g. (Moscow 1957).
(*Yakovlenko*)
Yakushkin V. E., *Gosudarstvennaya Vlast* (Spb 1906). (*Yakushkin* I)
Yakushkin V.E., i Rozenberg V. A., *Russkaya Pechat i Tsensura* (Moscow 1905).
(*Yakushkin* II)
Yarmolinskiy A., *Road to Revolution* (London 1957). (*Yarmolinskiy*)
Yaroslavskiy E. E. (Gubelman M. I.), 'Dekabrskoye Vostaniye 1905g. In Pokrovskivy
M. N., *1905. Istoriya Revolyutsionnogo Dvizheniya V Odtelnykh Ocherkakh*,
vol. III, part II. (*Yaroslavskiy* I)
Revolyutsionnyy Put Gorkogo (Moscow 1933). (*Yaroslavskiy* II)
Yegorov A. (see *Martov Yu. O.*).
Yelnitskiy A., *Istoriya Rabochego Dvizheniya v Rossii*, 4-ye izd (Moscow 1925).
(*Yelnitskiy*)
Yerman, K. K., 'Borba Bolshevikov Za Demokraticheskuyu Intelligentsiyu v
1905g', *Voprosy Istorii*, no. 2 (1955), pp. 17–31. (*Yerman* I)
'Demokraticheskaya Intelligentsiya Rossii v Revolyutsii 1905–1907gg', ibid. no.
12 (1966), pp. 23–38. (*Yerman* II)
Intelligentsiya v Pervoy Russkoy Revolyutsii (Moscow 1966). (*Yerman* III)
'Vserossiyskaya Pochtovo-Telegrafnaya stachka 1905g', *Istoricheskiye Zapiski*,
vol. 53 (1955), pp. 110–43. (*Yerman* IV)
Yermanskiy A., 'Krupnaya Burzhuaziya do 1905g', *O.D.* vol. I, pp. 313–48.
(*A. Yermanskiy*)
Yermanskiy O. A. (Kogan O. R.), *Iz Perezhitogo* (Moscow-Leningrad 1927).
(*O. Yermanskiy*)
(Yermolov A. S.), 'Zapiska A. S. Yermolova', *K.A.* VIII (1928), pp. 49–69.
(*Yermolov*)
Yevreyskaya Letopis (Petrograd 1923–4).
Yevreyskoye Istorichesko-Etnograficheskoye obshchestvo. Kommissiya Po Isledo-
vaniyu Istorii anti-Yevreyskikh Pogromov v Rossii, 2 vols (Petrograd 1919,
1923).
Yezhov N. M., 'Russkiya Metamorfosy', *Istoricheskiy Vestnik* (1910),
vol. 120, pp. 149–60, 555–71, 906–22, (*Yezhov* I)
vol. 121, pp. 467–79, 875–908. (*Yezhov* II)
Yordanskiy N. I., *Zemskiy Liberalism*, 2-ye izd. (Spb 1906). (*Yordanskiy*)

Bibliography

(*Yubileynyy Sbornik*), Veselovskiy B. B. and Frenkel Z. G. (eds.), *1864–1914, Yubileynyy Zemskiy Sbornik* (Spb 1914).

Yudovskiy V. (ed.), *Nashi Protivniki, Sbornik,* 2 vols (Moscow 1923–9).

(*Yudovskiy* I, II)

Yuvachev I. P., 'Mogila Gapona', *Istoricheskiy Vestnik,* vol. 118 (1909), pp. 206–10.

(*Yuvachev*)

(*Za stol Let*), Burtsev V. L. (ed.) (London 1897).

Zalevskiy K (Turevich S. S.), 'Natsionalnoye Dvizheniye', *O.D.* vol. IV, part II, pp. 149–242. (*Zalevskiy* I)

'Natsionalnyye Partii v Rossii', *O.D.* vol. III, pp. 227–344. (*Zalevskiy* II)

Zarnitsy, Literaturno-Politcheskiy Sbornik, no. 2, parts I–II (Spb 1909). (*Zarnitsy*)

Zaslavskiy D. O., *M. P. Dragomanov* (Moscow 1934). (*Zaslavskiy* I)

'M. P. Dragomanov i Volnoye Slovo', *Byloye,* no. 27/28 (1924), pp. 90–122.

(*Zaslavskiy* II)

Rytsar Chernoy Sotni V. V. Shulgin (Leningrad 1925). (*Zaslavskiy* III)

Vzvolnovannyye Lobotryasy (Moscow 1931). (*Zaslavskiy* IV)

'Vzvolnovannyye Lobotryasy', *Byloye* (1924),

no. 25, pp. 72–91, (*Zaslavskiy* V)

no. 26, pp. 256–82. (*Zaslavskiy* VI)

'S. Zubatov i Manya Vilbushevich', ibid. no. 9 (1918), pp. 99–128.

(*Zaslavskiy* VII)

Zavarzin P. P., *Rabota Taynoy Politisii* (Paris 1924). (*Zavarzin* I)

Zhandarmy i Revolutsiya (Paris 1930). (*Zavarzin* II)

Zayonchkovskiy P. A., *Krizis Samoderzhaviya Na Rubezhe 1870–1880gg.* (Moscow 1964).

(*Zayonchkovskiy*)

Rossiyskoye Samoderzhaviye v Kontse XIX Stoletiya (Moscow 1970).

(*Zayonchkovskiy* I)

Zelikson-Bobrovskaya Ts., *Bolshevitskiye Taynyye Tipografii v Moskve, 1904–1910* (Moscow 1923). (*Zelikson Bobrovskaya* I)

Pervaya Russkaya Revolyutsiya v Peterburge 1905g (Leningrad 1925).

(*Zelikson-Bobrovskaya* II)

Zapiski Ryadovogo Podpolshchika, 2nd edn (Moscow 1924).

(*Zelikson-Bobrovskaya* III)

Zemskiy Syezd 6-go i Sl. Noyabrya 1904g, Kratkiy otchet (Paris 1905).

Zenzinov V., *Iz Zhizni Revolyutsionera* (Paris 1919). (*Zenzinov* I)

Perezhitoye (N.Y. 1953). (*Zenzinov* II)

Zilli V., *La Rivoluzione Russa del 1905. La Formazione dei Parriti Politici (1881–1904)* (Naples 1963). (*Zilli*)

Zilliacus, K., *The Russian Revolutionary Movement* (London 1905). (*Zilliacus*)

(Zubatov S. V.), 'Pisma', *K.A.* XIX (1926), pp. 210–11. (*Zubatov* I)

'Pisma Zubatova Burtsevu', *Byloye,* no. 17 (1912), pp. 74–80. (*Zubatov* II)

'Zubatovshchina', ibid. no. 4 (1917), pp. 157–78. (*Zubatov* III)

Index

Index

Index

Index

Index

Index

mony' theory 69–70, 79, 95, 98, 102, 104–5; *Iskra* and *Zarya* 101, 104; Liberation of Labour 29–30; Marxist 73, 74, 76–8, 80, 84, 85, 98; personal vendettas 80–2, 92, 93, 94, 107; publication 81; SD Workers party 70, 77, 97, 215
Pobedonostsev, K. P. 20, 48, 115
Poland 90, 205, 215, 236, 240, 247
Police *see okhrana*
Police unionism 182–4
Polovtsev, A. A. 109n
Poltava 9, 14, 24, 119, 137
Populism 2, 29, 30, 33, 58, 60, 63–4, 66–8, 71–2, 87, 164
Potresov, A. N. 27, 84, 92–7, 101, 102, 103, 104
Pravo 112, 219, 234
Printers, Union of 249
Prokopovich, S. N. 61; abroad 65, 75–8, 81–2, 89, 119, 177; arrested 82, 243; Marxism 65, 71, 74–82, 89, 92, 95, 99, 177, 265; Peoples Rights Party 61, 65, 74, 75, 219; political groups 77, 99, 118, 164, 246, 249, 265; publications 75, 182; Union of Liberation 62, 65, 191–2, 219, 237, 243
Protection of Labour, International Congress on Questions of legislation for (Zurich) 77
Pskov 97, 115, 118
Pugachovshchina 9, 187, 255, 256, 257, 271

Radishchev, A. N. 269
Railway Workers and Employees, All-Russian Union of 248, 259, 262, 265
revisionism *see* Marxism
Revolution, First Russian (1905) 1, 232, 232n
Revolyutsionnaya Rossiya 164
Richter, N. F. 224
Rodichev, F. I. 15n, 26, 208; Cadet Party 247, 266; Lawyers Union 247; Schaffhausen Conference 177; Union of Unions 249; zemstvo congresses 17, 258; zemstvo member 15, 15n, 24, 27, 33, 199–200
Rodzyanko, M. V. 231n, 250
Rossiyskaya Sotsial-Demokraticheskaya Rabochaya Partiya see RSDRP
Rostov-on-Don 182, 233, 246
Rozhkov, N. A. 247
RSDRP (Russian Social-Democratic Workers Party) 1, 2, 70, 78, 84, 96, 107,

215–16, 219, 241, 243, 244, 246, 249, 264, 266, 270; congresses 89, 255
Russian Social Democratic Movement 30, 78, 82, 84, 93, 95, 96, 97, 106
Russian Social Democrats Abroad, Union of 76–7, 78, 81, 82
Russian Wealth *see Russkoye Bogatstvo*
Russkiya Vedomosti 19
Russkoye Bogatstvo: banquet campaign 233; Freedom Group 99, 100; Peoples Rights Party 60, 65; Peoples Socialist Party 265; Populists 2, 60, 123, 164, 189, 245, SRs 219, 253, 265; Union of Journalists 247; Writers Union 99
Ryazan 121
Ryazanov, A. I. 61
Ryazanov circle 60–1, 74

St Petersburg: banquet campaign 221, 233, 234, 235, 236; 'Bloody Sunday' 239–41, 243, 244, 271; Conferences 38, 43, 44, 119, 168, 169, 188, 200, 221, 224, 226, 228, 229, 262; Free Economic Society 62; Kazan Square 106, 113–15, 124, 160, 183; political groups 27, 65, 92, 94–5, 96, 100–1, 113–15, 122, 124, 127, 166–9, 188, 208, 221, 233, 264; radical intelligentsia 46, 82, 100–1, 113–15, 124, 127, 166, 167, 168, 169, 176, 188, 191, 221, 233, 244; Soviet, 168, 169, 249, 264–5; Unions 30, 184, 234, 235, 236–7, 246, 247, 249, 256; Union of Liberation ('Big Group') 118, 188, 192, 233, 237, 238, 239–40, 243, 249, 250, 258, 260, 264; 265; University 91, 121, 123, 261; unrest in 30, 91, 106, 113–15, 197, 237, 239, 241, 261, 264, 271
Samara 14, 88, 188, 233
Samarin, F. D. 52, 53, 54, 55
Samoderzhaviye i Zemstvo see Witte, memorandum to Tsar
Saratov, 24, 62, 64, 189, 256
Savelyev, A. A. 171, 224
Schaffhausen Conference *see* Liberation Movement
secret police *see okhrana*
Semevskiy, V. I. 239
Sergius, Grand Duke 183, 240
Shakhovskoy, Prince D. I.: *Beseda* 55, 110, 116, 119, 131, 145, 146, 192; Cadet Party 32, 266; Friends of Liberation 118, 119, 131; Liberation Movement

322

Index

Index

Index